THE STATE OF FOOD AND AGRICULTURE 2000

FAO Agriculture Series No. 32

ISSN 0081-4539

THE STATE OF FOOD AND AGRICULTURE 2000

FOOD AND AGRICULTURE ORGANIZATION OF THE UNITED NATIONS
Rome, 2000

Reprinted 2000

ISBN 92-5-104400-7

PÉR
HD
1401
.S73

Foreword

The last years of the twentieth century were generally unfavourable for world food and agriculture. *The State of Food and Agriculture 2000* reports only very modest growth in world agricultural production in 1998, and the estimates for 1999 do not appear to indicate any improvement. Particularly for the developing countries, where the performance of the agricultural sector is of special concern, prospects for 1999 are for a noticeable slowdown in crop and livestock production − reflecting a negative trend that is now in its third consecutive year. It has been a difficult period for many of these countries, which have been facing unusually adverse climatic conditions, together with the negative economic impact of the financial crisis that erupted in 1997, declining prices of several of their major commodity exports and, in a number of cases, political instability and conflicts. Food supply disruptions associated with these problems have led to the outbreak or persistence of serious food emergency situations in a large number of countries − currently more than 30 − around the world.

The close of a millennium is an opportune time for studying the past with a view to seeking lessons for the future. In its special chapter, "World food and agriculture: lessons from the past 50 years", *The State of Food and Agriculture 2000* reflects on humankind's achievements and failures in fighting poverty and hunger over the past half-century − a theme that stimulates both historic and prospective thought.

Overall, the past 50 years have been a period of unprecedented progress on many fronts. Major gains have been achieved by all developmental yardsticks − real income, life expectancy, infant survival and levels of education and nutrition. Science and technology have changed the daily lives of many beyond anything imagined in the mid-1900s; people with even modest means today can hope for better health care, mobility and communications than the richest in those days; some diseases that had afflicted humankind since time immemorial have disappeared; humans and their machines are now routinely voyaging into outer space; and innovations in computer and information technology are succeeding each other at a bewildering pace, at once offering answers to our practical problems and introducing profound changes to social and economic interactions and people's behaviour.

Among our achievements has been progress in fighting world hunger. Undernourishment, especially in populous Asian countries, has diminished, with initial constraints of gigantic dimensions and complexity successfully overcome. Famine, a threat that is as old as humankind and has claimed millions of deaths even in recent decades, now only occurs in exceptional circumstances − mostly in the case of war and conflict in countries already suffering from serious problems of undernutrition and institutional capacity.

Yet, the past 50 years have also left a backlog of unresolved problems, new challenges, risks and uncertainties. We must pose serious questions about the meaning and scope of our economic and technological achievements and their cost to us and future generations. Our technological and economic gains overall appear sadly ironic when contrasted with the squalor and hopelessness in which a large segment of humankind continues to live. More than 800 million people – 13 percent of the world's population – still lack access to the food they need and are therefore condemned to short and unfulfilled lives.

Observers of our time have termed it variously an "information", "atomic" and "globalization" age. It can also be characterized, sadly, as an age of "inequity". Indeed, it is difficult to find a more apt discription for a world in which disparities and inequities are as striking as they are unjustified – a world in which the poorest 20 percent of the population accounts for slightly more than 1 percent of global income, while the richest 20 percent claims 86 percent. We also find it hard to conceive of safe and civilized future societies in which such disparities would be allowed to widen further – a tendency that is, however, suggested by certain aspects of the evidence before us. For instance, between 1960 and 1994, the income ratio between the richest 20 percent and the poorest 20 percent inceased from 30:1 to 78:1.[1] Beyond these broad statistics are pervasive inequities and disparities – among and within countries – between rural and urban populations, between ethnic and minority groups, between women and men. The concept of inequity can also be seen in its intergenerational dimension: the culture of consumerism, on the one hand, and survival strategies of the poor, on the other, have often resulted in environmental damage that compromises the capacities and potential of future generations.

Inequities can also be found within agricultural and rural societies. It is a well-known fact that the poorest tend to be concentrated in rural areas, and this feature stubbornly persists. Within agriculture itself, this publication highlights the growing technological, productivity and income gaps between modern and traditional farming systems – a process that is leading to a progressive pauperization of small-scale farmers, who cannot possibly compete with modern capitalized farms in an increasingly open world economy.

There are powerful forces behind the trend of growing inequality. The ongoing process of globalization and market liberalization may unleash opportunities for all, but more so for those who have the resources, information and expertise to benefit from them.

We are convinced, however, that the battle against inequity, poverty and hunger can be won. *The State of Food and Agriculture 2000* advocates ways out of the "poverty trap" in which governments and institutional structures play a major role. It is fundamental that the public sector does not relinquish its role as provider of basic social services and does not neglect the poor and vulnerable, and it is crucial that it creates an institutional framework that unleashes and protects people's initiative and rewards their efforts. The publication also underlines the obvious but often neglected fact that, because the poor and undernourished are heavily concentrated in rural areas, any serious effort to alleviate their plight must

---

[1] World Resources Institute. 1998. *World Resources 1998-99,* p. 145. Oxford, UK, Oxford University Press.

necessarily begin with agricultural and rural development. The fact that many of the poor are staple food producers points to a clear policy orientation − that of helping the poor to produce more and better-quality staple food more efficiently in order to take the first step out of poverty. Painfully learned lessons show the importance of observing these simple policy principles.

Amazing gains have been achieved in agricultural productivity over the past half-century, thanks to progress in technology and expertise. The major challenge now is to reduce the technological gap by adapting improved technologies, old and new, to the local conditions and needs of low-income food-deficit countries as well as to specific areas within countries.

This does not mean that scientific research for new technological avenues should not be intensified. Indeed, it should. Biotechnology, in particular, holds much promise for the future, and its application in agriculture is still in its infancy. Its development, however, must be undertaken with full consideration of ethical issues as well as of quality and safety-related risks.

The general conclusion to be drawn from our experience of the past 50 years is that much has been achieved in reducing hunger in the world, but still much more remains to be done if the scourge of hunger is to be eradicated. The necessary technology and sufficient resources exist today. Therefore, if we do not fulfil our commitment to eradicate hunger, we will have no excuse to offer to new generations other than that of ignorance, shortsightedness and selfishness.

Jacques Diouf
FAO DIRECTOR-GENERAL

Contents

PART I
World review

PART II
World food and agriculture: lessons from the past 50 years

Boxes

Tables

Figures

Maps

Annex table

Time Series for SOFA 2000 – on diskette

Acknowledgements

The State of Food and Agriculture 2000 was prepared by a team from the Agriculture and Economic Development Analysis Division, led by F.L. Zegarra and comprising: A. Croppenstedt, F. Fiorenzi, R. Nugent, J. Skoet and S. Teodosijevic. Secretarial support was provided by S. Di Lorenzo and P. Di Santo. General supervision was provided by K. Tsubota and J. Vercueil.

Contributions and background papers for the World review were prepared by A. Whiteman, Forestry Department (Production and trade of forest products); FAO Fisheries Department (Fisheries: production, disposition and trade); L. Naiken and P. Narain, Statistics Division (External assistance to agriculture); L. Anderson and R. Nugent (Microcredit: effects on rural poverty and the environment); and J. Weeks and C. Cramer, with research assistance from M. de Araujo (Conflicts, agriculture and food security). The sections entitled Food shortages and emergencies, World cereal supply situation and outlook, Food aid flows and International agricultural prices were prepared by the staff of the Commodities and Trade Division, supervised by P. Fortucci, A. Rashid and A. Gürkan.

Contributions and background papers for the special chapter (World food and agriculture: lessons from the past 50 years) were prepared by M. Mazoyer and L. Roudart (The socio-economic impact of agricultural modernization), M. Lipton (Food and nutrition security: why food production matters), R. Evenson (Agricultural production and productivity in developing countries), and P. Bardhan (Political economy in the alleviation of poverty and food insecurity), with inputs from T. Aldington, A. Ayazi, F. Fiorenzi, A.C. Lopez, R. Sharma, H. Thomas and G. Zanias.

Glossary

AsDB   Asian Development Bank

BMI   body mass index

BMR   basal metabolic rate

CAP   Common Agricultural Policy (EC)

CCP   Committee on Commodity Problems (FAO)

CFS   Committee on World Food Security

CGAP   Consultative Group to Assist the Poor

CGIAR   Consultative Group on International Agricultural Research

CILSS   Interstate Committee for Combating Drought in the Sahel

CIMMYT   International Maize and Wheat Improvement Center

CIS   Commonwealth of Independent States

CSD   Commission on Sustainable Development (UN)

DAC   Development Assistance Committee

DES   dietary energy supply

ECLA   Economic Commission for Latin America (superseded by ECLAC)

ECLAC   Economic Commission for Latin America and the Caribbean

ECOSOC   Economic and Social Council (UN)

EEZ   Exclusive Economic Zone

EGS   Employment Generation Scheme (India)

EHDAEs   economies highly dependent on agricultural exports

EU	European Union
FAC	Food Aid Convention
FDI	foreign direct investment
GATT	General Agreement on Tariffs and Trade
GDP	gross domestic product
GIEWS	Global Information and Early Warning System
GNP	gross national product
HFA	household food adequacy
HFS	household food security
IARC	international agricultural research centre
IBRD	International Bank for Reconstruction and Development
ICA	International Coffee Agreement
ICCO	International Cocoa Organization
ICRISAT	International Crops Research Institute for the Semi-Arid Tropics
IDA	International Development Association
IDA	iron deficiency anaemia
IDD	iodine deficiency disease
IDP	internally displaced person
IFA	individual food adequacy
IFAD	International Fund for Agricultural Development
IFF	Intergovernmental Forum on Forests
IFPRI	International Food Policy Research Institute

IFS	individual food security
ILO	International Labour Organisation
IMF	International Monetary Fund
IPF	Intergovernmental Panel on Forests
IPR	intellectual property right
IRR	internal rate of return
IRRI	International Rice Research Institute
ISA	International Sugar Agreement
LIFDC	low-income food-deficit country
MFO	microfinance organization
MSA	most seriously affected (country) (UN)
MTNs	multilateral trade negotiations
NARS	national agricultural research systems
NFS	national food security
NGO	non-governmental organization
NSSS	national staples self-sufficiency
ODA	official development assistance
OECD	Organisation for Economic Co-operation and Development
OPEC	Organization of the Petroleum Exporting Countries
PDA	Population and Community Development Association (Thailand)
PDI	Population and Development International (Thailand)

PEM	protein-energy malnutrition
PFP	partial factor productivity
ROSCA	rotating savings and credit association
SACCO	savings and credit cooperative
SAP	structural adjustment programme
TNS	Technoserve (Ghana)
UNCED	United Nations Conference on Environment and Development
UNCLOS	United Nations Conference on the Law of the Sea
UNCTAD	United Nations Conference on Trade and Development
UNDP	United Nations Development Programme
UNICEF	United Nations Children's Fund
UNEP	United Nations Environment Programme
UNRISD	United Nations Research Institute for Social Development
VAD	vitamin A deficiency
WCARRD	World Conference on Agrarian Reform and Rural Development
WFP	World Food Programme
WHO	World Health Organization
WTO	World Trade Organization

Explanatory note

Symbols
The following symbols are used:

- = none or negligible (in tables)
... = not available (in tables)
$ = US dollars

Dates and units
The following forms are used to denote years or groups of years:

1996/97 = a crop, marketing or fiscal year running from one calendar year to the next

1996-97 = the average for the two calendar years

Unless otherwise indicated, the metric system is used in this publication.
"Billion" = 1 000 million.

Statistics
Figures in statistical tables may not add up because of rounding. Annual changes and rates of change have been calculated from unrounded figures.

Production indexes
The FAO indexes of agricultural production show the relative level of the aggregate volume of agricultural production for each year in comparison with the base period 1989-91. They are based on the sum of price-weighted quantities of different agricultural commodities after the quantities used as seed and feed (similarly weighted) have been deducted. The resulting aggregate therefore represents disposable production for any use except seed and feed.

All of the indexes, whether at the country, regional or world level, are calculated by the Laspeyres formula. Production quantities of each commodity are weighted by 1989-91 average international commodity prices and summed for each year. To obtain the index, the aggregate for a given year is divided by the average aggregate for the base period 1989-91.

Trade indexes
The indexes of trade in agricultural products are also based on the base period 1989-91. They include all the commodities and countries shown in the *FAO Trade Yearbook*. Indexes of

total food products include those edible products generally classified as "food".

All indexes represent changes in current values of exports (free on board [f.o.b.]), and imports (cost, insurance, freight [c.i.f.]), expressed in US dollars. When countries report imports valued at f.o.b., these are adjusted to approximate c.i.f. values. Volumes and unit value indexes represent the changes in the price-weighted sum of quantities and of the quantity-weighted unit values of products traded between countries. The weights are, respectively, the price and quantity averages of 1989-91 which is the base reference period used for all the index number series currently computed by FAO. The Laspeyres formula is used to construct the index numbers.

PART I

WORLD REVIEW

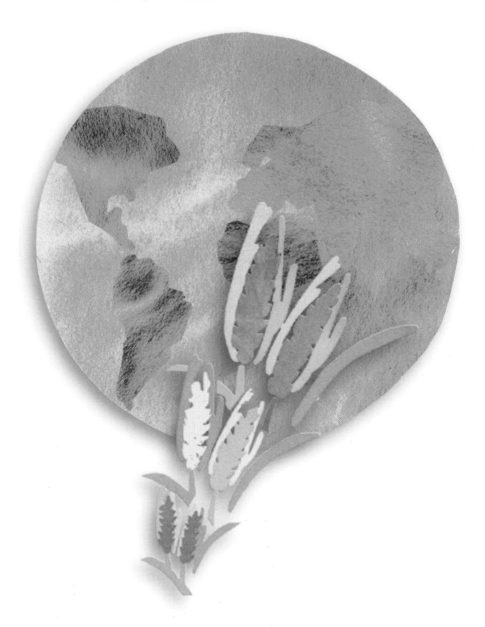

WORLD REVIEW

I. CURRENT AGRICULTURAL SITUATION – FACTS AND FIGURES

I. CROP AND LIVESTOCK PRODUCTION

• World crop and livestock production in 1998 is estimated to have expanded at a very modest rate of only 1.1 percent, the lowest since 1993. This unfavourable outcome is to a large extent the result of a decline in output in the developed countries, estimated to be 1 percent. However, the performance of the developing countries as a group was also relatively disappointing during 1998. Their agricultural production expanded by only 2.6 percent, lower than the already relatively modest rate of 2.9 percent in 1997, although this slowdown follows a series of high rates, in the range of 4 to 5 percent, recorded from 1993 to 1996.

• Estimates of agricultural production in 1999 are still provisional, but point to an expansion in global crop and livestock production of roughly the same limited order of magnitude, 0.9 percent, in 1998. For 1999, however, while the developed country performance appears to have improved slightly relative to 1998, the developing country group appears to have experienced a further deceleration in the rate of increase of crop and livestock production. If the provisionally estimated rate of expansion of 1 percent for the developing countries were to be confirmed, 1999 would be the third consecutive year of noticeable slowdown, representing the lowest recorded rate of growth in agricultural production in the developing countries since 1972.

• A major factor behind the slower growth of output in developing countries is the worsening performance of the Far East and the Pacific developing region. Production growth in this region slowed to only 1.8 percent in 1998. Bad weather conditions, in particular torrential rains from June to September in some countries and El Niño-related droughts in others, were the main common factors behind the worsening performance. The provisional estimates for 1999 indicate that regional production growth may have slowed further, to only 1.2 percent. Such developments are, to a large extent, determined by the situation in China where, after six consecutive years of output

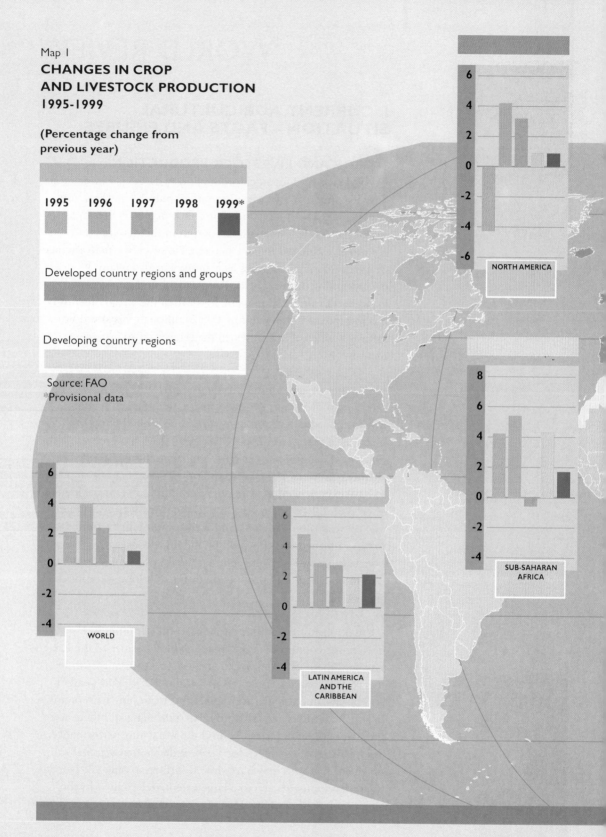

Map 1

CHANGES IN CROP AND LIVESTOCK PRODUCTION 1995-1999

(Percentage change from previous year)

1995	1996	1997	1998	1999*

Developed country regions and groups

Developing country regions

Source: FAO
*Provisional data

NORTH AMERICA

SUB-SAHARAN AFRICA

WORLD

LATIN AMERICA AND THE CARIBBEAN

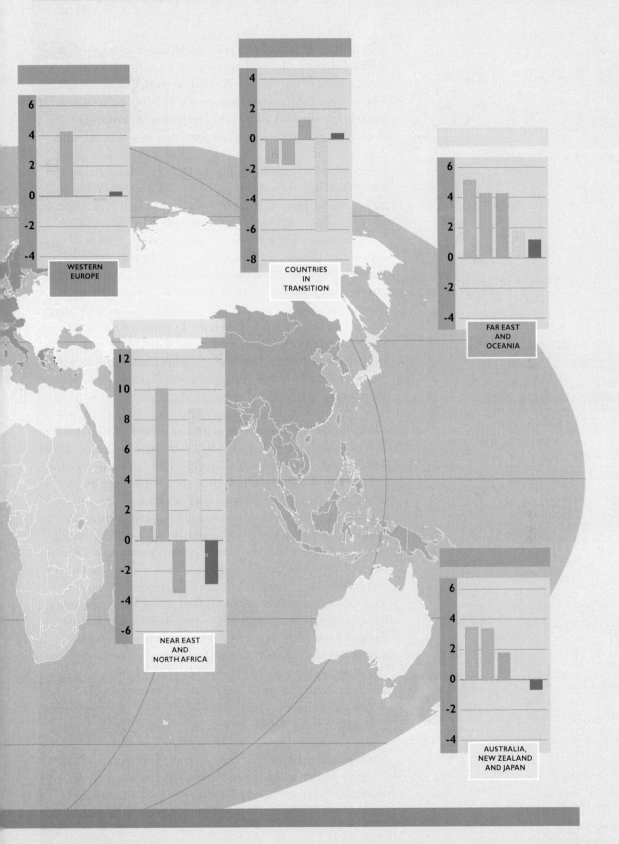

WESTERN
EUROPE

COUNTRIES
IN
TRANSITION

FAR EAST
AND
OCEANIA

NEAR EAST
AND
NORTH AFRICA

AUSTRALIA,
NEW ZEALAND
AND JAPAN

growth at more than 5 percent, agricultural output growth in 1998 fell to a more modest 3.3 percent, as floods in the central parts of the country affected, in particular, the rice and wheat crops. Provisional estimates for 1999 point to almost stagnant production, with output increasing by less than 1 percent. In particular, a slight reduction in paddy output is expected, partly owing to the lowering of the state purchasing prices for inferior quality grains and to crop damage caused by heavy rains in June and July. India recorded a slight reduction, of less than 1 percent, in agricultural output in 1998, while a modest recovery was expected to take place in 1999. Other larger countries in the region suffered either declines in agricultural production (Indonesia, the Philippines, the Republic of Korea, Thailand, Malaysia) or slowdowns in output growth (Bangladesh, Cambodia) in 1998. Resumed output growth was expected in 1999 in most of these countries, with the exceptions of Indonesia and the Republic of Korea. The production estimates now point to Viet Nam as the most consistently positive agricultural performer in the region, with rates of production growth near or above 5 percent for the past eight years.

• In Latin American and the Caribbean, agricultural production also experienced slower growth in 1998, at an estimated rate of 1.9 percent. The slowdown is largely accounted for by a below average rate of expansion in Brazil, where crops were hit by droughts in parts of the country and rains caused exceptional damage, affecting wheat-producing regions in particular. The Andean region was affected by severe dry spells, which caused output to stagnate in some countries and actually to decline in others. Hurricanes George and Mitch caused immense human and material losses and also damaged agriculture in several countries in Central America and the Caribbean. On the other hand, strong output growth was recorded in Argentina. Estimates for 1999 point to an expansion in agricultural production at a rate only slightly higher than that of 1998. While performance in 1999 should improve markedly in Brazil and Peru, Argentina and Chile appear to have witnessed stagnating or slightly declining levels of production and the rate of growth appears to have slowed in Mexico.

• In sub-Saharan Africa, agricultural output recovered in 1998 from the small decline of the previous year and grew by an estimated 4.3 percent, largely owing to strong expansion of production in Nigeria, which followed the contraction in 1997.

Particularly good performances were also recorded for Angola, Ghana, Mozambique and Uganda, while Ethiopia, Zambia and Zimbabwe witnessed a decline, estimated in the 3 to 5 percent range, and the Sudan and the Democratic Republic of the Congo saw stagnating levels of production. The provisional estimates for 1999 indicate that agricultural production growth may have slowed to less than 2 percent, with lower rates of growth in the strong performers of 1998 and actual declines expected in Angola, Kenya, the United Republic of Tanzania and Zimbabwe.

• In the Near East and North Africa region, agricultural production in 1998 more than recovered from the decline of 1997, growing by an estimated rate of more than 8 percent. A major factor behind this was increased production in the North African countries – Algeria, Morocco and Tunisia – which had suffered a sharp weather-induced downturn in 1997. But performances also improved markedly, with strong expansion of production, in such other countries as the Islamic Republic of Iran, the Syrian Arab Republic and Turkey. In Egypt, by contrast, agricultural production is estimated to have suffered a slight decline. Estimates for 1999 point to another decline in agricultural production in the region, currently estimated to be 3 percent. The major factor behind this is another sharp decline in Morocco, where the cereal crop has fallen by almost half as a result of inadequate rainfalls and reduced plantings, and declines in production are estimated also for the Islamic Republic of Iran, Jordan, the Syrian Arab Republic and Turkey.

• The transition countries experienced a 6 percent decline resulting mainly from a further severe contraction recorded for the Commonwealth of Independent States (CIS), where many of the major producing areas were seriously affected by drought. Production declined significantly, *inter alia*, in the Russian Federation, Ukraine and Kazakhstan. Outside the CIS, a major decline in agricultural production was also recorded in Romania, while strong output growth was recorded in Poland. Estimates for 1999 point to a marginal increase in production in the transition countries as a group, with further slight declines expected for the Russian Federation and Ukraine, strong recovery in Kazakhstan and more modest output growth in Romania. Only relatively minor variations in agricultural production have been estimated for the remaining developed country groupings in 1998 and 1999, with only North America recording increases in production in both years.

2. FOOD SHORTAGES AND EMERGENCIES

• The number of countries facing food emergencies as of February 2000 is estimated to be 32, compared with 38 in February 1999.

• In East Africa, substantial food assistance will be required throughout 2000, mainly because of drought-induced crop and livestock losses. Successive poor rains in most pastoral areas of the subregion have severely affected pastures and livestock, resulting in acute food shortages and the migration of thousands of people in search of water and food. Past or ongoing civil conflicts have also seriously disrupted food production and distribution in some areas, causing food shortages and mass population displacements. In Somalia, poor *Deyr* season rains have exacerbated food supply difficulties in some southern regions. In Kenya, food assistance is urgently sought for more than 2.7 million people in the drought-affected Northern Plainlands and North-Eastern Province. In Eritrea, nearly 600 000 people, affected by the war with Ethiopia and by drought, need urgent food assistance. In Ethiopia, the food supply situation is very tight for more than 8 million people, including some 400 000 displaced by the border war with Eritrea. In the Sudan, despite a stable food supply situation, about 103 000 tonnes of food aid is needed for some 2.4 million people affected by drought and the long-running civil conflict. In the United Republic of Tanzania, localized crop failures have affected thousands of people in several central and lake regions. In Uganda, despite an improved food supply situation in most parts of the country, serious food shortages owing to drought are reported in the eastern Karamoja region, while food assistance is being provided to people affected by persistent insurgency in the north and west of the country.

• In West Africa, following two consecutive above-average crops in 1998 and 1999 in most countries of the Sahel, the food supply situation is stable and markets are well supplied. Households and national food security stock managers have been able to replenish their stocks. However, some areas were affected by floods in September and October 1999, notably in Mauritania, the Niger and Senegal. In coastal countries along the Gulf of Guinea, floods also affected northern regions of Benin, Ghana, Nigeria and Togo. Following many years of civil strife, Liberia and Sierra Leone remain heavily dependent on international food assistance, despite some improvement in food production in Liberia.

• In the Great Lakes region, food shortages persist in several countries. In Burundi, the food supply situation is tight following reduced harvests caused by dry weather and persistent civil strife. In particular, the food and health situation is critical for some 800 000 displaced people in camps who have no access to their fields. In Rwanda, despite an improvement in food production, food shortages persist in certain areas that were affected by drought. In the Democratic Republic of the Congo, severe food shortages and malnutrition are reported among large numbers of the displaced population, mainly in the northeastern Katanga and south Kivu areas, which remain inaccessible owing to insecurity. The security situation is improving in the Congo, but displaced populations are still vulnerable.

• In southern Africa, the worst floods in 40 years struck Mozambique, South Africa, Botswana and Swaziland in early February, leaving tens of thousands homeless and causing considerable damage to infrastructure. In Mozambique, the worst hit country, the number of people severely affected by the floods and in urgent need of emergency food assistance is currently estimated to be 300 000 but is still rising. In Angola, emergency food aid continues to be needed for 1.1 million internally displaced people as a result of the protracted civil conflict; food aid is also required by large numbers of Angolan refugees in neighbouring countries.

• In the Near East, food production in Afghanistan is likely to be constrained by serious shortages of agricultural inputs and population displacement. In Iraq, despite recent beneficial rains, prolonged drought conditions and shortages of agricultural inputs continue to affect cereal production. In the Islamic Republic of Iran, Jordan and the Syrian Arab Republic, which were affected by drought last year, crop prospects have improved recently following favourable rains.

• In Asia, vulnerable populations in a number of countries continue to be affected by serious food supply difficulties resulting from past disasters and the effects of economic turmoil. Two large natural catastrophes affected the region in 1999. The first was the cyclone in northeastern India, which covered the states of Orissa, West Bengal and Andhra Pradesh and had a severe impact on household food security. The second disaster was in Viet Nam, where the worst flooding in decades affected central coastal areas in late October 1999. In

Map 2
COUNTRIES EXPERIENCING FOOD SUPPLY SHORTFALLS AND REQUIRING EXCEPTIONAL ASSISTANCE*

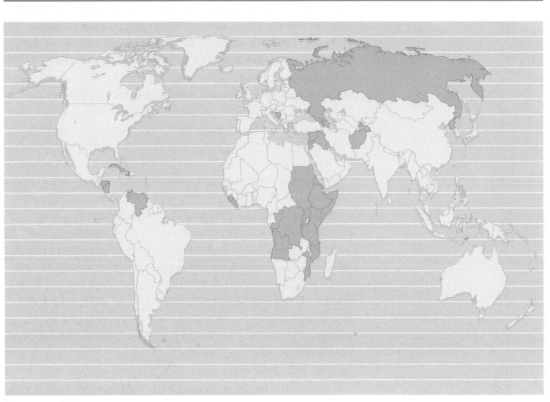

* In current marketing year

Source: FAO, Global Information and Early Warning System, June 2000

the Democratic People's Republic of Korea, the food supply situation continues to give cause for concern as domestic food production remains well below needs, while economic problems are heavily constraining the country's capacity to supply essential inputs to agriculture and to import commercially. In East Timor, overall food supply prospects in the medium to long term are less gloomy than envisaged at the height of the crisis following the August 1999 referendum. Concerns persist regarding the plight of refugees still in West Timor, with the United Nations Children's Fund (UNICEF) reporting moderate to severe malnutrition in camps. In Mongolia, the transition from a centrally planned to a market economy has resulted in the dismantling of various state structures, including state farms. As a consequence, productivity and production have fallen, resulting in deterioration in food security among vulnerable groups.

• In Latin America, unusually adverse weather phenomena have affected the whole region in the last few years. A prolonged drought in 1994 inflicted severe damage on the important first-season cereal and bean crops in Central American countries. Losses in the range of 25 to 30 percent of anticipated production were incurred. Hurricanes Lily (1996) and George (1998) in the Caribbean were followed by hurricane Mitch, one of the most destructive natural disasters of the century which swept across Central America in late 1998, devastating all crops along its path and leaving a large number of victims and immense damage to housing and infrastructure. To date, countries are still in the process of reconstruction. Furthermore, and most important, virtually the entire region was severely affected by the El Niño phenomenon for a long period, extending from early April 1997 to late September 1998 and resulting in diverse negative effects such as torrential rains, flooding, severe droughts and extensive forest fires in parts of the region. Finally, in December 1999, incessant torrential rains in Venezuela resulted in deadly slips and mudslides, aggravated by very serious flooding. There were more than 30 000 casualties and extensive damage to housing and infrastructure.

• In Europe, several of the Balkan countries remain affected, to a lesser or greater extent, by a decade of civil unrest which culminated most recently in war in Kosovo Province of the Federal Republic of Yugoslavia (Serbia and Montenegro) in the first half of 1999. The Federal Republic of Yugoslavia now has more refugees than any other European country and is in a state of acute economic crisis. This is characterized by, *inter alia*, the deterioration of public utilities, the destruction of fertilizer and fuel plants and the virtual collapse of social services. At the beginning of 2000, there are estimated to be more than 1.1 million refugees, internally displaced and economically and socially deprived people receiving food assistance in Serbia (excluding Kosovo Province) and Montenegro while, in Kosovo Province, a further 1 million persons are receiving food aid. Assistance continues to be provided also in Albania and The Former Yugoslav Republic of Macedonia for remaining refugees and other persons rendered vulnerable by the Kosovo war in 1999.

• In the CIS, civil strife in Chechnya has led to the destruction of the capital, Grozny, other villages and basic infrastructure. The situation in agriculture is critical, with severe damage inflicted on livestock and the grape growing industry and mined fields.

Hundreds of thousands of people have been displaced, either within the country or to neighbouring autonomous states, particularly Ingushetia, a small country of some 300 000 inhabitants who are hosting about 200 000 refugees. The food security of the civilian population trapped in Chechnya is rapidly deteriorating and the outlook for winter grain and fodder crops is bleak. Elsewhere in the CIS, economically vulnerable people and internally displaced or refugees in Armenia, Azerbaijan, Georgia and Tajikistan continue to need food assistance. In these countries, gross domestic product (GDP) is recovering, but slowly, from a level of less than half of that in 1990, but their economies remain fragile. The devaluation of the Russian rouble in August 1998 and the associated cutback in trade have slowed recovery. Many vulnerable people, notably the aged, disabled and recent refugees, are not in a position to benefit from market reforms, and targeted food aid is likely to be necessary in the years to come. In Tajikistan, serious crop losses caused by the infestation of wheat by yellow rust and smut in 1999 will need to be addressed if cereal output is to recover in successive years.

3. WORLD CEREAL SUPPLY SITUATION AND OUTLOOK[1]

• World cereal production in 1999 reached 1 865 million tonnes (including rice in milled terms), slightly below the previous year's level but above the average of the past five years. The decline was mostly a result of lower wheat and coarse grain production. Global wheat production fell in 1999, for the second consecutive year, to about 589 million tonnes, down 2 percent from 1998. Severe drought in the Near East and parts of North Africa, as well as excessive rainfall at planting time in northern Europe, were the main causes of the decline in 1999 wheat production. A 5 to 10 percent rise in compulsory set-aside in the European Union (EU), combined with planting cutbacks by several wheat growers in response to low prices – particularly on winter wheat plantings in the United States – also had a negative impact on global production. However, the decline was partially offset by favourable weather and higher yields in a number of other countries, including Argentina, Australia, Bangladesh, Canada, China, India and the Russian Federation.

• At an estimated 876 million tonnes, global output of coarse grains in 1999 was about 4 percent below the previous year. Smaller harvests were gathered throughout all regions of the globe with the exception of Central America, where production remained unchanged, and Europe, where it increased marginally. Significant declines occurred among some of the major producers, including Argentina, China, the EU, India and the United States. In several countries, such as China, exceptional dry conditions during the growing season were responsible for the reduction in output, while in the United States planted area declined but the yield was above average.

• World paddy output in 1999 is estimated to have returned to the trend prevailing in the 1990s, after the disappointing 1998 season caused by weather problems in major producing countries. Supported by an expansion in area and generally favourable growing conditions, paddy production rose by 2 percent, to 598 million tonnes in 1999, more than twice the growth rate of 1998. Much of the increase was concentrated in Bangladesh, Brazil, Egypt and the Philippines, but Argentina, India, Indonesia and the United States also performed well. By contrast, output contracted in China following the launch, in 1998, of new policies geared towards enhancing quality grain production, which discouraged the planting of early rice, considered to be an inferior grain.

• In 1998/99, total cereal utilization rose slightly above the level of the previous season, to 1 875 million tonnes. At this level, global cereal utilization returned to close to its long-term trend (1986-1998), after being above trend for the previous two seasons. The volume of cereals used for food consumption rose the most, while global feed usage was down slightly from the previous season. All of the increase in cereal utilization occurred in the developing countries. Overall, the growth in world food consumption slightly exceeded the rise in population, resulting in a small increase in per caput food consumption of cereals in 1998/99. Despite a continuing decline in grain prices during the 1998/99 season, which would normally stimulate demand, world utilization of cereals for feed declined slightly, mostly in response to the slow economic growth of several countries in Asia and a continuing contraction in the livestock sectors of the emerging economies of Eastern Europe and the CIS. Looking into the 1999/2000 season, world cereal utilization is forecast to increase by about 3 percent to 1 882 million tonnes. As in the previous season, overall consumption of cereals for food is expected to keep pace with population growth while the total volume of cereals destined for animal feed is expected to remain close to the previous year's level.

• World cereal stocks for crop years ending in 2000 are forecast to reach 332 million tonnes, down by 4 million tonnes from their opening levels. The main reason for this decline is the projected level of world cereal utilization in 1999/2000, which is expected to outpace production. A decline in the wheat and coarse grains inventories held by some of the major exporting countries would account for the bulk of this reduction, while rice carryovers are likely to increase for the second consecutive year. Overall, the ratio of global cereal carryovers to trend utilization in 2000/01 would be 17.4 percent, pointing to a small deterioration from the previous season but still within the 17 to 18 percent range that the FAO secretariat considers to be the minimum necessary to safeguard world food security. Moreover, the percentage share of global cereal stocks held by major exporters, an additional indicator of global food security, is expected to remain stable at last year's level of around 45 percent.

• The reduction in wheat and coarse grain production in 1999 is mostly responsible for the expected decline in wheat and coarse grains inventories. However, rice stocks are expected to recover from the reduced levels observed in recent years to the highest since 1994. Most of the rice stock buildup will be in the major exporting countries, particularly Thailand, Viet Nam, the United States and India.

• Global cereal trade in 1999/2000 is expected to reach 222 million tonnes, some 8 million tonnes, or 4 percent, more than in the previous season. The increase is attributed to an expansion in wheat and coarse grain trade as rice imports are projected to decline slightly. For the developing countries as a group, cereal imports are expected to rise to an all-time high of about 160 million tonnes. While larger wheat imports would account for the bulk of this increase, the gradual economic recovery in southern Asia is likely to result in some expansion in coarse grain trade as well.

• At the current forecast levels, the cereal import bill of the developing countries in 1999/2000 is expected to reach roughly $21 billion, which would be about $670 million, or 3 percent, below the previous year's value. Weaker international cereal prices during the course of the season are expected to more than offset the rise in import volume. In making this estimate, the total volume of food aid shipments during the 1999/2000 season is assumed to remain unchanged from the previous season. For the low-income food-deficit countries (LIFDCs), cereal imports are likely to remain at last year's estimated volume of around 70 million tonnes. However, given the prevailing low prices, the overall cereal import expenses for this group of countries are expected to fall by at least $670 million, or 5 percent, to around $9.1 billion.

• Based on the current evaluation of the latest official and trade sources and assuming normal growing conditions, the early outlook for the 2000 wheat crop suggests a global production level close to that of 1999. While plantings have yet to begin in the Southern Hemisphere, in the Northern Hemisphere a combination of good yields and higher plantings could result in greater production. Favourable weather conditions in many parts of Asia and North Africa could boost production in countries adversely affected by drought in 1999. Wheat planting in the EU is forecast to rise, as current large domestic supplies of rapeseed, combined with a reduction in aid to oilseeds under the first year of Agenda 2000 reform, could encourage increased wheat planting. In Canada, official estimates point to an increase in spring wheat area at the expense of canola and flaxseed because of favourable wheat prices. By contrast, the winter wheat seeding in the United States was officially set at its lowest level since 1972, apparently because farmers were responding to continuing prospects of low prices at planting time. In China too, latest estimates put winter wheat planting area down by nearly 7 percent from the previous year, mostly in response to low prices and the recent government decision to eliminate support prices for low-quality winter wheat. In the Southern Hemisphere, some of the 2000 coarse grain crops are already planted in the major producing countries. In southern Africa, early prospects are favourable, reflecting generally abundant rains and reports of increased plantings. Similarly, in South America, weather conditions are generally favourable. Although an increase in paddy production can be expected in 2000, it could be modest, as there are indications that low prices in 1999 have prompted some countries in the Southern Hemisphere − including Australia, Argentina and Brazil − to reduce plantings. While, in the Northern Hemisphere, planting for the 2000/01 season will not start until April or May, current policies in China could bring about a further cut in output. By contrast, Indonesia has already announced a production target that is about 1 million tonnes, or 2 percent, higher than the actual 1999 crop.

4. EXTERNAL ASSISTANCE TO AGRICULTURE

• According to provisional data for 1998, total commitments of official development assistance (ODA) from the major bilateral and multilateral donors to developing countries for agricultural development amounted to $12 316 million in current prices. This is almost exactly the same level as was recorded in 1997 ($12 340 million) but represents an increase over the level of 1996.

• When measured in constant 1995 prices, the multilateral and bilateral donors' commitments have increased since 1995, but still remain 8 percent below the level that opened the decade in 1990.

• The share of concessional assistance in total commitments is estimated at 65 percent in 1998, well below the shares of 1988, at 77 percent, and 1996, at 74 percent. The share of grants in total commitments has remained relatively stable throughout the 1990s and represented 28 percent in 1998.

Figure 1

COMMITMENTS OF EXTERNAL ASSISTANCE TO AGRICULTURE*

(At constant 1995 prices)

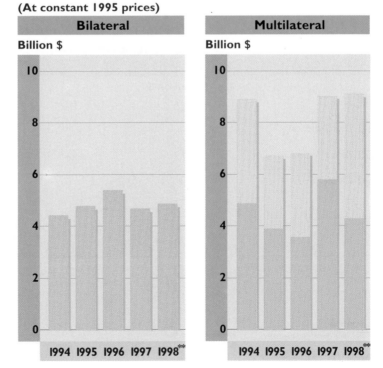

Concessional

Non-concessional

* Broad definition
** Provisional

Source: FAO and OECD

Figure 2
COMMITMENTS BY MAIN PURPOSE
(At constant 1995 prices)

Research, training, extension

Crop production

Regional and river development

Environment

Rural development

Land and water

Others

* Provisional

Source: FAO and OECD

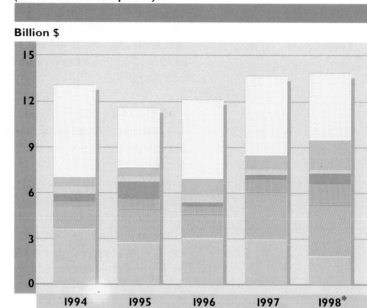

Billion $

Figure 3
COMMITMENTS BY MAIN RECIPIENT REGIONS
(At constant 1995 prices)

Asia

Latin America

Africa

Others**

* Provisional
** Including developed countries

Source: FAO and OECD

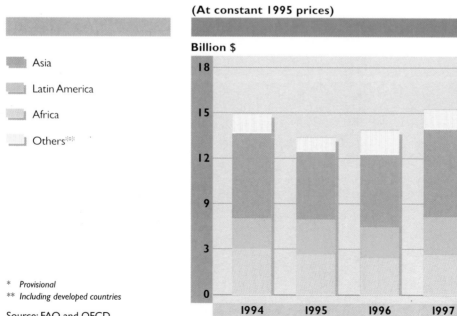

Billion $

• The contributions made by bilateral donors, mainly countries in the Development Assistance Committee (DAC), remained about $4.3 billion in both 1997 and 1998. Japan contributed $1 797 million and $1 853 million, respectively, for the two years, and thus remained the leading donor among DAC members. In 1997, Germany was the second donor in terms of volume, but was surpassed by the United States in 1998 with a volume of $402 million.

• The increased levels of assistance in 1997 and 1998 over that of 1996 were represented entirely by increased levels of multilateral assistance, particularly from the International Development Association (IDA), while bilateral assistance was actually lower than in 1996.

• Throughout the 1990s, the flow of funds to primary agriculture (including fisheries and forestry) have tended to decline, while there has been increasing attention to other areas, in particular environment protection and rural development and infrastructure.

• As for the geographic distribution of flows, there has been a declining trend throughout the 1990s in the share going to Africa. In 1998, the largest share of commitments went to Asia (46 percent), with Latin America and the Caribbean in second place (23 percent) and Africa third (21 percent). A smaller share went to Europe (2.5 percent) with an unallocated residual of 7 percent.

5. FOOD AID FLOWS[2]

• Total cereal food aid shipments, under the programme, project and emergency categories in 1998/99 (1 July to 30 June) reached 9.5 million tonnes, up by more than 3 million tonnes, or 53 percent, from 1997/98 and the highest since 1993/94. Shipments from the United States more than doubled to 5.6 million tonnes, while those from the EU also rose, by more than 30 percent to 2.4 million tonnes. Among other countries, larger donations were registered for Japan, whereas those from Australia and Canada declined slightly. The increase in cereal food aid shipments concerned mostly wheat, rice and rye.

• On the recipient side, the bulk of the increase in food aid shipments went to the Russian Federation in the form of cereals, which rose from only 42 000 tonnes in 1997/98 to more than 1.3 million tonnes in 1998/99. Shipments to Bangladesh also rose substantially, by more than 1 million tonnes to roughly 1.6 million tonnes. Cereal food aid to Indonesia exceeded 700 000 tonnes, compared with only 9 000 tonnes in the previous year. Larger shipments were also

Figure 4

RECIPIENTS OF SHIPMENTS OF FOOD AID IN CEREALS

(In grain equivalent)

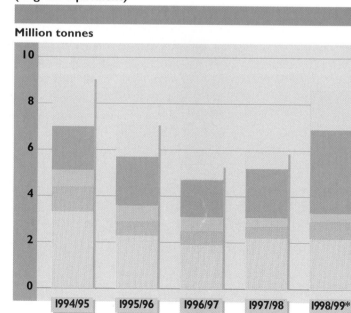

Countries in transition

Far East

Near East and North Africa

Latin America and the Caribbean

Sub-Saharan Africa

Provisional
Note: Years refer to the 12-month period July/June

Source: FAO

registered to the hurricane-ravaged countries of Central America, especially Honduras, Guatemala and Nicaragua. In Africa, cereal food aid to most countries fell; the exceptions being mainly Eritrea, Guinea-Bissau, Sierra Leone, the Sudan and Zimbabwe. In Asia (in addition to Bangladesh and Indonesia, which were mentioned earlier), larger food aid shipments were registered to Mongolia and Nepal, while cereal donations to many other countries fell drastically, including those to the Democratic Republic of Korea, one of the largest food aid recipients in recent years. Similarly smaller shipments were registered to Armenia, Sri Lanka, Azerbaijan, Georgia, Kyrgyzstan and Tajikistan.

• In June 1999, major donors approved the new Food Aid Convention (FAC) and confirmed their intention to implement it for an initial period of three years, starting in July 1999. The new FAC calls for a more flexible approach to food aid by expanding the list of eligible commodities and the methods of contribution. The commodity list has been extended to include edible oils, root crops (cassava, potatoes, etc.), skimmed milk powder, seeds for eligible crops, sugar, products that are part of the traditional diet of vulnerable groups or a component of supplementary feeding programmes, and micronutrients and fortified food products. These food items, in aggregate, will be limited to no more than 20 percent of any donor's commitment, with individual commodities limited to between 3 and 7 percent of the total donation, excluding transportation and other operating expenses. Overall, the total volume of commitments under the 1999 FAC is 4.89 million tonnes in wheat equivalent, compared with 5.35 million tonnes under the 1995 FAC . The difference is accounted for by the EU's pledge to provide 130 million euros in cash, equivalent to a volume of about 588 000 tonnes, including transportation costs. At current prices and transportation costs, the food aid volume commitment under the new convention is roughly equivalent to the previous one.

6. INTERNATIONAL AGRICULTURAL PRICES

• In the international wheat market, prices have remained under downward pressure during the first half of the 1999/2000 season, mostly reflecting good harvests in the major producing countries. In the futures market, soft red winter wheat values were under continuous downward pressure, particularly between October and December when they were quoted at some $10 to $18 per tonne less than in the corresponding period in 1998. Against the background of abundant global exportable supplies and the current favourable 2000 production prospects, support for a sustained recovery in international wheat prices would have to come from a strong rise in global import demand during the 2000/01 marketing season. However, considering that the trade expansion in 1999/2000 mostly reflected large purchases by a few drought-stricken countries, the likelihood of a further rise in import demand in 2000/01 could be limited should yields return to normal.

• World coarse grain prices also remained under downward pressure during the first half of the 1999/2000 season. Large exportable supplies and weak import demand have driven international coarse grain prices down, although some support has come from rising demand in southern Asia. The United States maize export prices between July and December averaged around $89 per tonne, $6 below the comparable period in the previous season. However, starting in January, maize prices began a slow recovery, mostly in response to an expected decline in stocks, especially in the United States. Nevertheless, with large export supplies in the United States and several other exporters, including China, any possibility of supply tightness in the short term is unlikely. In addition, reports of higher plantings in Argentina and the United States would reduce support for maize prices unless the improving economic conditions, especially in Asia, could fuel a much faster rise in feed demand than currently projected.

• International rice prices followed a downward trend during most of 1999, as good harvests in a number of the major exporting countries coincided with a production recovery in many of the major importing countries. The FAO export price index for rice (1982-84 = 100) started the year with a monthly average of 125 points in January and ended it with an average of 105 points in December. For 1999 as a whole, the index averaged 114 points, down from 127 points in 1998 and the lowest since 1994. The general weakness in rice prices is expected to continue at least through the early months of 2000, barring any major shocks from the demand or supply sides.

• Cocoa bean prices declined during 1999 to the lowest levels of the past five years owing to abundant world supplies and weaker than anticipated demand. Prices fell sharply for most of the 1999 calendar year, with the International Cocoa Organization (ICCO) average monthly price decreasing 37 percent over the year. Overall, the ICCO price averaged $957 per tonne during the year, about 30 percent lower than annual average price levels for 1997 and 1998. Continued economic difficulties in the Russian Federation, Eastern Europe, Brazil and the Far East contributed to overall downward price pressure. The potential for increased production and a larger than anticipated exportable surplus in Côte d'Ivoire, the world's largest cocoa producer, contributed substantially to the decline in 1999 prices. Growth in world production levels is expected to surpass consumption in 1999/2000, with total world consumption expected to grow by about 4 percent, potentially resulting in increased stock building and further downward price pressure.

• World coffee prices fell throughout most of the 1999 calendar year, with the International Coffee Agreement (ICA) composite price decreasing from 98 US cents per pound in January to 72 US cents per pound in September. The composite price averaged 86 US cents per pound during 1999, 22 percent lower than the previous year and the lowest since 1993. The composite price for the first quarter of the 1999 calendar year averaged 93 US cents per pound, 27 percent lower than the same quarter in 1998. The fall was principally in response to the devaluation of the Brazilian real, which encouraged exports from Brazil, the world's largest coffee producer, resulting in a decline in overall world coffee prices. In May 1999, prices showed a temporary surge in response to the forecast of colder than usual weather in Brazil, which would have affected the 1999/2000 crops. However, prices fell again soon after the weather pattern returned to the seasonal normal, and they continued to fall. By September, prices had declined to 72 US cents per pound as the market expected another surplus in the coming coffee year. As a result, the second quarter average declined to 87 US cents per pound, and the third quarter average was down to 76 US cents, both more than 20 percent lower compared with the same quarter of 1998. In response to the dry weather in Brazil, prices started to pick up in October.

Figure 5

EXPORT PRICES OF SELECTED COMMODITIES*, 1997-2000

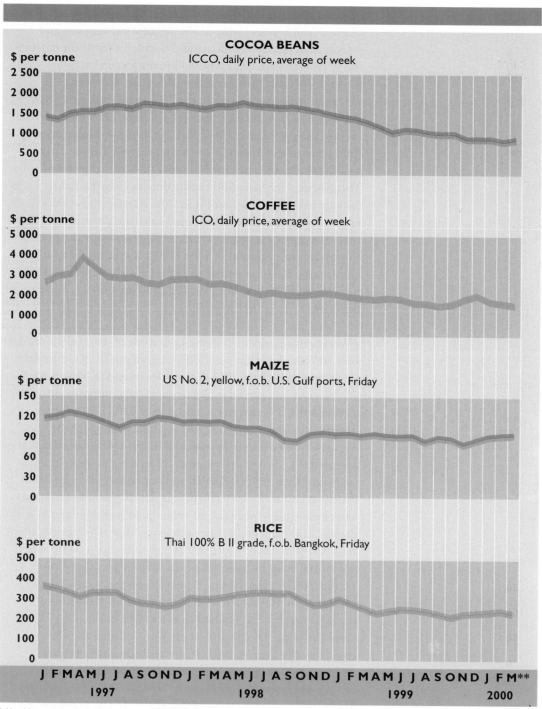

COCOA BEANS
ICCO, daily price, average of week

COFFEE
ICO, daily price, average of week

MAIZE
US No. 2, yellow, f.o.b. U.S. Gulf ports, Friday

RICE
Thai 100% B II grade, f.o.b. Bangkok, Friday

* Monthly averages calculated from the   *** Provisional*
available weekly price quotations

Figure 5 (continued)
EXPORT PRICES OF SELECTED COMMODITIES*, 1997-2000

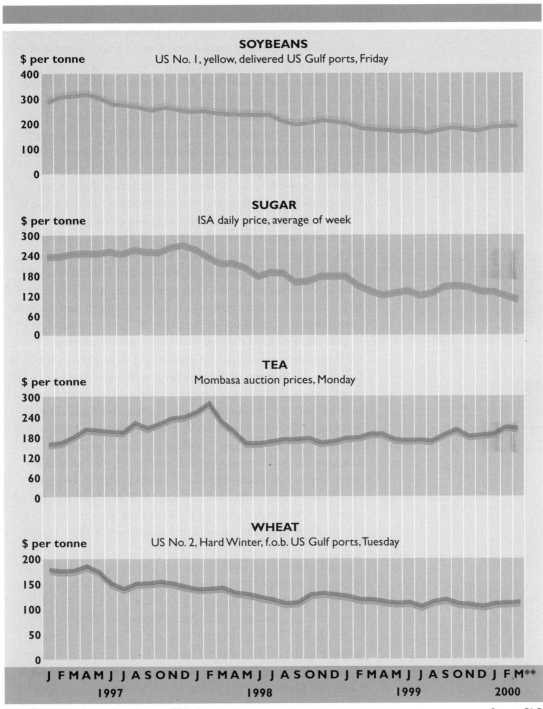

SOYBEANS
US No. 1, yellow, delivered US Gulf ports, Friday
$ per tonne

SUGAR
ISA daily price, average of week
$ per tonne

TEA
Mombasa auction prices, Monday
$ per tonne

WHEAT
US No. 2, Hard Winter, f.o.b. US Gulf ports, Tuesday
$ per tonne

J F M A M J J A S O N D J F M A M J J A S O N D J F M A M J J A S O N D J F M**
1997   1998   1999   2000

* Monthly averages calculated from the available weekly price quotations   *** Provisional*   Source: FAO

By December, they had improved to 96 US cents per pound as the markets anticipated possible reductions in the 2000/01 crop year.

• World cotton prices continued on a downward trend in 1999. The Cotlook A-Index, an indicator of world prices, plummeted to a 13-year low of 98 US cents/kg in December 1999. Abundant supply, a slow increase in demand and, in particular, the huge stocks built up over the past few years, were responsible for the lower prices. World cotton production is estimated at 19 million tonnes for the 1999/2000 crop year (1 August to 31 July), up nearly 500 000 tonnes from 1998/ 99, while global cotton consumption in 1999/2000 is expected to be 19.1 million tonnes, which is slightly higher than production. At the same time, the total volume of trade in 1999/2000 is expected to rebound from the depressed level of 5.3 million tonnes in 1998/99, to 5.8 million tonnes. However, given the huge stocks of nearly 10 million tonnes at the end of 1999, the slightly higher demand and imports will have little impact on prices. Cotton prices are therefore unlikely to bounce back significantly in the next few months although, if global demand continues to pick up and China continues to reduce its stock level through production and marketing reforms, cotton prices may be expected to strengthen in the next few years. In addition, the recent surge in the world price of petroleum, which is the key input in synthetic fibre production, may enhance the competitiveness of cotton and induce higher demand in the next few years. Moreover, implementation of the Agreement on Textiles and Clothing is programmed to eliminate all quota restrictions on textile trade by 2005. This, according to FAO/International Cotton Advisory Committee estimates, should induce an increase of about 2 to 3 percent in global cotton consumption and a significant increase in cotton trade, which should result in higher prices for cotton.

• Oversupply, record stock levels and depressed demand in key importing countries continued to exert pressure on world sugar prices in 1999, resulting in a 13-year low of 4.78 US cents/ pound in April. International Sugar Agreement (ISA) average prices were 6.3 US cents/pound in 1999, almost 30 percent lower than the 1998 average price of 8.9 US cents/pound and almost 50 percent lower than the average annual price of 11.4 US cents/pound for 1997. The sharp decline in world sugar prices between 1998 and 1999 essentially ended a four-year period (1993 to 1996) of relative price stability in the world market in which annual ISA prices averaged close to 11.9 US cents/pound. Continued downward price pressure over the short term is therefore expected, with upward price movements dependent on the economic recovery in Asia, the Russian Federation and Brazil. Brazil will continue to have an enormous impact on the world sugar market over the short term, with export volumes largely dependent on how much sugar cane production is diverted into fuel alcohol for domestic energy utilization in response to rising world oil prices.

• World market prices for black tea declined in all auction markets during the first half of 1999, in response to potentially larger crops in major producing countries and weaker demand in the Russian Federation, the world's second-largest importer. The FAO composite price index for tea (a weighted average price of tea traded in the major auction markets of Kenya, India and Sri Lanka) declined by 3 percent during the first two quarters of 1999, from an average of $1 660 to $1 610 per tonne. However, as the year progressed, reports of lower than anticipated production in Bangladesh, India, Indonesia and Kenya emerged, providing the basis for limited price recovery. Prices continued to improve in the last half of the year, recovering by 11 percent to $1 780 per tonne in the third quarter and increasing by an additional 3 percent, to $1 830 per tonne, by the final quarter of 1999. The FAO composite price for black tea for all of 1999 was $1 707 per tonne, 15 percent lower than prices in 1998 and 1997, when higher import demand in the Russian Federation and a drought-reduced crop in Kenya supported higher price levels. Although the annual composite price declined in 1999 compared with the past two years, average price levels were still 26 percent higher than the 1994 to 1996 average of $1 360 per tonne.

• Banana prices generally weakened in 1999. For instance, import prices[3] in the United States decreased by 13 percent from the preceding year, those in France by 20 percent, in Germany by 18 percent, and in Japan by about 6 percent. The weakening of prices was mainly the result of abundant supplies coupled with constrained demand growth in the emerging markets of the CIS and Baltic states and China. As a result of the general decline in international prices, banana export revenues from developing countries in 1999 were estimated to have declined once more, this time by around $495 million, or 15 percent.

7. FISHERIES: PRODUCTION, DISPOSITION AND TRADE

• Production of fish, shellfish and other aquatic animals declined from 122 million tonnes in 1997 to 117 million tonnes in 1998. While aquaculture continued to grow – by 2 million tonnes in 1998 – marine capture fisheries production

Figure 6

WORLD FISH CATCH AND SUPPLY

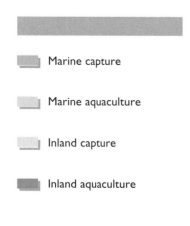

Marine capture

Marine aquaculture

Inland capture

Inland aquaculture

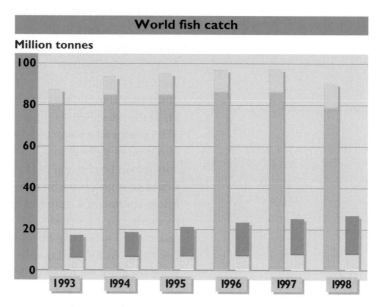

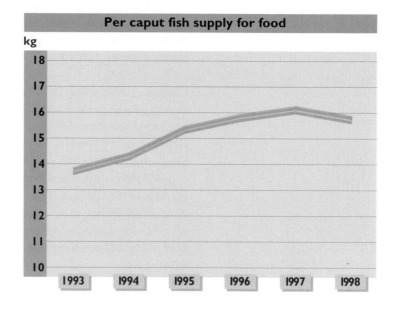

Source: FAO

fell by about 7.3 million tonnes, to 86.3 million tonnes. This
fall in landings was caused essentially by the El Niño
atmospheric phenomenon that affected fish stocks, particularly
in the Southeast Pacific. Landings of Peruvian anchovy and
Chilean jack mackerel declined from a total of 11.3 million
tonnes in 1997 to 3.7 million tonnes in 1998. However, in
1999 these fish stocks recovered rapidly. Elsewhere the picture
was uneven in 1998, the Western Pacific recording modest
increases in landings.

• China remained the world's top fish producer in 1998,
accounting for some 38 million tonnes, followed by Japan with
catches of about 6 million tonnes.

• Aquaculture production for both inland and marine areas
continued to increase, reaching a level of 30.8 million
tonnes (not including aquatic plants) in 1998. The Asian
region (particularly China) continued to dominate world
production.

• Fishmeal and oil production in 1998 was lower than
normal, as only about 24.5 million tonnes of fish were used
for reduction, 4 million tonnes less than in the preceding
year. Availability of fish for human consumption also fell,

Figure 7
TRADE IN FISHERY PRODUCTS

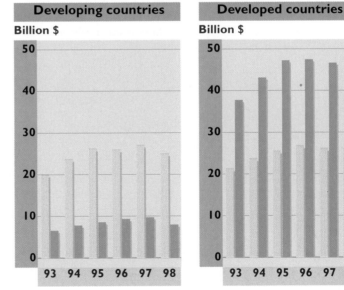

Exports

Imports

Source: FAO

to an estimated 15.7 kg/caput (liveweight equivalent) for 1998.

• In value terms, developed countries accounted for more than 80 percent of total fish imports in 1998. The three major markets for fish and fishery products were Japan, the United States and Europe. In spite of the recession, which brought a decrease in fish imports into Japan, the country remained the largest importer of fish and fishery products, accounting for some 23 percent of total imports in 1998. The United States was the second-largest importer. The share of fish imports in total fish supply continued to increase in the EU.

• Total fisheries exports amounted to $51 billion in 1998, a decline of about $2.4 billion from the previous year. The net foreign exchange receipts (after deduction of the value of fish imports from the total value of fish exports) earned by developing countries reached $17 billion in 1998. The exports of fish and fishery products for some developing countries represent a significant source of foreign exchange earnings.

• Twenty-five countries account for some 78 percent of total fisheries export products in value, and the first 11 countries account for as much as 50 percent of the total. With export earnings of about $4 billion in 1998 (8 percent of the world total), Thailand maintained its position as the leading world fisheries exporter. Norway, placed second with total exports of $3.7 billion, increased its export value by 7.7 percent over 1997. Denmark and China moved into the third and fourth positions, with exports amounting to $2.9 billion and $2.7 billion, respectively, in 1998.

8. PRODUCTION AND TRADE OF FOREST PRODUCTS

• Global markets for forest products weakened in 1998, owing to economic difficulties in some of the world's largest producer and consumer countries, particularly in Asia. Overall, global roundwood production fell by 0.9 percent to 3 270 million m³. In the developing countries, which account for about 60 percent of total roundwood production, production fell by 0.8 percent, while production in the developed countries fell by 1 percent.

• Industrial roundwood production (which excludes the production of wood used for fuel) accounted for about 46 percent of total roundwood production (including fuelwood) in 1998 and fell by 2 percent, to 1 520 million m³. Developed countries account for the largest share of industrial roundwood production (just over 70 percent) and production in these regions shrank by 0.9 percent, to 1 090 million m³. Developing country production fell much more dramatically, by 5.5 percent to 420 million m³.

• Global production of solid wood products (which include sawnwood and wood-based panels) also fell during 1998, by 3.7 percent to a level of 570 million m³. Sawnwood production fell by 3.6 percent, to 420 million m³, while wood-based panel production fell by 4 percent, to 150 million m³. Again, the decline in production was felt much more sharply in the developing countries, where production fell by 12.3 percent as opposed to a fall of 0.6 percent in the developed countries.

• In contrast to the markets for solid wood products, the global market for pulp and paper was fairly flat, and there were even a few moderate increases in production in some regions. Overall, global output of pulp and paper products increased by 0.3 percent in 1998, to 450 million tonnes. The economic slowdown in Asia and other developing countries had less effect on pulp and paper production, because developing countries account for only a 20 percent share of the global market. However, growth in pulp production in developed countries also continued to be held down by the increased use of recovered paper in the total fibre furnish.

• Global trade in forest products was also severely affected by the economic events in developing country markets in 1998. A significant proportion of forest products output is traded on

Figure 8
MAIN FOREST PRODUCTS

Developing countries

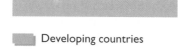
Developed countries

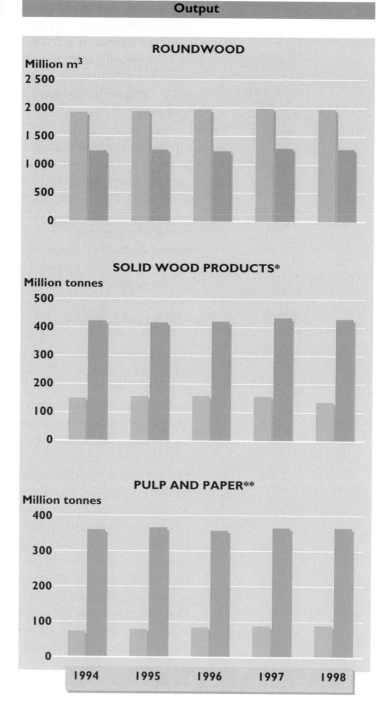

Output

ROUNDWOOD

SOLID WOOD PRODUCTS*

PULP AND PAPER**

* Sawnwood and sleepers and
   wood-based panels
** Wood pulp and paper and paperboard

Source: FAO

Figure 8 (continued)
MAIN FOREST PRODUCTS

Developing countries

Developed countries

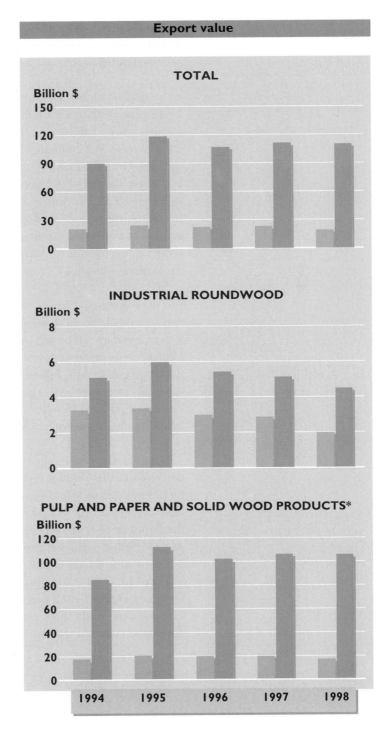

* Wood pulp and paper and paperboard,
  sawnwood and sleepers and
  wood-based panels

Source: FAO

international markets each year including, in 1998, 30 to 35 percent of sawnwood, wood-based panel and paper production in developed countries and 40 percent of wood-based panel and wood pulp production in developing countries. During 1998, exports increased in some regions and some product sectors, but fell in others.

• The value of global industrial roundwood exports in 1998 fell by 17.9 percent, to $6.5 billion. Developing countries recorded a much greater fall than developed countries, with a decline of 29.3 percent to $2 billion. However, only a small proportion of industrial roundwood production is exported (about 5.4 percent in 1998). The fall of 9.4 percent in the value of sawnwood exports, to $23.3 billion, is likely to have had a far greater impact on the sector. Developed countries account for about 85 percent of sawnwood exports, but the percentage fall in export revenues was roughly the same for both developed and developing countries.

• In the wood-based panels sector, the export situation varied considerably between developed and developing countries. Export revenues fell overall by 12.1 percent to $15 billion. However, exports from developing countries fell by a massive 39.6 percent, to $4.6 billion, while those from developed countries increased by 9.9 percent, to $10.4 billion. Lower exports of plywood from Indonesia accounted for most of the fall in developing country export revenues in this sector.

• Exports of paper and paperboard increased overall by 2.8 percent, to $69.4 billion. Developed country exports increased by 2.3 percent, to $62.9 billion, while developing country exports increased by 7.5 percent, to $6.6 billion. Indonesia and the Republic of Korea accounted for much of this increase in the developing countries. Exports of wood pulp fell overall, by 7.9 percent to $14.6 billion. Developed country exports fell by 9.5 percent, to $12.1 billion, while developing country exports increased slightly by 0.3 percent, to $2.5 billion. Reductions in exports from North America accounted for most of the fall in developed country exports.

WORLD REVIEW

II. OVERALL ECONOMIC ENVIRONMENT AND AGRICULTURE

WORLD ECONOMIC ENVIRONMENT

After the financial turbulence and slowdown in economic activity that followed the financial crisis initiated in Asia in 1997, risks of a global recession have receded. Current estimates of world economic growth in 1999 point to a rate of about 3 percent, up from 2.5 percent in 1998.[4] Prospects for the year 2000 are for a further acceleration, to 3.5 percent.

For the industrial countries, current estimates are for growth rates of around 2.8 percent in 1999 and 2.7 percent in 2000, with unbalanced cyclical patterns among the major economies. The long period of sustained growth in the United States is expected to continue, albeit at a slower pace in 1999 (3.7 percent, down 3.9 percent from the previous year) and 2000 (2.6 percent). In Japan, after a severe contraction in 1998, GDP only rose by an estimated 1 percent in 1999. With public investment and household confidence remaining weak, the economy is expected to recover only modestly in 2000. Japan's export sector did benefit from the rebound of its regional trading partners' economic activity, but these gains were offset by the strengthening of the yen.

Growth in the euro area fell to 2 percent in 1999, reflecting in particular weaker growth rates in Germany, Italy and the United Kingdom, but it was expected to recover to a level of 2.7 percent in 2000. The fall of the euro has stimulated exports and economic activity without creating inflationary pressure. In the second half of 1999, GDP growth strengthened, and hopes for a pickup in the world economy in 2000 now hinge to a large extent on increased demand in Western Europe. High unemployment has remained a problem despite some progress in job creation.

Economic recession in the economies in transition appeared to have bottomed out in 1998. The positive, if weak, economic growth forecast for 1999 was expected to gain momentum in 2000, thanks in particular to the forecast return to positive growth in the Russian Federation (2 percent). The very low petroleum prices in 1998, together with ineffective economic policies and the Asian financial crisis, had caused severe financial problems in the Russian Federation, but the subsequent strong rise in petroleum prices has improved the country's economic outlook. Growth in Hungary and Poland remained relatively strong, despite a slowdown in exports, but several other East European countries were experiencing difficulties in revitalizing economic activity.

For the developing countries as a whole, real GDP expansion in 1999 was estimated to be about 3.5 percent, only slightly above the previous year's rate, but an acceleration to 4.8 percent is forecast for 2000.

After the economic shock caused by the financial crisis, performances in Asia improved considerably, with growth forecast to be around 5.3 percent in both 1999 and 2000, up from 3.7 percent in 1998. In 1999, China's and India's economies expanded by 6.6 and 5.7 percent, respectively, despite generally disappointing performances of agriculture in both countries, and their growth was forecast to slow down only moderately in 2000. In China, however, private demand remains weak, and capital outflows and higher unemployment rates indicate strains. The implementation of further state enterprise and financial sector reforms remains a challenge. India benefited from past structural reforms and dynamic manufacture and service sectors.

In the rest of Asia economic performances also improved in 1999. The newly industrialized Asian economies saw real GDP contract by 1.8 percent in 1998 but recorded 5.2 percent growth in 1999. For four of the five countries most affected by the financial crisis (the Republic of Korea, Malaysia, the Philippines and Thailand), recovery is under way at a much more rapid pace than anticipated. In Indonesia, the fifth country, the economy seems to have turned around, but deep-seated structural problems remain and a modest growth rate of 2.6 percent is forecast for 2000. The initial catalyst for growth was a revival of exports, stimulated by competitive exchange rates and led by a global electronics boom. Improved agricultural output and the bottoming out and then gradual recovery of some commodity prices also played a role. Declining inflation allowed an easing of interest rates, while the region also saw a gradual recovery in capital inflows. However, private demand and, in particular, private investment remain sluggish, and unemployment high.

Africa's economies performed relatively well in 1998 and 1999, continuing the positive trend initiated in the mid-1990s. For the region as a whole, growth was in the order of 3.4 and 3.1 percent in 1998 and 1999, respectively, and was forecast

Figure 9

GROWTH IN WORLD ECONOMIC OUTPUT*

Advanced economies

Developing countries

Countries in transition

World

* Real GDP
** Projected

Source: IMF

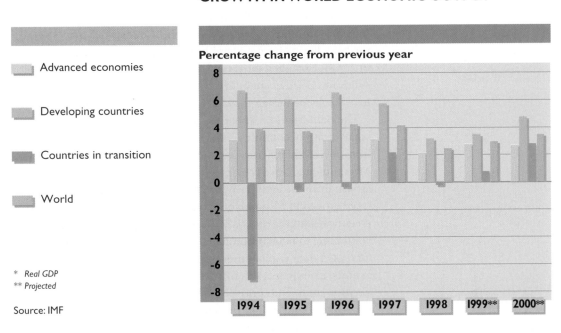

Figure 10

ECONOMIC GROWTH* IN DEVELOPING COUNTRY REGIONS

Africa

Asia

Near East

Latin America

* Real GDP
** Projected

Source: IMF

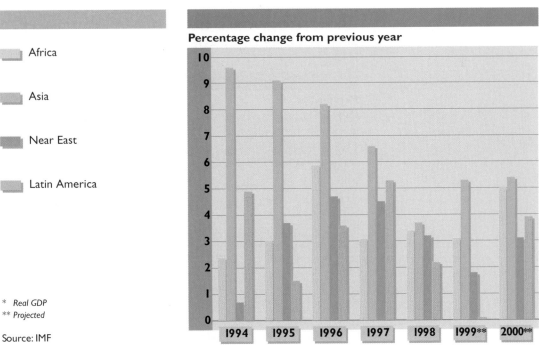

to gain strength, reaching 5 percent in 2000. For sub-Saharan Africa, growth was estimated to be only around 2.9 percent in both 1998 and 1999, but this aggregate performance was strongly influenced by the two largest economies, South Africa and Nigeria, the latter having been hit hard by the decline in petroleum prices in 1998. Excluding these two countries, growth in sub-Saharan Africa was 3.7 percent in 1998 and 4.4 percent in 1999, and it may accelerate further to reach 5.5 percent in 2000.

The performances within the subregion varied substantially. A small group of countries continued to grow robustly, benefiting from successful macroeconomic policies. Ghana, Uganda and Mozambique, in particular, underwent continuously strong growth from the early 1990s, although prospects for continuing rapid growth in Mozambique were severely compromised by the recent catastrophic floods. CFA countries also performed strongly, continuing to benefit from the 1994 devaluation which had increased their competitiveness and boosted investment and exports. Elsewhere, performances ranged from average to poor. Very low petroleum prices in 1998 hurt a number of petroleum-exporting countries, but proved very beneficial for net petroleum importers. Conversely, their subsequent strengthening will play a major role in the strong growth expected for Africa as a whole in 2000, but it will hurt many small net importer economies. The

Figure 11
GROWTH IN WORLD OUTPUT AND VOLUME OF TRADE

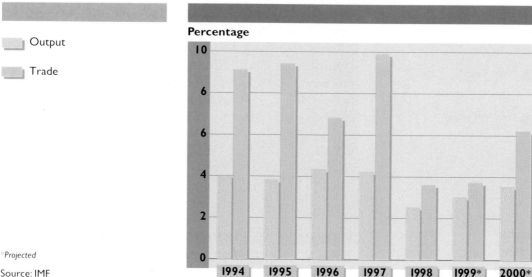

Output

Trade

Percentage

*Projected

Source: IMF

38

decline in agricultural commodity prices was a severe blow to many economies in the region.

Growth in the Near East and North Africa averaged 3.2 percent in 1998, down from rates of more than 4 percent in the previous two years. The slowdown was largely due to the low petroleum prices in 1998, which hurt petroleum-exporting countries but also contributed to a drop in workers' remittances to other countries in the region. The agricultural sectors of a number of countries, including Morocco, the Syrian Arab Republic, Jordan, Iraq and Turkey, were adversely affected by drought. Estimates for 1999 were for a further deceleration to 1.8 percent, not as much as anticipated, however. Short-term prospects for the region have brightened considerably, thanks in particular to the strong rise in petroleum prices in 1999 and the first quarter of 2000.

Real GDP growth in Latin America and the Caribbean fell from 5.3 percent in 1997, the best performance in 25 years, to 2.2 percent in 1998, and is expected to fall to -0.1 percent in 1999. The spread of the international financial crisis to Brazil and the devaluation of the real had a delayed and uneven impact on the region. While Brazil's economy stagnated, Mexico, Argentina and Bolivia managed to grow strongly in 1998. In addition to deteriorating terms of trade, reduced world export volumes and capital flows after the Russian default in August of 1998 meant that by the fourth quarter of 1999 Argentina, Brazil, Chile, Colombia, Ecuador, Peru and Venezuela all experienced recession. Lower commodity prices and natural disasters also contributed to the downturn.

Projections for 2000 point nevertheless to a sizeable recovery from the 1999 slump, with a 3.9 percent growth rate. Brazil is benefiting from the firm implementation of stabilization policies. While trade was depressed in the first half of 1999, the pronounced fall in the effective exchange rate of the real is expected to boost Brazil's export sector. Argentina's downturn, on the other hand, was stronger than anticipated; economic conditions did not improve in several other countries that were facing difficult political and social challenges and financial instability. Caribbean countries experienced an average per caput growth rate of 2.2 percent in 1999, but prospects were less than bright for 2000. In particular, countries depending on sugar and banana exports suffered from adverse terms of trade.

WORLD TRADE AND COMMODITY PRICES

Owing to the Asian financial crisis and the subsequent crises in the Russian Federation and Brazil, the volume of global trade grew at just 3.6 and 3.7 percent in 1998 and 1999, respectively, compared with an average growth rate of 6.9 percent in the period 1991-97. The drop in export and import volume for 1998 was more severe in developing countries. African countries, in particular, saw the value and volume of their exports decline by 13.5 and 1.4 percent, respectively, in 1998, reflecting their heavy reliance on petroleum and metal commodities exports. Rising import demand, especially from Europe, is expected to boost

Table 1

PERCENTAGE CHANGE IN WORLD TRADE: VOLUME AND TERMS OF TRADE

Year	World	Advanced countries			Developing countries		
		Exports	Imports	Terms of trade	Exports	Imports	Terms of trade
1997	9.9	10.3	9.2	-0.5	12.4	10.4	-0.3
1998	3.3	3.2	4.8	1.2	4.6	-1.3	-6.9
1999[1]	3.8	3.0	5.9	0.8	2.4	2.0	1.0
2000[2]	5.8	6.2	5.9	-0.3	6.1	8.0	1.3

Percentage change in the volume and terms of trade

[1] Estimate.
[2] Forecast.
Source: IMF.

Table 2

PRIMARY COMMODITY PRICE INDEXES BY QUARTER, 1997-1999

Year/ quarter	All primary commodities	Non-fuel primary commodities					Petroleum
		All	Food	Beverages	Agricultural raw materials	Metals	
1997:Q1	106.1	116.6	120.2	147.0	126.8	92.0	91.7
1997:Q2	101.7	117.2	116.5	189.6	123.0	92.8	80.5
1997:Q3	98.5	111.2	107.5	167.6	117.8	93.4	81.2
1997:Q4	96.1	106.4	110.4	157.8	108.7	85.4	82.0
1998:Q1	85.0	102.2	106.3	165.1	102.8	79.6	61.6
1998:Q2	81.1	98.2	101.4	141.8	102.0	77.6	57.8
1998:Q3	77.2	92.4	93.7	129.1	96.8	74.9	56.6
1998:Q4	75.1	92.3	96.4	125.3	96.8	72.2	51.6
1999:Q1	73.3	89.4	89.5	119.3	99.3	68.3	51.3
1999:Q2	80.9	88.0	83.8	110.9	99.4	72.2	71.2
1999:Q3	89.2	88.7	81.6	98.6	101.3	78.6	89.9
1999:Q4	97.0	92.3	82.3	113.2	106.2	81.9	103.3

Source: IMF.

international trade in 2000, including all main categories of primary and manufactured goods.

Commodity prices, which had been on a downward trend since 1995/96, further weakened in 1997 and 1998 in the wake of the Asian financial crisis and remained depressed during most of 1999. The index of non-fuel primary commodity prices fell by 30 points between early 1997 and mid-1999. Particularly hard hit were food products, beverages and metals. The index of petroleum prices fell from 91.7 in the first quarter of 1997 to 51.3 in the first quarter of 1999 and then recovered to 103 by the end of the same year.

Most commodity prices bottomed out during 1999 and some began to recover. In particular, in the first quarter of 2000, petroleum prices reached the highest level since the 1980s. The prices of several agricultural commodities also firmed somewhat in the same quarter (see Facts and figures, 6. International agricultural prices, p. 22). IMF forecasts a 4 percent rise in agricultural prices in 2000, although this modest upturn is subject to uncertainty. Indeed, supply generally failed to contract significantly in response to low prices and there are ample stocks for several commodities. Thus, barring output shocks or a strong upsurge in demand from the major importer countries, no sizeable price recovery can be expected in the short to medium term.

Implications for growth, trade and food security in developing countries

Economic developments have major and direct effects on agricultural performance and food security. It has been estimated that annual growth rates of 3 percent per caput should be required on a sustained basis to allow tangible improvements in living standards and poverty alleviation in the developing countries. According to the UN, a minority of only 23 of these countries met this criterion in 1998, and even fewer (including, however, the major cases of China and India), appear to have met it in 1999.[5]

Among the poorer countries, very few have shown such high levels of economic activity over protracted periods in the recent past. The revival of economic growth that has taken place in sub-Saharan Africa since the mid-1990s is remarkable in a historic context, but at best it enabled only modest gains in per caput terms.

For these and many other countries in the developing world, one factor of particular concern is the weakness of commodity prices on which many of these countries' economies depend. As pointed out, a demand-driven price boost for these products can only be expected to result from strong economic growth in the industrialized countries. The very high price of petroleum and overheated stock indexes bring the risk of inflation, which could lead to heightened interest rates slowing the industrial economies.

Most current forecasts appear to be cautiously optimistic for the medium term, however. As seen above, IMF expects a "soft landing" of the United States economy; growing momentum in growth in Europe; a gradual improvement in economic conditions in Japan; and a further solid recovery in Asian and several other developing country economies. These are also the general assumptions incorporated in the Project LINK economic and agricultural forecasts reviewed below.[6] For the developing countries, Project LINK forecasts average economic growth of more than 5 percent for 2000/01 (4 percent in Latin America, 4.5 percent in Africa, 5.6 percent in South and East Asia and 4.2 percent in West Asia).

Project LINK projections also suggest a recovery in the developing countries' agricultural output and trade:

- After the poor agricultural performances of these countries in 1998 and 1999, agricultural output is expected to expand by an annual average of 4.1 percent during the period 2000-03. The expansion would be above this average in the Near East and North Africa, sub-Saharan Africa and, to lesser extent, Latin America. The agricultural sector in India, and even more so in China, may experience slower growth over the period.
- Exports and imports of agricultural products, which contracted significantly in 1998 and 1999, are also anticipated to recover, especially on the side of imports. After having deteriorated in 1998 and 1999, the developing countries' agricultural barter terms of trade are expected to stabilize or slightly improve. This is broadly in line with IMF short-term (1999-2000) forecasts for developing countries' total terms of trade, which show a 6.9 percent decline in 1998 and a slight (about 1 percent yearly) improvement in 1999-2000.

Prospects for countries particularly dependent on agricultural trade

There are two country groups for which agricultural trade is particularly important, and they are therefore especially sensitive to changes in the international economic and agricultural market environment: i) low-income food-deficit countries

(LIFDCs) with the lowest capacity to finance food imports; and ii) economies highly dependent on agricultural exports (EHDAEs).[7]

Two forecast criteria are used: i) short-term economic (1999-2000) forecasts, estimated for FAO by IMF, and; ii) medium-term (2000-03) agricultural forecasts prepared by Project LINK.

i) Short-term economic forecasts

LIFDCs with the lowest capacity to finance food imports. IMF economic forecasts for these countries indicate:

- an expansion in real GDP of around 5.5 percent in 1999-2000, faster than the 3.2 percent average achieved during the 1991-95 period;
- steady progress in fiscal stabilization, with the fiscal deficit falling from an average 5.9 percent of GDP in 1991-95 to 2.9 percent in 1999-2000;
- a declining debt-service ratio from an average 30 percent in 1991-95 to 14 percent in 1999-2000. This would reflect both a reduction in the debt service, associated with positive developments in debt reduction and rescheduling, and an expansion in exports of goods and services. Nevertheless, the ratio remained very high in several African countries in the group.

EHDAEs. For this group of countries, IMF forecasts:

- a drop in real GDP growth from about 4.8 percent over the 1991-95 period to 1.1 percent in 1999 – mainly because of a contraction in the Latin American countries in the group – but a recovery to about 4 percent in 2000;
- a return to positive trade balances in 1999 and 2000 after eight consecutive years of deficit; this would enable a marked reduction in current account deficits which would, however, remain very high;
- a jump in the debt-service ratio from around 25 percent over the 1991-95 period to 37 percent in 1999-2000 (in 1999-2000, the ratio was 9 and 26 percent in the Far East and Pacific and the sub-Saharan region, respectively, but it stood at 85 percent in Latin America in 1999, with a forecast 67 percent for 2000);
- an increase in the fiscal deficit from an average 1.1 percent of GDP in 1991-95 to 3.1 percent in 1999-2000.

ii) Medium-term agricultural forecasts

LIFDCs with the lowest capacity to finance food imports. For this group, as for the developing countries as a whole, Project

LINK projections indicate a recovery in agricultural output and trade. In particular, LINK forecasts:

- an expansion in agricultural output of about 4 to 5 percent, slightly above the rate recorded between 1998 and 1999;
- a significant acceleration in agricultural trade growth, with imports expanding at a faster rate than exports;
- basically stable agricultural barter terms of trade, but a slight deterioration in the purchasing capacity of agricultural exports.

EHDAEs. For this group of countries, Project LINK projections for 2000-03 point to:

- a recovery in agricultural output growth from around 1 to 2 percent in 1998 and 1999 to 3 to 4 percent in 2000-03;
- an even more pronounced recovery in agricultural exports, which would expand by yearly rates of about 6 percent in 2000-03, following a cumulative 10 percent decline in 1998-99 – much of the increase should be volume-based, since export unit values are expected to increase only little;
- a small improvement in agricultural barter terms of trade, largely offsetting the strong deterioration in 1998-99 – thanks to expanded volumes of exports, EHDAEs' purchasing capacity would increase by a cumulative 9 to 10 percent over the 1999-2003 period.

WORLD REVIEW

III. SELECTED ISSUES

Microcredit: effects on rural poverty and the environment

INTRODUCTION

Lack of access to credit has plagued poor farmers and rural dwellers for many years. Rural people need credit to allow investment in their farms and small businesses, to smooth consumption, and to reduce their vulnerability to weather and economic shocks. Because they have little access to formal financing institutions, poor rural people follow suboptimal risk management and consumption strategies and rely on costly informal credit sources. Recognizing this, governments and international agencies created banks and lending programmes targeted at rural farmers. The track record of these programmes is mixed, especially with regard to reaching the poor. Reforms and innovations have emerged in recent years to improve credit market opportunities for the rural poor and increase the efficacy of rural finance.[8]

Microcredit helps the rural poor escape poverty by investing in small businesses and farms.

One such innovation is microcredit, or small loans targeting the poor, and this has transformed the way credit is viewed. Microcredit is intended to help the rural poor escape poverty by investing in their own small businesses and farms. Microcredit schemes overcome some of the problems of delivering rural credit to the poor by offering collateral-free loans at near-market interest rates, through community-based programmes operated by financing institutions or non-governmental organizations (NGOs).

Microcredit departs from traditional rural banking in three main ways:

- it aims at a more marginalized group of borrowers than credit institutions typically do;
- it generally includes non-credit services; and
- it employs a group lending approach.

Microcredit has not been portrayed as a substitute for agricultural credit, nor for traditional banking, as it is far smaller in scale and differently targeted than such lending. However, in its most modest form, it fills gaps in credit delivery that are not addressed by other providers; and, in its most ambitious form, it attempts to catalyse economic development that will reduce rural poverty.

THE HISTORY AND EVOLUTION OF MICROCREDIT

There are many antecedents to microcredit, which is a recently coined term that is applied to a diverse range of credit activities and types of institution. Locally managed credit arrangements have existed for hundreds of years and continue to serve small borrowers despite the advent of the "microcredit movement". Examples are rotating savings and credit associations (ROSCAs) and savings and credit cooperatives (SACCOs), both of which are found in communities around the world. Small loans to poor borrowers have also been part of the rural development strategies followed by many agencies and organizations since the early 1970s. The World Bank, FAO's Rural Finance programme, and major donors and other development agencies, including agricultural development banks, have incorporated small loan programmes and products in their rural finance strategies. Thus, microcredit is older than it appears at first blush, but the invention of the term "microcredit" as well as an organization to promote it globally and the high-level endorsement of specific outreach goals have recently elevated the movement to far greater prominence.

Several events in the past five years have sparked a social movement that has led to the development of a microcredit industry. The movement has been led by people outside the mainstream of rural finance and development and has posed a strong challenge to orthodox approaches. In very few years, an assortment of established and startup credit providers, advocates, evaluators, researchers, trainers and donors have focused their energies on microcredit and – in some cases – have bet heavily on its success. Debates have emerged over fundamental philosophy and technical details of microcredit delivery. Adherents have produced a flurry of examples and studies to support their view that microcredit is a revolution in social and economic development that will pull people from the depths of poverty, while critics staunchly maintain that it is not a panacea for reaching rural (or urban) poor where other credit systems have failed.

In 1976, Muhammad Yunus founded the Grameen Bank, the world's best-known provider of microcredit. Some trace the origins of microcredit in its recent form to this event. Through the Grameen Bank, Yunus was able to institutionalize features that provide a model for many – although not all – microcredit providers today. Microfinance organizations (MFOs) and programmes have since flourished, including "Grameen replications" in 45 countries. Today there are more than 1 200

Borrowing through microcredit schemes is growing rapidly in developing countries.

institutions providing microcredit at a national level.[9] 26 major institutions leading international microcredit programmes,[10] and 7 000 to 10 000 local and regional organizations providing microcredit as all or part of their development efforts.[11]

In 1997, two decades after Yunus began experimenting with loans to women in poor South Asian villages, more than 2 900 individuals, representing 1 500 organizations and 137 countries, gathered at the Microcredit Summit in Washington, DC. Headlined by Heads of State and dignitaries from the global development community, the Summit launched a campaign to reach 100 million of the world's poorest families by the year 2005. The significance of the Summit was to bring a certain aura of celebrity to the goal of poverty alleviation through microcredit, and to create an institution whose mission was to promote this goal at the global level.

It is widely perceived that growth in microcredit programmes has been phenomenal. The total number of borrowers reported through the members of the Microcredit Summit grew by 50 percent between 1998 and 1999 to reach 21 million globally; 12 million of these borrowers live on less than $1 per day.[12] The Grameen Bank alone has distributed $3 billion in loans to more than 2 million borrowers in Bangladesh, with $2.5 billion repaid to date.[13] Despite the fast growth, many believe the microcredit industry is still in an incipient stage relative to the potential demand for its services.[14] Moreover, microfinance is increasingly becoming less of a South Asian phenomenon. For instance, one donor is concentrating sustainable microfinance

Table 3

REGIONAL DISTRIBUTION OF MFOs AND GRANTS BY MEMBERS OF THE CONSULTATIVE GROUP TO ASSIST THE POOR (CGAP)

Region	Number of MFOs	CGAP grants (Million $)
Africa	988	7.1
Asia and the Pacific	822	7.0
Central/South America and Caribbean	335	9.2
Europe and North America	987	0.0
Near East and North Africa	n.a.	0.2
Eastern and Central Europe	n.a.	0.4
Global total (partial)	**3 142**	**24.0**

Note: Figures include all Summit Campaign members, including some that do not lend.
Sources: CGAP. 1998. *Focus* (various issues). Washington, DC, World Bank; Microcredit Summit Campaign, 1999.

Table 4

CHARACTERISTIC FEATURES OF MICROCREDIT

Lending	Borrowers
Small loan sizes	Poor
Little or no collateral required	Predominantly female
Non-credit services offered	Low education levels
Regular loan payments	Geographical remoteness
Peer group liability	Few assets
Donor-funded	Agriculture-related occupations

development efforts in Africa, "thereby pushing the frontier beyond what has been achieved to date".[15]

Table 3 shows the distribution of Microcredit Summit members, major donor grants and total disbursements by region.

A remarkable success story, or a new name for an old solution? What indeed are the impacts of microcredit and is it reaching its stated goals? Who benefits and who pays the costs of microcredit delivery? Finally, are there hidden effects − either good or bad − that should be recognized in our evaluation of what importance microcredit has as a development tool? This section describes the evidence and the arguments surrounding microcredit's broad impact to date.

Also discussed briefly is one "hidden impact" of microcredit delivery: its potential effect on the rural environment and natural resource use. Despite an escalating interest in microcredit and, more generally, microfinance, there has been almost no discussion about the relationship of these programmes to sustainable natural resource use. Given the primacy of poverty concerns over environmental protection, and the long-held tendency to take natural resources for granted, this oversight is not surprising. But it may be critically shortsighted, especially for the rural poor who depend on the natural resource base for their livelihood.

HOW MICROCREDIT WORKS

Microfinance organizations are more flexible than formal banking institutions, but more structured than informal rural lenders.

Many variants of microcredit have emerged as the geographical reach, clientele and aims MFOs have expanded.[16] Both in the conditions of lending and in the nature of the borrowers, microcredit is a hybrid of development tool and financial service. MFOs are more flexible in their terms of lending and repayment than many formal institutions, but more structured than informal lenders.

FAO/17552

Group lending approach
A training officer in Bangladesh helps village women to improve their income-generating abilities by making sarees to sell in the local market

Microcredit aspires to:
- reach potentially creditworthy borrowers who do not meet lenders' normal screening criteria; or
- reach potentially creditworthy borrowers who are geographically isolated; and
- offer related services such as basic financial management to increase borrowers' income-generation capacity;
- use financial services as a development tool at the household level; and
- catalyse female-based entrepreneurship.

The provision of a typical microcredit loan would involve the following steps:
1. Eligible poor borrowers are identified according to the target criteria and procedures.
2. A small group (five to eight people of common gender) of eligible borrowers is formed and rules are explained and agreed to.
3. Each member carries out compulsory saving.
4. One or two group members borrow the initial maximum amount.
5. The group meets weekly with other groups to discuss business and make instalment payments.

6. Financial management and other training is provided on a voluntary or mandatory basis to all members of the group.

7. When the initial loans are repaid, the next members of the group may borrow.

8. If a loan is not repaid on schedule, no member of the group may borrow until the loan is repaid by the borrower, or by other members of the group.

9. Eventually the repaid loans and group savings provide

Box 1

BORROWERS' STORIES

Almost 1.2 billion people, or about one out of four, in the developing and transition countries live on less than $1 per day – a globally recognized measure of poverty. Most of these people, including children, work long hours at physically demanding jobs just to survive. Many are entrepreneurs who run their own businesses in the "informal sector" and their lack of official standing prevents them from having access to formal credit sources. They turn to microcredit to purchase materials for weaving mats, sewing leather purses and baking bread, as well as to survive in times of emergency. Following are selected cases in which mircocredit loans have been used:

• An $80 loan was used by a young woman to purchase clay and glazes for a small ceramics business in the Dominican Republic. Since 1987 the owner has received eight loans from the microfinance institution and now has seven employees.

• A 22-year-old Pakistani woman lives with her husband and three children on his clerical salary and her occasional earnings from embroidery piecework. She received a loan of 4 500 rupees, which her husband took to the market to purchase two goats. The young woman maintains the goats while the loan instalment payments are made from her husband's salary. The goats are used primarily to provide milk for the children and the woman hopes eventually to sell them for a profit. She sufficient capital to maintain the revolving loan pool for all members.

Most recipients of microcredit are poor families with small income-generating businesses or potential to start up such a business. While this would appear to exclude farmers, effectively the microcredit programmes in rural areas do not preclude loans for the purpose of enhancing food production, and many rural farm families are also involved in non-farm economic

also uses the savings component of the microfinance programme.
• In the Philippines, a 2 000 peso (about $52) loan was used to purchase two piglets. The loan required weekly instalment payments of 88 pesos ($2.30) for six months. The piglets were fed table scraps, some garden produce and commercial feed. Both the weekly instalments and the purchase of feed had to be made out of household income. After six months, the fattened pigs were sold for 4 000 pesos ($104) each.
• An Indian woman purchased small bangles and cosmetics to trade at the market with a working capital loan of 1 000 rupees ($24) She borrowed for 20 weeks at a 20 percent flat interest rate, paying

instalments of Rs 60 ($1.42). She sells her wares at the market and door-to-door and earns about Rs 600 per week. After expenses, her earnings are Rs 120 per week ($2.84), half of which is devoted to the loan payment.
• One study examined the profits obtained by microentrepreneurs who received loans from the Bangladesh Rural Advancement Committee (BRAC), a large Bangladeshi MFO.[1] It found that there is a wide range of profits obtained from different enterprises. Poultry, potato cultivation, and net making were those with the highest profitability (about $21 per month), operating a grocery was in the middle category (profits about $12 per month),

paddy cultivation and goat rearing earned the least (about $2 per month) and bull fattening was unprofitable.

[1] H. Zaman. 1999. Assessing the poverty and vulnerability impact of microcredit in Bangladesh a case study of BRAC. Background paper for the WDR 2000/2001. Washington, DC, World Bank.

Table 5

SUBSECTORAL LENDING IN BANGLADESH, BY TYPE OF LENDER

Subsector	Percentage of loans disbursed by MFOs, 1997-98	Percentage of loans disbursed by informal lenders, 1991-92	Percentage of loans disbursed by formal lending institutions, 1991-92
Agriculture	12	22	23
Fisheries	4	n.a.	n.a.
Food processing	10	n.a.	n.a.
Small business	42	9[1]	8[1]
Cottage industry	3		
Transport	3	19	39
Livestock	18	0.4	2
Other	7	49	27

[1] Data are for small business and cottage industry combined.

Sources: Credit and Development Forum. 1999. *CDF Statistics*, Vol. 6. Dhaka, Bangladesh; and S. Khandker. 1998. *Fighting poverty with microcredit.* Washington, DC, World Bank. Categories do not match perfectly between the two sources and, because of rounding, totals do not add up to 100.

Small loans are used to finance non-farm rural activities, home gardening and small agricultural enterprises.

activities.[17] Rural non-farm income is becoming an increasingly important share of total rural income, averaging 42 percent in Africa, 40 percent in Latin America and 32 percent in Asia.[18] The types of enterprise that are supported by microcredit include handicraft production, simple agroprocessing operations, vending and marketing, rickshaw driving and, in some cases, the acquisition of improved farm inputs.

Table 5, shows the breakdown of microfinance loans (in value) in Bangladesh in 1997 and 1998, and the relative proportions provided by other lenders in Bangladesh in 1991-92. MFOs included the Grameen Bank, the Bangladesh Rural Advancement Committee (BRAC), NGOs and cooperatives. Formal lenders included the government, Krishi Bank and commercial banks; informal lenders included families, moneylenders, employers, input suppliers and others.

HOW MICROCREDIT OVERCOMES BARRIERS TO CREDIT DELIVERY

The borrowing needs of the non-bankable population are addressed largely by informal moneylenders and other providers of informal finance – including rotating credit groups and savings associations. Microcredit does not replace these local sources of credit and savings but combines characteristics of such mechanisms, such as the information advantages of village moneylenders and the rotational lending of ROSCAs. These traditional mechanisms have fulfilled the primary role of credit delivery to the rural poor. However, the astounding growth of

Microcredit fills a credit niche for certain population groups, especially women.

microcredit's philosophy and methods attests to the continuing existence of unmet needs. IFPRI[19] reports a significant number of poor in developing countries as experiencing real borrowing constraints.

The barriers hindering rural credit delivery to the poor derive from the lack of institutions for monitoring and enforcing credit transactions in rural areas.[20] The section entitled Political economy in the alleviation of poverty and food insecurity (p. 287 of this issue) describes some of the market and institutional failures that prompted the spread of microcredit directed at poor, rural populations. The author notes a history of credit market failures, including the capture of benefits by wealthy or politically advantaged élite groups and repayment disincentives. He also mentions several types of institutional failure, including the lack of practical mechanisms for reaching the rural poor.

The problems can be summarized as:
- Information asymmetries
- Low-potential profitability
- Lack of portfolio diversification

The novelty in rural credit introduced by microcredit is the way in which it tackles these well-known market and institutional failures. Microcredit attempts to overcome the market and institutional barriers and still be financially viable.

Information asymmetries are created when the parties to a transaction do not have access to equal information, thereby creating an advantage to the party with a greater amount of information. Such situations can arise either before a transaction takes place, when a borrower may appear to be less risky than she/he really is, and after the transaction has occurred, when a borrower may have an incentive not to repay the lender as originally agreed. To deal with the problem, lenders usually require borrowers to have good credit histories and meet other requirements (such as steady income) to ensure they are creditworthy, as well as requiring some collateral to be provided in exchange for granting credit. However, the usual remedies do not work with the borrower group aimed at by microcredit.

Microcredit resolves information asymmetries by creating peer group contracts in which liability is collectively accepted and regular payments are made at group meetings. In this way, peer pressure creates an incentive to remain current with loan payments, as well as to exclude those who might be considered poor credit risks.[21] Sometimes loan payments adjust over time to correspond to a borrower's increased ability to pay back.

Low-potential profitability is the second barrier to loans for the poor. It reflects a bank's perceptions of the high costs, high risk and small market inherent in serving such a borrower population. At the individual level, such borrowers generally do not have steady or adequate income or any assets to seize, and they face great economic and cultural barriers to earning income. At the community level, they are relatively isolated – so it is expensive to provide financial services to them, and their market opportunities are few. The sparse population of potential borrowers in such areas also inhibits reaching economies of scale in the provision of financial services.

Microcredit resolves this problem through several practices. Many microcredit programmes provide – sometimes require – *training and technical advice* to borrowers in an effort to increase their incomes. These include literacy programmes, enterprise management and education in family planning and nutrition. These "full service" programmes try to increase the skills and capacity of their borrowers. The value of this is obvious, especially for poor women who lack experience and knowledge in running businesses.[22] However, the costs are also high and must be supported by the interest payments of the borrowers, or by continued subsidies.

High repayment rates are also important to microcredit's ability to lend to the poor. This is believed to be attributable to the emphasis on female borrowers, who are more responsible than men in making payments, and to the peer joint-liability system. Loan default rates for female borrowers are 3 percent compared with 10 percent for men in the same programmes.[23] The Grameen Bank has repayment rates of about 98 percent, while other major microfinance organizations report loan repayment rates of 90 to 95 percent.[24] This compares with rates of less than 50 percent reported by agricultural development banks.[25] Even when the Grameen Bank's repayment rates are recalculated using a stricter definition of overdue loans that is more consistent with regulated banking practice, the repayment rate between 1985 and 1994 was 92 to 95 percent, and it has been slightly higher since then.[26]

Microcredit programmes generally charge market interest rates on loans to support their high costs. One might expect the rates to be concessional, based on the subsidy that is often provided to the MFOs by donors. In fact, real interest rates are frequently higher than those of commercial banks, but lower than those of village moneylenders.[27] This is a contributing factor to the formation of a market niche for microcredit borrowing, and it

The provision of training and technical advice to borrowers is sometimes required as a loan condition.

Borrowers generally pay market interest rates for microcredit.

helps overcome high costs. An eligible borrower would rather obtain microcredit than pay the higher interest charged by other informal credit sources.

Despite these practices, the presence of financial support suggests that most MFOs are not profitable if they follow standard accounting principles. This is an area of great controversy within the industry and is discussed in more detail below.

Portfolio diversification is the third problem barring poor rural populations from access to credit. Lenders operating in a given community or region face covariant risks. Among the most likely reasons for loan delinquencies in a region or country is a natural disaster (such as the Bangladesh floods of 1998) or an economic downturn (such as the 1997 financial crisis in Asia). Such events affect microcredit borrowers more than other borrowers because of their greater economic vulnerability.

Microfinance organizations have only partially resolved portfolio diversification problems. The peer group lending approach spreads the liability for repayment among the entire group of borrowers in a given village or peer group. This means that they accept responsibility for each other's debts. While this

Poor rural borrowers are usually considered a high risk for lending institutions because of their vulnerability.

Figure 12

THE MAIN AIMS OF MICROCREDIT

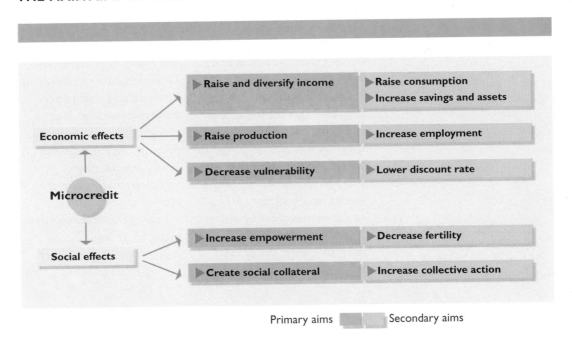

Economic effects

- ▶ Raise and diversify income
- ▶ Raise consumption
- ▶ Increase savings and assets
- ▶ Raise production
- ▶ Increase employment
- ▶ Decrease vulnerability
- ▶ Lower discount rate

Microcredit

Social effects

- ▶ Increase empowerment
- ▶ Decrease fertility
- ▶ Create social collateral
- ▶ Increase collective action

Primary aims   Secondary aims

approach does not overcome the risk of calamitous losses when a poor harvest or natural disaster occurs, it does reduce the risk exposure when losses are not widespread among borrowers.

Insurance products and emergency funds are also being adopted to address the lack of portfolio diversification. These sources provide compensation or additional credit during times of disaster, and they might include the suspension of loan repayment schedules until recovery is possible. This is analogous to the extra liquidity that a creditor might provide to a solid company undergoing a cyclical downturn, or to the action taken by central banks when the entire financial system undergoes stress.

Box 2

MEASURING THE IMPACTS OF MICROCREDIT

A great many studies have been performed in recent years, purporting to measure the impacts of microcredit. These have been done as a requirement of funding agencies, as an academic exercise and as a way of targeting funds better so as to achieve specific social or economic goals. Unfortunately, the results have been somewhat contradictory, fuelling debates over the effects and value of microcredit.

Different measures are used to assess the impacts of microcredit. The most common indicator is change in *household income* of the borrowing households. Also important are changes in *assets, net worth and labour*. The reason for this is straightforward: the primary purpose of microcredit is to raise people from poverty. The positive externality of poverty alleviation is the justification used for spending public funds on microcredit. Another common measure of impact is *household consumption*, which is a close proxy for income and is more easily measured in household surveys. Studies have measured changes in total household consumption, changes in food consumption and timing of consumption. Other indicators of individual or household welfare are also considered, such as change in *school enrolment* rates and *health* measures. Finally, indicators of *empowerment* and *effects on women* are measured.

Khandker[1] surveyed three major microcredit programmes in Bangladesh for impacts. His results show

During the Bangladesh floods of late 1998, the Grameen Bank and other microcredit lenders allowed borrowers to suspend payments on their loans until they were on a sounder financial footing. The savings component of microcredit programmes is sometimes used to finance such concessions. This is not a failsafe way to avoid losses. The risk of default does not evaporate when payments are postponed, and clientele facing frequent liquidity crises may never become current with their obligations. But this is one way in which microcredit lenders have shown flexibility in dealing with an institutional barrier that impedes credit availability to the rural poor.

an 18 percent increase in household consumption from microcredit borrowing by women, and an 11 percent increase in consumption when men are the borrowers (op. cit., p. 148.) He suggests that 5 percent of participating families can escape poverty each year because of the increased consumption resulting from microcredit. Other impacts of microcredit reported by Khandker are consumption smoothing, labour supply smoothing and improved child nutrition, especially for girls. However, Khandker warns that these effects will only be sustainable if microcredit is targeted at areas and economic activities with high growth potential. This is because of the emphasis among the poor to use loans for consumption purposes, which should eventually lead to production and income changes.

Morduch[2] examines the impacts of microcredit, being careful to exclude from the sample ineligible households. One reason is to avoid the problem of sample selection bias, which arises at the household level (when more creditworthy households enter the programmes), the village level (when better-off villages have access to microcredit) and the individual level (because success as a borrower will engender additional borrowing).

Morduch shows no increases in consumption among microcredit borrowers, and sometimes reveals lower enrolment rates. He attributes this to his use of control groups that correct for the selection bias inherent in many microcredit programmes. He does find beneficial impacts through consumption smoothing among borrowing households, as well as an increased ability to diversify labour supply. These effects reduce the vulnerability of borrowing households compared with non-borrowing households. (A summary of important impact assessments is provided in Table 6.)

[1] S. Khandker. 1998. *Fighting poverty with microcredit*, p. 11 Washington, DC, World Bank.
[2] J. Morduch. 1998. Does microfinance really help the poor? New evidence from flagship programs in Bangladesh. HIID, Harvard University (unpublished document).

EFFECTS OF MICROCREDIT ON BEHAVIOUR OF THE RURAL POOR

The primary aim of microcredit programmes is to alleviate poverty by increasing borrowers' earnings. In the process, there may be other impacts such as schooling and family planning decisions. It is difficult to determine the precise impact of microcredit because of the fungibility of loans. For the rural poor, in particular, it is difficult to separate out production and consumption decisions, since labour is the main productive asset and adequate nutrition is essential to work. Figure 12, p. 55, outlines the avenues through which

Table 6

EFFECTS OF MICROCREDIT ON SELECTED VARIABLES: THE RESULTS OF IMPACT STUDIES

Author	Morduch (1998)	Khandker (1998)	IFPRI (1998)	MkNelly (1997)	Zaman (1999)	Other[1]
Income/ poverty	No impact	Lower poverty; higher village income	Higher income	Higher off-farm income	Smoothed	–
Net worth, assets	–	Increase when female borrower	–	–	Increase	Increase
Labour supply	Diversified	Increase for females; decline for males	–	–	–	–
Consumption	Smoothed	Smoothed; increased	More food; no smoothing	Increased food security	Smoothed	Smoothed
Enrolment	No effect/ lower	Higher for boys; no effect for girls	–	–	–	Better access
Health measure	–	Better child nutrition	–	No nutrition impact	Better child nutrition	–
Contraceptive use	–	Reduced	–	–	–	–
Female empowerment	–	–	–	–	Increase	Increase

[1] Includes Jacoby (1994), Schuler and Hashemi (1994), Buckly in Hume and Moseley (1995), Foster (1995) and World Bank (2000) – these authors are cited in IFPRI (1998).

References: J. Morduch. 1998. Does microfinance really help the poor? New evidence from flagship programs in Bangladesh. HIID, Harvard University (unpublished document); S. Khandker. 1998. *Fighting poverty with microcredit.* Washington, DC, World Bank; IFPRI. 1998. *Rural finance and poverty alleviation.* Washington, DC; B. MkNelly. 1997. Freedom from Hunger's credit with education strategy. Sacramento, CA (unpublished document); H. Zaman. 1999. *Assessing the poverty and vulnerability impact of microcredit in Bangladesh: a case study of BRAC.* Background paper for the WDR 2000/2001. Washington, DC, World Bank.

microcredit directly and indirectly affects borrowers. Box 2 summarizes the empirical evidence for some of these changes from several major studies.

Economic effects

Increased income. The evidence suggests that microcredit raises the income of participants (see Box 2 and Table 6). As income increases, secondary changes in the quantity, composition and timing of consumption, savings and asset-holdings will occur.

Income diversification. Opportunities to diversify income are important, particularly for the rural poor, who are dependent on agriculture and subject to weather fluctuations and crop cycles. Income can be diversified into additional farm activities such as new crops and new or expanded non-farm activities.

Borrowers sometimes use microcredit loans for immediate consumption needs.

Consumption effects. A share of microcredit loans is used directly to increase consumption. While consumption behaviour may change immediately, other impacts of microcredit borrowing may show up only in the long term. For instance, a reduction of vulnerability through increased food purchases in the short term may change long-term economic outcomes for poor rural dwellers. Given the low income levels of microcredit borrowers, increments in income are often spent on improved food, shelter and other basic goods.

Savings effects. Either through forced savings, or diversion from increased income, microcredit borrowers increase their savings. This allows them to smooth consumption, invest in earning activities and prepare for emergencies. Research shows that microcredit loans are used largely for investment purposes (e.g. 80 percent of BRAC credit in Bangladesh), such as investing in housing and other productive assets.[28]

Production effects. Credit provides the opportunity to begin or expand new non-farm activities, such as agroprocessing, food distribution, small-scale manufacturing, equipment repair and rental, tourism, mining and service sector activities. It can also change production methods in farming with yield-enhancing inputs. These changes in production lead to new and different employment opportunities for the borrowers as well as others in the community.

Discount rate. Credit provides a way to shift the timing of consumption to reduce vulnerability, thereby changing the discount rate that borrowers place on future income. The higher an individual's income, the less they are preoccupied with satisfying current consumption needs. It becomes possible to trade off some current consumption for a higher, more sustained future return.

Social effects

Empowerment of women. As a group, MFOs overwhelmingly focus on recruiting and extending credit to women, especially compared with the emphasis of other lenders.[29]

The reasons MFOs prefer to target women may differ. Women have higher payback rates and are reputed to be better credit risks, easier to discipline and more inclined to use the income they control for improving children's nutrition and education, and they have more unrealized entrepreneurial capacity.

Economic empowerment of female borrowers can lead to reduced fertility rates.

Some MFOs may simply wish to increase women's economic power.

Some evidence suggests that microcredit programmes may reduce fertility rates.[30] This is not surprising, given the higher opportunity cost of bearing children for a successful female microentrepreneur, relative to a woman employed only in household or farm activities and where the child may be a more important source of labour. It may be that economic power, new information or a new support system has allowed women to take more control over childbearing decisions. Also, as women's income rises, child mortality rates usually fall, lessening the need or desire to bear as many children.

There may, however, be an even more direct avenue of influence on fertility from female participation in microcredit-related activities. This might explain cases such as Bangladesh, where fertility rates are plummeting, while child mortality remains high. Some MFOs provide, indeed encourage, family planning education as part of their programme and regular meetings. Participants with BRAC and the Grameen Bank, for example, are far more likely to practise contraception than the national average.

Collective action. MFOs forego traditional collateral and, instead, rely on participants' social collateral. Participants may be required to borrow in groups, act as mutual guarantors or receive loans that are contingent on others in the group paying their loans back. These group incentives and dynamics are reinforced through regular, often weekly, group meetings.

This social interaction has the effect of lowering the costs of collective action, which influences the provision of public goods, the use of common property resources and decisions about many other matters. Communication among participants greatly increases the chances of successful collective action. Ostrom, Gardner and Walker[31] have shown in a series of experiments that, given the right institutional framework to communicate, poor people make productivity-increasing and cooperative decisions.

MICROCREDIT'S LINK TO NATURAL RESOURCES

If the goal of microcredit is long-term poverty eradication rather than immediate poverty alleviation, sustainable natural resource use must be considered, particularly for the rural poor. The effect of microcredit on the environment is not clear a priori; rather, who receives microcredit and the uses to which it is put determine the manner and degree to which microcredit affects the environment. The extent of these effects has not been studied carefully, but it may become more apparent as experience with microcredit impact assessment grows. While a certain degree of these impacts is to be expected from any credit delivery, the primary reasons for making this connection an explicit and conscious component of microcredit programmes are that the poorest tend to be the most resource dependent and women tend to be the primary natural resource stewards.

The net direct impact of microcredit on the environment is probably detrimental in the short term, as is most economic activity. But the need of the poor to generate income cannot be compromised or delayed. Thus, it is paramount to search for ways to mitigate harmful environmental effects. Direct efforts that promote environmental management and environmental products can offset harmful impacts. The net indirect impact is less easy to assess but, with the exception of increasing waste and by-products, other impacts such as increasing and diversifying income, targeting women, reducing fertility rates and facilitating collective action can be environmentally beneficial.

There are a growing number of programmes that are linking microcredit to environmental resources, either because they have realized that credit can promote their environmental agenda, or because they have discovered that environmental management can be good business and environmental products have a market. Further, choices are made in the methods used even for potentially harmful activities. Examples of such programmes are described in Box 3, p. 62.

Despite what we have learned about opportunities to enhance growth while protecting the environment, there is still a tendency to dismiss the relationship between microcredit and the environment. This may be an issue of scale. The cumulative effect, however, of millions of microentrepreneurs should not be ignored.

CURRENT DEBATES ABOUT MICROCREDIT

Neither the growth nor the reception of the microcredit movement has been without controversy. Like most development efforts, particularly those that compete for scarce

Box 3

INTERTWINING MICROCREDIT AND ENVIRONMENTAL GOALS

There are few examples of MFOs that explicitly tie environmental management to lending, although environmental practices often appear in the members' conditions of lending. This may be due in large part to the precedent set by the 16 conditions that the Grameen Bank encourages its borrowers to respect. Members pledge the following: "… we will keep our children and the environment clean, we will build and use pit-latrines [and], during the plantation seasons, we will plant as many seedlings as possible." These conditions have been copied by the hundreds of Grameen replicates around the world and they have laid the foundation for microcredit lending that embraces environmental objectives.

Microcredit and environmental factors are frequently coupled by conservation NGOs, or development NGOs with a conservation agenda. In some cases these organizations have microcredit capacity themselves, while others partner with more specialized credit suppliers,

such as local or international banks or other NGOs.

There is also a small but growing group of MFOs concerned with producing "green" products or technologies. For example, Grameen Shakti is dedicated to providing renewable energy sources (e.g. solar panels, biogas digesters and wind turbines) to villages in Bangladesh that do not have electricity. Likewise in the Dominican Republic and Honduras, the solar-based rural electrification concept (SO-BASEC) uses microcredit to promote solar-based renewable energy.

Technoserve – Ghana

In Ghana, population growth is leading to encroachment on forest reserves near the Red Volta and Morago Rivers. Further, declining soil fertility is forcing agricultural activities to move closer to elephant migration corridors. For coexistence to be possible, the local communities will have to reduce their dependency on food crops and find other income-generating activities.

The NGO Technoserve (TNS), in collaboration with the Ghanaian Government and local organizations, is developing the marketing and processing of the shea nut, which grows wild on native trees. Shea butter has export potential for use in the natural cosmetics market (e.g. The Body Shop) for United States and European buyers. It is important as a native resource that supports sustainable development activities. In Ghana, TNS works with 300 self-employed women, who receive training and credit and organize themselves into groups in order to increase income-earning ability. The income earned by these women helps to support up to 2 100 family members.

The NGO is supporting the prefinancing of such women's groups by export companies – in essence, providing seed capital for the women to purchase materials. The women have difficulty in smoothing their income because they need cash when nuts are harvested and processed but they only receive income from sales later. In the past, the groups received loans from agricultural development banks, used the money to collect nuts, which they then auctioned before

paying back the loan. However, only registered groups could afford this procedure. The process was slow and cumbersome, requiring guarantors and securities that frustrated the women's work and, ultimately, required high interest payments. Moreover, the slow response of shea nut exporters to tender bids for the purchase of shea nut stores (via auctions) resulted in further delays in the sale of the nuts, thereby increasing interest accumulation on the loans.

Through TNS, borrower groups avoid the necessity of registration and can obtain the prefinancing loan enabling them to approach the exporters themselves. They then gather nuts and supply the contracted volume. Access to working capital loans increases their ability to stockpile the nuts, add value through processing, increase income and create local employment.

TNS works with the export companies on behalf of the women's groups to negotiate the terms of contracts, coordinate activities on the ground in order to ensure that both

parties are fulfilling their requirements and provide basic business training to the identified groups. All this helps the women involved to plan and assess the profitability of the shea marketing activities, as well as to determine how they might invest some of the profits to enhance their livelihood strategies.

PDA and PDI – Thailand
The Population and Community Development Association (PDA) is a well-established NGO in Thailand that uses the microcredit tool for environmental conservation and natural resource management. It was founded in 1974 with the aim of promoting family planning in urban and rural areas but, over time, its scope of work has enlarged. Today it covers income-generating activities and development in rural areas as well as sanitation, environmental conservation and educational training.

Population and Development International (PDI), an affiliate of PDA, has used microcredit to provide farmers with in-kind loans of seeds and fertilizers or cash, tied to specific environmental protection conditions. The interest rate on the loans is equivalent to the bank rate (1 baht/month). The value of the loan depends on village capacity as well as local interest in preserving the environment.

PDI uses microcredit to create savings groups, mainly comprising women. After taking out a loan, the women's savings groups choose between using the funds to leverage a larger bank loan (which can be up to five times the amount of the funds) or acting as their own credit organization, providing small loans to individual members of the savings group.

The Western Forest Complex (WFC) project in Thailand's Kanchanaburi Province began in 1996. Its purpose is to decrease deforestation in the long term, while increasing the level of conservation awareness in the short term. The project is financed by local and international funds and targets 15 villages in the western part of the country.

In this project, PDI uses microcredit to implement sustainable, alternative livelihood practices with the aim of reducing dependency on natural resources, especially in areas affected by slash-and-burn agriculture. In particular PDI encourages planting of native trees and fruit-trees by providing credit in-kind in the form of saplings. The programme offers saplings and training to a farmers' conservation group, which distributes trees to individual farmers. In return, farmers agree to refrain from clearing more land. If a planted sapling dies within one year, the farmer pays back the group that received the sapling.

Significant results have been achieved in a few years. One thousand seedlings have been planted each year. Beneficiaries have increased their knowledge and practices of agricultural activities such as fruit gardens and animal husbandry. Farmers have substantially decreased their use of chemical inputs in agricultural activities as well as their gathering of non-timber forest products. The future aim of the project will be to solidify the pilot activities into sustainable operations that can be implemented and managed directly by the farmers, eventually forming cooperatives for selling and buying trees without the need of intermediaries.

donor funds, there are disagreements over the appropriate role and vision of microfinance. The three most vociferous debates concern the financial sustainability of microfinance organizations, the targeting of the poorest of the poor, and impact assessment.

Financial sustainability. Microcredit is provided by a range of organizations, from commercial banks to local NGOs, whose goals range from profit maximization to long-term poverty eradication. With this range of objectives, it is not surprising to find that programmes vary tremendously in their approaches, functions and underlying philosophy. Some of the debates are indicative of a healthy and maturing industry, such as questions about assessing credit risk, appropriate information systems, responding to natural disasters, providing for refugees and monitoring and evaluation. At root, however, a fundamental philosophical divide has emerged within the industry regarding the emphasis on "poverty alleviation" as opposed to "financial sustainability". The subsidy to MFOs has been a subject of debate, with many financial specialists and donors insisting that subsidies must be removed.

There is concern that some MFOs are dependent on donor subsidies.

Arguments for an emphasis on the goal of financial sustainability tend to:
- separate organizations and borrowers who can be financially viable from those who cannot;
- extend limited donor resources to the greatest number of viable microcredit efforts;
- maintain that a reliance on subsidies will limit the growth of MFOs; and
- maintain that, without cost-cutting market incentives, inefficiencies may be perpetuated.

Arguments for an emphasis on the goal if poverty alleviation maintain that:
- microcredit reaches the poor who do not have access to market-based financial services; and
- microcredit programmes can achieve social goals more cost-effectively than alternative forms of aid delivery.[32]

In the past few years, major donors have imposed time limits on the subsidies that they offer for microcredit programmes in the hope that MFOs – whether they be public or private – will eventually achieve financial sustainability. For CGAP recipient organizations, that period is five years. The Grameen Bank reduced the subsidy proportion of loans outstanding from between 22 and 23 percent in 1986-87 to 8 percent in 1993-96, while rapidly expanding their clientele.

Targeting the poorest. The second debate currently raging in the microcredit world revolves around targeting the poorest. There are some who question whether it is appropriate to lend to poor people who cannot meet normal standards of "bankability", especially with donor funds. The crux of this debate concerns the ability of very poor people to pay back loans and avoid further cycles of impoverishment.

Arguments for targeting the poorest maintain that:

• payback records of the poor are as good as or better than those of higher-income borrowers and that the income level of recipients is not a determinant of "bankability"; and

• donor funds directed towards better-off recipients are siphoning funds from where they are most needed, i.e. development programmes.

Arguments for not targeting the poorest maintain that:

• social service organizations are better able to serve the real needs of that population;

• microcredit should be targeted at any borrowers who have the skills and resources to be financially viable, and not those selected on the basis of poverty;

• the poorest cannot escape poverty by borrowing, and may actually become worse off.

Impact assessment. The third major controversy concerns whether it is necessary to devote resources to measuring changes in the behaviour of microcredit borrowers owing to their ability to borrow funds. Impact assessments have become a requirement of most lending programmes, and yield a confusing array of results.

Several major impact reports are summarized in Box 2, p. 56. They generally show beneficial effects on income and consumption; however, there are substantial methodological disagreements remaining. Efforts have been spent in recent years on establishing best practices, monitoring systems and reporting requirements for MFOs. These practices should do much to resolve the remaining disputes regarding the impacts of microcredit.

It is clear that the maturation of MFOs reveals an economically viable market among clientele that do not need subsidies to carry out their economic activities. Many of these microcredit borrowers thrive merely from having access to credit and/or other services provided by MFOs. It could be argued that these clients do not need subsidized microcredit, nor perhaps the training and education that sometimes comes with it. It is also clear by now that there are microcredit borrowers

FAO/17873

Loan repayment patterns
In debt repayment, the poor
perform as well as, if not better,
than higher-income borrowers

who succumb to a cycle of increasing debt, or who face other
difficulties in maintaining the demands of financial
responsibility imposed by MFOs. It could be argued that these
clients would be better served by other development approaches
and tools.

Finally, there is a group of clients and potential clients for
whom subsidized microcredit provides an opportunity to move
out of poverty, but at a pace consistent with their income-
generation abilities and the economic capacities of their region.
MFOs can cite a multitude of examples of these borrowers or
former borrowers who have successfully used their microcredit
to become more financially stable. For this group, an excessively
swift removal of subsidies would be a mistake.

CONCLUSION
Microcredit has introduced some major innovations in
development and rural finance approaches. Its long-term
potential to free people from poverty is not yet clear. Studies
indicate that microcredit should be targeted at those borrowers
who have the potential to carry out sustained economic
activities and who are credit-constrained. The limited potential
of many borrowers to absorb additional capital may also limit

Microcredit is sometimes used to prevent or mitigate environmental damage.

the positive economic growth and poverty-reducing effects of microcredit.

Further analyses should consider the long-term outcomes for individual borrowers and the contribution made to the development of villages and rural communities. It is important to use local knowledge of the demand for economic activity when identifying appropriate microenterprise and other borrowing purposes, and to be aware of the opportunities as well as the risks. Microcredit, like other forms of credit, can result in environmental degradation and loss of natural capital. However, a conscious approach to the use of microcredit could hold potential for mitigating that damage and may even lead to environmental improvements. Further empirical work will identify whether or not the environmental impacts of microcredit justify its use as a tool for sustainable development.

Conflicts, agriculture and food security

"A peaceful and stable environment in every country is a fundamental condition for the attainment of sustainable food security."

World Food Summit Plan of Action, paragraph 3

INTRODUCTION

Armed conflict and civil strife were major sources of food insecurity in the 1990s and will continue to be this century, although their number and the losses associated with them may have passed their peak (see Figure 13). Depending on which of the various definitions of the term is used, from 30 to 40 countries were conflict-affected at the end of the twentieth century.[33] Overall, hundreds of millions of people were involved. The vast majority of these people lived in low-income countries, in which agriculture represents a major source of livelihood, foreign exchange and social stability. A disproportionate number of the countries were in sub-Saharan Africa.

The economic losses and the disruptions to food supply and access associated with conflicts can be disastrous, especially in low-income countries where there are no effective social safety nets. While conflicts are at the basis of food insecurity situations

Figure 13

NUMBER OF DEVELOPING COUNTRIES WITH CONFLICTS CAUSING REDUCED AGRICULTURAL OUTPUT, 1970-1997

 Number of countries

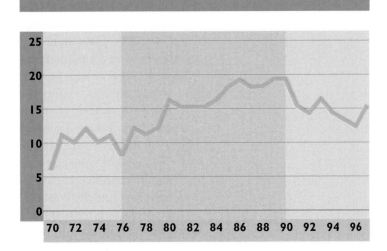

Source: FAO

in many countries, it is also true that raising agricultural productivity and reducing hunger and malnutrition in poor countries is an obvious path to peace. However, this is often overlooked – as was recently emphasized by the former President of the United States, Jimmy Carter.[34]

QUANTIFYING LOSSES RESULTING FROM CONFLICT IN DEVELOPING COUNTRIES

For all conflicts, as for all natural disasters, the most important impacts are the suffering, injury and death of men, women and children. The losses in output, means of production and infrastructure seem insignificant in comparison. Yet these material losses are also important, for they undermine the ability of conflict survivors to subsist and recover. This is most obvious in agriculture, where the destruction of crops and livestock results, at best, in reduced food security and, at worst, in famine and death. Indeed, in many cases, deaths resulting indirectly from conflict (through famine, for example) exceed deaths from direct violence. The estimation of material losses, narrow as it is, represents an important aspect of assessing the severity of a conflict. It also provides a guide to the design of long-term policy for dealing with conflict situations.

It has been found that the indirect costs of war are typically greater than the more straightforward direct costs; and that they continue long after the end of a conflict.[35] However, estimating the total direct and indirect costs of conflict is a complex procedure.[36] The outcomes of war should not be assessed against a static framework, but it is hard to accommodate changes in technology, changing institutions and shifting social relations during conflicts. It is also extremely difficult to assess the economic value and employment impact of the loss of human life.

In this section, which focuses on developing countries, estimates of war losses are limited to the *direct impact on agricultural output*, with no attempt to include capital losses or indirect effects, for example, on rural non-agricultural activities.[37] Direct losses may arise from various mechanisms: the migration of population from conflict-affected areas, leaving land idle and livestock abandoned; a reduction in marketed output because transport services are disrupted; the destruction of crops in the field or of post-harvest stocks and livestock by armed groups; and declines in yields resulting from lack of access to key inputs. (These are considered in more detail in the section Characteristics of agriculture and the impact of conflict, p. 83).

It must be emphasized that cost estimates are tentative. The accuracy of estimates is undermined by the frequent lack of

Deaths resulting from reduced food security and famine, i.e. long-term effects of conflicts, can exceed the deaths caused directly from violence.

reliable statistics. Many of the conflict-affected countries are low-income countries where agricultural statistics are of questionable accuracy even during peacetime.[38] Conflict frequently disrupts the normal data collection and estimation process. Furthermore, in wartime the unmeasured proportion of output is likely to increase because it is channelled through unofficial marketing networks.

The estimated output losses for all developing countries are illustrated in Table 7, p. 73, and they are extensive. Over the 28 years from 1970 to 1997, the estimation yields an aggregate of almost $121 billion at 1995 prices, or an average of $4.3 billion per year. This can be compared with the estimated costs

Box 4

CONFLICT AND FOOD ENERGY CONSUMPTION IN AFRICAN COUNTRIES

A study conducted for FAO on the determinants of food energy consumption levels[1] included estimates of the impact of war and civil strife in a number of African countries during 1971-92. The study used regression analysis to explain the evolution of per caput food energy consumption, calculated in terms of the dietary energy supply (DES) level minus its food aid component, for a number of countries that experienced situations of civil war and/or strife (data on such situations were obtained from the United States Department of Agriculture [USDA]). Civil war and/or strife was represented in the analysis by a dummy variable.

The study concluded that the impact of civil war/strife on food energy consumption varied widely according to the frequency and severity of such situations but was in some cases considerable. Thus, among the countries for which the impact of this variable was significant (i.e. at the 10 percent statistical level), the lost food energy in Uganda during each year of civil war/strife amounted to 56 kcal, or 2.5 percent of the average DES levels. The figure of lost food energy was as high as 362 kcal in Liberia (16 percent of the total), 438 kcal (20 percent) in Somalia and 120 kcal (6 percent) in Ethiopia.

[1] Prepared for FAO by Professor George P. Zanias from Athens University of Economics and Business, Athens, Greece.

Box 5

CONFLICTS AND FOOD EMERGENCIES

The last 15 years have seen a large number of food emergencies arising from natural or human-induced factors. Their number has fluctuated from about 20 to 30 in most years, but has tended to increase during the 1990s, particularly the latter part of the decade. This increase has been associated primarily with the greater incidence of conflicts.

The Figure below shows, in fact, a discernible shift in the causes of food emergencies. Whereas human-induced disasters contributed to only about 10 percent of total emergencies in 1984, by late 1999 they were a determining factor in more than 50 percent of cases.

*Source:*FAO.

Figure A

TRENDS IN CAUSES OF FOOD EMERGENCIES

Number of countries affected

— Human-induced disasters

— Natural disasters

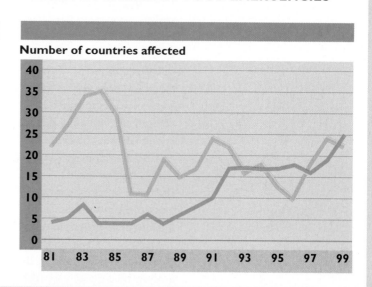

Source: FAO

Table 7

AGRICULTURAL OUTPUT LOSSES RESULTING FROM CONFLICT, BY REGION: 1970s, 1980s AND 1990-97

Region	1970s		1980s		1990-97		Total losses
	Countries	Losses *(Million $ – 1995 prices)*	Countries	Losses *(Million $ – 1995 prices)*	Countries	Losses *(Million $ – 1995 prices)*	
Latin America and the Caribbean	Colombia, Nicaragua, Honduras (3)	1 328 (7%)	Nicaragua, Peru, El Salvador, Guatemala, Colombia, Honduras, Panama (7)	8 686 (12%)	Nicaragua, Peru, El Salvador, Guatemala, Colombia (5) [Haiti, no data]	5 011 (8%)	15 025 (10%)
Sub-Saharan Africa	Angola, Burundi, Chad, Dem. Rep. Congo, Guinea-Bissau, Ethiopia, Mozambique, Namibia, Rwanda, Sudan, Zimbabwe (11)	9 427 (15%)	Angola, Cent. Afr. Rep., Chad, Dem. Rep. Congo, Ethiopia, Liberia, Mozambique, Namibia, Nigeria, Sudan, Zimbabwe (11)	21 951 (26%)	Angola, Burundi, Cent. Afr. Rep., Congo, Dem. Rep. Congo, Ethiopia, Kenya, Liberia, Mozambique, Somalia, Sudan, Zimbabwe (12)	21 005 (40%)	52 383 (30%)
South and Southeast Asia	Cambodia, Lao People's Dem. Rep., Sri Lanka, Viet Nam (4)	4 346 (21%)	Cambodia, Philippines, Sri Lanka (3)	6 707 (13%)	Cambodia, Philippines, Sri Lanka (3)	6 360 (10%)	17 413 (14%)
West Asia and North Africa	Iran, Iraq (2) (no data for other CACs)	206 (6%)	Afghanistan, Iran, Iraq (3) (no data for other CACs)	13 211 (11%)	Afghanistan, Algeria, Iraq (3) (no data for other CACs)	22 382 (58%)	35 800 (40%)
TOTAL	Countries: 20 Per year: 10.3	15 307 (16%)	Countries: 24 Per year: 16.9	50 556 (18%)	Countries: 23 Per year: 15.3	54 758 (41%)	120 620 (28%)

Notes: The countries listed are those for which the model (see below) produced statistically significant results for the conflict variable (except for exceptions noted below). Omitted are conflict-affected countries (CAC) for which the method showed statistically insignificant results, or countries without data. Percentages in parentheses are the share of losses in agricultural value added for the conflict-affected years, weighted across countries by total value added for each country. Losses are estimated by the following regression model *by country:*

agric = a_0 + a_1(ag/man) + a_2(Trd/ntrd) + a_3(T) + a_4(conf) + e

Where (with variables in logarithmic form except T and conf):

    agric = agricultural value added in constant 1995 dollars

    ag/man = the ratio of the agricultural to the manufacturing relative price among tradables

    Trd/ntrd = ratio of tradable prices (agriculture, mining and manufacturing) to non-tradables (services), the real exchange rate

    T = time trend

    conf = conflict variable, which takes the value of 1 in conflict years, and

    e = the error term

If the conflict variable was significant at the .1 level, in the war-affected years this was multiplied by the actual output to obtain estimated losses. For several countries, this method could not be applied and another method was used.

Economic losses from conflict in developing countries exceeded total food aid to those countries in the 1980s and 1990s.

of raising nutrition to minimum required levels. Notional estimates calculate that it would cost approximately $13 per caput/year to provide enough food to feed the undernourished at a minimally adequate level.[39] Dividing the estimated loss of $4.3 billion per year by $13 produces a figure of 330 million undernourished people who could have raised their food intake to minimum required levels for the year. Such a decrease in malnutrition would rival the combined impact of all food aid. In both the 1980s and the 1990s, conflict-induced losses in developing countries exceeded the total food aid of all types to those countries (see Table in Box 6). For the full decade of the 1980s, the former were about $37 billion and the latter $29 billion (both in current prices).

From 1976 until 1990, the estimate of constant price losses grew at an alarming 12 percent per year (see Figure 14, p. 76), levelling off in the 1990s to about $6.5 to $7 billion per year. The pattern of output losses supports the conclusion that a peak was reached in 1990, although there has been no reversal of the previous trend. While this is cause for a degree of optimism, in the 1990s conflict remained a major cause of output loss and food insecurity in developing countries. The relative size of the losses can be indicated by comparing them with the agricultural trade of all developing countries (average imports and exports). While the comparison is not rigorous (trade involves gross output and losses refer to value added), the numbers are startling (see Figure 15, p. 76). After oscillating between 1 and 3 percent from 1970 until 1980, losses began an upward trend, peaking at slightly more than 7 percent of total agricultural trade in 1990.

The situation by region

Among the regions, Latin America and the Caribbean, and South and Southeast Asia show substantially lower levels of conflict-induced losses (see Figure 16, p. 77 and Table 8, p. 78). The former was unique in that, at the end of the 1990s, only one Latin American country, Colombia, remained at serious risk of conflict. In this region, losses were concentrated in the 1980s and early 1990s. In Central America, the conflicts in El Salvador, Guatemala and Nicaragua were caused by a variety of political problems and socio-economic instability, but they also arose from long-term disputes over the distribution of land (especially in El Salvador and Guatemala). The losses resulting from conflict in Honduras were primarily "collateral" effects of armed struggles in the other states.[40] While the right of indigenous peoples to resources has been a major issue in Latin

Latin America is the developing region to have been least affected by conflicts since the 1980s.

Box 6

FOOD AID AND CONFLICT

Food aid can, and does, play an important role in reducing the impact of conflict on food-insecure groups. Food aid assigned in response to conflicts would provide an indication of agricultural conflict losses, were it possible to make the necessary disaggregation. Available data make it

possible to disaggregate only "emergency" food aid, which includes disbursements for the full range of emergencies, both natural and human-induced. The Table below reports shipments of cereal food aid to the conflict-affected countries listed in Table 7, with the exception of the

Lao People's Democratic Republic and Viet Nam (their internal conflicts were over by 1989/90 when the Table begins). The overwhelming majority of emergency food aid to the conflict-affected countries went to the sub-Saharan Africa region during the 1990s – 86 percent over all years.

EMERGENCY CEREAL FOOD AID TO CONFLICT-AFFECTED COUNTRIES, BY REGION (1989/90 TO 1997/98)

	Thousand tonnes					Percentage			
	Latin America	Sub-Saharan Africa	South and Southeast Asia	North Africa and West Asia	Total	Latin America	Sub-Saharan Africa	South and Southeast Asia	North Africa and West Asia
1989	85	994	9	68	1 156	7.4	86.0	0.8	5.9
1990	37	1 846	38	120	2 041	1.8	90.5	1.9	5.9
1991	12	2 513	75	261	2 861	0.4	87.9	2.6	9.1
1992	13	3 082	125	174	3 394	0.4	90.8	3.7	5.1
1993	12	2 306	55	276	2 649	0.4	87.0	2.1	10.4
1994	33	2 209	60	265	2 567	1.3	86.0	2.3	10.3
1995	14	1 526	68	274	1 881	0.7	81.1	3.6	14.5
1996	9	1 147	36	320	1 512	0.6	75.9	2.4	21.2
1997	15	1 177	55	174	1 421	1.1	82.8	3.9	12.2
Total	230	16 800	521	1 931	19 482	1.2	86.2	2.7	9.9

Note: Figures cover the same countries as Table 7, except for the Lao People's Democratic Republic and Viet Nam in South and Southeast Asia. The first year of the 12-month period is given, i.e. 1989 = 1989/90.
Sources: FAO and WFP.

Figure 14

LOSSES IN AGRICULTURAL OUTPUT RESULTING FROM CONFLICT IN DEVELOPING COUNTRIES, 1970-1997

Output losses

Source: FAO

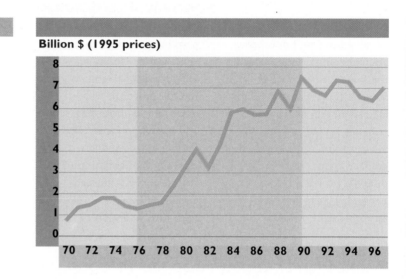

Billion $ (1995 prices)

Figure 15

CONFLICT-INDUCED LOSSES IN DEVELOPING COUNTRIES AS A PROPORTION OF THEIR AGRICULTURAL TRADE, 1970-1997

Losses

Source: FAO

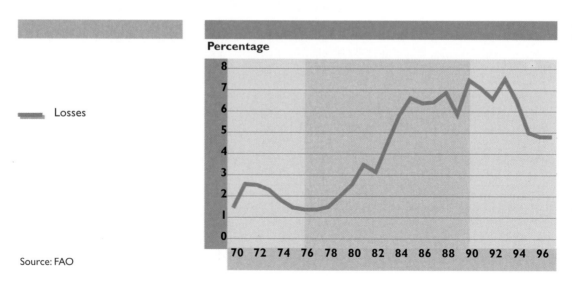

Percentage

Figure 16

AGRICULTURAL LOSSES RESULTING FROM CONFLICT, BY REGION, 1970-1997

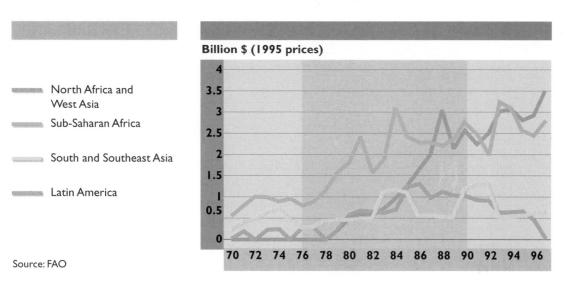

Billion $ (1995 prices)

North Africa and
West Asia

Sub-Saharan Africa

South and Southeast Asia

Latin America

Source: FAO

Figure 17

PERCENTAGE LOSS OF AGRICULTURAL GDP RESULTING FROM CONFLICT IN AFFECTED COUNTRIES, 1970-1997

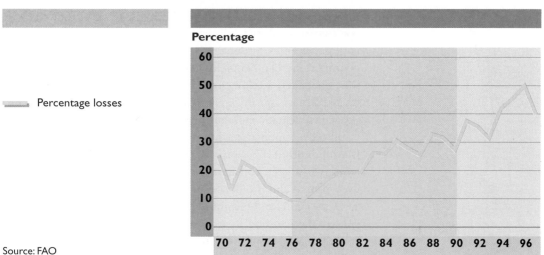

Percentage

Percentage losses

Source: FAO

Table 8

PERCENTAGE DISTRIBUTION OF AGRICULTURAL OUTPUT LOSSES, BY REGION AND DECADE

Region	1970s	1980s	1990s	Total
Latin America and the Caribbean	9	17	9	13
Sub-Saharan Africa	62	43	38	43
South and Southeast Asia	28	13	12	14
North Africa and West Asia	1	26	41	30

America, only in Guatemala was ethnicity an important contributing factor to a major conflict. Losses by country were generally lower in relative terms than in other regions, below 10 percent of total output in affected years. Nicaragua is the exception: in the late 1970s, estimated losses from conflict represented more than three times this percentage. In Nicaragua land disputes also continued to fuel conflict in the 1990s to a greater degree than in the other Central American countries. Despite a long history of rural insurgency in Latin America, typically over the distribution of land, at the end of the twentieth century it was the least conflict-affected region.

In South, Southeast and East Asia, none of the countries with large populations (i.e. Bangladesh, China, India, Indonesia and Pakistan) showed statistically significant losses as a result of conflict. In Southeast Asia, conflict was closely associated with cold war rivalries, evidenced by two major conflict-affected countries, the Lao People's Democratic Republic and Viet Nam, which achieved a lasting internal peace in the mid-1970s. In tragic contrast, war in Cambodia continued into the 1990s, with peace problematic even at the end of the century. The case of Cambodia demonstrates how easily losses can accumulate. If, from the early 1970s onwards, agricultural output in the country had been constant (even accounting for the great loss of lives in rural and urban communities), per caput production in 1997 would have been more than double its actual value. In spite of the Cambodia case, across all countries during their conflict years output losses in the region were a relatively low 14 percent of the sector's production (see Table 7, p. 73).

Losses from conflicts were especially severe in sub-Saharan Africa. Over the entire period, this region suffered the greatest losses in absolute terms, $52 billion (in 1995 prices). Across all

Economic losses from conflict in sub-Saharan Africa amount to almost 30 percent of agricultural output in affected countries since 1970.

affected countries during their conflict years, this represented almost 30 percent of agricultural output (Table 7). Unlike the two regions previously discussed, the estimates for sub-Saharan Africa show no marked tendency for either the incidence of conflict (number of countries) or the losses caused by conflict to decline in the 1990s. The number of countries affected was virtually the same in each decade. Relative to the total agricultural output of the affected countries in conflict years, losses grew at almost 5 percent per year from 1976 until 1996, with a sharp drop in 1997. While peace has come to several countries, including Mozambique, after long and devastating wars the region remained seriously plagued by conflict at the end of the century.

For most countries in sub-Saharan Africa, conflicts were relatively short, but often recurred. In a number of cases, conflict dominated the entire 28-year period. Angola was an extreme case, with virtually continuous internal warfare since before 1970 and no peace imminent at the turn of the century (despite a formal peace accord earlier in the 1990s). Estimates suggest that, at the end of the 1990s, agricultural output in Angola was well below half of what it would have been in the absence of war. The Sudan has suffered for almost as long, although the relative conflict losses were less.

The severity of the impact of conflict on sub-Saharan African countries is shown in Table 9 in dollar terms (1995 prices). For the conflict-affected countries, estimated agricultural losses were 75 percent of ODA for the 28 years, a percentage that increased with each decade. Conflict losses in sub-Saharan Africa were considerably greater than foreign direct investment (FDI) in the affected countries. Since more than 80 percent of FDI went to two conflict-affected countries, Angola and Nigeria,

Table 9

AGRICULTURAL LOSSES AND CAPITAL FLOWS IN CONFLICT-AFFECTED SUB-SAHARAN COUNTRIES, 1975-1997

	1975-79	1980-89	1990-97	Total
	(Million $ – current value)			
Losses	11 924	31 160	21 916	64 999
ODA	7 999	50 811	65 715	124 525
FDI	2 740	5 984	14 030	22 753
	(Percentage)			
Losses/ODA	149	61	33	52
Losses/FDI	435	521	156	286

Box 7

AGRICULTURE, CONFLICT AND GENOCIDE IN RWANDA

The two central features of Rwandan agriculture are high population density in rural areas and the concentration on export crops – tea and coffee. Coffee production increased by an average 4.4 percent per year between 1969 and 1981, while tea output grew by 17 percent per year. However, the quality of coffee, the main export crop, deteriorated after the late 1970s. This left Rwandan coffee farmers and the economy less able to capture windfall gains from price increases, and more exposed to price declines. During 1985-1992 the world price of coffee fell by 72 percent in real terms and that of tea by 66 percent. While Rwanda produced 40 percent more coffee in volume during 1989/90 compared with the early 1980s, earnings were down by 20 percent. After 1992, coffee price stabilization transfers to farmers were terminated, as part of the country's structural adjustment programme. In addition to this crisis, rapid population growth over a longer period generated a drop in the size of landholdings, and there was little effective intensification

of production. Droughts in the 1980s worsened conditions. According to one estimate, by 1989 one in six Rwandans was affected by famine. According to official estimates, food energy output fell from 2 055 kcal per farmer/day in 1984 to 1 509 kcal in 1991. Thus, during the 1980s a variety of severe pressures built up within Rwandan agriculture.

The onset of war in 1990 led to the displacement of 15 percent of the population, according to some estimates. The effect of the 1994 war on agriculture was dramatic. When the Rwandan Patriotic Front came to power, effectively ending the genocide, 2 million people had fled the country and hundreds of thousands were classified as internally displaced people.

In the aftermath of the genocide, many sources predicted unprecedented famine. However, these fears proved to be exaggerated. Later estimates of the conflict losses suggested that they varied substantially between and within provinces. Furthermore, they indicated that the problems of Rwandan agricultural production and rehabilitation were more complex than seed and harvest problems and extended to the entire organization of rural production. Far from being self-sufficient, most farmers relied on cash for crucial inputs such as seeds. The two most important income sources, apart from selling marketed farm output, were interprefectural seasonal migration by males and agricultural wage labour on commercial farms by females. Both were disrupted in the 1990s, the former by direct conflict and the latter by the flight or death of large-scale farmers. In 1995 the Ministry of Agriculture estimated that, since April 1994, three out of four farmers had been displaced and that the December-January harvest had fallen to 50 percent below normal output.

The recovery of agriculture after 1995 was uneven, as farmers returned to their lands, legal conflicts were partially resolved and labour migration revived. However, the problem of post-conflict rehabilitation, and agricultural policy more generally, was not merely one of restoring production levels and institutions to their pre-war status quo. Long-term solutions require a reorganization of the entire agricultural production system.

Sources: P. Gourevitch. 1999. *We wish to inform you that tomorrow we will be killed with our families.* London, Picador; J. Pottier. 1996. Agricultural rehabilitation and food insecurity in postwar Rwanda: assessing needs, designing solutions. *IDS Bulletin*, 27(3); A. Storey. 1999. Economics and ethnic conflict: structural adjustment in Rwanda. *Development Policy Review,* 17: 43-63; and P. Uvin. 1996. *Development, aid and conflict: reflections from the case of Rwanda.* Research for Action No. 24. Helsinki, UN University/World Institute for Development Economics Research.

agricultural losses far exceeded these private capital inflows for the other countries.

Work by Luckham, Ahmed and Muggah[41] supports these estimated losses and suggests that, of the 11 most war-affected countries of sub-Saharan Africa, measured per caput agricultural production declined most sharply in the four where the state collapsed during the 1990s (Sierra Leone, Liberia, Somalia and Rwanda). One of the 11 was Chad which, although conflict-affected, showed no significant losses according to the estimation. This may be because warfare was relatively small-scale and took place outside the main agricultural production areas.

North Africa and West Asia were, according to some indicators, even more conflict-prone than sub-Saharan Africa, with internal wars or invasion affecting a long list of countries. However, agricultural losses were statistically significant in only four cases: Afghanistan, Algeria, the Islamic Republic of Iran and Iraq. According to the statistical estimates, conflict losses did not begin until the late 1970s, after which they increased dramatically (see Figure 16 and Table 8), rising by 26 percent per year in constant prices between 1979 and 1988. This was overwhelmingly the result of conflicts in Afghanistan and the Iran-Iraq war. So severe was the estimated effect of these conflicts that, in the 1990s, the losses of three countries alone – Afghanistan, Iraq and Algeria – exceeded the total for sub-Saharan Africa. These countries were on average the most intensely affected of all regions. Across affected countries in conflict years, losses amounted to 58 percent of total output for the 1990s.

THE NATURE OF CONFLICTS

The impact of conflict on agriculture can be placed in the context of the nature of contemporary conflicts, which has changed since the Second World War. Until then, wars typically involved conflict between governments. For the most part, these wars were fought with regular armies, a well-defined division was made between combatants and civilians, there were recognized battle lines and the termination of conflict was relatively clear.

Since the Second World War there have been few and usually only brief intercountry conflicts (although the wars in Korea and Viet Nam and between the Islamic Republic of Iran and Iraq were notably prolonged). Most contemporary conflicts are not between countries, but between a government and political or military groups seeking to overthrow that government or create a separate state. Such conflicts are typically not fought by two regular armies, but involve a complex struggle between the government and various contestants, which may be hostile to one another.[42] In some cases it is difficult to determine who is officially or de facto in charge of the government. Because conflict is not formalized,[43] its beginning and its end are ambiguous. As the conflict in Angola shows, not even a formal peace settlement signed by the warring parties need signal an end to war.[44]

Recent conflicts have tended to be between governments and opposition groups within the same country.

Since the distinction between combatant and civilian cannot be made with any precision, intracountry conflicts tend to be indiscriminate in their effect on the population. In fact, the bulk of the casualties tend to be among civilians. The instruments of war are often of a low technological level, involving small arms and land mines. Land mines wreak particular havoc with agriculture, excluding vast areas of arable land from cultivation until they are cleared, a problem discussed below. Thus, it should not be surprising that the estimates of agricultural output losses are large; it is in the nature of intracountry wars. However, even more than their effects on the productive capacity of farmers, these conflicts are likely to create food insecurity situations because of the disruptions they cause to the transportation and distribution of food.

Intracountry conflicts harm rural populations more than intercountry conflicts.

Another characteristic of intracountry conflicts is that they are usually fought in the countryside rather than in cities. For this reason, they tend to have devastating effects on the rural population and agriculture (see Box 8, which discusses survival strategies). This is in contrast to the intercountry wars of the past (and the recent conflicts in Iraq and the Balkan states), in which aerial bombing brought destruction chiefly to cities.

There is evidence that competition over scarce resources, such as land and water, enhances the probability of conflict. The control of fertile lands, water and food stocks is likely to be a strategic aim of all parties in a conflict. Conversely, the destruction of food stocks and the means of agricultural production may be a military objective of both the government and the insurgents. A "scorched earth" tactic may be pursued by either side, but particularly the government, as a means of undermining support for insurgents. This tactic has a long history.[45] In such an approach to warfare, food insecurity becomes a powerful weapon, with disastrous effects on the rural population.

CHARACTERISTICS OF AGRICULTURE AND THE IMPACT OF CONFLICT

By their nature, intracountry wars affect agriculture in a variety of ways. The impact also varies with the characteristics of each country's agriculture. In some countries there may be surplus labour in rural areas. In such cases, war casualties, regardless of their obvious human cost, would not necessarily weaken agricultural productivity and output trends. In other circumstances, agriculture may be constrained by labour shortages, especially, at seasonal peaks (harvesting, weeding, etc.). When this is so, war casualties or the diversion of men from agricultural production to the armed forces will undermine the viability of agriculture.

The direct cost of war damage tends to be higher when

Box 8

THE BREAKDOWN OF SURVIVAL STRATEGIES DURING CONFLICTS

When households are in danger of becoming food-insecure, they employ various types of coping strategies to maintain their access to food and to protect their livelihoods during the crisis. They may collect wild foods, look for credit, sell their labour or reduce consumption. People's reactions depend mainly on their perception of the severity of the crisis and their economic and social position.

In deciding which options to employ, a household will carefully weigh the economic and social costs of each action, although during conflicts people may be forced to take greater risks more suddenly, since their first goal is to save lives. In

addition, freedom of movement is often restricted because of insecurity, and this limits access to foods. Collection of unfamiliar wild foods can be risky; many contain natural toxins and, when procedures for their preparation and utilization are unknown, their consumption may lead to toxicity and poisoning. Very often homes and farms are destroyed when people flee, which makes it extremely difficult for them to re-establish normal lives when they return to their home communities. In addition, many of the economic and social networks that households normally employ during times of crisis may be shattered in conflict situations; the community, or

even the family, may no longer be available as a safety net. In those cases the range of successful coping strategies may be severely limited.

A good knowledge of the various survival strategies available to households is fundamental for any efficient system of prevention and protection against food insecurity in conflict-prone areas.

Source: Adapted from A. Hussain and M. Herens. 1997. Child nutrition and food security during armed conflict. *Food, Nutrition and Agriculture* No. 19.

The costs incurred by war are greater for mechanized agriculture than for subsistence agriculture.

Livestock operations are highly vulnerable to war, as animals are left untended and disease spreads easily.

agriculture is more capitalized, i.e. when mechanization and irrigation are more advanced, purchased inputs are used and a large portion of the output is marketed. Disruptions in marketing channels may have costs for commercialized output, but might not necessarily force households into food insecurity, should they still produce for own consumption.

Conflict can affect agriculture and food security in many other ways. In areas that specialize in labour-intensive export crops, war will have an impact on foreign exchange earnings, which may have severe implications for development and food security. If the rural population consists of net food purchasers, who perhaps provide wage labour for commercial farms, the disruption of incomes and marketing networks will expose people to greater food insecurity than if there is a preponderance of subsistence food production. In cases where commercial farming areas depend, at least partly, on labour migration, war can interrupt established flows of seasonal labour migration and, therefore, damage productivity on commercial farms. This disruption also reduces income in areas that are not directly affected by war but that send migrant labourers to conflict zones. For example, workers from southern Kordofan in the Sudan could no longer migrate to jobs in other regions during phases of civil war. Guest workers who were repatriated to Bangladesh and the Philippines from Iraq, together with households dependent on their remittances, became victims of the Persian Gulf conflict through loss of earnings.[46]

The long-term effects of war on agriculture will vary with, among other factors, the composition of cropping patterns. For example, in areas with tree crops such as coffee or cashew nuts, refugee flight and conflict are likely to cause neglect or abandonment of trees and, subsequently, greater exposure to pests and diseases.[47] This was the case with the production of bananas in Rwanda and Burundi, where the fruit is a staple. As a result, there will be a delay in the postwar recovery of agricultural productivity, as trees and bushes lose productivity through age, and the costs of reviving competitive export production will rise. Similarly, one of the most vulnerable agricultural activities during wartime appears to be livestock raising. Estimates suggest that more than half the total livestock was lost through direct and indirect conflict effects in Somaliland during the mid-1990s.[48] The estimate for Mozambique is roughly 80 percent.[49]

Large farms, whether state-run, private, or joint ventures between the two, may be relatively protected from direct war impacts, but still be vulnerable as targets for insurgents. For

85

example, a state farm will often be a target for rebels whose strategy includes the selective destruction of government property. Governments may use troops to protect such enterprises, but it is likely that the linkages between large and small farms will be weakened, if not altogether severed, by wartime insecurity.

Agriculture's other linkages may suffer disruption during war. Rural people in low- and middle-income countries draw income from a portfolio of sources, including subsistence production, processing of crops for local and distant markets and small enterprises such as transport and crafts. There are linkages between the agricultural and the manufacturing sectors: in many instances the core of early industrialization is agroprocessing, such as cotton ginning, sugar refining, soft drinks production, industrial brewing of beer, furniture making and pulp and paper mills. There are also resource flows between sectors. All of these linkages are liable to be disrupted by war.

If links between rural and urban areas are weakened by conflict, or if tourism in rural areas is reduced by war, many of the diverse income sources of the rural population are likely to be curtailed by lack of demand or inputs. Agro-industry may be badly affected by conflict if the supply of raw materials is

Land mine victims

Farmers are sometimes forced to cultivate fields dotted with land mines

FAO/21328

disrupted, the marketing of raw material from producers to industrial enterprises is severed, or the demand for raw materials is reduced. Even if intersectoral resource flows remain in place, the mechanisms may be undermined by war. Marketing boards may have less ability to purchase crops, or their organization and personnel may be weakened by the diversion of resources to the war effort. The positive effects of resource transfers from agriculture to other sectors and of reinvestment in agriculture will suffer. A further mechanism of violence disrupts agriculture: the targeting of transport and communications infrastructure during war.

Land mines expose agricultural workers to danger and reduce their ability to produce.

Land mines are commonly scattered over rural areas − indiscriminately in some cases (see Box 9). They may be laid in crop fields, along footpaths linking villages to fields and rivers and on rural feeder roads, major highways and bridges. They have a direct and significant impact on agricultural production simply by making production too dangerous. Neutralizing the effect of land mines requires mapping their location. Often, however, neither the ruling regime nor its adversaries have records of where they have laid mines. In Afghanistan, Angola and Cambodia, countries with a particularly high density of mines, the overall impact on agricultural production is immense and likely to last for years after the end of conflict.

Production and communications infrastructure is critical to the vitality of agricultural production.[50] Poor transport adds to production and marketing costs, and damage to infrastructure clearly worsens this situation by, for example, raising traders' margins. Added to this, it is common in wars for access to petroleum to be disrupted, and for transport equipment, especially trucks, to be commandeered by the government or armed groups.[51]

During war, marketing and distribution systems are disrupted and food becomes more expensive.

A corollary of the increased risk of marketing agricultural produce and inputs is that traders' profits tend to rise. For those willing to take the risks, there are substantial war-monopoly rents; indeed, such profits may be necessary for marketing to continue and are sometimes referred to as "war taxes". This is a specific example of how, in a civil war, the established checks and balances of social and economic rules are eroded, are poorly monitored or collapse. In these circumstances, agricultural production and related activities may continue at a reduced level under conditions that have been characterized as a "vicious market fundamentalism".[52] Some people do very well out of such conditions.[53] While the activities of "profiteers" may offer a lifeline for people whose income-earning opportunities might otherwise be non-existent in war, the conditions that

Box 9

LAND MINES IN ANGOLA

Angola has experienced warfare almost continuously since 1961. Land mines were first used in mid-1961 in the war between Portuguese colonial authorities and nationalist groups. With the growth of foreign support for nationalist movements, which started in 1968, land mines became an increasing feature of the conflict. One of the most intense phases of military activity occurred in the late 1980s, during major battles in the southern Cuito Cuanavale area. Both sides laid large numbers of mines. Mine laying intensified after the failure of the peace process and elections between 1990 and 1992. The People's Movement for the Liberation of Angola (MPLA) government and UNITA both laid thousands of new mines to obstruct roads and bridges around besieged towns. There were mine "belts" up to 3 km wide.

One estimate puts the total number of land mines laid in Angola at some 20 million, with 4 million still in the ground in 1999, 6 million removed or detonated, and 8 million unaccounted for. Sixty different types of anti-personnel mines from 19 different countries have been identified. However, there is no comprehensive survey of their dispersion and no one knows precisely how many mines have been laid. The country has one of the highest rates of land mine injuries per caput in the world. Out of a population of some 9 million, there are tens of thousands of amputees, most caused by mines. With a conservative estimate of 20 000 serious land mine injuries, this implies a rate of injury that would be equivalent to 5 million people in the United States.

A great number of mines were laid on footpaths to rivers and small agricultural plots. Others were placed on roads and bridges. The effects on agriculture, although impossible to quantify, are clear: mines restrict access to farmland and prevent cultivation; when people are injured or killed by mines, the agricultural labour force is affected, with potentially severe effects on household labour allocation and food security; and mines on roads and bridges undermine trading and hinder effective relief efforts. Together with active fighting, refugee flight and recruitment into armed forces, land mines are responsible for destroying much of the agricultural supply base in the country and for reducing many Angolans to periodic famine.

"The rebuilding of rural communities after conflict can be made impossible by the presence of mines and ordnance. New buildings cannot be constructed and land use cannot be extended to support more people. Refugees and people displaced by the fighting, desperate to restart their lives, must either remain separated from their homelands or return despite the mines. An inability to grow crops or safely collect fruit, wood or other natural resources is a common product of land mine contamination. In some cases the local economy and the pattern of land mine contamination mean that land is not only denied altogether, but the land that can be farmed cannot be used to best effect. By denying land for agriculture, and making land use less efficient, land mines and unexploded ordnance (UXO) can create food insecurity. This in turn can promote dangerous activities, such as salvaging scrap metal from UXO, as people look for ways of supporting themselves or supplementing their income. Spurred on by the need to feed their families, people are forced to farm land that is known to be mined – often trying to clear mines themselves. This desperation causes accidents and a spiral further into poverty."

Sources: Africa Watch. 1993. *Landmines in Angola.* London; Human Rights Watch. 1999. *Landmine monitor – toward a mine-free world.* New York; S.H. McCormick. 1994. *The Angolan economy: prospects for growth in a postwar environment.* Washington, DC, Center for Strategic and International Studies; Mines Advisory Group. 1999. *The effects of landmines on the community.* www.oneworld.org/mag/effectstxt.htm

allow people access to income sources are likely to be worse than they are in peacetime.

An extreme example is when producers suffer a direct levy on their products in order to feed military forces for little or no payment. In Sierra Leone, for example, "... [Armed] young men ... discovered that control over business operations gave them access to additional benefits, such as the opportunity to extort food from farmers, set up roadblocks to levy tolls on internal commerce and organize protection and looting rackets.... This promise of survival, exemption from widespread exploitation of local populations, and even material gain amid the destruction of war, is a major incentive drawing young men and boys to be fighters."[54]

Alternatively, war may include, either directly or as a by-product, land and other asset accumulation by some at the expense of others; i.e. an increase in inequality, of which the long-term economic implications are not straightforward.[55]

POLICY ISSUES

Macroeconomic policies can be designed to prevent the worsening of tensions and conflicts that can lead to war.

That conflicts tend to be closely associated with low levels of development combined with inequity and competition over scarce resources points to an obvious conclusion: countries should seek to promote growth that is both rapid and inclusive. If the bases for growth are to be created through measures aimed at macroeconomic stabilization and reform, the challenge is to manage such measures in a manner that contains social stress and reduces, or at least does not accentuate, inequities. This view is now widely supported, despite difficulties experienced in translating it into fact. In a 1997 World Bank report,[56] it was observed that:

"The Bank needs to integrate concern for conflict into development operations. It must ensure that its interventions do not aggravate existing inequities ... and that they ameliorate potential conflict situations, through judicious social analysis and adequate attention to distributive policies...."

An excessive emphasis on rapid stabilization involving stringent fiscal austerity might conflict with the investments required to rehabilitate the agricultural sector, as well as with the so-called peace dividend (see Box 10, p. 92). While stabilization and adjustment programmes usually call for reduced state intervention in markets, post-conflict situations frequently require an increased role of the state in aiding local communities during reconstruction, for example through the direct provision of goods and services for food security and the supply of agricultural inputs.

Distribution issues are especially important, including those in the agricultural sector where conflicts over resources are often direct and take place in a context of increasing inequity and scarcity. It is fundamental that competition over scarce resources should take place in an equitable environment, within an enforced legal framework, with commonly accepted standards of commercial behaviour and respect for property rights, be they individual or communal. The enforcement of legislation supporting equitable landownership structures is a major step in this direction. In the short term, for many conflict-affected countries, "adequate attention to distributive policies" might imply moderating the impact of competition on smallholders during a transitional period when normal marketing services, transport facilities and agricultural extension are being re-established.

It has been observed that the most conflict-prone countries include many of those where agriculture is a major component of the economy and where the majority of the population is rural. In these situations, not only does the promotion of agricultural and rural development foster development and food security overall, but it is also a powerful way of reducing the risks of conflict.

The maintenance of strategic food stocks would appear to be an obvious response to the food insecurity situations caused by conflict. Stockholding is, however, notoriously costly and difficult to manage – especially during conflicts, when transportation is disrupted and silos become natural targets of attacks.

The building and maintenance of farm storage facilities in conflict-prone areas is only a viable option if they can be protected and controlled, and if the stored food can be effectively channelled to the areas in need. It should also be noted that it is very difficult and costly to maintain food stocks adequately in tropical and humid zones.

The World Trade Organization (Uruguay Round) Agreement on Agriculture allows countries to stockpile commodities for the purposes of food security and to sell from stockpiles at below market prices to the urban and rural poor. In general, the Agreement on Agriculture is quite flexible towards agricultural policies that are explicitly directed at poverty reduction, and these are of great relevance to conflict situations. Under the Agreement, the Decision on Measures concerning the Possible Negative Effects of the Reform Programme on Least-Developed and Net Food-Importing Developing Countries (the so-called Negative Effects Decision) is of particular relevance. This

Promoting rural development can reduce the risk of conflict in agriculture-dependent countries.

Box 10

IS THERE A PEACE DIVIDEND?

Disarmament and the resolution of a conflict appear to offer the prospect of shifting public expenditure towards economic growth and social welfare, generally known as the "peace dividend". A number of factors might prevent the realization of the peace dividend:

- There are costs associated with the transfer of resources from military to civilian uses. These costs include the retraining of personnel, the funding of resettlement (perhaps including equipping people with agricultural tools) and the conversion of military bases.
- Where there is no immediate reallocation of labour from military to civilian employment, there will be unemployment.
- The peace dividend depends on a decisive end to conflict, but the nature of civil war is such that there is no clear end to hostilities. Political,

economic and physical insecurity often persists after the formal end of a war, and this creates a disincentive for the reallocation of resources to productive purposes, particularly by the private sector. At the same time, continued tension creates a need for continued expenditure on national security.

- There are fiscal problems associated with the realization of the peace dividend.
- Revenue raising might not increase after the end of war. For example, in Ethiopia the state used coercive revenue-raising measures during the war and, when these were abandoned with peace, there was a decline in government revenue.
- Any putative peace dividend can easily disappear when there is a need, and external pressure, for deficit reduction.
- There is no automatic mechanism for realizing a

peace dividend. It is ultimately a political matter, within a context of extremely sensitive social tensions.

Evidence of a peace dividend is elusive. After eight years of peace, the Ugandan economy was still far below its pre-war peak.[1] In South Africa and the southern African region, the economic benefits of the peace dividend have yet to be realized, despite a 45 percent decline in the defence budget between 1989 and 1995.[2] Nonetheless, there are examples of possible peace dividend effects. Although the Mozambican economy also remains below the levels it had achieved at independence, since the peace agreement in 1992 the country has been among the fastest growing in the world.

The implications of the peace dividend for agriculture are ambiguous, and there has been no direct analysis of its impact on the sector. The most obvious mechanism through which a peace dividend can be expected is the return of refugees, internally displaced people and demobilized soldiers, all representing a shift of labour back into agriculture. Some agriculture-related buildings and equipment may be repaired or replaced relatively quickly after a war, and there will be greater security as well as a potentially significant improvement in the efficiency of markets. With the assistance of donors, seed stocks may be replaced quickly. However, a number of problems are likely to hamper the smooth realization of an agricultural peace dividend. Land mines in many conflict areas can take years to remove. In Zimbabwe, some areas were still fenced 20 years after the country's conflict.[3]

The revival of markets and poverty reduction after a war are likely to be affected by how thoroughly and quickly the rural infrastructure can be rebuilt. This is not just a question of reconstructing infrastructure but also of deciding on priorities in infrastructure investment. FAO's

monitoring of the impact on food and agriculture of conflict in Sierra Leone and Liberia stressed the immense damage to infrastructure. Finally, in many post-war situations, institutional change affects agricultural output, access to land and food security. In most of these situations, land tenure disputes continue after peace has returned.

In summary, the peace dividend is not a magic wand. Realizing the scope for a peace dividend is not an automatic process, but one that depends on choices made by relevant actors, not least by foreign donors. Donors have to consider carefully how their interventions might reduce conversion costs and maximize potential peace dividend benefits. Given that peace dividend benefits are likely to emerge in the medium to long term, donors need to make long-term commitments to support the process of realizing the dividend.

[1] J.-P. Azam et al. 1994. Some economic consequences of the transition from civil war to peace. Policy Research Working Paper No. 1392. Washington, DC, World Bank.
[2] P. Batchelor and S. Willett. 1998. Disarmament and defence industrial adjustment in South Africa, p. 170. Oxford, UK, Stockholm International Peace Research Institute and Oxford University Press.
[3] S. Willett. 1996. Military spending trends and developments in southern Africa: South Africa, Angola, Zimbabwe, and Mozambique, p. 36. Report for the Development Co-operation Directorate, OECD. 3 January 1996, London, Kings College, University of London. (mimeograph)
Sources: C. André and J.-P. Platteau. 1995. Land relations under unbearable stress: Rwanda caught in the Malthusian trap. Namur, Belgium, Centre de Recherche en Économie du Developpement, Faculty of Economics, University of Namur; P. O'Brien. 1988. The economic effects of the American civil war. Studies in Economic and Social History. Basingstoke, UK, and London, Macmillan; S.J. Stern. 1998. Shining and other paths: war and society in Peru, 1980-95. Durham, UK, and London, Duke University Press.

decision states the intention of parties to establish mechanisms to ensure that the rules stipulated by the Agreement on Agriculture do not adversely affect the food security of the least-developed and food-deficit countries (i.e. almost all conflict-affected countries) by: i) reviewing the adequacy of food aid; ii) ensuring that foodstuffs are provided to these countries on an increasingly concessionary basis; and iii) making a commitment to consider requests for technical and financial assistance to foster agricultural growth and food security. Unfortunately, at the end of the 1990s, no concrete steps had been taken to implement these commitments.

Policies to aid recovery

Countries' different experiences indicate a tremendous variation in the speed of agricultural recovery after conflict. In Mozambique, recovery was extraordinarily rapid, while in Nicaragua it was frustratingly slow. The policy lessons from these experiences are not always conclusive. Further research is required to determine the extent to which policy (as well as the particular type and combination of policies) facilitates the post-conflict recovery of agriculture. A number of general observations can be made, however.

The public sector has several functions in the recovery process. First, there are the immediate needs for resettlement of refugees and ex-belligerents, rehabilitation of land and infrastructure, and reintegration of communities into marketing networks. In addition, there are programmes that go further towards resolving the structural tensions that generate conflict – through such action as the decentralization of authorities and resources, the promotion of participatory rather than top-down decision-making and clarification of rural property rights. In post-conflict situations, however, the public sector is likely to see its means of intervention considerably weakened, and the process of capacity building may take time. In these circumstances, the speed of rehabilitation is particularly dependent on the dynamism of the private sector and civil society, and on the work of NGOs who often play a crucial role in such activities as relief delivery, advice to communities and support to local planning and programming activities.

Agricultural policy in all post-conflict situations requires the balancing of relief activities with development efforts. It has been noted, in fact, that a "gap has emerged between relief and development which has implications for the agencies that have traditionally been involved in either activity. The need for interventions that can bridge this gap and facilitate a faster transition from emergency response to sustainable development is compelling."[57] As far as possible, the emphasis should be on long-term development objectives. Even agricultural recovery programmes that are initiated very close to the end of hostilities and aim at relief and the repair of infrastructure could be linked to a longer-term development strategy. There are many constraints to the effective promotion of long-term sustainable development in immediate postwar conditions. Not the least of these is the need for political will and institutional capacity. Tensions may arise between the pursuit of long-term capacity building and the immediate maximizing of the benefits of employment-intensive public works schemes, which must be resolved with regard to concrete conditions.

Emergency relief efforts should be linked to longer-term development goals.

Development efforts can be made during the emergency phase through capacity building for local and national government services that provide agricultural inputs, extension services and marketing advice. This frequently requires the training of civil servants in activities that provide services to rural communities. Training provision can be combined with a strengthening of the links between private and public sector activities, which have proved important for achieving rapid growth in various parts of the world. Fostering these links is, in part, a matter of developing effective rural institutions such as public sector employment promotion offices and networks of local development agencies. It also involves encouraging the relationships among both private and public institutions. Rehabilitation of the agricultural sector after conflict is, by its nature, public sector-driven, although the participation of the private sector needs to be fostered.

Recovery of the agricultural sector requires action by external donors as well as a strong national effort. A number of UN organizations have policies for operations in conflict-affected countries. Participation of international organizations covers a spectrum of activities, from physical reconstruction, institution building and demobilization, to the creation or re-creation of an inclusive, non-discriminatory society. WFP can provide relief, FAO can advise on agricultural development and food security concerns and the World Bank can fund infrastructure. It is important for the speed of recovery, however, that assistance from these and other agencies is provided in close harmonization and collaboration among themselves and with the government. The latter, in turn, has a crucial role to play in creating a political, economic and institutional environment capable of maximizing the benefits of external assistance.

FAO's role in conflict-affected countries covers a broad range of activities. As soon as the security situation permits, FAO mounts missions to carry out assessments aimed at quantifying needs for both food and emergency assistance in agriculture. The types of assessment carried out may include the impact of the conflict on national food supply and demand, the food security and nutrition situations of affected groups, the population's need for international food assistance, the agricultural production capacity in the affected area, the need for agricultural relief to enable production to resume quickly, and the need for longer-term rehabilitation and reconstruction measures. Assessments are used as a basis for FAO's own relief efforts and are disseminated quickly to the international community in order to enable timely and effective donor responses.

FAO also provides "agricultural relief", defined as agricultural rehabilitation assistance provided on an emergency basis. Such relief is aimed at the rapid reduction of dependence on emergency food assistance and at providing a basis for longer-term rehabilitation. Assistance includes the provision of essential agricultural inputs such as seeds, tools, fertilizers, livestock and veterinary supplies to enable affected populations to resume basic productive activities quickly − in time for the next agricultural season where possible.

Agricultural relief is not, however, limited to the supply of agricultural inputs. Special agricultural relief operations also include the provision of services and technical advice that are not available from other UN agencies or from NGOs.

In its relief interventions, FAO also gives specific attention to the food security constraints of at-risk households in the areas affected, as well as to the need for appropriate information that allows affected households to make informed choices regarding food acquisition, preparation and distribution in unfamiliar situations.

As follow-up to immediate agricultural relief, FAO provides assistance in restoring extension, veterinary, plant protection and input supply services and institutions where these have been disrupted, and in the physical reconstruction of agricultural infrastructure such as dams and irrigation systems, markets and crop storage facilities.

FAO also provides policy and strategy support for recovery and development programmes in the food and agricultural sectors. This assistance is geared towards bringing the need for relief to an end and enabling development to proceed. It includes activities that help to make development sustainable by preventing and preparing for the possibility of further disasters and emergencies. A major emphasis is put on strengthening the coordination of locally active emergency and development institutions and on encouraging the participation of the affected population in designing and implementing interventions to promote household food security and nutrition. Priority is given to the needs of food-insecure households and to the promotion of sustainable and healthy livelihoods.

NOTES

1 This report is based on information available as of March 2000. Current information on the wheat market can be found in FAO's bimonthly *Food Outlook* report.

2 More detailed statistics on cereal and non-cereal food aid shipments are available at: www.fao.org/ under Statistical databases and then All databases.

3 Expressed in local currency.

4 Unless otherwise indicated, economic estimates and forecasts in this section are from IMF. *World Economic Outlook*, October 1999.

5 UN. 1999. *The World Economy in 1999*. Washington, DC.

6 These forecasts were prepared for FAO by the Institute for Policy Analysis, University of Toronto, Canada, associated with Project LINK.

7 "Low-income food-deficit countries with the lowest capacity to finance food imports" is a subgroup of the FAO category of all LIFDCs. The subgroup comprises 31 countries (17 in Africa, 3 in Latin America and the Caribbean, 8 in Asia and the Pacific and 3 in the Near East) for which food imports represent 25 percent or more of total export earnings. The group of EHDAEs comprises 47 countries (24 in sub-Saharan Africa, 18 in Latin America and the Caribbean and 5 in Asia) for which agricultural, fishery and forestry exports are equivalent to at least 20 percent of their total exports, or 20 percent of their total imports.

8 Failures in rural credit delivery have been extensively documented. See FAO/GTZ. 1998. *Agricultural finance revisited: Why?* Agricultural Finance Revisited No. 1. Rome (see also other publications in this series); World Bank. 1975. *Agricultural credit.* Washington, DC; and World Bank. 1993. *A review of Bank lending for agricultural credit and rural finance, 1948-1992.* Washington, DC.

9 Officially registered as members of the Microcredit Summit Campaign.

10 Members of the Consultative Group to Assist the Poor (CGAP), major donors of microcredit. The CGAP consortium was created in 1995 and has its headquarters at the World Bank.

11 Microfinance organizations (MFOs) range in size, expertise, funding base, clientele, purpose, geographical coverage and other characteristics. They may be run by the state or local government, private bankers, local or international NGOs or community organizations. Microcredit may be a primary activity of an MFO, or part of the overall development strategy of a government or NGO.

12 Other estimates of borrower numbers are lower, including 6.9 million estimated by the United Nations Development Fund for Women (UNIFEM, 1999) and 16 million estimated by the World Bank (1999).

13 S. Khandker. 1998. *Fighting poverty with microcredit*, p. 11. Washington, DC, World Bank.

14 UNCDF. 1999. *Working paper on microfinance.* New York.

15 Ibid.

16 An MFO generally includes a savings component. This paper focuses only on the credit aspect of microcredit.

17 Khandker (p. 150, op. cit., note 13) reports that marginal farmers receive 72 percent of the microcredit loans made to agriculture, compared with 3 percent of the agricultural loans made by agricultural development banks.

18 FAO. 1998. *The State of Food and Agriculture 1998*, p. 290. Rome.

19 IFPRI. 1998. *Rural finance and poverty alleviation*. Washington, DC.

20 These issues have been extensively discussed, among others, by: World Bank. 1993. op. cit., note 8; and K. Hoff and J. Stiglitz. 1990. Introduction: imperfect information and rural credit markets: puzzles and policy perspectives. *The World Bank Economic Review*, 4(3).

21 J. Morduch. 1998. Does microfinance really help the poor? New evidence from flagship programs in Bangladesh. HIID, Harvard University (unpublished document).

22 Although J.D. von Pishke (1999. *Poverty, human development and financial services*. UNDP Occasional Paper No. 25) has found that these programmes do not affect repayment performance, they do seem to affect earnings ability.

23 Khandker, p. 145, op. cit., note 13.

24 Women account for 95 percent of the Grameen Bank's borrowers.

25 Khandker, p. 155, op. cit., note 13.

26 J. Morduch. 1999. The Grameen Bank: a financial reckoning (unpublished mimeo). Available at: www.wws.princeton.edu/~rpds/macarthur/workingp1.html

27 Real interest rates charged on microcredit loans range from 2.5 to 6 percent per month, compared with 7 to 40 percent per month among moneylenders, according to sources in various countries.

28 Khan *et al.*, cited in H. Zaman. 1999. *Assessing the poverty and vulnerability impact of microcredit in Bangladesh: a case study of BRAC*. Background paper for the WDR 2000/2001. Washington, DC, World Bank. The World Bank (2000, Part 5.35) also reports that, when microcredit loans are used as an *ex ante* coping device by borrowers, the proceeds are usually devoted to building assets rather than direct consumption.

29 Some research suggests that control of the loan and productive activity may rest with males in the household (e.g. L. Mayoux. 1999. *Women's empowerment and microfinance programmes: approaches, evidence and ways forward*. Milton Keynes, UK, Development Policy and Practice Working Paper No. 41.), but the point is debated in the literature.

30 S. Schuler, S. Hashemi and A. Riley. 1997. The influence of women's changing roles and status in Bangladesh's fertility transition. *World Development*, 25(4).

31 E. Ostrom, R. Gardner and J. Walker. 1994. *Rules, games and common-pool resources*. Ann Arbor, USA, University of Michigan Press.

32 Khandker (p. 7, op. cit., note 13) reports a higher return and more cost-effectiveness of Grameen Bank loans compared with other microcredit programmes, targeted food programmes and agricultural development banks.

33 In one document, the World Bank estimated that more than 50 countries had been involved in civil conflicts between 1980 and 1995 – see World Bank. 1997. *A framework for World Bank involvement in post-conflict reconstruction*, p. 3. Washington, DC. In this paper, the count used is 33 (see Box 5).

34 J. Carter. 1999. First step toward peace is eradicating hunger. *International Herald Tribune*, 17 June 1999.

35 See R.H. Green. 1987. *Killing the dream: the political and human economy of war in sub-Saharan Africa.* IDS Discussion Paper. Brighton, UK, Institute of Development Studies; R.H. Green. 1994. The course of the four horsemen: the costs of war and its aftermath in sub-Saharan Africa. *In* J. Macrae and A. Zwi, eds. *War and hunger: rethinking international responses in complex emergencies.* London, Zed Books; F. Stewart. 1993. War and underdevelopment: can economic analysis help reduce the costs? *Journal of International Development,* 5(4): 357-380; and F. Stewart. 1998. The root causes of conflict: evidence and policy implications. Paper prepared for conference on War, Hunger and Displacement: the Economics and Politics of the Prevention of Humanitarian Emergencies, Stockholm, 15-16 June 1998. UN University/World Institute for Development Economics Research.

36 For a critical discussion on the costs of war, see C. Cramer. 1999. The economics and political economy of conflict in sub-Saharan Africa. Paper presented to the Standing Committee on University Studies of Africa (SCUSA) conference, Norwich, UK, September 1999. For a historical parallel for the First World War, see: A.S. Milward. 1984. *The economic effects of the two world wars on Britain,* second edition. Studies in Economic and Social History. Basingstoke, UK, and London, Macmillan.

37 The method followed specifies a simple equilibrium model in which the level of agricultural output in the absence of conflict is determined by relative prices and a trend variable. The former seek to capture the short-term output-optimizing decisions of farmers, while the latter approximates the growth of the labour force and technical change. Conflict losses are estimated within this framework by a binary ("dummy") variable that takes the value of unity for conflict years. In this study, conflict years for each country were identified through the compilation of information from a number of sources that specialize in conflict monitoring. Figure 13 shows the number of developing countries for which there were statistically significant conflict losses. While other countries were also conflict-affected, either the impact on agriculture was not statistically significant or data for estimation were not available. The country count shows that, after increasing for almost 15 years, the

number of output-reducing conflicts peaked in 1990 and then declined.

38 P. Svedberg. 1990. Undernutrition in sub-Saharan Africa: a critical assessment of the evidence. *In* J. Dreze and A. Sen. *The political economy of hunger*. Oxford, UK, Clarendon Press.

39 FAO. 1996. Food assistance and food security. *World Food Summit Technical Background Documents*, Vol. 3, No. 13. Rome. This estimate is based on the assumption, albeit unrealistic, that food assistance can be targeted perfectly.

40 Losses from conflict in Central America are estimated by a similar method in J. Weeks. 1997. Trade liberalization, market deregulation and agricultural performance in Central America. *Journal of Development Studies*, 35(5).

41 L. Luckham, I. Ahmed and R. Muggah. 1999. The impact of conflict on poverty in sub-Saharan Africa. Background Paper for World Bank Poverty Status Assessment for sub-Saharan Africa. Brighton, UK, Institute of Development Studies, University of Sussex, p. 21-22.

42 A good example of this was the conflict in Angola, in which at least two of the anticolonial movements were at war with each other and with the Portuguese army.

43 On occasion, insurgents can obtain a degree of international recognition by being granted "belligerent" status, as was the case with the insurgents in El Salvador in the 1980s.

44 In Angola, the death and destruction wrought in the two years after the 1992 peace accord was greater than that suffered between 1961, the start of the anticolonial conflict, and 1992. See the Preface to E. Medi. 1997. *Angola: study of vocational rehabilitation, training and employment programmes for persons disabled by the conflict: experiences and issues.* Geneva, ILO.

45 For a review of the history of agricultural disruption during conflict from the twelfth century onwards, see PRIO. 1999. *To cultivate peace: agriculture in a world of conflict.* PRIO Report No. 1/99. Oslo. International Peace Research Institute.

46 E. Messer, M.J. Cohen and J. D'Costa. 1998. *Food from peace: breaking the links between conflict and hunger.* Food, Agriculture and the Environment Discussion Paper No. 24. Washington, DC, IFPRI.

47 For example, before independence Angola was the world's fourth largest coffee exporter. Intermittent drought, policy neglect, the direct effects of war and political insecurity combined to reduce annual export production from 220 000 tonnes in 1973 to 3 000 tonnes in 1993. See S.H. McCormick. 1994. *The Angolan economy: prospects for growth in a postwar environment.* Washington, DC, Center for Strategic and International Studies. On a similar war and its effects on cashew production in Mozambique, see C. Cramer. 1999. Raising agricultural output capacity and productivity in low-income countries: with special

reference to Mozambican cashew production. Background paper for UNCTAD. *Least Developed Countries Report, 1999.* London, School of Oriental and African Studies, University of London.

48 I. Ahmed and R.H. Green. 1999. The heritage of war and state collapse in Somalia and Somaliland: local-level effects, external interventions and reconstruction. *Third World Quarterly,* 20(1): 113-128.

49 T. Bruck. 1997. Macroeconomic effects of the war in Mozambique. QEH Working Paper No. QEHWPS11. Oxford, UK, Queen Elizabeth House.

50 On the economic implications of infrastructure provision, see Y. Hayami and J.-P. Platteau. 1997. *Resource endowments and agricultural development: Africa versus Asia.* Cahiers de la Faculté des Sciences Économiques, Sociales et de Gestion – Namur, Série Recherche No. 192, 1991/12. Namur, Belgium, Centre de Recherche en Économie du Developpement; R. Ahmed and N. Rustagi. 1984. Marketing and price incentives in African and Asian countries: a comparison. *In* E. Dieter, ed. *Agricultural marketing strategy and pricing policy.* Washington, DC, World Bank.

51 Wartime diversion of transport vehicles and equipment from rural trading activities has long been acknowledged as one of the features that determines a strong relationship between war (even where this is not a civil war) and famine. See: J. Illiffe. 1987. *The African poor: a history.* African Studies Series No. 58. Cambridge, UK, Cambridge University Press.

52 M. Chingono. 1995. *The state, violence and development: the political economy of war in Mozambique.* Aldershot, UK, Avebury.

53 P. Collier. 1999. Doing well out of war. Paper prepared for the Conference on Economic Agendas in Civil Wars, London, 26-27 April 1999.

54 W. Reno. 1998. Humanitarian emergencies and warlord economies in Liberia and Sierra Leone. Paper presented at the conference on War, Hunger and Displacement: the Economics and Politics of the Prevention of Humanitarian Emergencies, Stockholm, 15-16 June 1998. United Nations University/World Institute for Development Economics Research (UNU/WIDER). p. 17-18.

55 D. Keen. 1994. *The benefits of famine: a political economy of famine and relief in Southwestern Sudan, 1983-89.* Princeton, New Jersey, USA, Princeton University Press. See also Luckham, Ahmed and Muggah, op. cit., note 41. For an analysis of the role of agriculture in the origins of conflict, see: PRIO, op. cit., note 45; Stewart, 1998, op. cit., note 35; Collier, op. cit., note 53; and Cramer, op. cit., note 36.

56 World Bank, op. cit., note 33.

57 E. Muehlhoff. and M. Herens. 1997. Household food security and nutrition in agricultural relief and rehabilitation programmes. *Food, Nutrition and Agriculture* No. 19, p. 5.

PART II

WORLD FOOD AND
AGRICULTURE:
LESSONS FROM THE PAST
50 YEARS

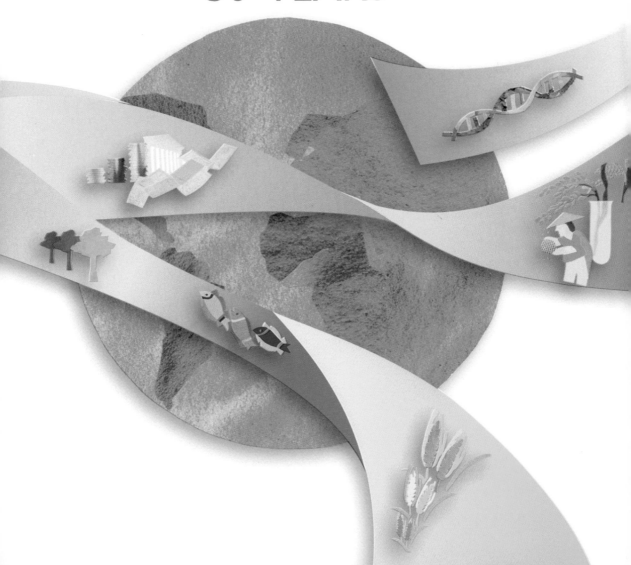

WORLD FOOD AND AGRICULTURE: LESSONS FROM THE PAST 50 YEARS

If you want the present to be different from the past, study the past.

Baruch Spinoza

INTRODUCTION

This review covers changes in the world food, agricultural and food security situation over the past half-century, with a view to deriving policy messages for the years to come.

Fifty years of world food and agriculture make up a canvas that can only be painted with a broad brush. It is not only a long period but also an extraordinarily eventful one – indeed, no other 50-year period in history has seen such wide-ranging and rapid changes in humanity. These changes have not left agriculture untouched. Food and agricultural techniques and systems have undergone major transformations, as have agricultural and rural societies. Different food security situations have also evolved across regions, countries and groups of people. Progress has been spectacular in some areas, disappointing in others. The world today appears overall to be a rich and peaceful place compared with what it was 50 years ago. Yet, millions of people, even in rich societies, are still bowed down by the suffering imposed on them by hunger and related diseases. Such contrasts are certainly not specific to the contemporary world, but advances in technology and resources have made hunger more avoidable and, therefore, more intolerable today.

From this wide field of research, five themes have been chosen for discussion in this year's special chapter. The first section presents a retrospective overview, largely drawn from the stock of historical and institutional memory contained in past issues of *The State of Food and Agriculture*; the second describes the process of agricultural modernization and its asymmetric effects on farmers and rural societies; the third focuses on the interrelated issues of staple food production and food and nutrition security; the fourth analyses agricultural

The past 50 years have seen a revolution in agricultural practices and production and a consequent transformation of rural societies.

productivity, its sources, scope and benefits; and the fifth discusses the role that political and institutional mechanisms can play in reducing or – as has often been the case – perpetuating poverty and food insecurity. A final section summarizes some of the main lessons of the past half-century, as they emerge from the various sections of this review. Overall, it is hoped that the review will contribute both to a greater understanding of the problems faced and to greater commitment towards, in Spinoza's words, "making the present different" – that is, making hunger a thing of the past.

Half a century of food and agriculture

This is a historical overview of the main events and trends affecting food and agriculture over the past 50 years. It draws primarily on the annual series of *The State of Food and Agriculture*, which was first published in 1947. These past publications record more than half a century of achievements as well as failures in agricultural and rural development and food security. They show recurring themes and concerns but also major transformations that make world agriculture today very different from that of half a century ago. The economic and political environments have changed profoundly, technologies have progressed enormously and policy perceptions and priorities have evolved.

This section attempts to trace the changes as reported by FAO in *The State of Food and Agriculture*, particularly – since 1957 – in the special chapters on selected topics. Some events that, in hindsight, appear to be important, but have either been overlooked or reviewed in an incomplete or inaccurate way in contemporary issues of the report, have been inserted or supplemented by additional information in the present review. This is necessarily selective in its coverage, and FAO's many activities and initiatives that are widely publicized in other documents have not been included, except for selected important events in which the Organization has played a prominent role.

It is hoped that this retrospective overview will be of interest, not only as a reminder of past events, but also as material for reflection on how far we have come towards achieving world food security and promoting agricultural and rural development. It should also prompt us to consider how much remains to be done and, judging from past experience, what action is most likely to contribute to further improvements.

THE SITUATION HALF A CENTURY AGO

Devastation and reconstruction, Food shortages
Geographic concentration of wealth and food supply
Asia – the focus of concerns

The Second World War had a profound affect on world agriculture. According to early issues of *The State of Food and Agriculture*, world agricultural production at the end of the war was 5 percent – 15 percent in per caput terms – below pre-war levels. However, the impacts of the global conflict differed widely across regions.

Agriculture suffered massive war devastation throughout Europe, in the USSR, in large areas of Asia and the Pacific and in North Africa. Sharp falls in agricultural production in those regions,[1] coupled with a widespread inability to finance food imports, resulted in acute food shortages even when hostilities ceased. These problems were compounded by a series of droughts during 1946 and 1947 in the USSR, North Africa and large areas of the Far East. Shortages were also acute in the fisheries sector, which was affected by the loss and requisition of fishing craft and equipment. Four fifths of world fish supplies had formerly been produced in the areas affected by the war. In forestry too, the impact of the war was severe. Direct damage to forests and forest industries was most serious in Central and Eastern Europe, including the western part of the USSR, and in some countries of the Far East. The war effort, combined with the cessation of coal trade, led to overcutting for fuel and to forest destruction in many parts of the world. In addition, there was generally less concern for forest management.

In sharp contrast, food supplies were abundant in a number of large producer countries that had been relatively spared by the conflict – Canada, the United States, Australia and Argentina. As in the First World War, those countries took on the role of food suppliers for their allies and made a special effort to stimulate output. In fact, especially for North America's agriculture, the war years were a period of expansion and prosperity. Agricultural production in this region increased by one third compared with pre-war levels, and net cereal exports rose from about 5 million tonnes in 1938 to an annual average of 17.5 million tonnes in 1946-48. Europe's net annual cereal imports rose from 9.5 million to 14 million tonnes during the same period. Among the developing country regions, both Asia and Africa turned from having a surplus to a deficit in cereals, with the shift being especially pronounced in the case of Asia (which registered a drop from +2.2 to −3.7 million tonnes between 1934-38 and 1946). Latin America and the Caribbean, Africa, the Near East and Oceania only suffered from the indirect effects of the war (with shortages of production requisites, or loss of import supplies or export markets), and the war had relatively little effect on their agricultural performances at the regional level.

In reviewing such diverse regional performances, already in 1948 *The State of Food and Agriculture* (probably recalling the depression-induced agricultural surpluses of the 1930s) warned against the paradoxical existence of burdensome excess food supplies in some parts of the world while there were acute scarcities elsewhere. It expressed the fear that food production in countries with a surplus might exceed the import capacity of food-deficit countries – many of which were acutely short of foreign exchange – and that the excess capacity of large producers and exporters could become structural in nature. It also noted that demand, particularly for forestry products, would shrink when reconstruction needs were met, and that synthetics would displace several agricultural raw materials. In contrast with some economists who advocated measures to reduce supply, FAO advocated action to raise demand, given the very low nutrition levels to which the populations of even some industrialized countries had fallen.

Excess food supplies in some parts of the world coexisted with acute scarcities in others. An increase in demand was needed to improve nutrition levels.

Developing country regions

Early issues of *The State of Food and Agriculture* reveal a balance of regional concerns profoundly different from the situation today. The regional reviews devoted much attention to the problems of Asia, with relatively less coverage of other regions. Africa, in particular, was recognized as the least economically advanced region, but one for which economic and social development and improved welfare were just a matter of time (see Box 11). This perception of "African hope-Asian drama" was reversed only after an extended period of contrasting development experiences in the two regions.

For *Asia*, the report depicted problems of an almost unsurmountable nature. This region had about half of the world's population but only one fifth of the earth's land, yet its economy was still dependent on agriculture to a great extent. Furthermore, agricultural productivity in much of the region was very low. For instance, cereal production per hectare of harvested land in India was estimated to be, on average, 20 percent below that of developing countries as a whole; and cereal production per worker in India, Indonesia and China was significantly lower than the average for developing countries.

Agricultural structures in South Asia presented a grim combination of extensive land use and a high person-land ratio. Not only was agricultural productivity low but almost three quarters of the labour force was tied up in the production of a meagre diet. Calorie intake was barely 2 000 kcal per caput/day and most people lived on small farms, producing most of what they ate and eating most of what they produced.

The war brought these long-term problems of Asia into sharper relief. The food sector suffered considerably from war, political instability and displacements of people. Per caput calorie intake declined during the war in all but three large rice-producing countries: Burma (Myanmar), Siam (Thailand) and Indochina (Viet Nam, Lao People's Democratic Republic, Cambodia). In India and Pakistan, Japan and the Philippines, it fell to around 1 700 kcal/day. The great fishing industries of Southeast Asia suffered heavy loss of fishing vessels and human resources. The region emerged in the postwar period as a net importer of food, a reversal of its traditional food surplus situation. This shift was perceived to be of great significance to world food trade and raised the question, still debated today in the case of China, of the extent to which food demand in densely populated countries in Asia would exceed their domestic production capacity and cause tightness in world food markets.

A very different picture emerged in postwar *Latin America*. Throughout and after the war, the region continued the rapid economic expansion recorded during much of the 1920s and 1930s. Such expansion was achieved more markedly than in other developing country regions through development strategies based on industrial growth and import substitution, which engendered considerable growth in industrial activity. Between 1934-38 and 1947 industrial output almost doubled, while agricultural production expanded by only 20 percent. Industrialization also contributed to a massive expansion of urban centres where most of the manufacturing activity was located, a phenomenon that would be amplified in the following decades.

Nevertheless, agriculture still dominated the region's economy, contributing about one fifth of total GDP and employing close to half of the labour force in 1950. A high level of employment and rapid increases in real incomes created a strong demand for food, especially in the cities. Indeed, yearly rates of population growth in the late 1940s were in the order of 2.7 percent, the highest of all regions, and per caput GDP growth was 2 to 3 percent. Despite the policy bias against

Box 11

AFRICAN DEVELOPMENT PROSPECTS AS SEEN IN *THE STATE OF FOOD AND AGRICULTURE 1948*

"From the standpoint of the highly developed regions, Africa appears as a comparatively empty continent with large potentialities of production – a soft-currency area with possibilities of a much greater exchange of goods with Europe. Indeed, in the last half of the twentieth century, Africa may in some cases be to Europe what 'the West' was to the United States in the latter half of the nineteenth century". However short in foresight, this vision of the role and future of African colonial territories reflected the conventional view of the time. Despite recognized nutritional shortcomings, Africa was not a focus of concern from a food security standpoint. Rather, adequate domestic food supplies were taken for granted in a demographically "empty" continent, where population was growing at moderate rates (1.3 percent yearly between 1920 and 1950), and with rich agricultural resources which constituted the region's area of specialization.

The fact that early issues of *The State of Food and Agriculture* may have misjudged the gravity of Africa's human and natural resource constraints is also suggested by the comparatively light treatment of this region in the publication's developing country reviews. Ignorance of facts, rather than neglect, probably explained this shortcoming. The report repeatedly emphasized the lack of information available to allow an adequate assessment of Africa's agricultural situation and the great uncertainty surrounding its development prospects. The 1948 report states that "... it is the least well-documented continent, and until more work has been done by governments in ascertaining the facts in each territory, only a very fragmentary idea of the food and agriculture situation is possible". This appeal for improved systems of collection and analysis of information on the African situation as a prerequisite for efficient policy action was to become a recurring theme of the publication over the years.

agriculture, caused by the industrialization drive (partly compensated by direct public support in various forms), the sector performed remarkably well, with food production generally coping with expanding demand. The region also remained a net exporter of food and agricultural products, although several countries became increasingly dependent on food imports. Satisfactory agricultural performances and expanding incomes translated into improved diets. Regional food intakes, estimated to be about 2 400 kcal per caput/day in 1947 (up from 2 200 before the war), were relatively high in relation to those of other developing country regions. Levels were, however, uneven among countries (Argentina 3 100 kcal, Peru 1 900 kcal) and income groups.

The war years had generally been years of economic progress for much of *Africa*. Demand was strong for many of its agricultural commodities and minerals. Many territories were able to expand economic activity and agricultural production. Average income levels were reported to be significantly higher than before the war. Basic food production in Africa increased in response to strengthened demand but, in contrast with other regions, the production of industrial crops − notably cotton, sisal and tobacco − increased faster than that of food crops. Higher income levels, chiefly in the cities, intensified the demand for foodstuffs, many of which had to be imported, and this created growing financial difficulties for several countries. However, despite generally satisfactory food production performances and increasing effective demand, dietary standards remained low. The 1947 estimates pointed to per caput calorie intakes of 1 500 to 2 000 kcal/day in North Africa (significantly below pre-war levels, especially in Algeria and Morocco); and 2 000 to 2 300 in most other countries.

The *Near East* was depicted as a backward region that was undergoing, however, the most rapid economic transformation. *The State of Food and Agriculture 1948* notes: "Only [recently] did this region emerge from a long period in which distances and time were reckoned on the speed of the dromedary caravan. Suddenly the Near East found itself a crossroad of world trade and traffic.... Mineral oil is now available in increasing quantities. Oil pipelines cross the once mysterious deserts. New ports, new towns, new activities are growing continually. Modern Turkey is vastly different from the Ottoman Turkey of 30 years ago, and this is also true [to a] degree of all other countries of the region." The report concludes: "It is difficult to appraise what sort of agriculture may come out [of] this economic transformation during the next generation." In fact, the region's agricultural systems were still dominated by environment and tradition. Water was, as it is now, a predominant concern. Only 4 percent of the land area was under cultivation. Farming systems were characterized by age-old practices and structures. Animal husbandry was divorced from crop farming and monopolized by nomads. Sheep, goats, camels and horses were the most important livestock, with beef cattle farming almost unknown.

Against this background, the war period had been generally one of expansion for agriculture in the Near East. This was true in particular for cereals, meat and other animal products, which generally supplanted cash crops such as cotton in order to satisfy the food demand of the allied forces present in the region. Domestic consumers did not appear to have benefited from this emphasis on food production, however, as available data (mainly concerning Egypt and Turkey) suggest a significant decline in per caput calorie, protein and fat intakes in 1947/48 in relation to levels in the period 1934-1938, especially in Turkey. Average daily intakes in 1947/48 were about 2 050 kcal per caput in Turkey and 2 390 in Egypt, down from about 2 500 prior to the war in both countries.

Fisheries and forestry

The fisheries and forestry sectors were the object of only passing reference in early issues of *The State of Food and Agriculture*. It was then an accepted fact that the high seas belonged to everybody and that they contained inexhaustible stocks of fish. The FAO Conference in 1946 stated: "The fishing grounds of the world are teeming with fish of all kinds. Fisheries are an international resource. In underdeveloped areas, especially, the harvest awaits the reaper." A similar consideration applied to forestry. Early issues of this publication did mention the importance of conservation and long-term development of forests, but the focus of their attention was on the production of forest products. Conservation issues would only come to the fore decades later – in the 1970s – when the public in some countries began to worry about the destruction of tropical forests, forest fires and forest dieback.

THE 1950s

Recovery, Industrialization, Development planning

Food self-sufficiency, Surpluses

Reassessing Africa

Uneven recovery and bipolarism

Growing political and economic bipolarism characterized the 1950s. The "cold war" and ideological confrontation rendered international cooperation more problematic. At the same time, the gap between rich and poor countries and societies widened. The Marshall Plan and reconstruction activity contributed to a rapid economic recovery in war-affected countries in Western Europe while, by contrast, many economies in the developing world suffered from instability in agricultural markets, acute shortages of foreign exchange and, particularly in Asia, severe problems linked to the process of establishing newly independent political systems. During this period, the growing gap between rich and poor was mentioned repeatedly in *The State of Food and Agriculture*, which also emphasized the importance of agricultural development in improving the economic situation of countries and societies. For developing countries to raise their living standards significantly, it was estimated that their food production would have to rise to between 1 and 2 percent above population growth. Such an increase in output, however, was felt to be beyond the resources and technological capacity of many developing countries.

Developing countries lacked the resources and technology with which to raise their living standards.

Industrialization

Industry-driven growth, already the cornerstone of many Latin American countries' development strategies, became the orthodox development paradigm during the 1950s. Thus, the phenomenon of "urban bias-agricultural discrimination" gained ground. There was direct discrimination against agriculture through policies, widely implemented by parastatal marketing boards, which drove a "wedge" between prices received by farmers and border prices of tradable commodities; and indirect discrimination arising from currency overvaluation that tended to depress prices of exportables and import substitutes, together with policies that protected industry and favoured industrial import substitution, thereby raising the prices of non-agricultural goods while reducing farmgate prices.

The industrial bias was based on the thesis that for an economy to develop, it had to grow rapidly, and to do so it had to industrialize. This view was reflected in the ample coverage of developments in industrial production found in early years of this publication, which introduced a regular section on this issue in the 1950s. Other than the fundamental ingredient of development, because of its positive effects on income growth, industrialization was also seen as the "basic factor behind effective purchasing power for farm production" (*The State of Food and Agriculture 1952*). It was also recognized that, since industrialization involved urban migration, it would be necessary to keep food prices low in order to mitigate social hardship in the cities. Subsidies on agricultural inputs, such as fertilizers and machinery, and cheap credit were intended to compensate agriculture. However, these measures tended to benefit the larger commercial farms rather than small-scale peasant farming. "Cheap food" policies in favour of urban consumers heavily penalized the farm sector. Such policies endured in many countries until the 1980s when they were swept away in the process of structural adjustment.

Development planning

Partially as a result of the Great Depression of the early 1930s and the ensuing collapse of effective demand, which in turn led to calls for greater state intervention in the economy and in managing markets, development strategies involved a strong state role in the marketing of inputs and outputs and in the planning of production and the allocation of resources. *The State of Food and Agriculture* reported extensively on developments in programming and planning in agriculture, highlighting in particular the pioneering experiences of some Asian countries. It was felt that the vicious circle of low income, low consumption and stagnant production could only be broken by public sector planning and financing of agricultural and economic development. Planning typically involved the establishment of production targets, the programming of investment and even detailed schemes for land reclamation, irrigation and the provision of inputs.

India was singled out as a particular case for the degree to which it planned an integrated development of its mixed economy on the basis of self-help, yet without undue regimentation. State control was applied at strategic points in order to ensure that the pattern of development was in line with the objectives of India's first Five-Year Plan (1950/51-1955/56). The Plan envisaged important public financing of food and fibre production, with the objective of restoring pre-war levels of consumption and diverting any savings into investment for further economic development.

Another, more radical, example of state planning and

intervention was that of China. Its first Five-Year Plan (1953-1957) was considered a success. Government investment in agriculture and industrial planning had reportedly increased GDP by 12 percent in real terms. In 1958, a new strategy was introduced, known as the "Great Leap Forward", in order to consolidate and reorganize rural agriculture and industry. The new strategy emphasized the adoption of new technologies in the countryside and the concomitant development of more rural-based light industry. It also involved the elimination of private rural property and the forced consolidation and collectivization of farms. The 1959 issue of this publication reported that, already by the end of 1958, more than 740 000 agricultural cooperatives in China had been transformed into 26 000 communes. Each contained some 2 000 families whose workload was divided between agricultural production and light industry.

However, although China's production increased significantly between 1957 and 1958, major problems emerged soon after. Production reports by the People's Communes were often overestimated, yet they served as a basis for the government's requests for increasing production quotas. Thus, government pressure on the peasantry to extract greater levels of output left rural communities with ever less of their production for their own consumption. The problem was compounded by the failure of rural industries to provide machinery, tools, fertilizer and other materials for agriculture as well as by widespread shortages of labour and the introduction of untested farming methods. These factors, coinciding with poor weather, contributed to a drastic reduction in agricultural production and led to food shortages.

The State of Food and Agriculture 1960 made some reference to the problems occurring in the communes and reported on measures used to counter them: "A reorganization of the communes was found necessary in August 1959, as food supplies for the commune kitchens had fallen below the previous year's level, and as overcentralization with the pooling of all income had meant that the more efficient 'brigades' were supporting the rest. Small plots were handed back to families for the cultivation of vegetables and the raising of poultry to improve rural food supplies." The report also alluded to the easing of other regulations that were enforced within the commune system and to the organization of urban communes.

Self-sufficiency
One common feature of many development plans was the emphasis on partial or total self-sufficiency in food, often

motivated by strategic considerations. Wartime and postwar shortages had impressed on many countries the importance of assured food supplies and had made them mistrustful of too great a dependence on imports. These concerns were powerfully reinforced by payment difficulties and the reluctance to spend scarce foreign exchange on imports of agricultural products rather than on capital equipment needed for development. Food self-sufficiency (or "reasonable levels" of it) became a standard feature of most national development plans, even in cases where such an objective was clearly out of reach, except at extremely high costs and in situations of ample food supplies in world markets. The emphasis on increased food production and self-sufficiency, clearly at odds with the anti-agricultural bias of industry-driven development strategies, created ambiguous policy settings in many countries.

One important factor behind the emphasis on self-sufficiency in the early 1950s was the payments crisis that emerged in those years. This was a period of growing demand for goods of all kinds, especially from areas where imports had ceased during the war and where a vigorous process of recovery was under way. Because North America was the major supplier of industrial and agricultural goods, importers had to pay in dollars, which soon became scarce. Many deficit countries, even those receiving concessional payment terms and other forms of aid from the United States, were forced to curtail their overall and food imports. In particular, Latin American countries had to introduce severe import restrictions.

The problem of agricultural surpluses
The State of Food and Agriculture followed the problem of growing agricultural surpluses in some countries closely. It covered it extensively in 1954, referring in particular to the 1953 FAO Conference, which had discussed at length the complex issues involved. The central ones were: how to dispose of surpluses without disrupting world agricultural markets and what to do to ensure that production would expand in line with world requirements without adding to the surpluses. The Conference led to the establishment of a standing subcommittee of the FAO Committee on Commodity Problems (CCP) in order to provide a regular forum for intergovernmental consultations on these issues. The idea of using surplus food commodities to alleviate food emergencies and promote development – "surplus disposal" – gained ground and led to the introduction of food aid as a form of development assistance. This publication also discussed the price

equalization schemes adopted by some exporting countries to attenuate price fluctuations, underlining the value of moving towards international commodity agreements to stabilize production and prices at a level that was satisfactory to both exporters and importers

Reassessing Africa

Africa began receiving ample coverage from this publication in the late 1950s. A special FAO study of food and agricultural development in Africa South of the Sahara was included in *The State of Food and Agriculture 1958*, which depicted a mixed record of agricultural performances since the conclusion of the war. In general, food production had kept pace with population growth, fish production had increased to three times its pre-war level, and dietary levels were considered by and large to be in line with requirements – despite cases of serious food shortages, especially in the periods preceding the harvests. While it was still regarded as an "empty" continent (with only 5 percent of the world's population and seven people/km^2 overall), Africa had areas of population density that were too high for the maintenance of soil fertility under shifting cultivation and its forest cover was being ruthlessly destroyed, with serious consequences for its soil and water resources.

Forests

Chapter IV of *The State of Food and Agriculture 1958* was entitled The growth of forest industries and their impact on the world's forests. It reviewed the development of forest industries from their early stages through to their enormous growth in the postwar period. For instance, wood pulp production had doubled in the ten years following the war to reach 56 million tonnes in 1956. Such expansion imposed enormous pressure on forest resources, the effects of which were, however, grossly understated ("Tabloid educators have familiarized most people with the fact that 50 ha of forest is consumed by a single Sunday edition of a New York newspaper"). The study emphasized that the world's forests were adequate to meet these demands and that the forest industry was in many cases the best friend of forests. It stated that "in many parts of the world, large-scale industrial exploiters of the forest are today setting a shining example of forest care and conservation". Opposing views were to come to the fore in the following decades.

THE 1960s

Technological progress
Concern about the poor and hungry – and famine in China
Rediscovering agriculture
Trade – the Kennedy Round of MTNs and UNCTAD
Development assistance – the unsuccessful attempt to set targets

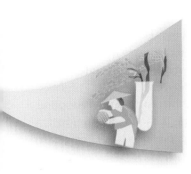

Technological progress

Of all of the past five decades, the 1960s could possibly be characterized best by the rapid advance of agricultural technology, although the first initiatives − including the establishment of the first international agricultural research centres (IARCs) such as the International Maize and Wheat Improvement Center (CIMMYT) − had been taken in the late 1940s and the 1950s. There were high hopes that rapid gains in agricultural productivity would alleviate rural poverty and underpin economic and social development while reducing the incidence of hunger.

Twice during the decade (in 1963 and 1968) special chapters of *The State of Food and Agriculture* discussed the issue of raising agricultural productivity and its underlying factors. With Asia the focus of development assistance efforts, it was logical that much attention and a large amount of development resources were directed at irrigation development, although the increased use of fertilizer (consumption by developing countries grew at record rates during this decade) and improved seeds were also key contributing factors to what was to become known as the "green revolution". FAO's own successful Fertilizer Programme, established under the aegis of the Freedom from Hunger Campaign, stems from this period.

The interlinked issues of science, technology, education and extension also received particular attention. It was noted that basic agricultural research, and still more its adaptation to local farm practice, was carried out predominantly in the developed countries with temperate climates. The crucial task ahead was to adapt the growing body of knowledge to the arid or tropical climates of most developing countries and to persuade farmers there to accept and apply this new knowledge.

The opportunities being opened up by new improved varieties and the good agricultural performances of a number of Asian countries in the latter part of the 1960s were the object of discussions in the 1968 and 1969 issues of this publication. To what extent were such improved performances a reflection of the conscious efforts to accelerate output, in particular through the more widespread use of improved cereal varieties and other inputs associated with them? While the reports offered no definite answer, they did point to a number of elements suggesting that something like a "green revolution" was in fact under way. The rate of adoption of the new cereal varieties had been much faster in Asian countries, where cereal crop yields had shown the greatest improvement. Improvements had been dramatic – the rate of growth in output in 1968 had doubled in those countries in relation to past trends – despite unfavourable weather conditions in many cases. It was suggested that government commitment, triggered by the urgency of the threat of food shortages, may have been crucial in this process. It was probably no coincidence that the fastest rate of adoption had taken place in the Far East, where the food situation had been particularly precarious, and that progress had been greater

Box 12

THE GREEN REVOLUTION IN AGRICULTURE

The "green revolution" is referred to several times in this review. It refers to a spectacular improvement that took place in the yields of major food crops (rice, wheat, maize), mainly during the late 1960s and early 1970s, and most impressively in Asia. The improved yields helped turn heavily populated food-deficit countries into self-sufficient producers in the space of just a few years. It clearly averted a major food crisis in Asia, and served as the foundation for startling economic growth in China and Southeast and South Asia.

The green revolution was characterized by the fast dissemination of high-yielding varieties, i.e. improved seeds resulting from science-based research, as part of a technological package that included irrigation or controlled water supply and improved moisture utilization, fertilizers and pesticides and associated management skills. Its development and dissemination among millions of farmers were possible thanks to enabling socio-economic and institutional environments where active market opportunities also played an important role.

Within 20 years, almost half the wheat and rice land in developing countries was being sown with the new varieties. In Asia, almost 90 percent of wheat fields were

In improving agricultural productivity, issues associated with land tenure and agrarian reform were the most difficult to address.

in food-importing countries than in exporting countries. It had been well perceived by the early 1960s that raising agricultural productivity was not simply a matter of developing and introducing new agricultural technologies. Land tenure and agrarian reform issues, reviewed in particular in *The State of Food and Agriculture 1960*, were seen as key aspects of agricultural development, but perhaps the most difficult ones to tackle. Moves towards agrarian reform had gained momentum since the end of the Second World War and, as the report stated, "in no comparable period of history were there such widespread efforts, affecting so many people, to establish systems of land tenure better adapted to the changing needs". However, achievements had been limited, agrarian structures continued to be dominated by extreme inequalities in most

planted with modern varieties, and plantings of high-yielding rice had increased from 12 to 67 percent.

These developments enabled major increases in farm production and yields. The most rapid increases in output occurred during the 1963-1983 period of the green revolution. In developing countries, total production of paddy rice, wheat and maize rose by 3.1, 5.1 and 3.8 percent annually. During the next decade (1983-1993) annual production increases were reduced to 1.8, 2.5 and 3.4 percent, respectively.

The green revolution technologies were not without their problems: the need for a significant use of agrochemical-based pest and weed control in some crops raised environmental concerns as well as concern about human health; as irrigation areas expanded, water management required skills that were not always available; gender roles were shifted; and there were new scientific challenges to be tackled. Furthermore, lack of access to appropriate technologies remains a constraint for many farmers in areas with unfavourable conditions.

Consumers may be the greatest beneficiaries of the green revolution. Real food prices in Asia, indeed throughout the world, have steadily declined over the past 30 years through the application of yield-increasing, cost-reducing technologies built around improved seed-fertilizer-weed control components. Lower real food prices benefit the poor relatively more than the rich, since the poor spend a larger proportion of their available income on food. The green revolution technologies have also led to increased rural incomes.

developing countries and, when actually implemented, schemes of agrarian reform met with uneven success. The report stressed the importance of providing adequate credit, marketing and technical services if measures of agrarian reform were to achieve the results intended.

Addressing hunger and malnutrition

Despite growing optimism regarding the possibilities for raising agricultural productivity, a number of important institutional events in the first half of the 1960s indicated growing concern about the problems of hunger and malnutrition and the development prospects of poorer countries. The first was the creation in 1961 of the World Food Programme (WFP), initially introduced on an experimental basis as a joint responsibility of the UN and FAO. WFP was "to explore methods of using the surplus of food production of the more developed countries to aid economic development in less developed countries, and to combat hunger and malnutrition. Though small in relation to some bilateral programmes, it is potentially of great significance" (*The State of Food and Agriculture 1962*).

The World Food Congress, held in June 1963 in Washington, DC, drew world attention to the problems of hunger and malnutrition. It called on all governments and international and other organizations to take up the challenge of eliminating hunger as a primary task of that generation. It emphasized, however, that any sustained attack on the problem of hunger would have to come from a much more rapid growth of food production in the developing countries themselves. The Congress passed numerous recommendations to overcome the technical, educational and economic constraints facing agricultural development. These were often reiterated in such major meetings as the 1974 World Food Conference and the 1996 World Food Summit, and still remain fully relevant. They underline that the solution to the problem of hunger lies less in seeking new remedies and more in implementing, with the weight of political commitment, what is already widely known.

As emphasis to the prevailing concern about the prevalence of hunger, the 1960s opened with news that food shortages that had been developing since 1958 in China were reaching dramatic proportions. *The State of Food and Agriculture* reported disastrous harvests in large areas of the country, with more than half of the farmland affected by drought, typhoons, floods, insect infestation or other damage. The extent of the catastrophe in terms of human losses was to be known, however, only decades later. Estimates of the death toll vary but some point to tens of

World food conferences over the decades have emphasized that the solution to the problem of hunger lies less in seeking new remedies and more in implementing what is already known.

millions. Writing in 1993, Sen[2] estimated that, during the period 1958-1961, between 23 million and 30 million people died as a consequence of this disaster, which marked the failure of the agricultural programme of the "Great Leap Forward".

Agriculture and development

The surge in interest in problems of hunger, poverty and development coincided with an intense debate over distributional issues and the economic role of agriculture. *The State of Food and Agriculture 1970* recalled the late 1960s when, after a long period of sustained economic growth, issues regarding distribution of income gains received increasing emphasis, to the point of making equity considerations an integral part of economic development policy. While earlier development theory had tended to stress the likelihood that rapid economic growth would lead to greater income inequalities between leading and lagging sectors, although the incomes of the poor would still rise, by the late 1960s quite the opposite perspective gained respectability. A "basic needs" approach took hold, stressing the alleviation of poverty as the central concern of economic development. The emphasis on distribution tended to benefit agriculture, since it was in rural areas that the majority of the poor were found and agriculture was often the lagging sector relative to industry.

The debate extended to other aspects of agriculture and development. On the one hand, there was a "rediscovery" of agriculture by neoclassic economists who claimed that freer markets, more liberal trade regimes and a growing agricultural economy were conducive to overall economic growth. They also claimed that export pessimism was largely unfounded and that agricultural production and exports did respond to incentives (and disincentives). This position was opposed by the "structuralists", including social scientists from the UN Economic Commission for Latin America (ECLA). Strong supporters of import-substitution industrialization, structuralists had long contested the theory of comparative advantage, noting that it was not to the advantage of developing countries to specialize and to export primary and agricultural products when industrialized nations were exporting manufactured goods with greater value added. The thesis of a secular decline in the terms of trade of agricultural exports then evolved and has been the object of considerable literature since.

Although *The State of Food and Agriculture* did not enter directly into the debate, its position during this period – and thereafter – remained on the side of agriculture as an active

Box 13

AGRICULTURAL OUTPUT PATTERNS BETWEEN 1955 AND 1995

Significant increases in agricultural output occurred across geographic regions and products during the second half of the twentieth century. Figure A shows the growth in value of agricultural production between roughly 1955 and 1995, for all major products, as well as changes in land area planted. Figure B shows the agricultural output of the top producing countries in 1955 and 1995, in value and in proportion to the world total, along with per caput production and crop yields.

Major changes in total production

- Output value increased in every product category, in spite of a limited area expansion for most crops.
- There was a particularly strong expansion of cereal production, which almost tripled.
- Meat production value tripled and milk production value doubled – fed by the huge increase in cereals grown for feed use.

Major changes among the top ten producer countries

- China's total agricultural production surged, doubling as a proportion of total world output and more than quadrupling in value. China overtook the United States as the world's largest producer.
- China also doubled the per caput value of its agricultural output, which was far more than any other of the large producer countries.
- India retained its position as the world's third largest producer by tripling its agricultural output, although this was less than the increase achieved by China in the same period.
- In per caput terms, India only expanded its agricultural production by 35 percent, again less than China.
- Brazil gained several positions to become the world's fourth largest agricultural producer.
- Argentina maintained its position as the world's

highest per caput producer, although per caput production actually declined, and France also substantially increased the value of its per caput output – inching past the United States.

Figure A

WORLD TOTAL AGRICULTURAL PRODUCTION (GROSS), 1955 AND 1995

Crops

Million ha

Area

■ 1955
□ 1995

Million International $*

Production

□ 1955
■ 1955

* Based on producer prices around 1990
** To avoid double counting, seed cotton area has been distributed between cotton seed and cotton lint

Livestock

Million International $*

Production

■ 1955
□ 1995

Source: FAO

Figure B
TOTAL AGRICULTURAL PRODUCTION: TOP TEN COUNTRIES AROUND 1955

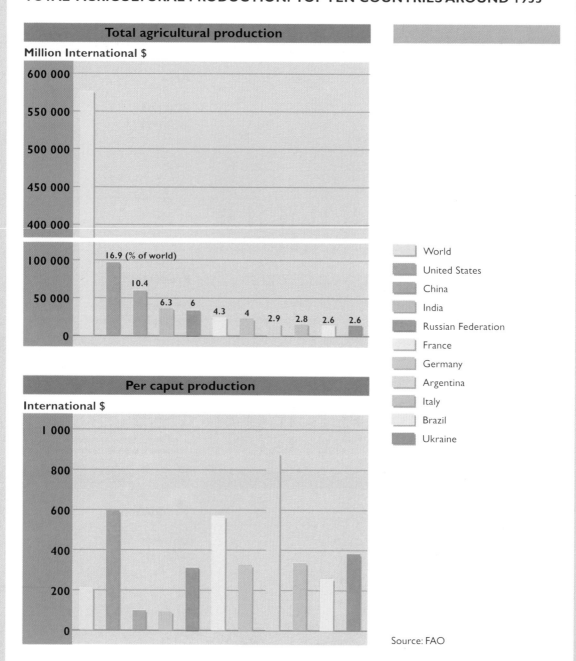

Source: FAO

Figure B (continued)

TOTAL AGRICULTURAL PRODUCTION: TOP TEN COUNTRIES AROUND 1955

Livestock production

Million International $

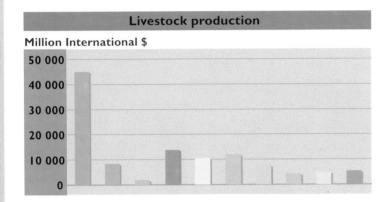

Cropped area

Million ha

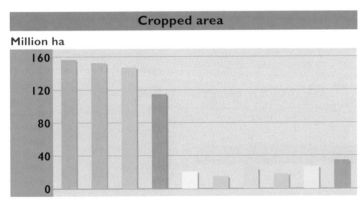

- United States
- China
- India
- Russian Federation
- France
- Germany
- Argentina
- Italy
- Brazil
- Ukraine

Crop production

Million International $

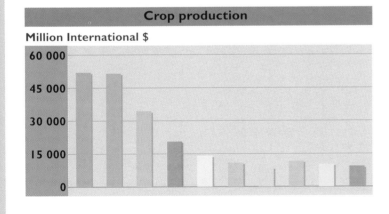

Source: FAO

Figure B (continued)

TOTAL AGRICULTURAL PRODUCTION: TOP TEN COUNTRIES AROUND 1995

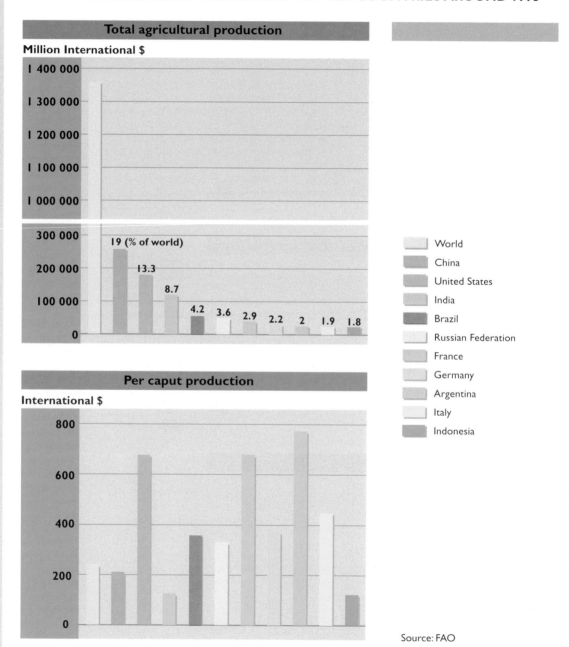

Source: FAO

Figure B (continued)

TOTAL AGRICULTURAL PRODUCTION: TOP TEN COUNTRIES AROUND 1995

Livestock production

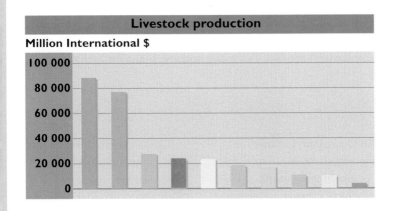

Million International $

Cropped area

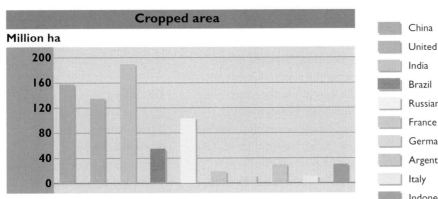

Million ha

China
United States
India
Brazil
Russian Federation
France
Germany
Argentina
Italy
Indonesia

Crop production

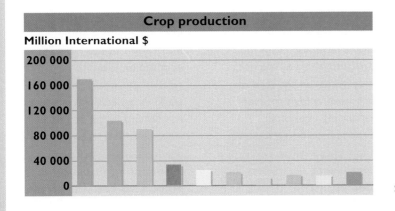

Million International $

Source: FAO

source of development; equity as a *sine qua non* condition to development; and farmers as responsive economic agents who, however, require government assistance to improve their productivity. The importance attached by the publication to agricultural production, productivity and the international competitiveness of developing countries implicitly suggested its faith in an agricultural path to development, if not agricultural specialization, for many of them. The 1962 issue, in particular, emphasized the fact that many ongoing plans for agricultural

Box 14

AGRICULTURAL TRADE – CHANGING TRENDS AND PATTERNS

Amid profound changes in the structure, direction and composition of world agricultural trade, a number of paradoxical features have emerged during the past decades. While losing relative importance in total trade, agricultural exports have remained a key element in the economies of many countries. Nevertheless, those economies that depend less on agricultural trade have generally made the largest gains in agricultural market share, while economies that are more firmly based on agriculture have not only lost market share but, in many cases, have also seen their agricultural trade balances deteriorate in the face of persistently high or even increasing economic dependence on agricultural exports as well as dependence on imports for food security.

Other general tendencies have been a decline in the real international prices of agricultural products and the growing importance of value-added products compared with primary products in total agricultural trade.

Declining importance of agriculture in world trade

Agricultural trade has expanded significantly faster than agricultural production over the past decades, underlying the growing interdependence and integration of the world's economies. Despite its relative dynamism, however, trade in agricultural products has tended to lag behind trade in other sectors, particularly manufactures. An important factor behind this process has been the decline development were, as they should be, closely integrated with those for general economic development. Although overambitious in many cases, these planning efforts were seen as signs of awareness of the importance of agriculture and its potential contribution to overall development.

Trade issues

Trade issues were prominent in *The State of Food and Agriculture* during the 1960s, especially in the latter part of the

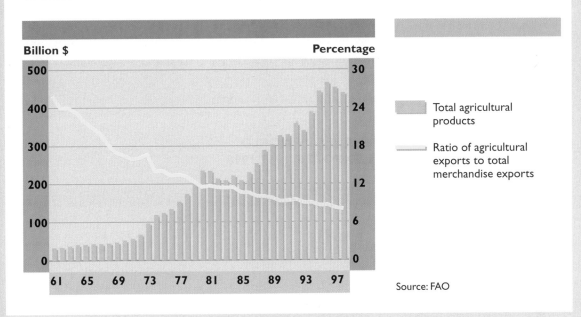

Figure A
WORLD AGRICULTURAL EXPORTS, 1961-1998

Billion $ **Percentage**

Total agricultural products

Ratio of agricultural exports to total merchandise exports

Source: FAO

in agricultural prices relative to manufactures. On a global basis, agricultural exports now account for less than 10 percent of merchandise exports, compared with about 25 percent in the early 1960s (Figure A). The tendency for agricultural trade to lose importance in external trade has been common to all regions, but in the developing country regions the process was particularly pronounced in the 1960s and early 1970s.

However, in Latin America and the Caribbean and in

sub-Saharan Africa, agricultural exports still finance about one fifth of the total import bill. Economic dependence on agricultural exports has remained very high in many individual countries. In 1998, 12 out of 48 countries in sub-Saharan Africa depended on agriculture for half or more of their total export earnings. In Latin America and the Caribbean, 10 out of 37 countries were in the same situation (four in the Caribbean). Extreme cases, where 70 percent or more

of export earnings were agriculture-based, included Belize and Paraguay in Latin America, and Burundi, Côte d'Ivoire, Ethiopia, Kenya, Guinea-Bissau, Malawi, Uganda and the Sudan in Africa.

Contracting developing country share in agricultural markets
The regional distribution of world total and agricultural trade has undergone significant changes. While the developing countries gained market share for total

merchandise exports between the early 1960s and recent years (from about 20 to more than 25 percent of the world total), their share for total agricultural exports has declined from more than 40 to about 27 percent (Figure B).

All the developing country regions, with the exception of Asia and the Pacific, progressively lost world market share for their exports. That Asia and the Pacific has actually increased its share in world agricultural exports since the mid-1970s

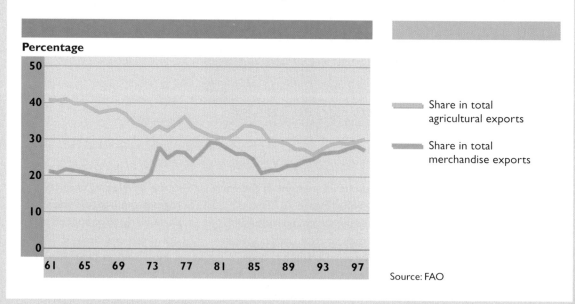

Figure B

DEVELOPING COUNTRIES' SHARES IN WORLD TOTAL AND AGRICULTURAL EXPORTS, 1961-1998

Percentage

Share in total agricultural exports

Share in total merchandise exports

Source: FAO

is all the more remarkable given that this is also the region that has been most successful in diversifying its export base away from agriculture. In contrast, despite the persistently strong agricultural component of its external trade, sub-Saharan Africa's presence in world agricultural markets has tended to lose significance since the early 1970s. Latin America and the Caribbean experienced pronounced market losses after the second half of the 1980s, a period of slow growth in the volume of agricultural exports and of strong decline in export prices (Figure C).

Falling real agricultural prices

Throughout the 1950s and 1960s international prices of food and non-food products remained relatively stable and only lagged slightly behind those of manufactured goods. The 1970s marked a new period of greater price volatility and divergence between agricultural and manufactured goods prices, with the latter tending to rise significantly faster than the former (Figure D). As a result, the net barter terms of trade (or "real" prices) of agricultural exports deteriorated markedly (Figure E). The decline in real agricultural prices was more pronounced for the developing than for the developed countries, reflecting the commodity composition of their exports, with those of temperate products typically exported by the developed countries showing a relatively firmer

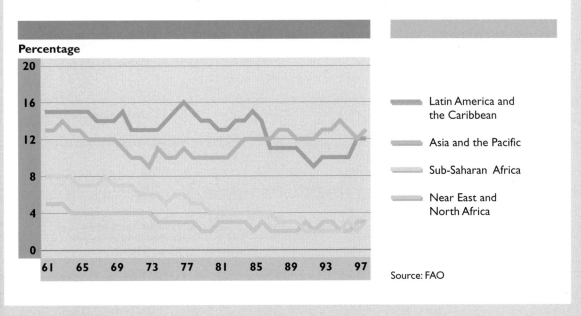

Figure C

DEVELOPING REGIONS' SHARES IN WORLD AGRICULTURAL EXPORTS, 1961-1998

Percentage

Legend:
- Latin America and the Caribbean
- Asia and the Pacific
- Sub-Saharan Africa
- Near East and North Africa

Source: FAO

Figure D

REAL PRICES* OF FOOD AND NON-FOOD COMMODITIES, 1948-1997

Base year 1990

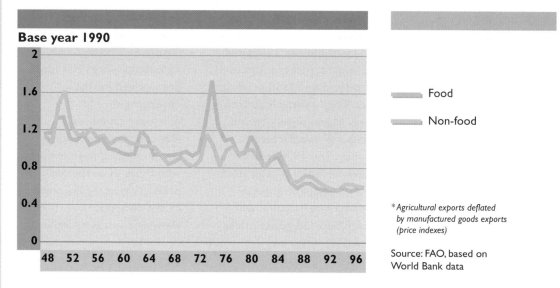

Food

Non-food

*Agricultural exports deflated
by manufactured goods exports
(price indexes)

Source: FAO, based on
World Bank data

Figure E

REAL PRICES* OF AGRICULTURAL EXPORTS FROM INDUSTRIAL AND DEVELOPING COUNTRIES, 1955-1996

Base year 1990

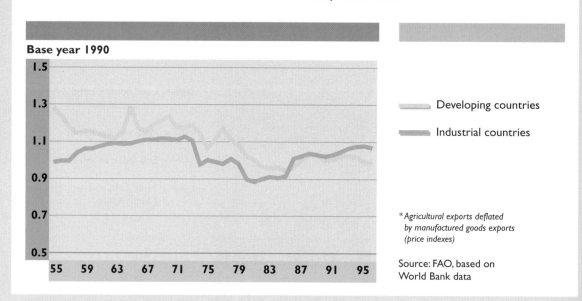

Developing countries

Industrial countries

*Agricultural exports deflated
by manufactured goods exports
(price indexes)

Source: FAO, based on
World Bank data

behaviour than those of tropical products overall.

The volumes of exports, by contrast, showed a steady upward trend throughout much of the period. Nevertheless, because of the price increase differential, the current value of agricultural exports rose on the whole much faster in the developed countries than in the developing ones.

Shifting from primary to processed exports

An issue of considerable importance is the extent to which the developing countries have been able to shift from exports of non-processed primary commodities towards value-added products. The different developing country regions recorded varying degrees of success on this account. In both Asia and the Pacific and Latin America and the Caribbean the share of processed products in total agricultural exports rose from around 10 percent in the early 1960s to about one third of the total in recent years. This share has risen to considerably higher levels in the more industrialized countries in these regions. Thus, in Argentina and Brazil the comparable figure is about 50 percent, while in Malaysia it is more than 70 percent.

In sub-Saharan Africa, on the other hand, the share of processed products in agricultural exports has remained at about 15 percent throughout the past three decades. Behind this stagnating pattern some countries showed pronounced temporal variations. For most countries in the region, however, the general picture is one of a high and undiminished dependence on a limited range of primary product exports. In the Near East and North Africa, the high share of value-added products in the total generally reflects the strong weight of a few processed products in a relatively small agricultural export base. Processed shellfish and other sea products, as well as canned and preserved fruits and vegetables, accounted for much of the total.

decade. Two main features marked this period: the conclusion of the Kennedy Round of trade negotiations in 1967 and the establishment of the United Nations Conference on Trade and Development (UNCTAD) in 1964 "to serve as an agent of accelerated development for all countries by means of formulating and carrying into effect new development-oriented trade policies ...",[3] with the aim of raising the export earnings of the developing countries.

The Kennedy Round resulted in reductions of industrialized participants' tariffs with an estimated average of 35 percent. Although exports from developing to developed countries responded positively to the concessions made in the Round, the products that were most affected were those traded among industrialized countries. Agricultural trade was absent from the negotiations, but there was an agreement among the negotiating parties to contribute food aid to the extent of 4.5 million tonnes of grain annually.

The State of Food and Agriculture noted that the proximity of the World Food Congress and UNCTAD's establishment illustrated the close link between the problems with which they dealt. Freedom from hunger could come only from the economic development of the poorer countries. Even more than foreign aid, the key to development for these countries was their ability to earn foreign exchange from their exports.

The second UNCTAD session of 1968 in New Delhi was remarkable for the scope of its agenda, which covered issues that remain at the centre of developing country interests to this day. These included access of primary commodities to markets in industrialized countries; volume, terms and conditions of development aid; trade expansion, economic cooperation and integration among developing countries; and the world food problem, on which conclusions largely echoed the principles promulgated at the 1963 World Food Congress.

Considerable attention was given to the question of international commodity agreements, then at the height of their popularity. One visible result was the revival of the International Sugar Agreement, which had been inoperative since 1961. After negotiation under the auspices of UNCTAD, it was enforced for a period of five years from 1 January 1969. Agreements covering other food and non-food commodities were also negotiated with varying degrees of success. There were also discussions on the possibility of introducing schemes of compensatory finance and more comprehensive forms of world commodity agreements, although FAO itself advocated the commodity-by-commodity approach as the more practical method.

Development assistance

The last years of the 1950s and the early 1960s also saw the gaining of political independence by several former colonial territories, particularly in Africa. While in some cases this otherwise welcome development led to political instability and civil strife, it also opened the way for a broadening of development assistance flows, particularly from multilateral sources. *The State of Food and Agriculture 1969* reported on the "Pearson report", published by an independent commission sponsored by the World Bank and chaired by Lester B. Pearson. The report reviewed the results of 20 years of development efforts by both donors and recipients and concluded that the aid effort was "flagging" at the very time that the drive for economic development was beginning to produce results. It called for a large increase in government aid, to 0.7 percent of the GNP of the industrial countries by 1975, and urged that 20 percent of the total be channelled through multilateral institutions, compared with the 0.4 percent and 10 percent, respectively, that had been committed in 1968. This objective was to prove unattainable by all but a few donor countries.

Calls for increased official development assistance failed to produce the desired results.

On a more positive note, the same issue of *The State of Food and Agriculture* also reported a much greater emphasis on agriculture in financing by the International Bank for Reconstruction and Development (IBRD). This policy shift was reflected by an expected fourfold increase in the level of loans to agriculture. One consequence of this development was the establishment in early 1964 of a new Cooperative Programme between FAO and IBRD to identify and help formulate many more agricultural and rural development projects for IBRD financing.

THE 1970s

Food and energy crises and a less stable development environment
the World Food Conference,
Famines in Africa
the World Conference on Agrarian Reform and Rural Development
Environmental concerns, Trade issues
Fisheries and the Law of the Sea

Soaring petroleum prices had an adverse effect on most developing countries and the agricultural sector, although they brought large income gains to petroleum-exporting developing countries.

The early 1970s marked a turning point in the pattern that had characterized the postwar environment for development. A series of shocks introduced elements of instability to an international order under which steady economic growth, relatively predictable markets and prices and large international food stocks were taken for granted in the case of many developing countries. The new unstable environment resulted from the de facto devaluation of the US dollar; a sharp increase in the price of petroleum; and, in the area of agriculture, large grain production shortfalls and soaring prices of food, agricultural inputs and petroleum-based energy. This radical shift in the economic order brought large income gains to some countries (mainly petroleum exporters) and created export market opportunities for others but damaged the development prospects of many less developed countries.

The world food crisis

In comparison with the previous ten years, the 1970s were marked by a series of relapses in world agriculture. Global food production declined in 1972 and again in 1974, reflecting in both cases unfavourable weather conditions in major food-producing areas. In 1972, world production of cereals was reduced by 41 million tonnes, shared equally between developed and developing regions, and by 30 million tonnes in 1974. These declines resulted in a sharp depletion of stocks, especially in the traditional cereal-exporting countries: world stocks of wheat were drawn down from 50 million tonnes in 1971 to 27 million tonnes in 1973, the lowest level for 20 years. Rice was also in short supply owing to falls in production in the major rice-consuming countries of Asia. Consumer prices of food items rose in all regions of the world, causing hardship for the poor and reducing the level of nutrition, particularly of vulnerable population groups. Hardship was more severe in sub-Saharan Africa, where per caput food production had remained stagnant during the first half of the 1970s.

Although world food production recovered in 1973 (cereal ouput increased by 100 million tonnes), the recovery was

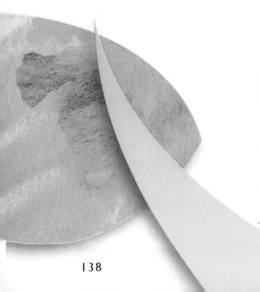

insufficient to prevent the depletion of cereal stocks in the main exporting countries, especially in North America, nor could it halt the steady rise in the prices of food. World agriculture was also afflicted by the energy crisis, inflation, monetary instability, the slowing down of economic growth in the industrialized countries and a general atmosphere of uncertainty.

This global relapse of agricultural production coincided with grave food shortage situations at regional and local levels in the first half of the 1970s. A dramatic food crisis erupted in Africa following two catastrophic droughts. One was the prolonged drought in the Sahel countries (Burkina Faso, Chad, Mali, Mauritania, the Niger and Senegal), which reached its peak in 1973. In that year, net food production per caput in the Sahel countries was one third less than the average for 1961-65 and some 100 000 people died as a result of the famine, which was also instrumental in the spread of epidemic diseases, especially in the relief camps. To save lives, a massive international emergency relief operation was started in early 1973. The creation of the Permanent Interstate Committee for Drought Control in the Sahel (CILSS) was the direct consequence of this prolonged drought.

The other drought caused the Ethiopian famine which lasted from 1972 to 1974. International aid arrived too late and between 50 000 and 200 000 lives were lost in a population of 27 million. The areas worst affected were the provinces of Wollo, Tigrai and Harerghe. The people who suffered most were the Afar community of nomadic pastoralists.

The Ethiopian famine and its causes and consequences have been extensively discussed within and outside FAO but contemporary issues of *The State of Food and Agriculture* were surprisingly silent about it. As for its causes, several years later Amartya Sen wrote: "The Ethiopian famine took place with no abnormal reduction of food output, and consumption of food per head in the height of the famine in 1973 was fairly normal for Ethiopia as a whole. While the food output in Wollo was substantially reduced in 1973, the inability of Wollo to command food from outside was the result of the low purchasing power in that province. A remarkable feature of the Wollo famine is that food prices in general rose very little, and people were dying of starvation even when food was selling at prices not very different from pre-drought levels. The phenomenon can be understood in terms of extensive entitlement failures of various sections of the Wollo population."[4]

Devaluation of the dollar and the energy crisis

The early part of the decade was marked by two other events with long-lasting effects on the world economy, including agricultural production and trade. The first was the decision by the United States Government in August 1971 to suspend the fixed-gold convertibility of the US dollar, which meant a devaluation of the US dollar *vis-à-vis* other internationally traded currencies. For the developing countries, the currency realignments had major negative repercussions because of the vulnerability of their economies to international price fluctuations.

The second event, which caused worldwide panic, was the sharp rise in the price of crude petroleum, decided in 1973 by the Organization of the Petroleum Exporting Countries (OPEC) in response to the devaluation of the US dollar (since petroleum prices are based on the dollar). The world export price index of crude petroleum rose from 196 in 1973 (1970 = 100) to 641 in 1974. For agriculture, this implied a sudden increase in the cost of petroleum-based inputs such as fertilizers and pesticides as well as fuel and power, which are of crucial importance for irrigation and agricultural transport, marketing and processing. Fertilizer prices tripled and even quadrupled in the course of one year and, in 1974, the world consumption of fertilizer dropped by nearly 4 million tonnes, resulting in an estimated shortfall of
1 million tonnes of plant nutrients in relation to projected demand. The UN, at its Sixth Special Session (9 April to 2 May 1974) identified 42 developing countries as being most seriously affected (MSA) by the sharp rise in the prices of essential imports (food, petroleum, fertilizers). It established a Special Fund to assist these countries in mitigating their economic hardships. FAO established the International Fertilizer Supply Scheme, which provided 73 000 tonnes of fertilizers to MSA countries in the 1974/75 crop year.

The subject of "energy and agriculture" was covered in a special chapter of *The State of Food and Agriculture 1976*, which concluded that the rise in prices of fuel and fertilizers was causing sharp declines in the profitability of using energy-intensive inputs, particularly in horticulture and livestock production and capture and culture fisheries. It stated that there was much room for the economic use of domestic sources of energy for agriculture, raising efficiency in the use of imported inputs, recycling of plant and animal residues and being selective in the use of farm machinery.

The World Food Conference

The world food crisis of the early 1970s and the difficulties created by the sharp rise in the cost of petroleum prices led to the convening of the World Food Conference in November 1974 under the joint auspices of FAO and the UN. The aims of the Conference were to secure international consensus on policies and programmes to increase food production and productivity, especially in developing countries; to improve the consumption and distribution of food; to put in place a more effective system of world food security, including an early warning system, effective stockholding policies and emergency food relief; and to bring about a more orderly system of agricultural trade and adjustment.

The 1974 World Food Conference created institutions for agricultural development and the monitoring of agricultural and food supplies.

The building and maintenance of adequate levels of food stocks at national and/or regional and international levels were a central theme of the Conference. These stocks were expected to provide food security guarantees against local, national or regional emergencies and also to cover international relief needs. *The State of Food and Agriculture* reflected this concern by providing regular accounts of developments in national stock policies. Thus, the perception of food security in the first half of the 1970s was still firmly supply-side oriented. Nevertheless, the World Food Conference also stressed the need for lowering the population growth rate and reducing rural unemployment and underemployment by diversifying agriculture and expanding on-farm and off-farm income-generating activities. Of its institutional initiatives (see Box 15), three remain today – the International Fund for Agricultural Development (IFAD), the Global Information and Early Warning System (GIEWS) and the Committee on World Food Security (CFS).

The World Conference on Agrarian Reform and Rural Development

The disproportionate emphasis on industrialization resulting from the policy of import substitution, and the consequential migration of rural people to urban centres, brought to the surface the need for greater attention to rural development.

A number of studies carried out by the International Labour Organisation (ILO) stressed that economic growth alone was not enough to ensure balanced and sustained development. The distribution of wealth and political power also had to be taken into account. In this respect, access to land and the reform of tenancy laws were given special attention. The United Nations Second Development Decade (1970-1980) also underlined the need for treating rural development as an integral part of the

Box 15

THE SIX INTERNATIONAL INITIATIVES OF THE WORLD FOOD CONFERENCE

The 1974 World Food Conference called for:

1. A World Food Council to be established "to serve as a co-ordinating mechanism to provide overall, integrated and continuing attention for the successful co-ordination and follow-up of policies concerning food production, nutrition, food security, food trade and food aid, as well as other related matters....";

2. An International Fund for Agricultural Development (IFAD) to be established immediately "to finance agricultural development projects primarily for food production in developing countries," focusing in particular on poor peasant farmers;

3. A Consultative Group on Food Production and Investment in Developing Countries to be established and "be composed of bilateral and multilateral donors and representatives of developing countries....";

The Conference:

4. Endorsed the objectives, policies and guidelines of the International Undertaking on World Food Security[1] and

welcomed the creation by FAO of GIEWS.

5. Urged FAO to establish the Committee on World Food Security (CFS) as a standing committee of the FAO Council to, *inter alia*, "keep the current and prospective demand, supply and stock position of basic food stuffs under continuous review, ... to make periodic evaluations of the adequacy of current and prospective stock levels, in aggregate, in exporting and importing countries....";

6. Recommended the concept of forward planning for food aid and called on donor countries "to provide commodities and/or financial assistance that will ensure in physical terms at least 10 million tons of grains as food aid a year, starting from 1975, and also to provide adequate quantities of other food commodities".

[1] The International Undertaking on World Food Security, launched in 1974, called on countries to participate voluntarily in programmes to secure adequate food reserves for use in times of shortages and emergencies and for reducing fluctuations in production and prices.

development strategy in combating poverty and narrowing the income gap between rural and urban families. The Second Development Decade had further stressed the importance of establishing national employment objectives and the need to absorb an increasing proportion of the national working population in modern types of non-agricultural activity. *The State of Food and Agriculture 1973* conducted a survey of employment in agriculture covering the period from 1950 to 1970, with projections for 1980, 1990 and 2000. The survey revealed that, in the developed countries as a group, the share of agriculture in the total economically active population declined from 38 percent in 1950 to 21 percent in 1970 and was projected to drop to 5 or 6 percent by 2000 (a fairly accurate projection). The corresponding ratios for the developing countries as a group were 79, 66 and 43 percent, respectively (currently it is around 55 percent and so the flow of labour out of agriculture has been slower than expected).

An earlier contribution of *The State of Food and Agriculture* to the development debate was a special chapter in 1972, entitled Education and training for development. This provided a bird's-eye view of rural education in the developing regions and outlined the strategy for human resources planning, the process of priority setting in rural education and training and the identification of special areas of concern such as the training of trainers, extension workers, capacity building for the young, teaching aids and communication media.

The deepening appreciation of these and other social issues concerning rural development resulted in the 1979 World Conference on Agrarian Reform and Rural Development (WCARRD), which was a landmark in the search for ways of alleviating rural poverty. WCARRD, which was sponsored by FAO, adopted a Declaration of Principles known as the "Peasants' Charter", involving 17 major areas and a Programme of Action that included national programmes of action in developing countries and international policies for agrarian reform and rural development. The latter covered the monitoring of agrarian reform and rural development; the analysis and dissemination of knowledge; the provision of technical assistance; and support for the mobilization of resources.

The United Nations Conference on the Human Environment

Growing concern for the environment was aroused by the publication of *The limits to growth* by the Club of Rome in

1971. The publication raised alarm about the deterioration in the status of the world resources in relation to population growth and mounting economic waste. The collapse of the Peruvian anchoveta fisheries in the early 1970s was a reminder of the fragility of what had been perceived to be a virtually inexhaustible resource.

The question of environmental deterioration and means of combating it was the subject of the United Nations Conference on the Human Environment, held in Stockholm from 5 to 16 June 1972. The Conference approved the Stockholm Declaration and a Plan of Action including 109 resolutions on the environmental aspects of all sectors of the economy, 51 of which related to natural resources management. The majority of the resolutions were specifically addressed to FAO and covered such diverse areas as rural development, environmental planning, soil management and fertility, pest control, recycling of agricultural waste, genetic resources, monitoring of forests and aquatic resources and the management of fisheries. The Stockholm Conference expedited the establishment of the United Nations Environment Programme (UNEP) in Nairobi in 1973. Yet its far-reaching recommendations were probably in advance of contemporary public thinking. It was to take another decade or more for the accumulation of evidence of profound environmental deterioration on a global scale – forest destruction, ozone depletion, increased greenhouse gases in the atmosphere, marine pollution, etc. – to raise public support for the initial remedial steps to be taken.

Concern for the environment had been high on FAO's agenda since its establishment. In a special chapter in 1971, *The State of Food and Agriculture* reviewed the effects of water pollution on living aquatic resources and fisheries. It identified the major characteristics of water pollution and traced its biological and ecological effects on fisheries. The chapter drew attention to the regional differences in aquatic pollution and proposed criteria and systems for monitoring this phenomenon as well as proposing legal and institutional measures required to reduce water pollution as part of the larger effort in pursuit of sustainable development.

As follow-up to the 1972 Stockholm Conference, *The State of Food and Agriculture 1977* included a special chapter on the state of natural resources and the human environment. The assessment covered soil, water, grazing land and forage resources, forests, wildlife, fisheries and genetic resources. It provided an analysis of the impact of agricultural intensification on the environment and the legislative aspects of avoiding natural resource degradation and environmental pollution. It attributed the major causes of pollution in the developed countries to the high level of industrialization and reliance on energy-intensive agricultural systems. On the other hand, the major environmental problem in the developing countries was not pollution but the degradation and depletion of natural resources. The chapter proposed a better and more coherent method of data collection; multidisciplinary research in assessing the impact on the productivity of natural resources of the application of different land use planning; adaptation of local knowledge for raising the efficiency of natural resource use; and developing the appropriate institutional and legal systems in the management of natural resources.

Population and food supply

The pervading concern about the possible imbalance between the natural resource base and the demands placed on it from a rising rate of population growth underlay the United Nations World Population Conference, held in August 1974 in Bucharest.

The Conference adopted the World Population Plan of Action, which paid special attention to the importance of increasing food production and productivity so that food could be made available at reasonable prices for the developing countries. FAO's contribution to the Bucharest Conference was contained in a special chapter (Population, food supply and agricultural development) in *The State of Food and Agriculture 1974*. The chapter took stock of the trends in population growth and food supply for the period 1952-1972, noting possibilities for increasing food production. It stressed the dimension and causes of hunger and malnutrition and the factors affecting the long-term demand for food.

Fisheries

The third United Nations Conference on the Law of the Sea (UNCLOS III) took place in Geneva from 17 March to 9 May 1975 but ended without any definite agreement on the major issue of exploitation rights over the sea and seabed. Nevertheless, an increasing number of coastal states were extending their jurisdiction over fisheries beyond the 12 nautical mile limit, which had broadly prevailed for the previous 300 years. In 1979, the adoption of Exclusive Economic Zones (EEZs) by the FAO Conference added a new dimension to FAO's work in fisheries. As a result of the new legal regime of the oceans, fishery resources of coastal states were brought under their direct national jurisdiction in the form of EEZs.

Marine fisheries in the new era of national jurisdiction was covered in a special chapter in *The State of Food and Agriculture 1980*. The chapter reviewed the opportunities and challenges to coastal fisheries arising from the international community's acceptance of the EEZ-based jurisdiction. It explained the consequences of the changes in the Law of the Sea on fish catch of the coastal states, the effects of open access, problems of adjustment for coastal states, repercussions on countries with large distant-water fleets, the effects of EEZs on international trade in fish and the management of coastal fisheries under this new system.

Expansion in trade: the Tokyo Round of multilateral trade negotiations

The 1970s witnessed a vast expansion in international trade, spurred by the rise in the price of petroleum and the radical redistribution of national wealth that this entailed. Agricultural trade also increased, although the benefits were not shared by all countries. The less developed exporters of mainly tropical agricultural commodities suffered from severe declines in their income terms of trade as price inflation of their industrial imports and higher energy bills more than offset increases in the value of their mainly agricultural exports.

The Tokyo Round of multilateral trade negotiations (MTNs) under the General Agreement on Tariffs and Trade (GATT) was launched in 1973. Attempts to extend interventions in domestic agricultural markets into international trade through a series of international commodity agreements covering grains, oilseeds, dairy products and meat failed to materialize, and the Round, which concluded with only a modest agreement on agriculture, marked a turning point in the extent of government involvement in international agricultural markets – a trend that was to continue in the turbulent decade that followed.

THE 1980s

A "lost decade" for many countries in Latin America and Africa
Economic stabilization and structural adjustment
Famine in Africa, Environment and sustainable development
Trade tensions and the launching of the Uruguay Round

Economic crisis and adjustment

The decade of the 1980s was largely dominated by the protracted economic recession that affected many countries – developed and developing – at various times, with negative effects on their overall and agricultural development. *The State of Food and Agriculture* reported, year after year, a seemingly endless process of deteriorating conditions in many developing countries, despite strenuous efforts to stabilize and recover their economies and the introduction of harsh policy packages. The 1990 issue drew a number of conclusions regarding this crisis period in a special chapter entitled Structural adjustment and agriculture.

The crisis emerged in the early 1980s following a sudden and unexpected change in the international economic environment, formerly characterized by abundant liquidity in financial markets and expansionary fiscal and monetary policies in many developing countries. The second oil shock of 1979, unlike that of five years earlier, led many developed countries to tighten their monetary and fiscal policies, causing a severe slowdown in their economic activity. This slowdown caused a reduction in those countries' import demand, which coincided with and reinforced a sharp decline in international commodity prices. International credit suddenly dried up and capital inflows into developing countries all but ceased. Many countries that had borrowed heavily in the 1970s but had invested the funds in low-productivity projects could no longer repay their external loans. The admission by Mexico in 1982 that it lacked the necessary funds for debt repayment unleashed a global financial crisis that evolved into a deep recession in much of the developing world. Countries in Latin America that were particularly dependent on external trade and heavily indebted were especially affected. Asia was the only region that experienced no declines in per caput incomes during the decade. The crisis also led to a contraction in trade in 1982, the first in 25 years, and to low growth in trade for the rest of the decade. There was an alarming rise in the burden of external debt of the developing world.

This publication noted on various occasions that the policy response to the crisis in the developing countries had recessive

A spiral of deteriorating macroeconomic conditions in developing countries impeded progress in agricultural trade, food security and development assistance.

elements which, at least initially, further aggravated the crisis. Countries were to stabilize their economies in the shortest possible time, and this could only be achieved through cuts in budgetary expenditures and imports. Structural adjustment programmes (SAPs), which were imposed on many countries by international lending institutions, became the means by which governments were forced to restore health to their economies. SAPs, including access to their lines of credit, entailed "conditionalities": reductions in state spending, currency devaluations, market liberalization and the privatization of public enterprises. They came as a severe economic and social shock to many developing countries. Real wages were reduced together with the provision of public social services, and unemployment increased, so the urban sector was also affected. Government intervention, including social programmes, was eschewed in favour of liberal markets. *The State of Food and Agriculture* made the point that if stabilization was inevitable (to restore economic balances) and adjustment advisable (to create a sounder basis for growth), the immediate social cost of these measures was unacceptable and required particular consideration ("adjusting adjustment") by governments and financing institutions.

The crisis and measures to cope with it had direct effects on agriculture. Many farmers, especially in countries where agriculture was more exposed to market forces, were caught in a price squeeze with lower commodity prices coinciding with high real interest rates. Public support schemes in favour of agriculture were downscaled or abandoned. Programmes that helped the politically weak poor people were often among the first to be cut back. Economic priorities postponed the improvement of farming, marketing and input supply systems. Income losses and credit restrictions forced many farmers to reduce employment as well as the purchase of fertilizers and other production requisites. All these factors translated into deteriorating agricultural performances and rural hardship in many countries. In Latin America and the Caribbean, agricultural production growth declined from an annual average of 3.5 percent during the 1970s to 2.2 percent during the 1980s. For the other regions the impact of the crisis on agricultural output growth was less discernable in the aggregate but, in the case of Africa, the expansion in food production remained below population growth.

Agricultural trade was also badly hit. For the developing countries as a whole, agricultural export growth slowed down from 15 percent yearly during the 1970s to less than 3 percent during the 1980s. This was largely due to a dramatic decline in commodity prices. In real terms, the general level of agricultural export prices in the developing countries was one third lower in 1989 than in 1980, despite a short-lived price boom in 1987/88. The collapse of commodity prices stemmed from various causes: massive indebtedness in many countries – forcing them to expand production for export while reducing imports – combined with a slack demand for agricultural exports and inadequate access to developed country markets. At the same time, the ability of developing countries to compete for the markets of several commodities had been seriously weakened by the farm protectionist policies of industrialized countries, including heavy export subsidization. The adverse economic climate exacerbated protectionist pressures and heightened trade tensions while also impeding international efforts to strengthen multilateral arrangements related to agricultural trade, food security and development assistance. International commodity agreements, already languishing, collapsed during this period.

Far-reaching reforms in China
Yet not all programmes of radical shifts in economic and agricultural policy were to have such negative connotations. In the late 1970s, China's policy-makers introduced a series of rural sector reforms aimed at overcoming what were seen as unsatisfactory performances of agriculture. The measures introduced in 1978 initially focused on increasing agricultural production by providing farmers with improved price and income incentives, but they were quickly followed by a complete restructuring of the agricultural sector. In less than five years, policy changes shifted the control of resources and production from the collective farming system to a household-based farming system. By the early 1980s, the government had dismantled the commune system, embraced the household responsibility system and allowed prices and markets to determine input use and production decisions.

Contemporary issues of this publication did not refer to these reforms, which it first discussed in 1985 in the context of a global mid-decade review. *The State of Food and Agriculture 1985* largely credited the policy reforms in China for extraordinary improvements in its farm productivity and rural incomes. It reported an acceleration in the annual rate of growth in food production (from an average 3 percent in 1971-80 to nearly 8 percent in 1980-84) and per caput farm incomes (from 0.5 to 5 percent per year during the same period). Yet, with the benefit of hindsight, we can now understand that these remarkable productivity gains were also based on a period of investment in agricultural infrastructure, extending from the 1950s, that the prevailing centralized agricultural marketing and procurement policies had failed to exploit. This experience of adjustment underlined the importance of agricultural development policies being appropriate across a range of policy aspects, and not just with respect to one aspect.

Food security

In the mid-1980s, concern about the gravity of the economic crisis and its widespread effects on the poor led FAO to reappraise the concept of food security. The new concept focused on three pivotal elements: food availability, stability of supplies and access to supplies. Former approaches to food security emphasized the supply side – food availability and supply stability – in particular through the building and maintenance of adequate levels of food stocks at the national and/or regional and international levels. The new concept added demand-side considerations relating to access to food through own production or exchange for earnings from agricultural or non-agricultural activities.

The first half of the 1980s also witnessed another major shock: famine in Africa. In January 1983, FAO's GIEWS reported for the first time on the catastrophic consequences of drought in southern Africa. This was followed by increasingly alarming news from this and other regions of the continent. In the course of 1984, one of the region's worst droughts of the century reached its peak, searing countries mostly in the Sahel and in southern and eastern Africa. In some cases, the disruptions caused by crop failures were exacerbated by civil strife. Famine engulfed an estimated 20 percent of Ethiopia's population, and entire traditional cultures in the Sahel were on the verge of collapse. Hundreds of thousands of people died in the countries affected.

The response to the crisis in Africa was generous and prevented an even greater catastrophe. The existing systems of information, including GIEWS, functioned much more efficiently than at the time of the previous major African food crisis, 12 years earlier. A historically unprecedented outpouring of food aid – about 7 million tonnes of cereals in 1985 and 1986 – arrived in stricken areas. The lessons of the emergency prompted FAO to propose the adoption of a World Food Security Compact, whereby member countries were called on to make every effort to uproot the causes of hunger. Although the

Compact had special relevance to the food crisis in Africa as well as to the situation in many countries in other regions where agriculture had long been neglected and where the economy was vulnerable to external shocks, it was not widely supported. Possibly, the idea of a "Compact" was too legally binding at a time when governments were avoiding commitments.

Financing agricultural and rural development

Flows of financial resources to developing countries, often under concessionary terms, increased rapidly from the early 1970s and continued into the 1980s. Such external flows rose by between 5 and 6 percent per year in real (i.e. constant price) terms during this period. Flows from domestic sources, often arising from loose fiscal policies and resulting in rising budgetary deficits, also increased. This trend was possibly spurred by the Pearson Report of 1969, but also by the widely held belief that government-sponsored investments funded by increasing flows of financial resources would accelerate economic growth and agricultural and rural development. However, following the financial crises of the early 1980s and the process of economic stabilization and structural adjustment noted above, these flows stagnated and even declined from the middle of the 1980s as aid fatigue on the part of bilateral and multilateral donors, together with harsh economic realities, took their toll – private foreign direct investment (FDI) virtually ceased, except to a few privileged countries, mainly in Asia. *The State of Food and Agriculture 1986* dedicated a special chapter to this issue. Entitled Financing agricultural development, the chapter's analysis drew attention to the unsustainable financial imbalances faced by many developing economies. It also noted the shift that had taken place in conventional thinking, after 30 to 40 years of development efforts based on belief in the primal role of the public sector, and particularly its fiscal policies, in promoting economic growth.

Another line of thinking that had supported the major role of external assistance in this effort was based on the "two gap" thesis: chronic shortages of capital and foreign exchange posed severe constraints to development. The experience of the first half of the 1980s raised serious questions regarding such thinking. Balanced government budgets and investment project quality became overriding concerns. The chapter drew attention to ways of mobilizing domestic rural savings for investment, instead of relying excessively on external assistance or loose fiscal policies, and to the need to search for policies that would attract private funds that did not create external debt, i.e. equity.

A new emphasis on effective institutions for development led to new policy recommendations.

It may now be noted that this period marked a shift in the ongoing analysis of the development process towards a deeper appreciation of the importance to development of institutions, including markets forces, transaction costs, property rights, etc., and hence it signalled the emergence of the "new institutional economics" in the 1990s.

Environmental protection, natural resource management and sustainable development

Public concern in these areas evolved considerably during the 1980s. Concern was mobilized by ever increasing alerts against forest devastation, depletion and waste of fisheries resources, the greenhouse effect of increased emissions of carbon dioxide and other gases on global temperatures, or the long-term damage being done by some industrial gases to the world's protective ozone layer.

The year 1987 marked an important step in the publication of two reports: the *Report of the World Commission on the Environment and Development* (the "Brundtland Report"), which was submitted to the UN General Assembly that year; and UNEP's *Environmental perspective to the year 2000 and beyond.* These reports drew widespread attention to the concept of sustainable development, a concept that evolved further in the following decade.

The State of Food and Agriculture 1989 revisited the issue of sustainable development and natural resource management, already partially addressed in 1977. It sought to make the concept of sustainable development operational and identified a number of areas for concrete action along the following lines:

- the developed countries must pursue economic goals without the current levels of inacceptable environmental damage to themselves and other nations;
- there must be a serious examination of the survival strategies of the poor, to the extent that these result in overexploitation of the resources on which they depend;
- broad strategies must be devised for the various types, combinations and quality of land and water resources and the uses they serve – low- and high-potential lands, forests, fisheries and, through these, genetic reserve areas;
- there should be greater integration of economic and environmental considerations and an adequate accounting of the costs of environmental degradation involved in development strategies, programmes and projects.

Several important events took place addressing issues of concern to the fisheries and forestry sectors. UNCLOS III completed its work at the end of April 1982 when it adopted the International Convention on the Law of the Sea, which was opened for signature in December 1982. This Convention, together with state practice, resulted in the expansion of the coastal state authority over fisheries resources to a distance of 200 nautical miles from the shore. Many coastal states thus acquired not only new opportunities but also weighty problems, responsibilities and challenges.

In mid-1984, FAO organized the World Conference on Fisheries Management and Development, which was the first international initiative to confront the practical realities of the new legal regime of the sea, signed in 1982. The Conference was an important occasion in the evolution of governance of the world's fisheries. It was the first time that nearly all nations came together to reach agreements on comprehensive action to confront the practical implications of the new ocean regime and to improve management of the potential of fisheries as a vital source of food, employment and income. To assist developing countries in boosting the productivity and conditions of fishers, the 1984 Conference endorsed a strategy and an integrated package of five programmes of action on: the planning, management and development of fisheries; the development of small-scale fisheries; aquaculture development; international trade in fish and fishery products; and the promotion of the role of fisheries in alleviating undernutrition.

In Mexico in July 1985 – the International Year of the Forest – under the theme "Forest Resources in the Integral Development of Society", the Ninth World Forestry Congress focused in particular on forest degradation and destruction arising from poverty in tropical and arid regions. The Congress emphasized the importance and urgency of the Tropical Forestry Action Plan, adopted by the FAO Committee on Forest Development in the Tropics earlier that year.

It was also in 1985 that the FAO Conference adopted the International Code of Conduct on the Distribution and Use of Pesticides. This code constituted the first step towards the establishment of international rules for the safe handling and use of pesticides and their trade.

Trade negotiations and issues

An important event in international trade, which took place against a background of increasing tension among agricultural trading nations, was the launching in September 1986 of the Uruguay Round of MTNs. For the first time in a GATT round of MTNs, special prominence was given to agriculture. In the

Declaration that formally announced the launch of the Uruguay Round, ministers agreed that "there is an urgent need to bring more discipline and predictability to world agricultural trade by correcting and preventing restrictions and distortions, including those related to structural surpluses so as to reduce the uncertainty, imbalances and instability in world agricultural markets".

There was a marked turnaround in the world agricultural market situation in 1987/88. Some important agricultural commodity markets shifted from a situation of surplus to one of relative scarcity and, after having fallen to their lowest levels in many years, international prices increased significantly. World stocks of many commodities were sharply reduced from previous high levels. The first significant year of recovery for agricultural commodity prices in the 1980s was not until 1988, and this recovery was mainly confined to sugar, cereals and oilseeds and their products. Tropical beverage prices remained depressed. In the case of cereals, a dramatic rise in prices was the result of two years of reduced production, with the 1988 drought in North America being of particular significance. However, for many commodities, prices during this boom period still did not reach the levels of the early 1980s, even in nominal terms. In real terms, export prices of agricultural commodities in 1988 averaged only three quarters of their 1980 levels.

Social issues
In anticipation of the 1985 World Conference to Review and Appraise the Achievements of the United Nations Decade for Women, which was launched in 1975, the special chapter of *The State of Food and Agriculture 1983* aimed at raising wider awareness of gender issues in the field of food and agriculture. Entitled Women in developing agriculture, it discussed the particular problems of women on farms and in rural areas, as well as their important contributions to food production and marketing and to rural entrepreneurship. It also discussed current issues relating to the difficulties and inequities encountered by women, the effects of agricultural modernization on their condition and the need for development projects to reach them. A further aim was not to have development activities and institutions set aside for women but to "mainstream" gender issues within the overall development effort.

Also in line with the rising concern shown for social issues during the 1980s, the 1984 issue had a special chapter on Urbanization, agriculture and food systems. It examined the problems and opportunities created by urbanization in developing countries as they relate to the production of food and its distribution to urban populations. It made the point that urbanization and migration were not self-adjusting processes and, if not controlled or directed to some degree, could result in deteriorating living conditions for both rural and urban people. It concluded that rural-urban migration, rapid urbanization and the excessive rise of major cities could be modified by government actions so that the negative effects of overly rapid modernization on agrarian societies could be eased. Such measures might consist simply in the removal of an urban bias in agricultural policies or the coordination of such policies. In other cases, more specific measures might be required, involving movements of people from one area to another or the transfer of jobs to rural people. These measures could range from assisting spontaneous rural-rural migration to more elaborate and expensive government-sponsored settlement schemes and rural industrialization programmes. Policies designed to control the overall rate of population growth over the long term would make the situation easier to manage.

Box 16

THE EVOLUTION OF INTERNATIONAL TRADE RULES

The General Agreement on Tariffs and Trade (GATT) came into force in 1947 as a framework for negotiating tariff concessions and for regulating international trade. GATT was initially envisaged as part of an International Trade Organization (ITO) designed to deal with a broad range of trade-related issues (e.g. employment, development, restrictive business practices and commodity policy) in addition to the specific subject of tariffs and trade (commercial policy). However, Member Governments never ratified the ITO Charter. As a result, GATT came into being as a "provisional" or "interim" arrangement, and remained without a formal organizational framework until the conclusion of the Uruguay Round Agreement in 1994. At this point, it was subsumed under the World Trade Organization (WTO) – which took effect on 1 January 1995 – as GATT 1994.

When GATT began in 1947, there were 23 contracting parties (countries) and the value of world trade was US$10 billion. By the end of the Uruguay Round, the 8th trade negotiating round under GATT, there were 128 contracting parties and the value of world trade had reached US$5 000 billion, of which 12 percent was trade in agriculture.

Trade rules established under GATT were based on four general principles: reciprocity, i.e. one country grants tariff concessions in exchange for similar concessions from other partners; non-discrimination, embodied in the "most favoured nation" (MFN) clause, which says that any concession granted to one contracting party is to be automatically extended to all; national treatment, which prohibits discrimination in importing countries between imported and domestically produced products; and a "tariff only" regime, whereby only ordinary tariffs – bound in schedules of concessions – are to be used for regulating imports.

GATT 1947 contained 38 Articles or rules to give effect to these basic principles as well as to address several other issues, particularly the settlement of disputes and remedies (trade measures) against, for example, unfair trade practices (dumping, export subsidies) and sudden surges of imports (safeguards). In the case of trade in agricultural products, some of these articles also provided exceptions to the general GATT rules.

The treatment of agriculture in GATT

Although the original GATT did not have an explicit set of rules for agriculture (e.g. as under the current WTO), there were two notable exemptions for agricultural products from the general rules. One exemption was from the general prohibition on the use of quantitative import restrictions, and the other was from the prohibition on the use of export subsidies.

These exceptions for agriculture were partly due to the existence of extensive price and income support programmes in the leading countries of the postwar era. Many of these policies had been introduced in response to the Great Depression of the 1930s and the associated collapse of agricultural incomes, and also as part of the wartime regulation of the agrifood sector in many countries. It was expected

that many of these measures would have to continue for some time to promote agricultural recovery and to offset the expected slump in postwar agricultural prices.

By 1947, there were only a small number of countries where agricultural policies were being implemented in a systematic manner. Among these countries, the United States was the only major agricultural exporter, followed by Australia and some others, notably Canada, Argentina and New Zealand. The United States Agricultural Adjustment Act of 1933, with its extensions and amendments, permitted the United States authorities to utilize tariffs and quantitative import controls as well as export subsidies to stabilize domestic producer prices, and the concept of "parity" between farm and non-farm incomes continued to command strong support. For its part, Europe was just recovering from the war and food security was a critical issue – although the formation of the European Economic Community and its Common Agricultural Policy (CAP) came much later with the Treaty of Rome in 1956. A great majority of the

developing countries were still under colonial rule or had just gained independence.

It was against this background – the widespread food insecurity problems in most parts of the world, including Europe, and the declining ratio of farm to non-farm incomes in some countries – that the exceptions for agriculture were written into GATT.

The original GATT rules did not prohibit export subsidies initially, nor did they prohibit domestic subsidies. However, in 1955, a Protocol to the General Agreement added the prohibition on export subsidies on all but primary products, subject to the condition that a subsidizing country does not capture "more than an equitable share" of world export trade in the subsidized agricultural product.

As regards the prohibition of quantitative import restrictions, initially GATT rules exempted agricultural and fishery products from this rule only when such restrictions were used in order "to implement domestic policies that operate to restrict the production or marketing of the like products, or to remove a temporary surplus". However, in 1955, the United States obtained a GATT waiver to apply import restrictions even where there were no production-limiting or marketing policies in place. This affected in particular the imports of sugar, groundnuts and dairy products. This waiver lasted until the Uruguay Round Agreement on Agriculture came into effect.

In retrospect, many emerging agricultural trading nations took advantage of this precedent as well as the other exceptions for agriculture from the general GATT rules. These, together with a proliferation in the use of "grey area" measures (e.g. voluntary export restraints, minimum export prices, variable levies) in the 1960s and 1970s, effectively kept agriculture out of GATT. It was thus on the three areas of quantitative restrictions, domestic support and protection and export subsidies that much attention was focused during the Uruguay Round negotiations on agriculture and in the resulting Agreement on Agriculture.

The Uruguay Round – what it achieved and what remains to be done

By the early 1980s, as a result of increasing frictions in trade relations in the agricultural sector, it became widely recognized that world agricultural trade was in "disarray", a term used to characterize distortions caused by the lack of effective GATT disciplines. These distortions were widespread mainly in the "temperate zone" food products. The Uruguay Round was thus launched in 1986 against the background of very high levels of domestic support to producers (about 60 percent of the value of agricultural production in OECD countries in 1986-88), which necessitated export subsidies to dispose of the surpluses on world markets; growing trade tensions including export subsidy wars; and, high budgetary costs of farm policies of the industrialized countries. An important factor during the negotiations was the explicit recognition that domestic agricultural support policies mattered for trade and also needed to be disciplined.

The key results reflected in the Agreement on Agriculture may be summarized as follows:

- On *domestic support measures,* rules were laid down to stipulate which measures have the potential to distort trade, and so need to be disciplined, and which should be permitted. The outlays on the former were benchmarked for the base period and were to be gradually reduced over the implementation period. WTO members must not exceed their support outlays over the set limits.

- On *market access*, it was agreed that all non-tariff import restrictions should be prohibited and that trade should be regulated with ordinary tariffs only. Most of the agricultural tariffs were bound for the first time, and agreed percentage cuts were to be phased in over the implementation period. Given the high level of tariffs resulting from the conversion to a tariff-only regime in agriculture (tariffication), "minimum" and "current" access tariff quotas were introduced.

- On *export competition*, an agreement was reached on what constitutes export subsidies and, as with domestic support outlays, benchmarks were established for the base period and were to be reduced over the implementation period. WTO members may not exceed the subsidy limits thus determined.
- Provisions were made for *special and differential treatment* for the developing countries, which were allowed a longer implementation period, lower rates of reductions, exemptions from certain disciplines that applied to the developed countries and promises of technical and financial assistance.
- The Agreement on Agriculture was also complemented by a number of other Uruguay Round Agreements and Decisions, such as the Decision on Measures Concerning the Possible Negative Effects of the Reform Programme on Least-Developed and Net Food-Importing Developing Countries, which addresses some remedial measures in the event of food import difficulties related to the reform process in agriculture.
- The *Agreement on the Application of Sanitary and Phytosanitary Measures* and the *Agreement on Technical Barriers to Trade* were formulated to ensure that regulations that have a trade-restrictive effect are applied only to the extent necessary to protect human, animal or plant life.

In conclusion, the most important contribution of the Uruguay Round was to bring the rules governing agricultural trade "much closer" to but not fully in line with the GATT rules because current rules still permit certain measures that are not allowed for non-agricultural products, notably export subsidies. As a result, the Uruguay Round Agreements may not have significantly reduced distortions in world agricultural trade. Nevertheless, the Agreement on Agriculture provides a framework for further reforms and Article 20 of this Agreement provides for further negotiations to continue the reform process through substantial and progressive reductions in support and protection. These negotiations were started in March 2000.

THE 1990s

Emergence of a new political, economic and trade order

Liberalization, globalization and financial upheavals

Food security – the World Food Summit

UNCED – sustainable agricultural and rural development

Trade – conclusion of the Uruguay Round

The years bridging the 1980s and 1990s marked what were possibly the most momentous political changes since the end of the Second World War. An extraordinary sequence of events heralded the effective end of communism in the USSR and Eastern Europe and raised expectations of a new era of closer collaboration in international relationships to replace the former political and ideological confrontation.

The subsequent transformation of formerly centrally planned systems into market-based economic systems took place in the context of serious economic, social and institutional problems and, in some countries, dramatic political events. Ethnic and political tensions also developed and degenerated into devastating ethnic confrontations in former Yugoslavia as well as in some countries in central Africa. The dismantling of previous economic and trade structures and the ensuing disruptions in production and distribution systems did not spare the agrifood sector in Eastern Europe. Severe shortages of even the most essential products arose in some of these countries, creating a new focus of attention for international assistance, including food aid. Nevertheless, several countries of Eastern Europe showed a growing capacity to adjust to the new circumstances and entered into a process of greater economic and political integration with the rest of Europe. Several of them began to show convincing signs of recovery.

The 1990s showed an uneven pattern of economic activity among the major *industrialized countries*. Integration gained momentum in the EU, despite complex political issues and difficulties linked to slow economic growth, pressure to adhere to fiscal and monetary discipline and a seemingly intractable unemployment problem in much of the EU. Japan, formerly a star performer in the industrialized world, was hit by a serious recession from which it is still struggling to emerge. In contrast, in 1992 the United States entered into an unprecedented process of economic growth, accompanied by low unemployment and inflation and dynamic trade.

For many *developing countries* the 1990s were a period of recovery from the disastrous performances of the 1980s. Their overall GDP growth averaged more than 5 percent during the

The end of the cold war brought optimism regarding international collaboration and greater attention to countries in transition.

period 1991-1999 and exceeded 6 percent for five consecutive years (1992-1996) despite the global recessionary conditions prevailing during the early part of the decade and pronounced swings in growth rates. These were caused by conflicts, unusually severe climatic disasters (including a particularly destructive El Niño phenomenon) and a series of financial shocks. The general environment for growth and food security was improved by a move towards democratic regimes, particularly in Africa, and a consolidation of economic reforms that began to yield long-awaited results. Many developing countries, including some of the largest and most populous, benefited from this process and made further inroads into the longstanding problems of hunger and malnutrition. This was particularly the case of Asian economies, seen for a long period as archetypes of dynamism and stability. However, the Asia region had its exceptional growth performances interrupted in 1997, following a severe financial crisis that erupted in Southeast Asia. Initially affecting several fast-growing economies in the subregion, the crisis transmitted destabilizing and recessionary shockwaves to other countries within and outside the region as a whole. By the end of the decade, however, economic recovery was rapidly gaining ground in Asia.

The Asian financial crisis also affected countries in Latin America and the Caribbean, which had already been hit by an earlier crisis of a similar nature (the Mexican crisis) in 1994, from which they had shown an unexpectedly firm recovery. Recent developments suggest that most of the region is absorbing the new crisis relatively well, a feat that can be attributed to improvements in economic fundamentals and lessons learned over the past decade. Nevertheless, the crisis has already involved considerable costs, particularly in Brazil, in terms of reduced economic growth and social stress, while it has also slowed the momentum of reform and regional integration. In Africa, much improved economic performances were recorded by a large number of countries since 1995, sustained in particular by a dynamic agri-export sector. While much of the turnaround was related to transient factors, in particular higher commodity prices during 1996/97 and the successful currency devaluation of countries in the CFA franc zone, *The State of Food and Agriculture* stressed that the unusual length of the improvement and its breadth across countries suggested that other more fundamental forces, in particular reform policies and progress in debt cancellation, may also have played a role. The still relatively high growth rates expected for 1999 and 2000 (more than 3 and 5 percent, respectively, according to IMF) tend to support this view. This publication also noted, however, that the improvement in Africa had to be seen in the context of a long period of regression that had brought many countries in the region to extreme levels of economic and social hardship.

As regards the Near East, *The State of Food and Agriculture* also noted generally improved economic conditions during the 1990s and progress by practically all countries in raising the nutritional standards of their populations to more satisfactory levels. This occurred despite considerable problems: a mediocre growth of the agricultural sector, pronounced swings in performances linked to climatic factors and fluctuations in petroleum and other commodity prices as well as conflicts in the region. *The State of Food and Agriculture* also noted, however, the increased efforts made towards achieving regional peace and cooperation and the comprehensive economic and agricultural reforms carried out in several countries.

Against this general background, the publication also reviewed a number of unsolved problems and risks for the developing world, with direct implications for food security: recurrent food emergencies and civil strife, which appeared as frequently and severely as in previous decades; unabated poverty and social stress in many countries, not least in rural areas, and even in countries registering a significant macroeconomic improvement; a process of liberalization that promised a sounder basis for growth but also involved clear risks of accentuating inequalities in incomes and opportunities among and within countries; a largely unresolved external debt burden affecting many countries; and increasing risks of financial upheavals arising from the liberalization of financial markets.

Nutrition and food security
The International Conference on Nutrition, jointly sponsored by FAO and the World Health Organization (WHO), was held in Rome in December 1992. The initiative arose from the realization that about 800 million people in the world were undernourished and that the incidence of malnourishment was worsening rather than receding in many countries; the need for closer identification of the causes, nature and magnitude of the problem so as to define coordinated strategies and realistic objectives; and the need to enhance international solidarity and mobilize the necessary resources. The Conference issued the World Declaration on Nutrition, affirming the commitment of the participant states to work together to ensure sustained nutritional well-being for all people; and a global Plan of Action

for Nutrition, containing recommendations for policies, programmes and activities aimed at the achievement of these objectives.

The awareness that the International Conference on Nutrition and other events and initiatives had not mobilized sufficient political commitment at the highest levels to remove the stigma of widespread hunger from the world prompted the convening of the World Food Summit in 1996. A major institutional event, it brought together delegations from 185 states and the EU, many of which were represented at the highest political level, as well as international institutions, religious leaders and more than 1 000 NGOs from 80 countries, totalling close to 10 000 participants. The Summit conveyed the fundamental message that, although more than 800 million people around the world still suffered from undernourishment, world food security was an achievable goal.

The Plan of Action adopted by the Summit participants reaffirmed the commitment of the international community to eradicating the hunger and malnutrition affecting about one fifth of the developing world's population, and specifically to halving the number of undernourished people in the world within a period of 20 years. The Summit also confirmed a consensus on several important points: that the problems of hunger and malnutrition are associated primarily with poverty and are intensified by conflict or political instability; and that food security is not just a matter of ensuring food supplies, but also of ensuring their availability and stability as well as access to them. To accomplish the complex task of halving the incidence of hunger by 2015, combined efforts were to be made at all levels of society: international, national and community.

The Rome Declaration on World Food Security reaffirmed the "right of everyone to have access to safe and nutritious food, consistent with the right to adequate food and the fundamental right of everyone to be free from hunger"; and the World Food Summit Plan of Action included seven commitments (see Box 17).

Environment, natural resources and climate change

A number of meetings of major importance to these issues took place in the 1990s: the United Nations Conference on Environment and Development (UNCED), in Rio de Janeiro in 1992; the Convention on Biological Diversity, in the Bahamas in 1994; the creation by the UN Committee on Sustainable Development of an open-ended, ad hoc Intergovernmental

Panel on Forests (IPF), which held its first session in New York in 1995; the first session of the United Nations Convention to Combat Desertification, in Rome in 1997; and the Third Conference of the Parties (COP-3) to the UN Framework Convention on Climate Change, in Kyoto in 1997.

Although UNCED attracted considerable attention, the results fell short of the high expectations. Major differences persisted on such key issues as the time scale for reducing carbon dioxide emissions; the sustainable and equitable use of biodiversity; and the establishment of a Special Fund to assist developing countries in the implementation of its Agenda 21, the "plan of action for the twenty-first century". Nevertheless, UNCED did alert world opinion and policy-makers to the high stakes involved, and it provided operational guidelines for future action. It also contributed substantially to the forces advocating a change in the way natural resources are utilized. Apart from

Box 17

WORLD FOOD SUMMIT COMMITMENTS

1. Ensuring an enabling political, social, and economic environment.
2. Implementing policies aimed at the eradication of poverty and inequality and improving physical and economic access to food by all.
3. Pursuing participatory and sustainable food production and rural development policies and practices in both high- and low-potential areas.
4. Ensuring trade policies conducive to fostering food security for all.
5. Preventing and forestalling natural and human-induced disasters and meeting transitory and emergency food requirements.
6. Allocating public and private investments to foster human resources, sustainable agricultural systems and rural development in high- and low-potential areas.
7. Implementing, monitoring and following up the Plan of Action.

Agenda 21, the main products of UNCED were: the Rio Declaration on Environment and Development, laying down the guiding principles concerning the rights and duties of states to achieve a global partnership in sustainable development; two framework conventions – on climate change and on the conservation of biodiversity; a statement of non-legally binding principles for the management, conservation and sustainable development of all types of forest; a decision to start a negotiation process for an international convention to combat desertification; and an agenda for action on freshwater resources, arising mainly from the Conference on Water and the Environment, held in Dublin in 1992.

The United Nations Framework Convention on Climate Change in 1992 recognized the need to reduce greenhouse gas emissions and agreed that developed countries in the first place should aim at reducing emissions to 1990 levels by 2000 and beyond, although caveats provided exemption for some countries.

The 1997 conference in Kyoto pursued these issues further and agreed that industrialized countries as a whole should decrease their emissions by an average of 5.2 percent by 2005. A "flexibility clause" was built into the agreement, allowing countries to trade emissions quotas among themselves to encourage reductions where they were most "cost effective". The issue of global warming was also discussed in *The State of Food and Agriculture 1997*, which focused on the implications, positive and negative, of greenhouse gas abatement policies for the developing countries and their agriculture.

In the field of resource management and environment, problems relating to freshwater availability and use also attracted global attention – UNCED and the Dublin Conference on Water and the Environment in 1992 and the 1990 Montreal meeting "NGOs Working Together". In 1993, the special chapter of *The State of Food and Agriculture*, entitled Water policies and agriculture, examined the problems and policy options behind agricultural development and water use. It noted that water was already in short supply in many areas of the world; that agriculture was by far the largest user of freshwater and that it was a relatively low-value, low-efficiency and highly subsidized user of the resource.

The 1992 special chapter, Marine fisheries and the law of the sea: a decade of change, focused on sustainability and economic issues in the area of fisheries. It discussed developments that had occurred in the previous ten years and their implications for the future management of fisheries.

The chapter discussed the massive waste in fisheries under conditions of open access. For the first time, it presented tentative global estimates of fishing costs and revenues, reaching the remarkable conclusion that the annual operating costs of the global marine fishing fleet in 1989 were approximately US$22 billion greater than the total revenues obtained. This chapter provoked a lively debate.

UNEP opened the first session of the Conference of the Parties to the Convention on Biological Diversity in November 1994. The objectives of the Conference were "the conservation of biological diversity, the sustainable use of its components, and the fair and equitable sharing of the benefits arising out of genetic resources". For the first time, an international legal instrument described the rights and obligations of the parties involved with regard to scientific, technical and technological cooperation.

During its third session in April 1995, the Commission on Sustainable Development (CSD) established the IPF to continue and stimulate the intergovernmental forest policy dialogue that had been initiated at UNCED.

The UN Economic and Social Council (ECOSOC), in its annual substantive meeting in Geneva in July 1997, established the ad hoc, open-ended Intergovernmental Forum on Forests

Land cleared by fire for agricultural production

Deforestation has been a major means of increasing arable land, with dramatic environmental consequences

FAO/13925

(IFF) to continue the dialogue on a number of outstanding issues left by the IPF at the end of its mandate. Since then, the IFF has held four organizational meetings – the latest took place in New York from 31 January to 11 February 2000.

The first session of the UN Convention to Combat Desertification was held in Rome in 1997, with the intention of promoting a "fresh approach" to managing dryland ecosystems, as well as managing development aid flows which, in the past, have been a point of contention between aid agencies and recipients. The Convention was to address the major problems of dryland degradation, now caused by economic or social factors including overcultivation, overgrazing, deforestation and poor irrigation as well as violent national or international conflicts. More than 250 million people are directly affected by desertification and nearly 1 billion people are at risk. Programmes to help prevent or reverse the process of desertification were at the core of the Convention, which was signed by 110 countries. Action programmes at the national level were developed to "address the underlying causes of desertification and drought" and to identify appropriate prevention measures. The national action programmes are to be supplemented by regional and subregional programmes for more accurate assessments and implementation.

The changing international trade order
In April 1994, the Final Act of the Uruguay Round of MTNs was signed in Marrakesh. Launched in 1986, the Round concluded with an agreement to create the World Trade Organization (WTO) to replace GATT. *The State of Food and Agriculture 1995* reported that, given the importance of the issues and the seven years of strenuous negotiations involved, the outcome of the Uruguay Round in terms of market access and reductions in domestic support and export subsidization fell short of what might have been expected. Agricultural protectionism remained high and was likely to continue to plague agricultural markets in traditional and new forms in the future.

The special chapter of the 1995 issue (Agricultural trade: entering a new era?) analysed the achievements and shortcomings of the Uruguay Round, with particular reference to the Agreement on Agriculture, and raised a number of questions that remain pertinent in the current context of preparations for a new round of MTNs. It suggested that a "new era" may be emerging with the deregulation of the world economy; the increasing presence of the developing countries in

The open trade regime promises the increasing integration of agricultural trade markets but threatens to exclude some countries from the gains.

world markets, new trade patterns arising from the transformations in Eastern Europe and the CIS and Baltic states, and changes in world markets and trading rules following the conclusion of the Uruguay Round and the creation of the WTO. The chapter said there were risks, however, that this open trade regime would remain unjust, with an asymmetric distribution of opportunities and gains, risks and losses among countries.

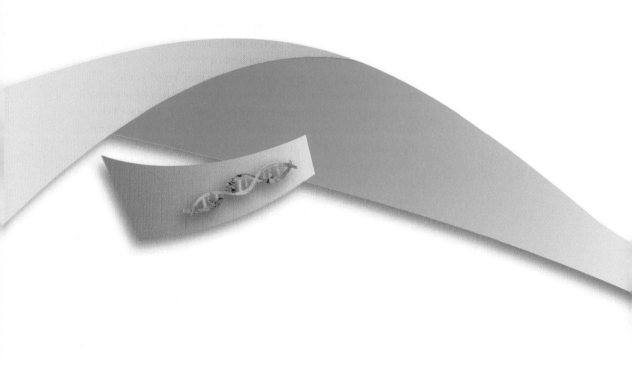

CONCLUDING REMARKS

The past half century has seen changing perceptions of what constitutes the main developmental challenges, shifting policy priorities and a dramatic transformation of the perceived role of the state in fostering welfare and social progress. In this evolving policy context, agriculture and food security have not always occupied a priority position, suggesting an inadequate awareness of the irreplaceable role of the agricultural sector in economic and social development. Such relative neglect on the part of the authorities has mirrored a similar neglect by the media and, therefore, by public opinion at large. Although recent decades have increasingly become known as the "information age", hunger and food insecurity have tended to attract media coverage and priority attention only when exceptional events bring to light their most dramatic manifestations. The same holds true for positive developments, which have "made the news" to a lesser degree still. Indeed, surprisingly little attention has been paid to what can be seen as the most significant achievement of humankind over the past 50 years: the major retreat of world hunger, particularly in densely populated Asian countries – demonstrating that even massive and extreme food insecurity situations can be overcome.

Now that we have entered the new millennium, there is a growing consensus at the international level on the need to address poverty and food insecurity as critical factors in achieving a more just and safe world for all. This tendency is gaining ground in a context of international economic integration and interdependence, with a convergence of views on the potential benefits of freer and more open markets. The international order that will emerge from this complex interplay of factors and influences is difficult to foresee. One major challenge, discussed in the following sections of this chapter, will be to integrate marginalized and disadvantaged countries and populations into world economic and social progress and to ensure that the benefits of liberalization and globalization are shared by all.

World hunger has been substantially reduced over the past 50 years as a result of a greater understanding of the problem as well as improved institutions and increased agricultural productivity.

NOTES

1 In both Europe and Asia, it was not until the early 1950s that cereal production reattained the average levels of 1934-38.

2 A.K. Sen. 1993. *Scientific American*, May 1993.

3 UNCTAD document TD/L 37. April 1968.

4 A.K. Sen. 1981. *Poverty and famines: an essay on entitlement and deprivation*, p. 111-112. Oxford, UK, Clarendon Press.

The socio-economic impact of agricultural modernization

INTRODUCTION

The world's population now exceeds 6 billion people, consuming a daily average of about 2 700 kcal per caput, compared with a population of 2.5 billion in 1950 and an average daily intake of fewer than 2 450 kcal per caput.[1] This means that, over the last 50 years, the increase in global agricultural production has been 1.6 times greater than the total production level obtained in 1950, after 10 000 years of agricultural history.[2]

This enormous increase in food production is attributable to:

- the spread in the developed countries of the modern agricultural revolution (involving motorization, large-scale mechanization, biological selection, use of chemicals, specialization) and its expansion into some sectors of the developing countries;
- the more noteworthy occurrence in the developing countries of the green revolution – a modern agricultural revolution that is not dependent on heavy motorized mechanization but instead involves the use of chemicals and the selection of high-yielding cereal and other domestic plant varieties suited to warm regions;
- the expansion of irrigated surfaces, from about 80 million ha in 1950 to about 270 million ha today;
- the expansion of arable land and land under permanent crops, from some 1 330 million ha to 1 500 million ha since 1950;[3]
- the development of mixed farming systems using high levels of available biomass (combining crops, arboriculture, livestock and, sometimes, fish farming) in the most densely populated areas that lack new land for clearing or irrigation.

However, even these considerable advances in agriculture cannot hide the fact that most of the world's farmers use inefficient manual tools and their plants and domestic animals have benefited very little from selection. Moreover, these underequipped farmers, with their inefficient production methods, are exposed to increasingly fierce competition from better equipped and more productive farmers as well as to the

FAO/15636/J. BRAVO

Traditional farming practices
Barley threshing using donkeys

strong decline in real agricultural prices. This continually condemns resource-poor farmers with low productivity to extreme poverty, making them vulnerable to hunger and prompting their migration to towns and cities that are themselves underequipped and underindustrialized.

The outcome is a contrasting situation between, on the one hand, the modern agricultural revolution, the green revolution, the expansion of irrigation, the clearing of land and the development of mixed farming systems using high levels of available biomass, and on the other hand, stagnation and impoverishment. This is the contradictory result of agricultural modernization in the second half of the twentieth century, and it raises a number of questions:

- How productive and well equipped were the world's farmers in 1950, and to what extent has the explosion of disparities in productivity been caused by the last 50 years of agricultural modernization?
- What means and economic development mechanisms of the modern agricultural revolution were used in the developed countries, and what have been the environmental, demographic, economic and social consequences?
- What are the limits of the modern agricultural revolution

FAO/10980/B. POLIMENI

Highly mechanized farming practices
A combine harvester at work on an extensive grain crop

and the green revolution in the developing countries? What are the mechanisms that lead to the impoverishment and marginalization of the underequipped peasant farmer sector in these countries? What other forms of agricultural modernization are under way in both developing and developed countries?

- What is the assessment of global agricultural production and food consumption at the close of these 50 years of modernization, and what are the prospects for the next decades?

MODERNIZATION AND THE EXPLOSION OF DISPARITIES IN WORLD AGRICULTURAL PRODUCTIVITY

In 1950, the agricultural sector employed 700 million people worldwide and used fewer than 7 million tractors (4 million in the United States, 180 000 in West Germany and 150 000 in France) and fewer than 1.5 million combine harvesters. Currently, 1.3 billion people are engaged in agriculture, and there are 28 million tractors and 4.5 million combine harvesters in use, mainly in the developed countries.[4] Only 17 million tonnes of mineral fertilizer were applied in 1950, four times more than in 1900 but eight times less than today. In

Figure 18

COMPARATIVE PRODUCTIVITY OF THE WORLD'S MAJOR AGRICULTURAL SYSTEMS IN THE MIDDLE OF THE TWENTIETH CENTURY

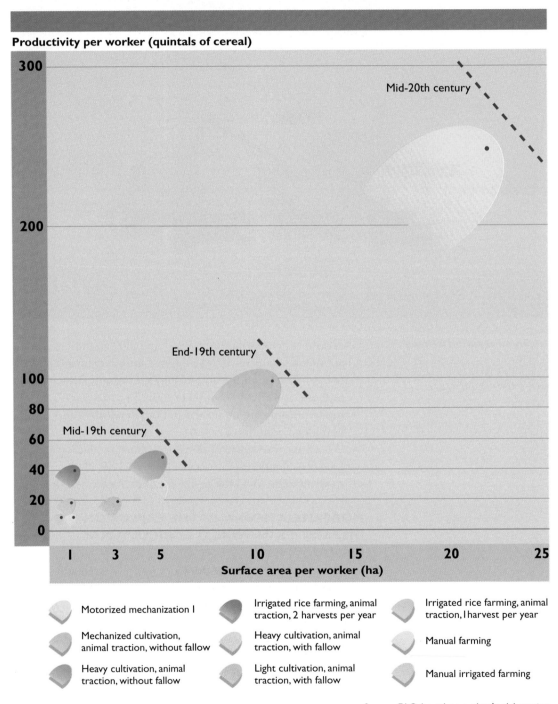

Productivity per worker (quintals of cereal)

Mid-20th century

End-19th century

Mid-19th century

Surface area per worker (ha)

Motorized mechanization I

Mechanized cultivation, animal traction, without fallow

Heavy cultivation, animal traction, without fallow

Irrigated rice farming, animal traction, 2 harvests per year

Heavy cultivation, animal traction, with fallow

Light cultivation, animal traction, with fallow

Irrigated rice farming, animal traction, 1 harvest per year

Manual farming

Manual irrigated farming

Source: FAO, based on author's elaboration

1950, 30 million tonnes of oilcake equivalent were used as animal feed, six times less than today.

Although the methodical selection of plant varieties and domestic animal species with high-yield potential had started decades earlier, it had not progressed far and only involved a limited number of species. A majority of the world's farmers still used local varieties and breeds. While there was already a wide range of phytosanitary products in 1950, it was minimal compared with the situation today where about 80 active ingredients are used for insecticides, 100 for fungicides and 150 for herbicides.[5] All of these products have been the subject of major toxicological studies. In 1950, average crop yields were 1 000 kg/ha for wheat, 1 500 kg/ha for maize, 1 600 kg/ha for paddy rice and 1 100 kg/ha for barley – much the same as at the beginning of the century. Since then, yields have doubled or tripled. Similarly, the average yield of a milking cow in France, for example, came to less than 2 000 litres per year compared with about 5 600 litres today.[6]

Progress in agricultural production hides a growing disparity among agricultural systems and populations.

These figures give an indication of the progress made in 50 years, but they fail to reveal the growing disparity in productivity among the different agricultural systems, based on quality of machinery and use of inputs. This calls for a comparative economic analysis of the major production systems in each period.

In the mid-twentieth century, after thousands of years of agricultural history with extensive regional variation, the peoples of the world found themselves in widely differing agricultural situations and engaged in production systems that had very uneven productivity levels.[7] Figure 18 illustrates these disparities by comparing potential net productivity for each system.[8]

As the Figure indicates, these systems can be ranked in order of increasing net productivity as follows:
- manual farming, with maximum net productivity of around 1 000 kg of cereal equivalent per worker;
- irrigated rice cultivation, using animal traction, with one harvest per year;
- light cultivation, using animal traction (swing plough, packsaddle, etc.), with fallow, with a maximum net productivity of 2 000 kg per worker;
- heavy cultivation, using animal traction (plough, cart, etc.), with fallow, with a maximum net productivity of 3 500 kg per worker;
- irrigated rice cultivation, using animal traction, with two harvests per year, with a similar net productivity to that of the previous system;

Figure 19

PRODUCTIVITY DIFFERENCES BETWEEN CEREAL SYSTEMS USING MOTORIZED MECHANIZATION AND CHEMICALS, AND MANUAL OR ANIMAL TRACTION CULTIVATION IN DEVELOPING COUNTRIES

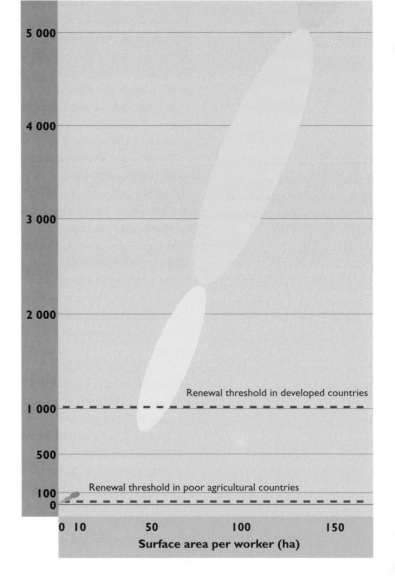

Net productivity per worker (quintals of cereal)

Extensive cereal cultivation in developed countries

Motorized mechanization V

Motorized mechanization IV

Motorized mechanization III

Manual cultivation and cultivation using animal traction in developing countries

Renewal threshold in developed countries

Renewal threshold in poor agricultural countries

Surface area per worker (ha)

Source: FAO, based on author's elaboration

- heavy cultivation, using animal traction, without fallow, with a net productivity of 5 000 kg per worker;
- mechanized cultivation, using animal traction, without fallow, with a net productivity of 10 000 kg per worker;
- first systems of cultivation using motorized mechanization (motorized mechanization I), with a maximum net productivity already exceeding 30 000 kg per worker.

Thus, the ratio in 1950 between the least efficient system (manual farming) and the most productive system (motorized mechanization) was 1:30.[9]

The gap between the most productive and least productive farming systems has increased twentyfold in the last 50 years.

At the end of the twentieth century, after another 50 years of agricultural history, the productivity of manual farming, which is the least efficient but most widespread type of farming worldwide, is still about 1 000 kg of cereal equivalent per worker, while the net productivity of the most motorized and input-intensive farming system exceeds 500 000 kg. The ratio between these two systems is therefore about 1:500 (Figure 19): almost a twentyfold increase in the ratio over 50 years.

THE MODERN AGRICULTURAL REVOLUTION IN DEVELOPED COUNTRIES

The modern *agricultural revolution* that triumphed in the developed countries from the late 1950s onwards was based on the development of new means of production and trade which, in turn, resulted from revolutions in industry, biotechnology, transport and communications.

The second *industrial revolution* provided the means for: motorization (internal combustion engines, electric motors, tractors and increasingly powerful machinery, fuels and electricity); large-scale mechanization (increasingly complex and efficient machinery for tillage, treatment and harvesting); heavy mineral fertilization (ammonium, nitrate, nitro-ammoniacal, phosphate, potassium and compound fertilizers); treatment of pests and diseases (herbicides, insecticides, fungicides, veterinary drugs, etc.); and the conservation and processing of vegetable and animal products (industrialization of preservation techniques through cold, heat, drying, smoking, freeze-drying, ionization, fermentation or the addition of salt, sugar and other food preservatives).

The *biotechnology revolution* supplied, through selection, high-yielding plant varieties and animal breeds that were adapted to the new means of industrial production and were capable of making these profitable.

The *transport revolution*, which began in the nineteenth century with the development of railways and steamboats, received a new boost with the motorization of transport by truck,

Figure 20

STAGES OF DEVELOPMENT OF AGRICULTURAL MACHINERY AND MOTORIZED MECHANIZATION IN CEREAL CULTIVATION

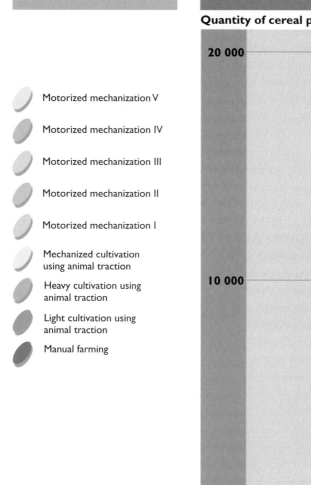

Motorized mechanization V

Motorized mechanization IV

Motorized mechanization III

Motorized mechanization II

Motorized mechanization I

Mechanized cultivation using animal traction

Heavy cultivation using animal traction

Light cultivation using animal traction

Manual farming

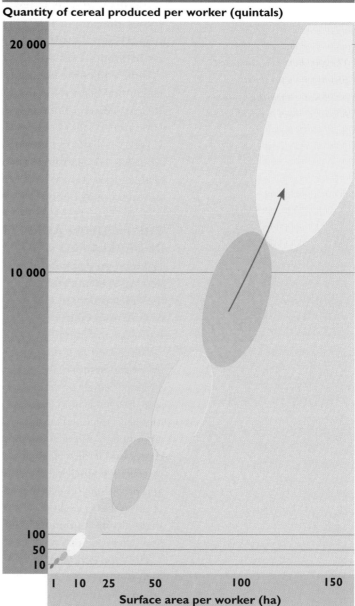

Quantity of cereal produced per worker (quintals)

20 000

10 000

100
50
10

1   10   25   50   100   150

Surface area per worker (ha)

Source: FAO, based on author's elaboration

train, boat and aeroplane. This opened up farms and agricultural regions and enabled them to procure their fertilizer, feed and other inputs from further afield and in larger quantities. It also allowed for the sale of their products, including perishable and unmanageable goods, in increased amounts and to wider areas.

Along the same lines, the *communications revolution*, based partly on the transport revolution and partly on telecommunications developments, provided the means for long-distance information supply and commercial transactions. This prompted distant trade and the organization of the large-scale administrative, productive, financial and trade structures that are integral to the modern industrial and agricultural revolution.

Agricultural modernization occurred gradually as a result of progress in industrialization, breeding technology and transport and communications, and in step with the enlargement of farms.

Agricultural holdings of a few hectares per worker, engaged in mixed crop and livestock farming using animal traction and producing much of their forage, manure, seeds, livestock and food, were still very common in the developed countries in the 1950s. How were these farms able to transform themselves within half a century into a small number of specialized production units of tens or hundreds of hectares per worker, operating as major purchasers of equipment and inputs and as sellers of almost all their production?

Rapid though it was, this major metamorphosis did not take place all at once. It occurred through progressive transformations in line with progress in industrialization, breeding technology and means of transport and communications, and in step with the enlargement and capitalization of an ever dwindling number of agricultural units.

Motorized mechanization. The development of motorization and mechanization varied according to the sphere of activity. Cereals and other large-scale grain crops (rapeseed, sunflower, soybean and other leguminous plants and cotton) were the first to benefit, and have always set the pace since. As these crops occupied a large proportion of arable land, they provided ample opportunity for the agricultural machinery industry. Motorized mechanization was then extended to the harvesting of roots and tubers, such as beetroot and potato, which are harder to handle because they are heavy, bulky and high in water content. It eventually spread to dairy cattle, forage harvesting, feeding and excreta disposal, viticulture and vegetable and fruit crops.

In large-scale field cropping, there are five stages in the process of motorized mechanization, each triggered by an increase in tractor power (see Figure 20). Before the 1950s, the first stage (motorized mechanization I) had relied on the use of low-horsepower tractors (10 to 30 HP) on farms of more than 15 ha. Faster than draught animals and – more important – tireless, these tractors helped increase surface area allocated per worker from some 10 to more than 20 ha.

From the end of the 1950s to the 1980s, the second, third and fourth stages (motorized mechanization II, III and IV) involved the use of increasingly powerful tractors and self-propelled machinery (30 to 50, 50 to 75 and then 75 to 120 HP) with higher tillage, sowing, field maintenance and harvesting capacity, leading to an increase in allocated land area per worker to 50, then 80 and finally 100 ha, respectively.

The fifth stage (motorized mechanization V), which began more than ten years ago, has involved the use of four-wheel drive tractors of more than 120 HP, extending the field crop area handled by one worker to more than 200 ha.

Similarly, for dairy production in 1950, one person could handmilk 12 cows twice a day. This number then doubled with the portable milking machine, rising to 50 cows with the herringbone milking parlour equipped with a milk tank and to 100 cows with the advent of the milking conveyor. With the latest fully automated milking parlour, it now stands at more than 200 cows. In this way, each stage in the motorized mechanization process has resulted in an increase in land area or number of livestock per worker, while concurrent progress in agricultural chemistry and breeding has increased yields per hectare or animal.

Agricultural chemistry and breeding. The considerable increase in major crop yields in developed countries over the last 50 years is mostly attributable to fertilizer use and to the breeding of plant varieties that are able to absorb and use enormous quantities of minerals profitably. Treatment against pests and improved mechanization have also played an important role.

From the late 1940s to the end of the 1990s, average wheat yields increased from 1 100 to more than 2 600 kg/ha in the United States, while mineral fertilizer use rose from 20 to 120 kg/ha of arable land. In France, wheat yields increased from 1 800 to 7 100 kg/ha for 45 and 250 kg of fertilizer, respectively.[10] Nowadays, on the rich loamy soil of northwestern Europe, wheat and maize yields sometimes exceed 10 000 kg/ha, with fertilizer applications of about 200 kg/ha of nitrogen, 50 kg/ha of phosphate and 50 kg/ha of potassium.

Obviously, the jump from landrace cereals producing 2 000

kg/ha to cultivars capable of producing 10 000 kg/ha did not occur overnight. Successive high-yeilding varieties were bred, marking as many stages in the profitable use of increasingly high fertilizer applications. In the case of wheat, for example, pure lines and, more recently, first-generation hybrids were obtained with increasingly shorter stalks, higher grain yields and resistance to cold, lodging, shrinkage, pre-harvest germination, foot rot, rust and powdery mildew. They were also of better quality for milling and baking, and suited the new processing appliances (homogeneity, ease of threshing).

The increased production of all kinds of grain (cereals and oilseeds) and crop by-products was such that a greater proportion could be used as concentrated feed. This, together with the increase in pasture and other forage crop production, helped raise livestock numbers and significantly improve their feed and yields. Therefore, animal breeds also had to be selected for their yield in meat, milk or eggs, and be able to consume increasingly nutritious feed rations in an economically profitable manner. While at the beginning of the century a cow consumed 15 kg of hay daily to produce less than 2 000 litres of milk per year, a highly bred milch cow now produces more than 10 000 litres of milk per year, consuming 5 kg of hay (or equivalent) and more than 15 kg of feed concentrate a day.

Livestock and crop protection. Such expensively bred and fed animals represent such an important capital investment with potential returns that the risks of animal or production loss through illness or accident become increasingly difficult to countenance; and the larger and more concentrated the animal population, the higher the risks. Therefore, very strict health precautions are taken and a wide range of expensive preventive and curative treatment is deployed, even veterinary surgery when necessary.

Annual crops undoubtedly represent a lower fixed capital than livestock or perennial plantations. However, as a crop develops, the capital investment (selected seed, fertilizer, fuel) accumulates and may represent as much as half of expected earnings. Moreover, the margin between earnings and expenditure must still cover the depreciation of expensive motorized machinery and wages, among other items. There is therefore no scope whatsoever for harvest losses, which means that phytosanitary products have to be used.

We can see how, from the technical and economic perspective, advances in motorized mechanization, breeding, mineral fertilization, livestock feeding and plant and animal

The protection of plant and animal health has become more important to safeguard investments in farm output and has led to greater farm and regional specialization.

health protection are very closely linked. Moreover, these advances have determined the simplification of production systems and, therefore, the specialization of production units and agricultural regions.

Specialization of crops/livestock. The use of fertilizers has led not only to increased harvests, but also to more straw and other crop residues that can then be ploughed into the soil and thus used to maintain acceptable levels of humus content. As a result, agricultural production units have been freed from the need to produce manure. In addition, with the introduction of tractors, they have been freed from the need to produce forage for draught animals. Consequently, agricultural holdings located in flat regions that are suited to mechanized farming and with good climatic and soil conditions for cereals, oilseeds or roots and tubers have abandoned fodder and livestock production to focus exclusively on growing field crops with motorized mechanization and use of mineral fertilizer.

By specializing in this way, these regions have produced higher marketable surpluses at a low cost, which they then export to regions less suited to large-scale mechanized cultivation. Conversely, farms in hill areas, in low-lying rainy, heavy-soil coastal regions and in arid, almost steppe-like Mediterranean or continental areas have focused largely on pasture and livestock (dairy or beef cattle, sheep, goats). At the same time, the use of agricultural chemicals has released farm holdings from the former crop rotation system used to control weeds, insects and disease. As a result, cropping systems have been simplified and further specialized, culminating in monocropping (or quasi-monocropping).

Trade between agricultural holdings and distant regions has grown and become more economical with the advent of road haulage (which took over from water and rail transport) and better means of communication. Farms can now be efficiently supplied with capital and consumer goods of every kind and no longer have to engage in mixed animal and crop farming for comprehensive localized self-supply. They have therefore been able to focus most of their production resources on the most profitable product (or simplified combination of products) as determined by environmental and trade conditions and local farmer expertise. Virtual monocultures of soybean, maize, wheat, cotton, vineyards, vegetables, fruit and flowers have thus spread over entire regions, giving rise to new specialized regional agricultural systems, each with very different agro-environmental and agro-economic characteristics.

Economic mechanisms for the development of the agricultural revolution

To move forward through all the stages of the contemporary agricultural revolution and establish the best-equipped and most appropriately sized farm, two or three farming generations have constantly had to discontinue less profitable operations and keep the most profitable one (or simplified combination). To do this, they have relied on improved seeds and new inputs, which they have combined so as to maximize profit margin per unit area. They have also continually bought new, more efficient machinery and have expanded operations in order to maximize unit area per worker.

By way of an example, the best located cereal production units in northwestern Europe, equipped with the most up-to-date and efficient machinery, have now attained a fixed capital of $300 000 (value of new material) and a surface area of 200 ha per worker, and have reached net productivity levels (after deduction of depreciation and maintenance costs) of $60 000 per worker. Most of the other specialized systems established during the second agricultural revolution have comparable maximum levels of potential capitalization and productivity per worker.

However, productivity does not equal income: to calculate net income per worker, it is necessary first to deduct interest on borrowed capital, land rent and tax, and add in any subsidies that might exist. Thus, working alone, a highly efficient cereal farmer who has a debt of about $300 000 at 5 percent interest and who leases his or her 200 ha at $150 per hectare, would earn an income (before tax and subsidies) of $15 000 per year.

More important, farms with such levels of capitalization, land and productivity are a minority; most have levels of capitalization, land productivity and income per worker of less than half these amounts.

On a financially viable farm in a developed country, the net income per farm worker is equivalent to the salary of an unskilled worker.

In the developed countries, a net income per worker of $15 000 per year more or less corresponds to the annual salary (including social contributions) of a relatively unskilled worker. If the net income per farm worker is at this level, the farm can renew its equipment and pay for its labour at market prices, but it will have virtually no margin for additional investment.

If income per worker is above this level, the farm has the capacity for net self-investment, and generally also has access to credit which will enable it to capitalize to increase productivity and income; all the more so, the higher the initial levels of capitalization and income.

However, if net income per worker is below this threshold of renewal and capitalization, the farm cannot renew its means of production and pay its workforce at market rates. Such a holding would in fact be in crisis and could only survive by underpaying its labour or by only partly renewing its means of production, resulting in a gradual decline of its productivity. However, remuneration for work must remain above the survival level, i.e. the minimum wage, otherwise farm workers will no longer be able to meet family needs and will have to abandon the farm. Agricultural holdings situated between the renewal and the survival thresholds generally have average-powered machinery that is obsolete and in bad condition. These farms are without plans for the future and without prospective buyers, but their productive resources could still be taken over, should they cease activity, by one or more neighbouring farms under expansion.

This divergent process has featured during each stage of the agricultural revolution: on the one hand, there has been an unequal and cumulative development of farms that are sufficiently capitalized and productive to be above the renewal threshold and, on the other, an impoverishment and elimination of units below this threshold. The farms that have invested and progressed the least in a given stage have found themselves relegated and then eliminated during the succeeding stage, while the most capitalized and productive units have moved on. Thus, most of the farms that existed in 1950 have disappeared, and only a minority have progressed through every stage and reached today's high capitalization and productivity levels.[11]

While the mechanisms of capitalization and the unequal and cumulative development of farms above the renewal threshold are easy to understand, it is necessary to explain the economic mechanisms whereby a majority of farms that had initially progressed and reached a certain level of capitalization and productivity were successively relegated below the renewal threshold and subsequently eliminated.

Falling commodity prices or higher costs can send a productive farm into an economic crisis.

A production unit that is above the renewal threshold may later fall below the threshold, despite having maintained its technical productivity. This can occur either because the unit's economic productivity has fallen owing to the unfavourable evolution of commodity or input prices or because of a rise in the renewal threshold (itself influenced by the wage levels on the work market), or both.

These two circumstances have actually occurred on a large scale during the past half-century. Real prices of agricultural food commodities have been on a sharp downward trend since 1950 because gains in agricultural productivity in the

developed countries have been superior to those of other
sectors during this period. Moreover, up until the 1980s, real
salaries of unskilled workers increased in these countries,
reflecting the fact that productivity gains in the economy as a
whole were directed not only towards capital earnings and
accumulation, but also in part towards increasing wages and
purchasing power.

Not only is this combination of declining real agricultural
prices and a rising in the renewal threshold detrimental to
underequipped farms, but it also acts in every region against the
least profitable products and product combinations, taking into
account local environmental and economic conditions.

In a given region, the levels of attainable productivity from the
various possible product combinations are very uneven, and the
least cost-effective eventually end up below the renewal
threshold and are progressively eliminated. The farms engaged
in these combinations are either themselves eliminated or they
abandon them in favour of a profitable product combination
that generally involves only a few very advantageous and
technically compatible production lines.

Thus, each region gradually determines its most efficient
specialized product combination and level of equipment (i.e.
the production system). As each region abandons the
unprofitable activities and focuses on a few profitable ones, the
resulting delocalization and then the relocation of all
agricultural activities produces a vast interregional division of
agricultural work which, taken beyond national borders, gives
some countries a very distinctive agricultural profile.

However, there are also regions in which all possible
production combinations have eventually sunk below the
renewal threshold, leading to the elimination of all farm units,
migration from rural to urban areas (when permitted by the
overall economy) and the spread of derelict land.

Consequences of the agricultural revolution

Beyond its intrinsic technical and economic aspects, the
agricultural revolution has also led to a series of associated
large-scale ecological, demographic, economic and cultural
changes.

Ecological changes. Specialization has brought about massive
spatial relocations and regional regroupings of field cropping in
some places, pasture and livestock farming in others, and
vineyards, market gardening, flower or other cultivation, fallow
land and afforestation elsewhere. Thus, today's cultivated

ecosystems differ from past multicrop/livestock ecosystems in which every village, every farm even, comprised a mosaic of land areas used for different purposes (cereals and other field crops, pasture, meadow, woodland, vegetable gardens, vineyards, orchards, etc.), each with a different crop and animal population.

Today's cultivated ecosystems are simpler and more uniform: wheat or maize fields, vineyards, or pasture and grazing herds sometimes succeed each other for hundreds of kilometres, and even the crop varieties and breeds vary little. What is more, being better nourished and protected, both crops and livestock are more vigorous and generally more densely stocked than in the past.

On the other hand, wild plants and animals have been seriously impoverished (there are more thistles, wallflowers, poppies and cornflowers and fewer insects, birds and rodents). The use of high concentrations of fertilizer and chemicals and the massive application of excreta from the large numbers of animals housed under the same roof can cause mineral and organic pollution, particularly of surface water and groundwater, and at times also adulteration of foods themselves (an excessive amount of nitrates in vegetables, pesticides on fruit and hormones and antibiotics in meat).

Tight economic conditions on a farm can make it difficult to maintain the productivity of natural resources.

The intensity of production and the cost-effective application of inputs, under the present system of comparative prices, frequently exceed ecological tolerance limits and a socially acceptable level of risk. However, clean-up operations are generally very expensive to the community, while the regulatory limitation of practices that may be optimal from a microeconomic point of view but pollute the environment inevitably reduces agricultural productivity. The cost of producing foodstuffs and maintaining an environment that both meet society's new quality expectations will have to be paid in one way or another.

Demographic changes. The replacement of most of the agricultural workforce by machines, together with the increase in land area per worker and the concomitant reduction in the number of farms, has generally led to very high agricultural outmigration, a process also fuelled by the reduction of allied activities (e.g. upstream and downstream trade and craftwork and public services). Thus, with 100 to 200 ha of field crops per worker, and 200 to 1 000 ha under extensive livestock production, without even considering the regions that have abandoned farming altogether, population density has fallen to below five and sometimes even one inhabitant per km²□.

This makes it very difficult to maintain services, such as post offices, schools, shops and health care, and to preserve local social life.

On the other hand, in some regions, specialization has led to agricultural and rural population densities equal to or even greater than in the past. With fewer than 5 ha per worker in quality viticulture, and less than 1 ha per worker in greenhouse market gardening or flower cultivation, population densities may amount to tens or hundreds of inhabitants per km^2.

Economic changes. The productivity gains from the agricultural revolution have been so vast that they have freed most of the workforce previously engaged in agriculture. During the first three postwar decades, this helped provide the large number of workers needed for industry and services in full development. Since the mid-1970s, however, economic growth has slowed and the continuation of agricultural migration has only fuelled unemployment. On the positive side, productivity gains in agriculture and other sectors have led to a shorter working week, a lowering of the retirement age and longer schooling. Finally, in the developed countries an active agricultural population, reduced to less than 5 percent of the total active population, has been able to feed the whole population − and better than before.

Cultural changes. As the new means of production are largely designed and manufactured in research and development centres and in concentrated industrial and service enterprises located far from the farm holdings and their immediate vicinity, the training of farmers and agricultural workers no longer takes place through apprenticeship on the farm, but increasingly in public and private institutes and using technical and economic information services. The former rural cultural heritage, produced and handed down locally, has given way to a relatively uniform culture, disseminated by education and the media.[12]

These immense ecological, demographic, economic and cultural changes indicate the extent to which the agricultural revolution has triumphed in the developed countries. Yet, looking a little further afield, this has clearly not been the case in the developing countries. Although motorized mechanization, high-yielding varieties and breeds, fertilizers, concentrated feeds, phytosanitary products and specialization have also reached these countries, more often than not they have been spread in an incomplete form and to a limited extent.

LIMITS TO THE AGRICULTURAL REVOLUTION
In the developing countries

The current agricultural revolution with all its attributes, in particular its heavy, complex and very expensive motorized mechanization, has not extended far beyond the developed countries, with the exception of small portions of Latin America, North Africa and South Africa and Asia[13] where it has only been adopted by large national or foreign farms that have the necessary capital. Alongside this, numerous small farmers continue to farm manually or using animal traction. Heavy motorized mechanization is also virtually non-existent in most parts of sub-Saharan Africa, in the Andes and in the centre of the Asian continent.

The agricultural revolution has reached few areas of the developing countries.

As a result of the green revolution, other regions and more farms have benefited from some of the components of the agricultural revolution: high-yielding varieties of maize, rice, wheat, cassava, broad bean, sweet sorghum and pigeon pea[14] selected in the course of the last decades in international research centres (e.g. the International Rice Research Institute and CIMMYT), fertilizer and phytosanitary products. There have been significant increases in yield in several countries, particularly with large-scale irrigated agriculture and proper water control. Water control throughout the year and the breeding of non-photoperiodic rice varieties suitable for cultivation in all seasons have permitted more than three harvests per year on the same plot of land.

Thanks to these achievements, the well-located and better-off farmers have been able to obtain animal traction – sometimes even power tillers or small tractors – and to some extent approach the productivity levels of developed countries. Also helped by low local wages, the production and productivity levels attained have enabled certain countries to reduce undernutrition significantly (e.g. India and China) or even to become rice exporters (e.g. Thailand, Viet Nam and Indonesia). Yet, despite these gains, extreme poverty and chronic undernutrition have by no means disappeared in these countries.

Even in green revolution regions, numerous small, poorly equipped and very low-income farms were unable to gain access to the new means of production. Unable to invest and progress, they saw their incomes fall as a result of the drop in real agricultural prices. Many of them sank to levels of extreme poverty and were eliminated. Above all, vast hilly and barely accessible regions of rainfed or scarcely irrigated agriculture were essentially bypassed by the green revolution. The varieties cultivated in these regions (millet, sorghum, taro, sweet potato, yam, plantain, cassava) benefited marginally, if at all, from selection. The same was true for varieties of major cereals (wheat, maize, rice) that were adapted to difficult local conditions (altitude, drought, salinization, aridity, waterlogging). For example, the average output of millet throughout the world today is barely 800 kg/ha, and that of sorghum is less than 1 500 kg/ha. These so-called "orphan" varieties, having been bypassed by the selection process, make the use of fertilizer and phytosanitary inputs unprofitable, which only adds to the problems of the regions where they are grown.

Integration into global markets can be a two-edged sword for farmers in developing countries.

Admittedly, the less accessible regions that were only marginally affected by the green revolution remained sheltered for a long time from the cheap imports of cereals and other staple foods from the more advantaged regions and countries. In this way, regions that had not been reached by modernization were able to maintain their production systems (diversity, breeds, implements, crop and livestock combinations and practices), their population and their culture longer than others. However, as soon as these regions were penetrated by the advance of motorized transport and commerce, they also found themselves caught up in interregional trade and were thus exposed to low-cost imports of cereals and other food commodities.

Based on the price paid to well-equipped cereal growers in developed countries (i.e. less than $15 per 100 kg of grain), a manual cereal grower producing 1 000 kg of grain net earns less than $150 per year. However, at least 700 kg of production have to be set aside for household consumption, so cash income does not even amount to $50 per year, and this is assuming that farmers do not have to pay land rent, interest on loans or taxes. At this income level, it would take a lifetime for manual cereal growers to purchase a pair of work oxen and basic animal traction equipment, assuming all their cash income could be spent on this purchase; and it would take three centuries to buy a small tractor.

Under these conditions, farmers try to take advantage of the widening access to external trade by diverting part of their resources and workforce to cash crops (cotton, oil-palm, rubber, coffee, cacao, banana, pineapple, tea). But this means that local food production declines and food dependence sets in; and, being underequipped and underproductive, most of these farmers are unable to invest and progress sufficiently to withstand the continuing and generalized decline in real agricultural prices. In such circumstances, hundreds of millions of underequipped peasant farmers in the more deprived regions sink into a three-pronged economic, environmental and nutritional crisis.

Because of falling agricultural prices, the already low cash income of these farmers becomes insufficient to maintain and entirely renew their equipment and inputs and thus further erodes their production capacity. At this stage, an able-bodied member of the family can still be sent out to find temporary or permanent work elsewhere, although this weakens farm production capacity still further. The temporary survival of the farm only becomes possible by means of decapitalization (sale of livestock, non-renewal of equipment), underconsumption, undernutrition and the migration of part of the workforce.

Increasingly poorly equipped and badly fed, these farmers are obliged to concentrate their efforts on short-term returns and to neglect the maintenance of the cultivated ecosystem. This neglect takes the form of poor maintenance of irrigation systems, slash-and-burn of ever younger fallow, insufficient weeding, sale of livestock and reduced transfer of fertility to the soil. The economic non-renewal of the productive system leads to the non-renewal of fertility of the cultivated ecosystem.

The reduction in equipment, the diminished workforce and the degradation of fertility of the cultivated ecosystem also lead farmers to simplify their cropping systems: "poor" crops, which are less demanding on the level of mineral fertility of the soil and require less labour, replace more demanding crops. This, coupled with the near disappearance of animal products, leads to serious protein, mineral and vitamin deficiencies. Thus, malnutrition resulting from the degradation of the cultivated ecosystem is compounded by undernutrition through poor crop quality.

These are the basic economic and environmental mechanisms that explain why the destitute peasant farmer population of poor agricultural regions constitutes the bulk (three quarters)[15] of the more than 800 million people suffering from undernutrition in the world today. Since a significant proportion of these peasant farmers and other rural inhabitants migrate each year to overpopulated urban areas, and since the number of chronically undernourished peasant farmers remains constant year after year, this means that the poor farmer population is constantly being renewed.

Reduced to the limits of survival, this impoverished peasant farmer population is thus at the mercy of the slightest adversity, whether climatic (flooding or drought), biological (plant, animal or human disease), economic (falling agricultural prices) or, more and more often, political (war) as extreme poverty and hunger are two further elements in the complex causes of local or regional conflicts.[16]

This process of impoverishment and exclusion has not yet affected the whole of the peasant farmer sector engaged in manual cultivation. It has affected the most deprived, who are especially numerous in resource-poor regions or where their condition is further aggravated by circumstances such as natural constraints (insufficient or excessive rainfall, cold, salinization), infrastructural obstacles (lack of irrigation), structural constraints (microholdings, precarious land tenure) and policies unfavourable to agriculture (overvalued currency, subsidies for food imports, taxation on agricultural exports, fluctuating prices, limited or inefficient public investment in agriculture).

The agricultural transformations of the past half-century are not limited to the two extremes of the contemporary agricultural revolution and green revolution, on the one hand, and impoverishment, exclusion and hunger, on the other. A closer analysis reveals that agriculture throughout the world is subject to change that does not originate from these agricultural revolutions but that contributes, in its own way and to its own extent, to the process of modernization.

In fact, agriculture does not stand still. Even the smallest-scale farmers in the African savannahs, the Andes and the high valleys of Asia routinely adopt new plants and new animals originating from other continents and, if they can afford them, new metal tools, either manual or animal-drawn. Above all, in order to adapt to ever changing economic, environmental and demographic conditions, they are continually combining and recombining crops and varieties, animal production systems and breeds and old and new tools to create new production systems, and the less favourable the conditions the greater the ingenuity.

For example, on the highly leached soils of the poor savannahs of the central plateaus of the Congo, during the last few decades the Batéké farmers have perfected systems that combine orchard gardens, annual crops (potato, bean, tobacco) on burn-beaten mounds, biennial cassava cropping on ridges and coffee plantations under the shade of restored woodlots on abandoned village orchard gardens.[17] Another example is the orchard garden with small livestock raising in the hills of Burundi or Haiti, practised under rainfed cultivation on sometimes very sloping terrain, and supporting populations of several hundreds of inhabitants per km^2. While the labour productivity of these systems cannot exceed the limits of their manual equipment, they are nonetheless modern and very sophisticated.

Most remarkable are the mixed systems with very intensively used biomass combining crops, arboriculture, breeding and sometimes even aquaculture, which are vigorously developed in the most populated regions of the world. For example, in certain plains, valleys and deltas of Southeast Asia (central-south Java, the Mae Klong delta in Thailand, the Mekong delta in Viet Nam), the cropping systems alternate raised beds (with the multicropping of cereals, tubers, roots and vegetables under plantations of banana, papaya, coconut palm and sugar palm) and aquaculture or rice basins with two or three harvests per year, supporting high densities of large and small livestock and providing jobs, subsistence and cash income to populations of 1 000 to 2 000 inhabitants per km^2. In the Nile valley, in Egypt, systems of two or three irrigated crops per year of fodder, cereals and vegetables under or alongside plantations of banana, citrus, palm and other fruit-trees support equally high animal and human densities.[18] These systems, often using little or no motorized mechanization and limited quantities of inputs, have a relatively modest productivity rate, but their production of usable biomass (including all forms of production) by unit of surface area largely exceeds the average production of large-scale specialized cropping in the developed countries. With the world's growing population, there is no doubt that these systems will become increasingly important in many regions.

In the developed countries

Even in the developed countries, the agricultural revolution has its limits and drawbacks. In temperate regions with only one cropping season, it is difficult to exceed annual yields of 12 000 kg of grain per hectare or milk yields of 12 000 litres per cow. Degradation of the environment and the quality of food worsens with overuse of fertilizers and agricultural chemicals, excessive concentrations of animal production and the recycling of possibly unhealthy organic waste in compound feed. At the same time, the huge mechanized capacity, rural outmigration and the abandonment of farmland pose increasingly acute problems of employment and land maintenance.

Alternative forms of agriculture are already developing in pockets of industrialized countries in response to these excesses. Including ecologically sound and organic agriculture, these alternative forms are less specialized, more economical in their use of non-renewable resources, more environmentally and socially friendly, and more geared towards product quality. They are in tune with the aspirations of the public and many farmers[19] and are destined to expand considerably.

ASSESSMENT AND FUTURE PROSPECTS

The first question is whether the conquest of new cropland, the extension of the agricultural and green revolutions to poor farmers and the development of sustainable forms of agriculture, in both developed and developing countries, will raise world food production to meet the quantitative and qualitative needs of the much larger human population of future decades.

The second question is whether these agricultural developments will take place under economic and social conditions that will finally give the more deprived population groups access to sufficient food.

After 50 years of modernization, world agricultural production today is more than sufficient to feed 6 billion human beings adequately. Cereal production alone, at about 2 billion tonnes or 330 kg of grain per caput/year and representing 3 600 kcal per caput/day, could to a large extent cover the energy needs of the whole population if it were well distributed.[20] However, cereal availability varies greatly from one country to another: more than 600 kg per caput/year in the developed countries, where most is in fact used as animal feed, but less than 200 kg per caput/year in the poorer countries. Moreover, within each country, access to food or the means to produce food is very uneven among households. Consequently, in many countries, large segments of the population do not have enough food. And, as noted earlier, the large majority of the 830 million chronically undernourished are in the poor peasant farming community.

World food security is determined by poor farmers' production methods and poor consumers' purchasing power.

World food security, therefore, is not an essentially technical, environmental or demographic issue in the short term: it is first and foremost a matter of grossly inadequate means of production of the world's poorest peasant farmers who cannot meet their food needs. It is also a matter of insufficient purchasing power of other poor rural and urban consumers, insofar as the poverty of non-farmers is also a product of rural poverty and migration from the land.

The demographic transition (i.e. the fall in fertility and thus population growth), which started a long time ago in the developed countries and which is spreading increasingly to the developing countries, leads many demographers to forecast a world population of about 10 billion in 2050, stabilizing at around 12 billion during the second half of the twenty-first century: twice as many people as in the year 2000. The experts estimate that present world food production will have to be tripled[21] if hunger and malnutrition are to be eliminated and if a population that has doubled, and consists of higher average build and age, is to be properly fed.

The question is, therefore, whether these estimated needs of humanity are not beyond the capacity of the earth's land and water resources. Indeed, many regions are already fully exploited and sometimes even dangerously overexploited and degraded by erosion, reduced organic fertility and pollution.

On the other hand, many regions with potential have not been exploited or are underutilized. FAO data suggest that rainfed and irrigated cropland could be significantly expanded in several regions without much difficulty and without harming the environment, particularly through appropriate land use management.[22]

Moreover, the current agricultural revolution can still produce higher yields in many regions, although its excesses need to be corrected. It can be extended to new land in developing countries and can even reclaim abandoned land in the developed countries (hilly, stony terrain) provided that its biological and mechanical resources are diversified and adapted. Similarly, the green revolution in its classic form can still make significant progress in yields and surface area in the regions where it is already developed.

A new green revolution should be extended to resource-poor regions and farmers and to "orphan" species and varieties that were previously bypassed.

Above all, a second green revolution could be extended to all hitherto neglected regions, including the most disadvantaged. However, this must be on condition that an in-depth study is carried out of the agricultural systems, experience, assets, constraints and farmers' needs of these resource-poor regions to serve as the basis for related projects and policies. Furthermore, selection must be resolutely applied to "orphan" species and to varieties and breeds appropriate to these regions. This large-scale renewal and revival of the green revolution to encompass more regions, populations, plants and animals is referred to by some as the "doubly green" or "evergreen" revolution.

Considering these different forms of agricultural progress and the experience of recent decades, many economists – very influential during the last 20 years and pushing optimistic liberalism to its extreme – believe that the productivity gains and falling real agricultural prices that result from trade liberalization and greater international competition will allow an abundant supply of low-cost food to be available to the majority of the world's population. They further believe that the redistribution of income and assistance targeting of the poorest will, in the short and medium term, lead to a reduction in the number of people suffering extreme poverty and hunger.

Under this long-term perspective, with the unrestricted circulation of capital, the development of industry and the service sector should be sufficient to eliminate unemployment and mass poverty worldwide, while bringing about a degree of convergence of human development in the different parts of the world.

However, liberalization thus envisaged concerns solely the movement of goods, services and capital, and certainly not the free movement of the mass of low-skilled labour excluded from the peasant farmer sector in the developing countries; nor does it imply the unrestricted access of the huge number of peasant farmers, who are excluded from agriculture in the South, to the land, infrastructures, credit and employment of the North.

While optimistic liberalism prevails today, such a perspective is nevertheless considered by many economists to be an unobtainable mirage. Quite apart from the imperfections of the real markets − for example, increased economies of scale, monopolies, monopsonies, asymmetry of information, transaction costs − we cannot fail to ignore the fact that, in just a few decades, the international food markets have been able to absorb vast historical national and regional economic entities, with significant disparities in development and productivity.

Under these conditions, agricultural prices set at the lowest international level have helped make agricultural commodities more accessible to consumers. At the same time, however, they have led to interruptions in development as well as to the impoverishment, and ultimately economic exclusion, of large segments of the most disadvantaged peasant farmer populations of the world.

In addition, over the last 20 years of free movement of goods, services and capital but not of people, the massive outmigration from agriculture has greatly exceeded the capital accumulation and employment-generating capacity of the world economy, notably in the South; and disparities among and within countries have widened, as has the scale of mass poverty.[23]

The experience of the last decades has also shown that, for all their merits and undeniable successes, international assistance, development projects and income redistribution policies have failed to eradicate poverty and hunger. In particular, assistance targeting of "vulnerable social groups" − the type of assistance that goes hand in hand with structural adjustment and stabilization policies − has fallen far short of the mark.

If, at the beginning of the twenty-first century, we continue down the path of liberalization of trade in food, other goods and services and capital, without the free movement of people and without providing the material and regulatory means for everyone to enjoy basic economic rights, extreme poverty and chronic undernutrition can be expected to persist in rural areas. The migration of agricultural workers, unemployment and low wages can also be expected to persist in the poorer countries that have no or few resources other than agriculture. This will contribute towards keeping the prices of exported goods and services and private and public incomes at very low levels in these countries, thus denying them the resources needed to provide the minimum public services required for development and good governance.

Finally, as the population of these countries accounts for more than half of humanity,[24] the signal weakness of their effective demand and their limited involvement in international trade will continue to hamper trade growth and will seriously compromise development of the global economy.

Definite action is required if enough food is to be produced and made accessible to the world's projected population of 10 billion to 12 billion people, and if their expectations of both environmental and product quality are to be fulfilled. First, approaches to development and food security need to prioritize the problems of the farming poor. Rescuing the most destitute half of the world's peasant farmer population from exclusion and poverty is in itself a fundamental social and humanitarian goal, but it is equally important to enable these farmers to play a tangible role in tripling world food production − the neccesary goal to be achieved in the next few decades.

Action targeting the most destitute farmers must aim at developing their food production capacity both to help them improve their nutritional status and to create employment and income for the poorer groups. The importance of these objectives and the policy measures required to achieve them are discussed in the next section of this review.

NOTES

1 FAO. 1999. *FAOSTAT '98. FAO statistical databases.* CD-ROM; FAO. 1954. *FAO Production Yearbook*, Rome.

2 M. Mazoyer and L. Roudart. 1998. *Histoire des agricultures du monde.* Paris, Éditions du Seuil.

3 The total net increase of 180 million ha is the result of an increase in the developing countries and a weak reduction in the developed countries. See FAO, op. cit., note 1.

4 FAO, op. cit., note 1.

5 *ACTA Phytosanitary Index*, 1999.

6 FAO, op. cit., note 1.

7 Mazoyer and Roudart, op. cit., note 2.

8 Estimated in kilograms of cereal equivalent (the quantity of cereals having the same calorie value as the total foodstuffs under consideration). Productivity is calculated as follows: maximum surface area cultivated by one farmer multiplied by potential yield per hectare of good soil, subtracting seeds, losses and quantity of grain needed to cover the cost of inputs and depreciation of materials. For each major system, the maximum surface area per worker and the maximum yield per hectare vary according to region, which explains why maximum productivity also varies to a certain extent.

9 Mazoyer and Roudart, op. cit., note 2.

10 The use of fertilizer and yields are very unequal in these two countries: they are low in the United States, where farmers dispose of a very large surface area, and higher in France, where the size of production units is much smaller. After the mid-1970s, the use of mineral fertililizer reached a peak and then declined in France, although yields have continued to rise because agriculture is tending to use fertilizer more sparingly (needs are calculated more carefully and split applications are made).

11 Mazoyer and Roudart, op. cit., note 2.

12 M. Mazoyer. 1999. Compte-rendu de l'atelier Agriculture, Ressources naturelles, Environnement. Colloque *L'enseignement agricole, quels apports à la société?* Paris, French Academy of Agriculture.

13 Today, with 1.3 billion people actively involved in farming, only 28 million tractors are used in agriculture worldwide.

14 FAO. 1995. *Dimensions of need. An atlas of food and agriculture.* Rome.

15 FAO. 1996. *Technical background documents. World Food Summit*, IPU. 1998. Inter-Parliamentary Union Conference – Attaining the World Food Summit's Objectives through a Sustainable Development Strategy, 26 November-2 December 1998, FAO, Rome.

16 M. Mazoyer and L. Roudart. 1997. Development of agricultural inequalities in the world and the crisis of the comparatively

disadvantaged peasant farming sector. *Land Reform*, 1: 7-17. Rome, FAO; M. Mazoyer and L. Roudart. 1997. L'asphyxie des économies paysannes du sud. *Le Monde diplomatique* (October).

17 C. Serre-Duhem. 1995. Les transformations d'un système agraire au Congo: le plateau Kukuya. National Institute of Agronomy Paris-Grignon. (thesis)

18 L. Roudart. 1998. Origines et transformations récentes des systèmes hydroagricoles de la vallée du Nil en Egypte – Le rôle de l'État. National Institute of Agronomy Paris-Grignon. (thesis)

19 Mazoyer, op. cit., note 12.

20 FAO. *The State of Food and Agriculture.* (various years) Rome.

21 P. Collomb. 1995. Population mondiale: conférences internationales et paradoxes du discours démographique. *Problèmes économiques*, 2.421: 20-23.

22 FAO. 1995. *World agriculture – towards 2010.* Rome.

23 UNDP. *Human Development Report* (various years). New York.

24 The population of the low-income food-deficit countries amounts to more than 3.6 billion people. See FAO (1999), op. cit., note 1.

Food and nutrition security: why food production matters

FOOD SECURITY AND NUTRITION IN THE LAST 50 YEARS

The years 1945 to 1952 saw Europe struggling to restore pre-war food production, consumption and security. Even in the mid-1960s, former levels still had not been reattained in Asia – rightly seen as the highest-risk area, where chronic undernourishment left people extremely vulnerable. Between 23 million and 30 million lives were lost in the Chinese famine of 1960-1962. In 1965 and 1966, famine was barely avoided in South Asia. More than 75 percent of Asians (and probably 90 percent of undernourishment victims) depended on food production for their income.

Then, in much of the world came rapid growth, green revolutions, land reform and poverty reduction. The proportion of chronically underfed persons fell in developing countries from 36 percent in 1970 to 20 percent in 1990. The proportion of underweight children under five years of age fell globally from 42 percent in 1975 to about 32 percent in the late 1990s. The reduction in undernutrition was rapid in East Asia, substantial in South Asia and Latin America but very slight in Africa, and it recently reversed in the republics of the former USSR. In these last two regions, related death rates are rising. Moreover, globally, progress in combating poverty and undernutrition was slower between 1987 and 2000 than between 1970 and 1985, corresponding to slowdowns in the yield growth of food staples, in land redistribution and, hence, in rural employment. Despite past progress, during the 1990s one in five people in developing countries ate less than the caloric minima for metabolic, work and other functions. Worldwide, there are still more than 150 million children under five who are underweight; more than 200 million – more than one in four – are stunted. These conditions appear to be implicated in about half of the 12 million deaths annually of children under five and, for some of the more damaged survivors, in physical and even mental retardation.

At the 1943 Hot Springs Conference, which set the blueprint for FAO, countries accepted responsibility for ensuring food and nutrition security.

Notwithstanding the slowdown in the progress against poverty and undernutrition, governments were increasingly given credit for such a large fall in food insecurity. At the national level, overt colonialism retreated massively twice, between 1947 and 1965 and in the early 1990s, leaving the state formally accountable to its own nationals. In both periods, many countries (not only former colonies) moved towards democracy. Moreover, national populations were becoming more organized in effective "civil societies" with more literacy, information, communication and power to put pressure on their governments for adequate food access. At the international level, food security was advanced by parallel changes in institutions and public awareness. Institutionally, the process began when the 1943 Hot Springs Conference (in part responding to President Roosevelt's 1941 designation of "freedom from want" as a human right) wrote the blueprint for FAO. For the rest of the century, international agencies obtained money and support, from taxpayers of almost all nations, to underpin major components of food and nutrition security.

IFAD, with a mandate to emphasize nutrition and food production for the poorest, was the harbinger of a growing focus on poverty as the main cause of food insecurity. In 1973, the World Bank began to express its increasing concern about the impact of poverty; but in the 1980s the focus shifted to country lending strategies. These initially emphasized stabilization but, increasingly in the 1990s, poverty impact also. The current World Bank President, James Wolfensohn, asks that the Bank be judged by its impact on poverty. Despite small (but significant) lending for nutrition as such, the Bank's approach implies that poverty reduction, together with increased agricultural output, is the main route to food and nutrition security. Yet the share of Bank lending (and of total aid) going to agriculture has fallen since the early 1980s, as have yield growth in food staples and the speed of poverty reduction and improvement in household food security.

A series of international conferences, most notably the World Food Conference of 1974, clarified the issues but led to sarcasm about "resolutions without resolution". Yet, in 1996, the Copenhagen World Summit for Social Development (the Social Summit) and the Rome World Food Summit culminated in targets to halve world poverty and undernutrition by 2015, and the Organisation for Economic Co-operation and Development (OECD) has supported moves to make this target country-specific, monitored and backed by aid.

The targets for reducing poverty and food insecurity can be

met. In East Asia the number of food-insecure fell faster between 1970 and 1985, owing in part to fertility transitions and bringing sharp falls in child-adult ratios as well as a rising ratio of workers to dependants (see the section Demographic transitions and food security, p. 203). Even larger shifts are now under way in Africa and South Asia. Can these heartlands of poverty and food insecurity expel them through this demographic "window of opportunity"?

Past and current trends and issues: implications for the early 2000s

Postwar experience suggests that, for rapid falls in undernutrition to continue in the low-income African and Asian countries where it remains worst, yield growth in main food staples will need to recover to the 3 percent level achieved in the 1970s – in the 1990s, as in 1950-65, it was barely 1 percent per year in developing countries. Growth in yields will also need to spread to some of the neglected staple crops and poorly watered lands, especially in Africa, that were bypassed by the green revolution. However, in real terms, funding for public agricultural research has been stagnant in international centres since the mid-1980s and has fallen in Africa and Latin America. Threatened water scarcities and the overfarming of marginal lands, although sometimes seen as reasons for not aiming at higher yields of food staples, are partly due to inadequate funds for research.

Increased food production is necessary but not sufficient to improve food security – entitlements must also grow.

In the 1940s and 1950s, the founders of FAO saw such needs clearly. So, in the 1960s, did the creators of the green revolution. Such production-oriented approaches are not *sufficient* to improve food security and health environments, but they are *necessary*.

Since 1945, the following global trends affecting food security and nutrition have emerged:

- increasing accountability on the part of nation states and the international community, not just for famine deaths, but for food and nutrition security;
- from about 1980, a shift from state action to reliance on markets;
- a shift from concern about national food security, measured by staples self-sufficiency, to potential household food security, measured by dietary energy supply (DES), and then to actual household food security, measured by the absence of protein-energy malnutrition (PEM);
- a shift towards consideration of food entitlements, rather than food availability, as the main guarantor of food security;

- major, although patchy, improvements in household food security and measures against undernourishment.

Consequently, attention is increasingly focused on the food-health-nutrient-activity balance and safety, involving micronutrients as well as calories; health (including bioabsorption and biodiversion), work and child care as well as food intake; and overnutrition as well as undernutrition.

Linked to the above, staples production for local employment and consumption has been downgraded since the early 1980s. This is also due to expanding European and Asian staples output and yields; falling real prices of staples; environmental concerns; failure to appreciate that many low-income people require extra staples production to obtain employment-based entitlements to food staples; and reliance on comparative advantages and trade options to permit a "switch" to cutting undernutrition mainly by non-food employment. Growth in such employment opportunities has seldom been substantial or nationwide until late in the development stage, even in East and Southeast Asia.

Staples yield growth, which was 3 percent per year in the developing world in the 1970s, fell to just above 1 percent in the 1990s. The need to raise yields, and thereby staples-related employment and entitlements, in poor areas will increase as workforces grow by 2 to 2.5 percent per year in much of Asia and Africa up to 2025.

The yield potential for tropical and subtropical staples surged for maize in the 1950s, and for rice and wheat in the 1960s, but has subsequently slowed down. In most countries with widespread undernutrition, contrary to general belief, rapid progress in food staples production implies renewal of growth in yield *potential*. The shift from states and international public action towards markets must be modified in at least one key area, biotechnology, if research is to be reoriented to the still pressing requirements for reduced undernutrition.

Three themes underly the trends described above:

i) The end of the dichotomy between "productionist" and "distributivist" approaches to individual food security – between failures of "food availability" and "food entitlements" as causes of famine (and chronic hunger). For most of the undernourished, extra employment income from local staples production has been the key to enhanced food entitlements in the period from 1950 to 2000, as discussed below. This will remain so until 2025, given the continued rapid growth of workforces and the need to restrain and stabilize local staples prices. Such employment is generated as a result of higher yields of food staples and better access to land, credit and institutions. The slowdown in food staples yield growth since the 1970s, and in its employment impact, offers new challenges. The experience of the green revolution shows how to address them in ways that enhance food entitlements and household food security. So far, however, the promising new tools of biotechnology have not been applied for the purpose of raising staples yields for poor smallholders.

ii) Increased policy focus on nutrition security (see the section From energy adequacy to nutrition security, p. 231) in response to new knowledge and new problems and in recognition of the fact that nutrition encompasses aspects such as nutritional quality and balance, food safety and physical activities that prevent obesity.

iii) The need for people and organizations wishing to improve food and nutrition security to respond correctly to changes in the role of the state vis-à-vis *markets.* This theme includes the joint action of these groups towards, and possible biases against, weaker or less politically active groups at special nutritional risk (e.g. rural or remote groups, children, females, minorities and refugees). The role of states and markets is crucial in determining whether such groups gain income, access to food and information to permit nutrition security. Many opponents of "free" or globalized markets fear that, as a result of perverse interactions between states and monopoly-like corporations, such markets do not help, and may harm, some of these vulnerable groups in their progress towards nutrition security. Even though competition can make some poor groups poorer still, there is much evidence to suggest that countries that liberalize their markets are generally those that are most likely to raise incomes, and this tends to reduce poverty faster.

FOOD SECURITY AS ENERGY ADEQUACY
For most of the world's poor, "food security" is knowing that future meals will provide enough dietary energy to meet their requirements. Box 18 reviews the concepts of food adequacy and security that are used in the text.

THE FRAMING CONDITIONS: PEOPLE, FOOD AND ENTITLEMENTS
Demographic transitions and food security
The past 50 years have seen an astonishing demographic

Box 18

FOOD ADEQUACY, FOOD SECURITY AND PROTEIN-ENERGY MALNUTRITION

Individual food adequacy (IFA) is shown, in the short term, by calorie intakes that are sufficient for needs, varying with age, health, work nd adult height; in the medium term, by the absence of acute protein-energy malnutrition (PEM),[1] for example low child weight for age (WA) or low adult weight for height (WH)); and in the long term by the absence of chronic PEM in children under five, of low height for age (HA). Inadequate HA (stunting), WA (underweight) or WH (wasting) are often equated with shortfalls of more than two standard deviations below the United States median (>2 SD).

Individual food security (IFS) refers to "access to *adequate* safe and nutritious food to maintain a healthy life ... without undue risk of losing such access"[2], i.e. IFA as well as the confidence that it can be maintained. Without such confidence, people take hypercautious decisions that forfeit their chances to escape from chronic hunger.

A poor person usually obtains 70 to 80 percent of his or her calories (and most other nutritional requirements) from one or two of the world's seven main food staples. These are by far the cheapest sources of energy, and of most other nutrients. For the poor, access to these staples is the key to achieving IFS.

Household food adequacy/security (HFA/HFS) is necessary for IFA/IFS, but not sufficient, because food may be distributed among household members disproportionately to their individual needs.

National food security (NFS) refers to a nation's capacity to ensure HFS/IFS without undue departure from other policy goals. NFS in a given year is often measured by: dietary energy supplies (DES) per person, allowing for the distribution of food and needs among individuals and times; or the ratio of food imports to total exports, although food aid must be allowed for; or staples stocks (publicly controlled or likely to be marketed if prices rise) as a share of normal consumption.

---

[1] The proximate cause of PEM appears to be energy deficiency relative to requirements and infection burdens. Although protein deficiency causes widespread and serious damage, most nutritionists now reject the earlier view that protein deficiency, let alone specific amino acid deficiency, is an independent problem requiring special protein-rich foods, supplements or cereal varieties. Only exceptionally is a protein problem not curable simply by providing "more calories".
[2] FAO. 1996. *The Sixth World Food Survey*. Rome.

transformation. Population growth accelerated between 1940 and 1960 in Asia and Latin America, and ten years later in Africa. The really massive improvement was among children under five, which raised the ratio of children to adults. Some 10 to 20 years later, the age groups that had been saved from child death increasingly entered the workforce, and parents, now more confident that their children would survive, began to reduce their fertility rates. As population growth slowed down, the ratio of adults – savers and workers – to children began to climb steeply.

Just as the early phase of demographic transition, with its rapid growth in child numbers, had harmed economic growth, income distribution and, hence, the reduction of poverty and PEM, so the later stage – with children reaching working age, and fertility falling – helped all these factors. The effects on food security are considerable. Directly, smaller families are less likely to be poor and, given their poverty level, less likely to suffer PEM. Indirectly, about one third of East Asia's growth in real income per person from 1965 to 1992 can be accounted for by rising adult–child ratios; across more than 50 developing and transitional countries for which adequate poverty data are available, the poverty-reducing impact of lower fertility rates is about as strong via better income distribution as via faster economic growth.[1]

The "demographic gift" of an increased worker-dependant ratio may help sub-Saharan Africa and South Asia to reduce food insecurity, as occurred earlier in East Asia.

The heartlands of world poverty, South Asia and sub-Saharan Africa, have entered their fertility transition and will face a very rapid rise in their ratios of workers and savers to dependants in the next two decades. For example, in Kenya, on the UN "medium variant" projection, the ratio of prime-age adults – the main workers and savers – to children under 15 years of age will rise from only 1:24 in 2000 to 1:87 in 2020. Will this "demographic gift" sharply cut poverty and, hence, PEM in Africa and South Asia – as it did in East Asia? This depends on whether extra workplaces offering rising incomes become attractive for the growing workforce and their employers – as was the case in East Asia – and whether extra investment opportunities, with a high impact on growth and poverty, attract the new savers. In East Asia this was achieved through a first phase of growth in staples yields and employment as a result of the green revolution between the mid-1960s and late 1980s; those countries that successfully continued the struggle to reduce poverty and malnutrition then moved into a second phase of rising non-farm employment, both urban and rural.

Sharp rises in adult-child ratios and thus in worker-dependant ratios and in savings, which were experienced in South Asia and Africa, are a "window of opportunity" for these regions to slash remaining poverty and PEM, as was done in East Asia. It has been proved that farm intensification through methods suited to local conditions *can* achieve similar results on a sustainable basis in large parts of South Asia and Africa. But the window is now curtained by threats to the growth in yields of, and employment-based entitlements to, main food staples and, in some cases, by severe land inequality.

Poverty and entitlements to food

Hunger, not just famine, mainly afflicts people who have insufficient "food entitlements".[2] As Sen emphasized, food production still matters: the poor rely on it for most of their food entitlements, whether based on small-scale farming or employment.

However, one would expect postwar improvement in food security to be associated with a substantial retreat of poverty (used here in the limited sense of "low real private consumption per equivalent adult"). Broadly speaking, this is correct. Poverty declined (and nourishment and DES improved) little in sub-Saharan Africa, in Latin America mainly in 1965-78, and in

Rural poverty in Honduras
Poverty does not completely explain undernourishment

FAO/20729/A. PROTO

Asia mainly in 1975-90.[3] Recent resurgences of poverty and undernourishment in the transitional countries are clearly linked.[4]

Yet, many poor households do not suffer undernourishment, owing to "positive deviance" in child care, low energy requirements or other behavioural adaptations. Many non-poor households, for opposite reasons, do suffer undernourishment. And, although the poorest show much higher responsiveness of calorie intake to extra income than others, the short-term responsiveness of the average household, even in quite poor communities, is often rather slight; poverty does not completely explain *current household* caloric inadequacy or PEM.

Nevertheless, poverty – and its main proximate cause, inadequacy of income from paid or self-employment and, hence, inadequacy of food entitlements – substantially "explains" *long-term group* undernourishment risk. Among and within countries, differences in the decline in poverty help to predict the improvements in both caloric underfeeding and anthropometric undernutrition. For several reasons, the relationship between poverty reduction and increased DES is imperfect:

- Anthropometric undernourishment measurements – stunting in children of normal weight for height, PEM at ages 12 to 24 months and micronutrient deficiency – may be a signal for some very poor victims of undernourishment that they should have other, perhaps higher, priorities for using extra income than simply acquiring more "empty" calories.
- A hard-worked poor person whose income rises because of a windfall or promotion to less heavy labour may well use and consume fewer calories. This person is more likely to use income increases to buy extra dietary energy when extra work is required, or in peak seasons.
- Estimates of calorie-income elasticity are usually based on the average sample member of the community. The poorest show much higher responsiveness.
- Different extents and speeds of response of household food security and DES to poverty reduction are also caused by variations in: health risk and care; work requirements; child care; intrahousehold gender discrimination; relative prices of foods and other needs; seasonality; and genetic factors affecting metabolism, weight, height and, therefore, food requirements.

However, these and other qualifications do not negate the strong causation between poverty and DES shortfall, food insecurity and PEM.

Self-sufficiency in staples is not an indication of national food security.

ENERGY ADEQUACY AND INADEQUACY: LEVELS AND TRENDS

Self-sufficiency in food staples and national food security

National food security (see Box 19) may be sought by increasing national staples self-sufficiency (NSSS), capacity to pay for staples imports, or stocks. A country's NSSS trends do not reveal trends in food security, although they help our understanding of its causes:

- For five of the eight staples of key interest to the food-insecure, trade affects a small and fluctuating proportion of total output; for at-risk countries where these are the main staples, trade dependence (the main indicator of NSSS trends) tells us little about food security.
- A country's degree of NSSS depends on global markets for wheat, rice and maize (which overwhelmingly dominate the staples trade), not just on the country's food security and policy towards it. Between 1948-50 and 1995-97, Western Europe's farm subsidies helped to cut its share in the world import volume of wheat, rice and maize from 62.6 to 16.1 percent; its export share rose from 5 to 17.9 percent. With

Box 19

NATIONAL STAPLES SELF-SUFFICIENCY: IS IT GOOD FOR FOOD SECURITY?

National staples self-sufficiency (NSSS) may or may not advance food security. India has attained NSSS, yet mass malnutrition remains. Indeed, NSSS in India is due not only to the green revolution's success in raising yields and output of rice and wheat, but also to persistent (albeit declining) poverty: staples output is "sufficient" for NSSS partly because the poor cannot afford adequate staples, i.e. they lack household food security (HFS).

As they develop, many countries shift production away from food staples, instead exploiting comparative advantages by increasing cash crop and/or industrial production, which is exported to buy more food. If these exports – as in Malaysia – raise employment incomes for the poor, the loss of NSSS can improve HFS. In Latin America and the Caribbean, staples imports rose from 0.9 percent of world food staples trade in 1962-70, to 5.7 percent in 1989-97, alongside big advances in nutrition. However, the rise during the same period in sub-Saharan Africa, from 2.7

such huge net supply rises, countries outside Western Europe are almost bound to move away from staples self-sufficiency.

- While policies aimed at NSSS, such as irrigation expansion and support for agricultural research in South Asia, have often been well conceived, in other cases the quest for NSSS readily turns into a policy of extracting rural produce cheaply to feed the cities, thereby creating perverse incentives that discourage farmers from growing more food, especially in Africa.[5]
- Above all, a greater degree of NSSS may mean better or worse HFS and PEM levels (Box 19).

A second indicator of NFS is the ratio of food imports to total exports. Given sufficient political will and functioning market and transport systems, countries with low ratios can respond adequately to poor harvests or sharp rises in food import prices. In 1988-90, 11 countries in Africa (including Ethiopia, Egypt and Mozambique) had food imports-total exports ratios of above 55 percent – levels that were seen elsewhere in the developing world only in Haiti, Samoa and Yemen. Such

to 4.7 percent, is less benign, since few countries achieved much expansion in non-staples employment or exports or, respectively, private or national capacity to buy staples imports.

Successful development usually involves two stages as regards NSSS. Stage one shows falling net staples imports as domestic staples production expands and is absorbed by people whose nutrition is thereby improved. Stage two shows rising net staples imports as later development shifts workers out of agriculture

and then shifts food consumption, as consumers become better fed and less poor, towards animal products – which require two to six times more grain per 1 000 human calories than direct cereals or bread consumption. The Far East's staples deficit as a share of world staples trade fell in stage one from 8.4 percent in 1962-70, to 4.7 percent in 1983-88. It then rose in stage two to 10.3 percent in 1995-97. Both stages saw big falls in PEM.

Can a greater degree of NSSS help HFS cost-

effectively, given its comparative advantage in:
- appropriate agro-ecologies;
- early development, where poverty reduction depends mainly on affordable rural workplaces; and
- countries or remote areas facing high risks or food transport costs?

Table 10
STAPLES IMBALANCES

	1961-63	1965-67	1975-77 (Million $)	1985-87	1995-97
Brazil					
1. Net staples imports	168.5	138.7	310.0	770.2	1 933.1
2. Non-staples exports	1 323.8	1 613.8	10 101.5	21 752.4	33 079.7
3. 1 as a percentage of 2	12.7	8.6	3.1	3.5	5.8
China					
1. Net staples imports	330.3	245.9	260.4	360.9	1 601.4
2. Non-staples exports	1 467.5	2 036.1	6 721.7	32 556.4	160 073.2
3. 1 as a percentage of 2	22.9	12.1	3.8	1.1	1.0
India					
1. Net staples imports	367.0	797.7	1 019.3	-175.3	-1 162.9
2. Non-staples exports	1 466.5	1 659.1	5 301.1	9 862.0	32 041.0
3. 1 as a percentage of 2	25.0	48.1	19.2	-1.8	-3.6
Indonesia					
1. Net staples imports	123.3	68.3	555.0	258.6	1 609.7
2. Non-staples exports	720.5	681.6	8 828.9	18 380.9	49 525.0
3. 1 as a percentage of 2	17.1	10.0	6.3	1.4	3.2
Kenya					
1. Net staples imports	-1.0	-1.3	-4.9	+17.1	112.4
2. Non-staples exports	169.6	234.7	810.5	1 041.9	2 074.3
3. 1 as a percentage of 2	-0.6	-0.6	-0.6	1.6	5.4
Mexico					
1. Net staples imports	19.6	74.6	329.4	434.0	1 397.2
2. Non-staples exports	840.9	1 036.7	3 382.2	20 332.7	57 340.6
3. 1 as a percentage of 2	2.3	7.2	9.7	2.1	2.4
Nigeria					
1. Net staples imports	18.6	21.0	296.5	378.5	422.0
2. Non-staples exports	496.3	741.1	10 102.1	9 045.4	16 246.5
3. 1 as a percentage of 2	3.7	2.8	2.9	4.2	2.6
Sudan					
1. Net staples imports	10.4	9.6	10.7	1 308.3	1 092.0
2. Non-staples exports	199.6	200.4	538.6	383.5	554.1
3. 1 as a percentage of 2	5.2	4.8	2.1	34.1	19.7
Former USSR					
1. Net staples imports	-378.3	69.3	2 138.0	3 612.0	1 906.7*
2. Non-staples exports	6 263.7	8 444.8	37 943.5	96 580.4	64 766.5*
3. 1 as a percentage of 2	-6.0	0.8	5.6	3.8	3.0*

* 1995 only.

*Source:*FAO.

countries tend to rely heavily on food aid. Table 10 tracks an even more relevant ratio, that of imports minus exports of food staples to non-staples exports, for some large countries.

This indicator gives a rather better guide to NFS than self-sufficiency. It does suggest the precarious food security situation in China in the early 1960s, in India when landless labourers' employment income was slashed by the successive disastrous monsoons of 1965 and 1966, and in the Sudan during episodes of civil war. However, the ratio must be used with care. Net staples imports can fall, not only because domestic supply is rising, but because people are becoming poorer and less able to afford sufficient staples. A rise in non-staples exports, as with petroleum in Nigeria, the former USSR and Indonesia, may do surprisingly little to improve staples availability via imports. If such export income accrues largely to owners of capital and/or governments who receive royalties but have other priorities than food security, little employment income is created for the poor and the income will not be used to buy food staples.

The ratio of stocks in public hands to normal consumption is also an indication of a country's NFS. In years of dearth, states can undertake large releases of staples. This helps the poor by suppressing the rise in prices. It also encourages the timely release of traders' hoards when prices start to rise; public capacity to act in this way in Bangladesh in 1984, but not in 1974, probably made the difference between famine and non-famine.[6]

Underfeeding: potential and actual DES

For the First and Second World Food Surveys,[7] FAO had measured *potential* underfeeding by setting national and regional mean daily "dietary energy supplies" (DES) per person against average requirements. Since the Third and, especially, the Fourth World Food Surveys, estimates of distribution of supplies were also taken into account. Supply estimates often depend on questionable output data, and requirements are controversial. However, sharp trends and major turning points in DES are usually significant, relating strongly to PEM outcomes and, hence, to HFS. Table 11, p. 212, provides summary DES data for a longer period.

Before 1939, "in areas containing over half the world's population, food supplies at the retail level [provided] less than 2 250 calories per caput daily.... Average total calorie supplies were around 2 000 or less in many large countries...".[8] Europe recovered rapidly from wartime shortages but the proportion of the world's people in countries with DES below 2 200 kcal per

Table 11

PER CAPUT DES IN SELECTED AREAS AND COUNTRIES, 1934-1997

	1934-38[1]	1946-49[2]	1961-63	1976-78	1988-90	1995-97
			(kcal/day)			
Africa			2 100	2 220	2 320	2 415
Sub-Saharan			2 040	2 060	2 080	2 190
Central[3]	2 060	2 080	2 150	2 150	2 050	2 080
East			1 980	2 040	1 960	2 010
West			2 090	2 030	2 200	2 400
Ghana			2 020	2 020	2 090	2 620
Uganda		2 100	2 240	2 250	2 170	
Kenya	2 230[4]	...	2 130	2 260	1 950	1 980
Mozambique			1 950	1 950	1 830	1 780
Nigeria			2 160	1 970	2 190	2 750
Asia			1 920	2 170	2 520	2 660
South	1 970	1 770	2 020	2 040	2 270	2 350
Bangladesh			2 090	2 040	2 050	2 080
Cambodia	1 850[5]	1 560	2 020	1 620	1 920	2 050
China	2 230	2 030	1 710	2 120	2 640	2 840
India	1 970[6]	1 700	2 040	2 040	2 290	2 470
Latin America/Caribbean			2 340	2 600	2 710	2 770
Central America			2 390	2 720	2 910	2 924
South America			2 350	2 570	2 650	2 790
Brazil	2 150	2 340	2 250	2 550	2 760	2 930
Mexico	1 800	2 050	2 530	2 880	3 080	3 110
Peru	1 860	1 920	2 170	2 120	2 120	2 360
Transitional countries			3 150	3 410	3 380	2 780
Eastern Europe	3 160	3 470	3 420	2 950		
Developing countries			1 960	2 200	2 490	2 627
Developed countries			2 970	3 190	3 300	3 220

[1] 1931-37 for China; 1935-39 for Brazil.
[2] 1949-50 for India and China.
[3] Central and Tropical for 1934-38 and 1946-49.
[4] Includes Uganda.
[5] French Indochina.
[6] Includes Pakistan.
Note: For this table, three-year averages were estimated from 1961-63 to 1995-97. Periods were chosen after 1961-63 to correspond to apparent "periods of change" in DES trends for several regions. FAO data are based on food balance sheets, i.e. they depend on the reliability of food production data which, for smallholder root crops and cereals in sub-Saharan Africa, are known to be weak. Small changes in short periods should be ignored. All data are rounded.
Sources: FAOSTAT; FAO. 1946. *The First World Food Survey.* Washington, DC; FAO. 1953. *The Second World Food Survey.* Rome.

day rose from about 40 percent just before the Second World War to about 60 percent in the late 1940s. "Over most of the Far East, where nearly one half of the world's population is concentrated, the declines [in DES] were about 10 percent." Average DES soon after the Second World War was 24 percent below requirements in India, 21 percent in French North Africa and 18 percent in Mexico.[9] Work effort, and to some extent basal metabolic rate and body size, "adapted" to such low intakes or requirements, fell but such adaptation was often harmful, resulting in widespread mortality, illness and mental and physical underperformance.

Table 11 suggests that DES in China, India and Kenya had, even by 1976-78, no more than recovered to the inadequate 1934-38 level, although DES in Latin America had improved sharply. The set of three-year averages confirms that 1976-78 was a turning point. India, China and some other Asian countries shifted from no change to rapid improvements in DES. In Central and East Africa, DES shifted from stagnation to steady decline. Interestingly, DES in West Africa showed no trend between 1961-63 (2 090 kcal) and 1982-84 (1 990 kcal), but then rose steadily to 2 400 kcal in 1995-97.

DES per caput in Asia and West Africa is now about 20 percent higher than in the mid-1970s, and in Latin America (from a much higher base) about 7 percent higher. In the same period, in East and Central Africa, DES appears to have fallen slightly by about 2 to 3 percent from already low levels. However, these DES estimates show that the national potential to reduce underfeeding has risen fast and far for the vast majority of inhabitants of at-risk countries – dramatically so in East Asia and Latin America. The fact that potential improvements in underfeeding (increases in average daily DES based on food balance sheets) do translate into actual improvements in the proportions of underfed people can be shown in two ways:

i) A few, long series of disaggregated, fairly reliable survey data measure year-round daily calorie intake directly per "consumer unit". In India the average intake rose from 2 061 in 1967 to 2 283 in 1989, but it rose faster among farm labourers (the poorest group) and children under five (those at greatest risk from a low DES).[10] Income distribution in India hardly changed over the period; clearly the poor were spending higher proportions of income on extra calories, thus translating a higher mean DES into better HFS.

ii) Box 20 reports regional FAO results, which estimate how

Box 20

CALORIC AND ANTHROPOMETRIC UNDERNUTRITION BY REGION

Region	Years	Undernourished population			
		Caloric[1]	Anthropometric status of children under five years		
		Population below 1.54 BMR	Wasted[2]	Stunted[2]	Underweight[3]
		(Millions) (%)	*(Millions) (%)*	*(Millions) (%)*	*(Millions) (%)*
ALL DEVELOPING COUNTRIES	**1969-71**	**918 35**			
	1979-81	**906 28**			**164.0 37.8**
	1990-92	**841 20**	**47.9 9.1**	**215.2 40.7**	**183.5 34.3**
East and Southeast Asia[4]	1969-71	476 41			
	1979-81	379 27			22.8 39.1
	1990-92	269 16	9.4 5.2	59.8 33.3	19.9 31.3
– China	1980				20.5 23.8
	1990				23.6 21.8
South Asia	1969-71	238 33			
	1979-81	303 34			89.9 63.7
	1990-92	255 22	26.6 17.1	92.7 59.5	101.2 58.5
Sub-Saharan Africa	1969-71	103 38			
	1979-81	148 41			19.9 28.9
	1990-92	215 43	6.1 7	33.7 38.8	28.2 29.9
Near East and North Africa	1969-71	48 27			
	1979-81	27 12			17.2
	1990-92	37 12	4.4 8.8	16 32.4	6.8 13.4

Region	Years	Undernourished population							
		Caloric[1]		Anthropometric status of children under five years					
		Population below 1.54 BMR		Wasted[2]		Stunted[2]		Underweight[3]	
		(Millions)	(%)	(Millions)	(%)	(Millions)	(%)	(Millions)	(%)
Latin America and Caribbean	1969-71	53	19						
	1979-81	48	14						
	1990-92	64	15	1.5	2.6	12.7	22.7	11.7	20.4
– Central America/Caribbean	1980							3.1	17.7
	1990							3.0	15.4
– South America	1980							3.1	9.3
	1990							2.8	7.7

Sources:
[1] FAO. 1996. *The Sixth World Food Survey*, Rome. More recent estimates of numbers of undernourished can be found in FAO. 1999. *The State of Food Insecurity in the World 1999.* Rome.
[2] FAO. 1996. *The Sixth World Food Survey.* Rome.
[3] UN ACC/SCN. 1992. *Second Report on the World Nutrition Situation*, Vol. 1, p. 67. Washington, DC; 2020 projections from M. Rosegrant, M. Agcaioli-Sombilla and D. Perez. 1995. *Global food projections to 2020: implications for investment.* Food, Agriculture and Environment Discussion Paper No. 5. Washington, DC, IFPRI.
[4] Southeast Asia only for "underweight", as separate data are given for China.
Definitions:
BMR: Basal metabolic rate.
Wasted: Wasting is a measure of a child's weight for height in relation to the median value of the US (NCHS) reference population. The cutoff point used here is -2 SD from the median. The figures in the table indicate the prevalence of *total* wasting (moderate and severe).
Stunted: Stunting is a measure of a child's height for age in relation to the median value of a standard reference population. The cutoff point is -2 SD from the median.
Underweight: Underweight is a measure of a child's weight for age in relation to the median value of a standard reference population. The cutoff point is -2 SD from the median.
(UNICEF. 1993. *Child malnutrition: country profiles.* New York.)

Higher food availability translates into reductions in undernourishment.

trends in potential undernutrition (measured in terms of average daily DES) between 1969-71 and 1990-92 translated into changing actual undernutrition: the numbers (proportions) of individuals with a basal metabolic rate (BMR) below 1.54 fell from 920 million (35 percent) to 840 million (20 percent) in 1990-92. The improvement was most dramatic in East and Southeast Asia (from 41 to 16 percent). It was substantial in other developing regions, except for sub-Saharan Africa where there was an increase from 38 to 43 percent, although improvements in the West African mean DES suggest that this may have been partly remedied since 1992 (Table 11, p. 212). Proportionate energy shortfalls for the underfed also fell, except in Africa. Thus, the regional pattern of increases in average DES or potential underfeeding is close to that of falls in actual underfeeding – proportion of populations with daily calorie intakes below 1.54 BMR – as estimated in the Sixth World Food Survey. These patterns are also close to those of trends in PEM. Both are fastest in East and Southeast Asia; moderate in the Near East and North Africa, in Latin America in the 1970s and in South Asia in the 1980s; and nil in sub-Saharan Africa. There have been huge improvements for some populations: in China DES rose by more than 60 percent from 1961-63 to 1994-96, and in the Republic of Korea at an even faster rate, so that obesity is more of a threat than PEM. However, although changes in PEM and DES are roughly consistent, continental levels show an HFS discrepancy. The results (see Table 11) suggest much worse underfeeding in sub-Saharan Africa than in South Asia, yet the proportions of stunted children – which are relatively reliable figures – are much lower (Box 20).

The recognized weakness of national food production estimates for most of Africa may suggest that estimates of mean DES in Africa are much too low – and, hence, the estimates of underfeeding, and implied lack of HFS, are much too high. But there is no evidence of a continentwide bias in that direction. Another explanation of the HFS discrepancy, which is borne out by mortality, famine prevalence and other evidence, is that smallness of body size, except at extremes, is less harmful in South Asia than in Africa. If this is so, South Asia's much more widespread smallness gives a less reliable guide to IFS than does Africa's much more widespread DES shortfall. In any case, countries and regions tend to show similar trends in stunting and DES (Box 20).

The huge improvement in DES, and also in PEM, is not a cause globally for easy optimism about food security. More than 800 million people are still seriously underfed in DES terms. Africa has not seen a secular improvement; and in the transitional economies, real DES may be declining. Above all, despite favourable signs in the heartlands of DES shortfall and of PEM (e.g. the spread of the fertility transition to Africa and the acceleration of growth in South Asia) the production and employment conditions for continuing rises in food entitlements may be fading, together with growth of employment and yields in food staples.

Household food security against PEM

The incidence of child PEM, measured as weight for height (wasting), height for age (stunting) or weight for age (underweight) is still shockingly high, even though it is falling. About 36 percent of children under five in the developing world – 197 million – were stunted in 1995, 29 percent were underweight and 9 percent were wasted, a condition that usually leads to hospitalization in rich countries. PEM is associated with

Table 12

DEVELOPING COUNTRY TRENDS IN PEM: PROPORTION OF CHILDREN UNDER FIVE WITH <2 SD BELOW US MEDIAN

UN region	Stunting				Underweight				Wasting
	1980	1990	1995	2000	1980	1990	1995	2000	1995
Africa	**40.5**	**37.8**	**36.5**	**35.2**	**26.2**	**27.3**	**27.9**	**28.5**	**9.6**
Eastern	46.5	47.3	47.7	48.1	24.9	30.4	33.2	35.9	7.0
Northern	32.7	26.5	23.3	20.2	17.5	15.6	14.8	14.0	7.2
Western	36.2	35.5	35.2	34.9	30.1	33.3	34.9	36.5	15.6
Asia	**52.2**	**43.3**	**38.8**	**34.4**	**43.9**	**36.5**	**32.8**	**29.0**	**10.4**
South and Central	60.8	52.2	48.0	43.7	58.1	50.9	47.3	43.6	15.4
Southeast	52.4	42.6	37.7	32.8	43.5	39.9	32.6	28.9	10.4
Latin America/ Caribbean	**25.6**	**19.1**	**15.8**	**12.6**	**14.2**	**10.2**	**8.3**	**6.3**	**2.9**
Caribbean	27.1	21.7	19.0	16.3	22.9	17.2	14.4	11.5	n.a.
Central America	26.1	25.0	24.5	24.0	15.1	15.2	15.3	15.4	4.9
South America	25.1	17.2	13.2	9.3	13.2	8.2	5.7	3.2	1.8
DEVELOPING COUNTRIES	**47.1**	**39.8**	**36.0**	**32.5**	**37.4**	**32.1**	**29.2**	**26.7**	**9.4**

Sources: ACC/SCN. 2000. *Fourth Report on the World Nutrition Situation.* Geneva; and WHO Global Database on Child Growth, 1990.

FAO/11231/Y. MULLER

Food insecurity as a result of natural disasters

A malnourished child is dwarfed by a ruined cereal crop in the Navrongo district of the Gambia, where two thirds of the crops were destroyed by drought

the deaths of some 6 million children each year, and with persistence into adulthood of incomplete mental development, reduced physical work capacity and damaged immune response for many millions more.

In terms of measurement, it is less problematic to assess PEM trends than levels. Table 12 shows a slow but consistent improvement in PEM indicators and, hence, in individual food adequacy outside sub-Saharan Africa. The pattern is confirmed by national surveys of children under five for stunting for 1980-1995[11] and low weight for age for 1976-1995.[12]

If we could compare all the 50-year periods in human history, 1950-2000 would almost certainly win first prize for speed, scale and spread of nutritional improvement. The falls in underfeeding came first in Europe; indeed, underfeeding (and probably PEM) rose in much of the developing world in 1945-60. The fall in PEM was most dramatic in East Asia, but it was also large in Latin America and South Asia. Only sub-Saharan Africa saw no improvement in DES and no fall in PEM. In 1985-2000, the decline in PEM slowed globally and reversed in transitional countries.

SECURITY AND INSECURITY: SPATIAL AND TEMPORAL VARIATIONS
Seasons, years and famines

Apart from inadequate "normal" energy supplies, vulnerable people are faced with the risk of sharp downturns – poor seasons and poor years. Improved average DES reduces food insecurity linked to poor seasons and poor years. So do the greater integration of food markets and public action to reduce nutritional and food price instability. Therefore, famines have been much rarer since 1945; since 1963 they have shifted almost wholly from Asia to Africa, and since the 1970s they have been largely confined to cases of war, civil war or the breakdown of a state. One reason for the retreat and relocation of famines has been the spread of political pluralism and openness; with rapid global communication technologies, including television, it is almost impossible for famine (as opposed to chronic, even fatal, undernourishment) to persist in an open and democratic society.[13] The risks of large famines have also been reduced by better early warning and response systems.

Famines causing more than 500 000 deaths in Asia have been virtually absent – in sharp contrast to the historical record – since the disaster in China in 1959-61. The worst subsequent Asian experience, in Bangladesh in 1974-75, cost fewer than 500 000 lives. Most deaths have been in sub-Saharan Africa, but only in Ethiopia (1984-85) did they approach 1 million.[14] Globally, there have been big swings in deaths resulting from famine or drought; periods such as 1982-86 saw "clusters" of war or civil breakdown in several drought-affected countries (Table 13). Seriously affecting 800 million

Table 13
DROUGHTS AND FAMINES, 1972-1996

Years	Average number of people killed by famine and drought	Average number affected	Average number made homeless
	(Thousands)		
1972-76	254	43 563	0
1977-81	0	52 123	0
1982-86	112	103 247	100
1987-91	2	75 852	10
1992-96	0.5	21 480	0

Source: International Federation of Red Cross and Red Crescent Societies. 1998. *World Disasters Report*. Oxford, UK, Oxford University Press.
Note: Entries of 0 and 0.5 obviously indicate very substantial underreporting.

Seasonal undernutrition has enduring consequences for physical and economic health.

people and causing 6 million deaths per year among children under five alone, since the mid-1960s chronic PEM has damaged far more people than have famines.

The incidence of severe seasonal worsening of nutrition has also almost certainly lessened, but there is much more evidence of the great harm that it does. In areas with fluctuations, people adapt to reduce stress, both behaviourally (storage, borrowing) and biologically (tending to deposit and release fat rather than lean).[15] However, some bad seasons are worse than normal, or follow previous bad harvests or economic downturns. And poor people, especially if they suffer low average DES and hence body size, face greater problems from seasonal stress and greater difficulties in coping with it. Human action makes a big difference: around 1994, some 370 million rural Asians and "only" 33 million Africans lived in areas that put them at nutritional risk from the effects of severe agricultural seasonality. However, the fact that irrigation and food entitlements are more widespread in Asia probably meant that more Africans than Asians were harmed by seasonal nutrition stress.

Seasonality especially harms food adequacy for three groups. Stillbirth rates increase if the hungry season occurs in the second trimester of pregnancy, and there is a higher mortality rate if it occurs at ages 6 to 12 months (as passive immunity is lost before it is fully replaced by active immunity).[16] Furthermore, children born in the hungry season face a sharply raised risk of age-specific death in adulthood. In the Gambia, the survival chances of more than 3 000 babies, born in different seasons, have been documented for more than 50 years, revealing "very marked ... raised mortality among adults born during the hungry season.... Infectious deaths [and their secondary effects] were the largest single [cause, suggesting] that early life events have caused permanent damage to the immune system".[17]

GROUP DISTRIBUTION AND FOOD SECURITY
Food and nutrition security is harmed for the rural, the remote, females, refugees and displaced persons, as well as for ethnic minorities and children,[18] by reinforcing disadvantages in three ways:
- Disadvantages *overlap* in food-insecure regions: disadvantages existing between gender and among ethnic groups, etc., overlap with those among illiterates, those in rural and remote areas, etc.[19]
- Disadvantages *cumulate* to reduce prospects of eating the right amount of the right foods, whether the main risk is undernutrition or overnutrition.

- Disadvantages harm many things at once, for example food consumption, access to production-based food entitlements (work, land and other assets) and mobility towards better prospects for production, consumption and, hence, nutrition.

Each of the following is normally more prevalent with than without each of the others: remoteness, rurality, discrimination against females, inadequate schooling, bad sanitation, absent or distant health care, poverty, heavy and seasonally peaked work even in pregnancy, and low calorie consumption per person.[20] In most developing countries, those in the "worst" quintile for all of these characteristics are likely to have 50 to 65 percent of the national average life expectancy and years of education, and double the age-specific death rate and periods of illness.

Rurality
Average energy consumption is usually somewhat higher in rural areas, but not among the poorest. In rural India, the poorest decile received only 1 212 kcal/person/day in 1972-73 (despite using 82 percent of consumption for food), as against a still shocking 1 316 (79 percent) in urban areas. Especially for employee households, work tends to be harder and infection more frequent and there are more pregnancies per woman in rural areas, so more food is needed. Confirming this, at the same level of income per equivalent adult, an increase leads to a larger rise in calorie consumption in rural than in urban areas. A greater food shortfall relative to requirements means that in rural areas stunting and wasting are typically at least 1.5 times more common than in urban areas.[21]

Since about 1980, owing to a reclassification of rural areas and to migration, the proportions of urban people suffering from PEM (and usually absolute urban numbers affected) increased. However, the already larger rural incidence of undernourishment usually diverged further from the urban incidence. The ratio of rural to urban incidence of stunting and wasting – as of poverty and early death – tended to rise, except in Africa, where the disparities had been greatest initially. The 60 percent of the world's population who live in Asia have seen big falls in undernourishment, child mortality and poverty risk, but mostly alongside some rise in rural-urban and regional divergence within nations.[22]

An aspect of the "reinforcing disadvantage" is that, even if both rural women and rural men fall behind their urban counterparts by the same proportion in nutrition indicators, rural women suffer more. Compared with urban women, their risk from low food consumption is worsened by less chance of trained attendance at childbirth and by a greater lag in education. To compound the damage in Asia and Africa, where undernourishment is worst, there is a larger proportion of rural women than rural men.

Region

In China, much of the rest of Asia and Latin America, remote, marginal, poorly watered or mountainous regions are the most liable to caloric undernutrition and to the other disadvantages that have an impact on death rates and on the development of those who survive: undersupply of health care, schools and roads, as well as a high proportion of residents suffering language or other discrimination, for example ethnic minorities. In Brazil, poverty explains only part of the much worse nutrition status in the north and northeast of the country than elsewhere; much of the rest is probably due to less access to health services.[23]

Assets

In some places (rural South Africa, northeastern Brazil) income is so unequal that even rapid growth has little impact on PEM or poverty. This is usually due in substantial part to extreme inequality of *assets*, especially land and education. Infant and child mortality, strongly linked to PEM, are often higher among landless labourers than among small farmers. Distributive land reforms have been linked with sharp falls in undernutrition and poverty.

There is ample evidence that households with an educated adult – especially a woman – have a higher standard of living and, even at a given level, have less PEM. Educated women marry later and have lower marital fertility. Their households are better nourished owing to more knowledge of food and farming and to higher worker-dependant ratios and less sibling competition.[24] Less widely recognized is the implication that, where education is especially unequally distributed (by region, gender or income group), PEM is higher than elsewhere – particularly among the most vulnerable (small children) owing to high fertility in uneducated households.

Gender

What is the role of gender in reducing PEM and/or overnutrition? In some countries, tests showed that stunting or low weight was much more prevalent than predicted from average DES. This is partly because of adaptation, but also partly because the gender distribution of DES and health care (and hence treatment of infections, which alters the efficiency of DES use) is especially unequal in some countries. This contributes to the unfavourable stunting and wasting status of India – North India, like Bangladesh and Pakistan, shows strong food discrimination against girls aged two to five years, with known harmful outcomes.[25] The same is probably true of Mauritania. The nutritional ill-effects of gender discrimination may rise even where nutrition is generally improving; in India, the incidence of adult body mass index (BMI) below 16 (third degree chronic energy deficiency) was 11.4 percent of men in 1975-79 but 8.8 percent in 1988-90, while for women the incidence only fell from 12.7 percent to 11.3 percent.[26]

Girls aged two to four years suffer serious disadvantages compared with boys in DES (relative to need) and/or access to health care – and as a result worse PEM – in many parts of Asia, but not in sub-Saharan Africa or Latin America.[27] Furthermore, girls almost everywhere have fewer chances of education than boys, so that women have less access to skilled work. Women also suffer discrimination in pay even for the same job or task, and more severely in access to land, legacies and credit. Although the evidence (especially in Asia) does not suggest a much greater poverty risk for women, their control over income is certainly less.

Apart from directly damaging the food security of women, these gender disparities harm children's food security, in two ways. First, income – including extra income – is more likely to be spent on improving the nutritional status of children under five if it accrues to women. Second, discrimination against small girls in feeding or health care not only cuts female life expectancy to the levels of males – elsewhere it is three to six years more – but is transmitted to later generations. Difficult pregnancies due to small womb size induce low birthweight, imperilling infant life and development. This helps explain why, for example, several South Asian regions suffer more frequent stunting and wasting than many African countries with lower calorie intakes and similar interhousehold distribution.[28]

International refugees and internally displaced persons

International refugees were estimated to total 1.8 million in 1960 and remained around 1.5 million to 2.5 million until 1976. They rose to a peak of 18 million to 19 million in 1991-92, then fell to about 12 million at the end of 1998. In sub-Saharan Africa, refugees and internally displaced persons (IDPs) fell from the 1995 peak of 16 million to 12 million in

1997; in Asia, the number of refugees fell from 5.8 million at end-1993 to 4.5 million at the end of 1995, plus more than 1.7 million IDPs.

However, IDPs often suffer extreme hunger or worse, especially when displacement is: sudden; results from violence, drought or natural disaster; is prolonged; separates victims from land or other means of production; or concentrates on women, children or the elderly. These victims, often without male heads of family (who are away fighting), face multiple threats to food entitlements, health and hence nutrition, especially among children. Well-funded refugee camps can substantially reduce PEM, as was the case for Afghan refugees to Pakistan and Kosovar refugees to nearby areas, or can achieve less (as in Angola and the Sudan) owing to underfunding, exacerbated by repeated bouts of civil violence, inducing inflows of refugees who are underfed even in normal times, disrupting food access, or obstructing food flows.

STAPLES PRODUCTION AND ACCESS TO FOOD
Changing perceptions of availability, entitlements and production, 1945-2000

This section shows that the conventional wisdom of postwar years – that very poor, mainly farming populations first escape poverty mainly by increasing their output of food staples – was quite wise after all, despite later swings of "development fashions". Between 1945 and 1965, emerging nations, which were accountable for food security but seeking to conserve foreign exchange for industrialization, emphasized self-sufficiency in food staples. Few analysts questioned tropical countries' comparative advantage in domestic staples production. This was therefore seen during this period as the key to *availability*, which was expected to ensure HFA/HFS. However, as land shortages began to be felt, price and allocation bias against agriculture, as well as distortions of farm markets, made it harder to attain food production goals.

Three changes occurred after the mid-1960s:
- The green revolution reached many Asian and Latin American smallholders.
- Land transfer to the poor – much more of it than conventional wisdom suggests – raised the rates of employment per hectare and (more modestly) yields per hectare, and resulted in greater emphasis on food in production.[29]
- From the mid-1970s, disincentives created by the anti-farm price bias weakened.

The resulting upsurge in smallholders' employment and

staples production provided a local source of food, together with employment-based income entitlements to it, thereby slashing poverty and PEM in much of Asia and Latin America between 1965 and 1988. Since the early 1980s, the following factors have weakened the emphasis on expanding staples production in areas where PEM remains:

- *Globally, population and effective demand have been far outpaced by staples output*, stimulated in Europe by subsidies, and in many developing countries by the green revolution. For 40 years, staples prices have fallen by some 0.4 percent per year relative to manufactures prices; despite droughts in Africa there has been no credible "global food scare" since 1972-74. From this it was concluded that extra staples production may be undesirable.
- *The global incidence of PEM (while still high) has fallen sharply.* Remaining PEM is seen to be due mainly to inadequate food *entitlements* – usually determined by poverty. From this it was concluded that more food production, even in places with PEM, will do little to reduce it; and that attention should shift from PEM to other nutrition issues, i.e. micronutrients, infections, food safety and problems of increasingly old, obese populations.
- *The progressive decrease in sustainable returns to water, land and agrochemicals have led to environmental stress.* From this it was concluded that one must beware both of intensifying staples production, especially on a narrow genetic base, in lead green revolution areas – irrigated, well-fertilized plains – and (more justifiably) of expanding production into marginal lands.

However, expanded local food production must still be seen as part of the cure for nutrition problems. PEM remains the world's main cause of death and misery. The great majority of its 800 million victims are afflicted mainly because they (or their working parents or children) lack employment-based entitlements to food, i.e. they cannot produce, or earn enough to afford, sufficient food. Extra food entitlements to reduce PEM and to accommodate the expected 50 percent increase in working-age populations in Africa and South Asia by 2020 to 2025 will continue to depend on rising employment or self-employment in farming, mainly food production.

Food staples production, yields and income from employment

In the developing world, falls in poverty, caloric underfeeding and PEM have generally accompanied rapidly increasing food

Those who are most food-insecure rely on nearby staple food production until they can diversify their income sources.

staples output. Table 14 shows why. People in these areas still depend mainly on farming and farm labour for employment income. For the poor, such income is overwhelmingly the main source of food entitlements. For the most food-insecure – the poorest, the rural, the remote – farm dependence is still higher. Increased staples production nearby, generating more employment and self-employment income to ensure entitlements to reliable supplies, is usually the key to food security, until enhanced farm growth followed by successful diversification has reduced employment dependence on farming towards current East Asian and Latin American levels.

The years 1945 to 1959 saw some acceleration of staples growth, based mainly on land area expansion and (in Asia) irrigation. From the late 1950s, with population growth and urban expansion, more and more prime agricultural regions ran out of quality spare arable land, while the number of people seeking work grew faster than ever, and industrialization proved either slower, or much less job-rich, than had been expected by the planners. Fortunately, 1965 to 1985 were golden years for yield growth of main staples in Asia and Latin America, as the green revolution increasingly provided varieties that were friendly to employment-intensive small farmers. Table 15 summarizes the outcomes since 1961.

As is shown in Table 15, yield growth in Asia and Africa shows a downward turning point around the mid-1980s, although timing varies among crops and regions. Moreover, although staples yield growth still generates much more employment per unit of extra GDP than, say, grazing, industry or construction (and than most urban activity), the employment effect declined: a 20 percent rise in wheat or rice yield in Asia

Table 14

PERCENTAGE OF WORKERS MAINLY DEPENDENT ON AGRICULTURAL INCOME

Region	1950	1960	1970	1980	1990	2000 [1]
East/Southeast Asia	76	71	64	56	51	41
South Asia	76	71	69	66	60	55
Sub-Saharan Africa	87	84	81	74	69	64
Latin America/Caribbean	55	50	43	35	26	21
All developing countries	**79**	**74**	**69**	**63**	**58**	**52**

[1] Estimate.
Source: FAOSTAT.

Table 15

RATE OF STAPLES YIELD GROWTH, 1961-1998

	Developing countries	East/ Southeast Asia	Latin America/ Caribbean	South Asia	Sub-Saharan Africa	All Africa
	(Percentage per year)					
Cereals						
1961-71	2.76	1.96	1.43	1.88	(0.29)	1.03*
1971-81	2.76	2.03	2.38	2.33	2.04	1.98
1981-91	1.86	1.67	0.74	3.09	(-0.07)	(0.75)
1991-98	1.55	0.86	2.72	1.7	(0.97)	(1.13)
1966-82	2.7	2.36	2.23	2.3	1.76	1.94
1982-98	1.67	1.35	2.05	2.69	(0.06)	0.75
Roots and tubers						
1961-71	2.95	(0.4)	1.57	4.13	0.65	0.65
1971-81	1.19	2.92	-0.77	1.73	1.44	1.52
1981-91	0.73	1.06	1.07	1.62	1.91	1.95
1991-98	0.99	(0.09)	1.02	1.09	(0.25)	(0.34)
1966-82	1.12	2.38	-0.56	2.04	0.52	0.61
1982-98	0.7	(0.21)	0.87	1.5	1.42	1.42

Sources: FAOSTAT. Author's regression data. Best-fit linear trend growth rates over each period.

Note: Numbers in parentheses mean trend is not significant; * significant at 10 percent; others significant at 5 percent.

led to about 8 percent more employment in the mid-1970s, but only 3 to 5 percent by the late 1980s. It is not surprising that the regional and temporal distribution of staples yield growth matches that of reduced poverty, underfeeding and PEM.

The "stylized facts" of poverty, food security and energy shortfalls are linked to those about staples production, employment and yields. This is not because more global food availability will cure hunger. It is because entitlements to more, nearby and reliable staples, generated mainly by work in producing them, remain for most of the world's at-risk people the initial escape route from both poverty and PEM; and because countries that industrialize almost always do so after successful staples yield growth.

The poor and malnourished obtain their claims to food largely from income, their own or that of parents or offspring, which almost always derives from work. The large majority of such income and work, as of the poor and malnourished themselves, is rural, and still will be in 2025.[30] Hence, the food entitlements of the poor and near-poor, who will remain mainly rural, will continue to depend largely on rural paid or self-employment income.

Growth in these rural work-based food entitlements can come

from growth in farming and growth in the rural non-farm sector (RNFS). RNFS growth, at least in low-income countries, usually depends on prior demand from a growing local agriculture, to which RNFS provides farm tools and inputs; processing and transport of farm outputs; and, above all, "consumption linkages" as rising farm incomes, especially among less well-off farmers and farm workers, are spent on local construction, trade, transport and other services.

Therefore, growth of rural employment income, and hence better food security for those at risk, will continue to depend mainly on nearby agricultural employment and income growth. Increasing migration to the cities does not invalidate this logic, for several reasons.

In most of Asia and Africa, where the majority of the food-insecure live and work, extension of farming into new lands is becoming, or is already, prohibitively costly (or even infeasible). Hence, expanded employment and self-employment income in agriculture is usually feasible only to the extent that:

- agriculture's total productivity factor grows enough to outweigh any falls in net farm prices, making it attractive or affordable for farmers to invest in more inputs, including family or hired labour; and/or

Employment in staple food production

Rural peasants in Myanmar use the land extensively for wheat production

- the organization of production changes, so that farm resources, especially land, are redistributed towards small and family farms, which produce more labour-intensively; and/or
- technology changes in a labour-using way, or incentives shift so that it is worth while for farmers to use a larger proportion of land labour-intensively, for instance, to produce vegetables instead of to carry out extensive grazing.

These three conditions usually stimulate each other, but agricultural productivity growth is the main source of extra demand for hired and self-employment on farms, and of better food security,[31] and it is mainly and increasingly constrained by land or water shortages. Therefore, agricultural employment and income growth, the main source of reduced food insecurity, will depend mainly on growth of farm output, usually implying higher yields per hectare or per litre.

Reducing food insecurity via farm employment: staples yield growth

Staple food production is a labour-intensive means of generating income.

Staples production is usually the main land use, employment source and output component of agriculture in most areas with serious food insecurity (i.e. in early development in low-income countries). Small farmers and landless labourers, the people most likely to be food-insecure, tend especially to concentrate on food staples production. This generates more employment per extra unit of land or of output than most alternative land uses. After successful early development in which extra employment and food security depend mainly on extra food staples production, land-scarce countries increasingly find that the comparative advantage shifts away from agriculture, and within agriculture away from food staples. But for food-insecure low-income populations, higher yields (per hectare and per litre) for food staples, and therefore extra employment and self-employment income in growing them, will be the main source of enhanced food security, at least until 2020.

Higher yields from staples production will be the main source of enhanced food security until at least 2020.

Three factors pose a threat to food security based on staples production: animal products, water availability and yield potential.

As incomes rise for the more affluent groups in the developing world, so more income is diverted from grains to animal products and total calorie intake is raised. Calories produced from meat or milk require three to seven times more cereal than grain. This may put upward pressure on staples prices and downward pressure on local availability, adversely affecting the poor. On the other hand, increased demand and prices for feedgrains may benefit farmers' incomes.

With urbanization and industrialization, both the demand and the need for water increase. There is considerable economic, ecological and political pressure to divert water away from agriculture. It will be difficult to obtain the increases in water-use efficiency needed to maintain, let alone increase, staples output in the irrigated heartlands of the green revolution in Asia and Central America. There will be increasing pressure to divert land to activities with more output per litre than staples production (and sometimes, although not always, lower employment). These problems will especially constrain output, yield and employment growth in rice, the thirstiest staple.

Cereal yield growth in developing countries has declined from an annual rate of almost 3 percent for 1967-82 to just above 1 percent in the 1990s. Yield potential, the best obtainable yield under trial plot conditions, with no limits on water, labour or agrochemical inputs, grew only very slowly for millets and sorghum in most semi-arid areas, including most of Africa. It was more rapid for maize, wheat and rice, as higher-yielding varieties became available in the early years of the green revolution in most of Asia and Central America. Farmers normally find it economically advantageous to achieve only 10 to 40 percent of yield potential, depending on agro-ecology, costs, risks and infrastructure for buying inputs and selling outputs. After a major improvement in yield potential, farmers normally move up to the new 10 to 40 percent economic "limit" in 10 to 15 years. After the early 1970s, yield potential rises resulting from the green revolution inevitably slowed down and shifted to improved defence against new pest biotypes. The slowdown in field yields in green revolution areas followed in the mid-1980s (in many areas no such improvement had taken place). The decline of real spending on agricultural research in Africa and Latin America, and its stagnation (and decline in 1999-2000) in the international system, signify a bleak future for yield potential and thus field yields in main staples.

Reducing food insecurity via distributive access: land, gender rights and food

It is sometimes said that no additional staples production is required to end PEM, given that it burgeons alongside vast unused grain stocks, not just globally or in rich countries, but even in India, because distribution is so unequal that the undernourished lack sufficient food entitlements. This lack is indeed the main cause of PEM. However, to rely solely on major, direct redistribution is to forget the slowness and/or rarity of this process and the political difficulties encountered.

More equal access to resources can improve the efficiency of farm production for some crops and in certain conditions.

Yet better distributive access can greatly help to get adequate food to the initially poor – via efficiency as well as via equity.

This is partly because small farms usually have higher yields and agricultural productivity, although not for all crops and conditions. Theory and (limited) evidence suggest that small farms do not usually lose their competitive edge following technical progress such as the green revolution, or most styles of liberalization and globalization. In addition to these efficiency arguments for land redistribution as a source of employment, and thus food security, there are equity arguments. Some countries and regions, despite upper-middle average real incomes, feature extreme inequality of landholding and income, resulting in widespread poverty and significant PEM; it is difficult to envisage their substantial reduction in, for example, South Africa or northeastern Brazil without land redistribution.

Even there, however, many of the poorest would not receive land from politically plausible redistribution. This is especially the case in countries such as Bangladesh, where some 25 percent of the farm population is functionally landless and where a 2 ha holding is large and a 10 ha holding exceptional. It is a mistake, however, to denigrate the contribution of land distribution to lowered PEM on these grounds. This contribution does not depend mainly on income from land, but on employment effects. The smaller the farm, and the larger the proportion of family workers, the lower the costs of screening, seeking and supervising labour, and the smaller the benefits of "shirking". Therefore, small farms normally use more hired labour per unit of land and much more family labour than large farms.

FROM ENERGY ADEQUACY TO NUTRITION SECURITY

Agriculture and health – combining food security and nutrition security

Over the last 50 years, the main global food issues have been famine, chronic hunger and PEM. These problems interact with other problems and, as they retreat, expose new problems. Hence, attention is paid increasingly to nutrition security. Although undernourishment still contributes to the deaths of 6 million children each year, other goals cannot be brushed aside: anaemia increases the mortality risk for more than 1.5 billion people worldwide; obesity (BMI >27.5) affects about a third of adults in the United States and will help kill at least another third. Yet, paradoxically, nutrition problems of late development, such as obesity, are genetically and behaviourally

Under- and overnourishment can exist simultaneously within countries.

rooted in those of underdevelopment, such as PEM. Moreover, a growing majority of countries are seriously affected by both sets of problems.

Moreover, in poor countries, adequate nutrition depends jointly on health and food. The huge fall in infant and child mortality is linked to the interaction between more (and more stable) food consumption and improved sanitation, immunization and health care. A classic study[32] proved this synergism in the poor villages of the Indian Punjab. A much larger fall in mortality and undernutrition was achieved when a fixed cash sum was divided between health care and nutrition supplementation, than when it was concentrated on one or the other.

Micronutrients – beyond food security in energy terms
Nutrition security requires overcoming key mineral and vitamin deficiencies, which often overlap and interact.

Iron deficiency anaemia (IDA) affects about one in three people worldwide and 43 percent of developing country populations. "All recent estimates of trends ... have failed to show significant improvement".[33] Global prevalence has risen since 1980 and increases among adult men have outweighed falls among women and children under five.

Severe IDA is the cause of one in five maternal deaths worldwide and is transmissible to children, causing stunting and vulnerability to infection. Even modest preschool IDA permanently reduces learning capacity and manual dexterity. A 10 percent rise in haemoglobin in a moderately anaemic person raises work capacity by 20 percent.[34]

Iron can be obtained from cereals, some vegetables and pulses, dairy products and meat – in sharply rising order of both iron content and bio-availability. As incomes rise, people turn from cereals to pulses and vegetables, and later to meat. Therefore, income growth should have reduced iron deficiency in Asia, where it is most serious. However, production changes have offset this: cereals showed more buoyant yields than pulses and displaced them, making pulse sources of iron scarce before most people could afford much meat.[35]

The risk of iodine deficiency diseases (IDD) in the 1990s affected some 2.2 billion people worldwide, of whom 740 million suffered from goitre. Estimates in about 1994 indicated 11 million people with cretinism and a further 43 million with mental impairment. IDD has declined dramatically: a great

FAO/20216/L. DEMATTEIS

Nutrition security

Adequate nutrition requires a diet that is both adequate and balanced, including essential micronutrients

success story for nutrition security policy. Following the iodization of salt, the proportion of people at IDD risk fell between 1994 and 1997 from 33 to 23 percent in Africa, from 23 to 7 percent in the Americas, from 43 to 30 percent in the eastern Mediterranean area, and from 29 to 14 percent globally.

Vitamin A deficiency (VAD) affects fewer people than iron or iodine deficiency. However, clinical (ocular) VAD can irreversibly harm children, while subclinical VAD raises mortality risk in pregnancy and impairs child development and iron utilization. Vitamin A is obtained largely from animal sources in high-income countries and Latin America, but elsewhere from green leafy vegetables, sweet potatoes and palm oil. The number of children under five in developing countries with clinical VAD fell from 5 million (1.1 percent incidence) in 1985 to 3.3 million (0.6 percent) in 1995. Subclinical VAD is much more prevalent, affecting an estimated 75 million to 250 million children under five.[36]

Other deficiencies, such as zinc, calcium and dietary fibre deficiency as well as excess sodium, are also probably widespread and are increasingly receiving attention. As people become richer, they diversify their diets and raise their consumption of animal products, fruit and vegetables. This reduces the risk of iron, zinc and Vitamin A deficiency substantially. These changes help the poor mostly in middle-to-late economic development. The very poor cannot afford to use income gains, if any, to buy micronutrient-rich fruit, vegetables or animal products. Yet these people are the ones most likely to be nutrient-deficient and untreated. Therefore, it is important to increase key micronutrient levels in their main cheap foods: staples. In 1999, much higher levels of iron and Vitamin A were introduced by transferring genes from other plants into rice. This indicates a vital line of research.

Overnutrition, diet-related diseases, development and diet composition

Overnutrition relative to reduced activity levels (and linked with diets containing excessive animal fats, salt and sugar, and deficient fibre) is a major cause of obesity, high blood pressure, coronary heart disease, diabetes and some cancers, leading to premature adult death and disability in old age − in developed countries.

Prevalence data show that nutritional diseases of "affluence" are already significant, not only among the poor in rich countries, but even (spreading down the income scale) in countries with widespread PEM. By 1995, 3.3 percent of children under five (18 million) were overweight in the developing world; in North Africa the proportion was higher than 8 percent (in the United States it was 7.4 percent). Obesity in urban areas far exceeds that in rural areas in a range of developing countries. By being obese, children under five more than double the risk of obesity in adult life.[37]

Lower-income groups are "differently food-insecure". In poor countries they are the most prone to PEM and deficiency conditions, eating too little food of which too small a proportion is from animal sources, which provide concentrated and accessible vitamins, iron and zinc as well as energy. In rich countries, they are the most prone to obesity and resulting disease and death and, often with low energy use, eat too many calories − and too many from fat and animal sources.

Food diversity is a main source of food security (against diseases of affluence as well as poverty, and to permit full discharge of "capabilities and functionings"). It is the indicated weapon against overnutrition and undernutrition alike, although that does not contradict the priority for increased income-based entitlements to cheap energy sources for sufferers from PEM. Food diversity improved between 1969-71 and 1990-92 in all regions and all types of economies, as is indicated by a falling proportion of calories derived from a country's main food group. Increasing trade, travel and urbanization have diversified food baskets in a large number of countries. Static health gains apart, this reduces the dynamic risk from crop failure or price rises for a single food source. Pressures towards diversity, except in the remotest areas and for some of the many people who are still too poor to consume enough calories, have more than offset "homogenization". In addition, globalizing shifts in local staples consumption have generally not damaged, but have rather been led by, or are conducive to, local staples production.[38]

POLICY IMPLICATIONS AND CONCLUSIONS

This review points to a number of areas for policy action to significantly reducing poverty and undernutrition. These areas concern smallholder staple food production, equity and redistribution, disadvantaged and vulnerable groups and nutrition security. Policy decisions relating to trade, market liberalization and the environment will also play a determining role in achieving food security on a sustainable basis.

Reducing poverty and improving nutrition through staples production

A first policy priority emerges from the fact that staples yield growth, which is a key factor for poverty reduction and food security in the early stages of development, has been on the decline since the mid-1970s. This requires renewing progress in staple yield potential.

Researchers and policy-makers must address the reasons why the green revolution:

- lost momentum (best areas fully exploited, new pest biotypes, water and plant micronutrient scarcities, and lack of promising intraspecific germplasm in robust low-yield crops);
- failed to benefit most "complex, diverse, risk-prone" semi-arid and marginal farming;
- became less employment-creating per unit of yield increase; and
- lost funds and skills from open-access public research in the age of biotechnology, as agricultural scientists and patents were "locked into" a few private firms in rich countries.

A second labour-intensive, nutrition-improving green

revolution requires more funds for public sector agricultural research; a renewed focus on plant breeding; buying in biotechnology skills from the private firms that now control them; and stress on less-favoured regions, sustainable water use and labour-intensive cultivation of staples on smallholdings.

The need to expand local food employment for individual food security, while mainly a national issue, validates international concern with agricultural, land-water environmental research and institutional prerequisites for rising smallholder food yields in developing countries.

The role of redistribution in achieving staples-based household food security

Household food security is assisted by higher yields of food staples, which in turn are facilitated by better access to land, credit and institutions. Land redistribution is particularly important given the extremely unequal landholding and farm income situation, resulting in widespread poverty and food insecurity in some countries and regions. Land redistribution (not tenancy reform, which has the opposite effect – encouraging landlords to evict and consolidate into bigger, less labour-using owner-farms) is a powerful source of employment-based entitlements to food, and also means more land sown to staples, as small farmers reduce the risk posed by price rises in retail food markets.

Land reforms between 1950 and 1980 achieved far more than fashionable scepticism suggests. But, as with the green revolution, revival requires awareness of why progress slowed (many countries have little land left in large holdings; political conditions, global and local, for old-style land reform are less favourable). Yet, in labour-surplus economies (where widespread undernutrition is found), market advantages favour labour-intensive small farms. It is therefore worth exploring land reform "with the grain of the market". A second wave of nutrition-improving land reforms might result in making farm units smaller and more equal voluntarily by: i) removing selective support from rich farmers' inputs (especially water); ii) focusing water, market-access facilities, training, credit and research on small farms (and on the poor people trying to buy them); and iii) assisted or voucher-based schemes for poor farmers to obtain farmland.

National staples self-sufficiency and food security

More food self-sufficiency may imply better or worse food security conditions for a country. It can be sought by "flexible", good policies such as irrigation programmes or agricultural research. But quests for self-sufficiency may turn to extracting rural produce cheaply to feed cities, creating perverse incentives, harming food output and employment and worsening undernutrition.

Development typically involves two stages with regard to food imports (see Box 19, p. 208), and policies need to work with the sequence: in the phase of declining recourse to food imports, sound food self-sufficiency policies (that take into account comparative advantage, logistic and agro-ecological conditions), achieved through labour-intensive activities (especially in smallholdings), can reduce undernutrition. In the later development phase, when net staples imports increase (financed by exported manufactures and services, which themselves employ the poor and give them more food entitlements), policy action will further contribute to reducing undernutrition by promoting labour-intensive shifts out of staples production.

It must be stressed, however, that stage two is a viable option only after the phase of staples employment and output growth. China's famine of 1960 and India's near-famine of 1965-66 show that sidelining local growth of food staples yields before non-farm employment takes off has disastrous results for food security.

Coping with fluctuations in food supply and access

Subsidized food distribution must be limited and well targeted.

Poor people, with a low calorie intake and, hence, body size, face greater problems from seasonal stress and greater difficulties in dealing with it. Policy options can help households' seasonal stress management. Fluctuations in employment income can be reduced by appropriate policies for robust and peak-spreading farming via irrigation, pest management and appropriate new varieties. A higher proportion of Asians than Africans is affected by severe agroclimatic seasonality, but a lower proportion is harmed. The difference is made by the existence in Asia of more widespread irrigation, public works and transport options.

Subsidized food distribution from public stocks is usually not directly targeted at the poor but helps them in years of dearth by encouraging the earlier release of traders' hoards, thereby limiting price rises. It is crucial to ensure that public stock releases reach needy, drought-affected and remote regions. No large country with undernutrition problems can sensibly dispense with public grain stocks, but their size in some countries such as India – often representing 10 percent and sometimes even 20 percent of domestic staples production –

237

involves huge costs in forgone public investment. Accordingly, policy managers should explore alternative methods (such as purchased liens on farmers' stores, or forward or options contracts in international markets) that might achieve more household food security at less cost. International agency guarantees for such market-friendly and cost-cutting national food security policies would be needed; they could feasibly be provided on a trial basis for small countries.

Household coping mechanisms that reduce vulnerability to shocks include credit and other arrangements for smoothing consumption; policy can support these, for example, by encouraging consumption microfinance for the poor where sustainable.

Focusing on vulnerable and disadvantaged groups
Household food security can be improved in these groups by direct food distribution, food-for-work, food subsidy or emergency relief schemes. Again, the employment link should be stressed: food-for-work can enhance working capacity, productivity and incentive; the work can produce further food and/or entitlements to it. Including the needy, excluding the greedy, cost containment and appropriate incentives are difficult issues. However, examples exist of strikingly cost-effective and well-targeted interventions that have accelerated nutritional improvement and avoided serious disincentive effects.

In a long-term perspective, basic education constitutes the best investment in favour of the most disadvantaged groups. Education improves farm productivity and income, among labourers as well as farmers. Educated women marry later, and have lower marital fertility. Their households are better nourished as a result of more knowledge of food and farming and of higher worker-dependant ratios and less sibling competition. Where education is very unequal (by region, gender or income group), undernourishment is higher than elsewhere – especially among the most vulnerable (small children), owing to high fertility in uneducated households.

In some areas, energy adequacy and household food security would be improved by redistributing control over income and assets towards women, for instance by reducing educational discrimination against girls and creating or enforcing women's legal rights to inherit land.

The environment and food security
Both food security and the environment can gain from better policies. Trade-offs exist but they are often a result of the wrong

incentives or institutions: "thirsty" food crops, notably rice, imperil sustainable water use where rice is subsidized relative to other crops, water relative to other inputs and urban relative to (potentially water-economizing) rural investment.

The environment and household food security gain from: correcting anti-employment and anti-environment incentives; and building on the key role of employment income for food entitlements, especially in periods of slack season and "off-year" employment. Schemes can be designed to substitute employment for environment, for example by using, or designing, soil- or water-saving public works.

From household food security to nutrition security: combined policy

Developing countries must tackle nutrition problems of late development, such as obesity, jointly with those of undernourishment, because: i) they have both already; ii) resource allocation between them is biased by political structures; and iii) mishandling present PEM and micronutrient deficiencies greatly increases death and illness from overnutrition 20 to 50 years later. Policy action is thus required in the form of incentives and public sector allocations. Two other problems, micronutrient deficiencies and food safety, which are shared in different forms by the wasted and the obese, underline the need for a combined nutrition security policy for agriculture, nutrition, health and the environment.

As the benefits of economic advances, and subsequent ageing of the population, spread from the better off to others, it is important that changes in diet and activity patterns spread too. This involves timely changes in incentives and institutions in agriculture, food markets, medical systems and education.

NOTES

1   R. Eastwood and M. Lipton. 1999. The impact of changes in human fertility on poverty. *Journal of Development Studies*, 36(1): 1-30.

2   A.K. Sen. 1981. *Poverty and famines: an essay on entitlement and deprivation.* Oxford, UK, Clarendon Press.

3   World Bank. 2000. *World Development Report 2000/2001.* New York, Oxford University Press.

4   S. Yaqub. 1999. *Poverty in transition countries: what picture emerges from UNDP's National Human Development Reports?* Working Paper No. 4. Brighton, UK, Poverty Research Unit, Sussex University.

5   A. Krueger, A. Valdes and M. Schiff. 1996. *The mulcting of agriculture in developing countries.* Washington, DC, World Bank.

6   M. Ravallion. 1997. Famines and economics. *Journal of Economic Literature*, 3: 1205-1243.

7   FAO. 1946. *The First World Food Survey.* Washington, DC. (5 July)

8   Ibid.

9   FAO. 1953. *The Second World Food Survey.* Rome.

10 K. Bagchi. 1992. *Impact of four decades of development on nutrition and health status in India.* Rome, FAO/WHO Joint Secretariat of the International Conference on Nutrition.

11 ACC/SCN. 1997. *Third Report on the World Nutrition Situation.* Geneva.

12 FAO. 1996. *The Sixth World Food Survey.* Rome.

13 Sen, op. cit., note 2.

14 Ravallion, op. cit., note 6.

15 P. Payne and M. Lipton. 1994. *How third world rural households adapt to dietary energy stress: the evidence and the issues.* Food Policy Review No. 2. Washington, DC, International Food Policy Research Institute; A.E. Dugdale and P.R. Payne. 1987. A model of seasonal changes in energy balance. *Ecology of Food and Nutrition*, 19: 231-245.

16 S. Schofield. 1974. Seasonal factors affecting nutrition in different age-groups and especially pre-school children. *Journal of Development Studies*, 11(1): 22-40.

17 A.M. Prentice. 1999. *Early nutritional programming of human immunity.* Annual Report 1998. Lausanne, Switzerland, Nestlé Foundation.

18 Children are disadvantaged indirectly, because concentrated where PEM is especially prevalent: the households of the poor, large families, rural and remote areas with delayed fertility transitions.

19 M. Lipton, S, Osmani and A. de Haan. 1997. Quality of life in emerging Asia. Background paper for *Emerging Asia: changes and challenges.* Manila, Asian Development Bank.

20 A household tends to have higher child-adult ratios, and hence reduced

caloric *requirements*, if (other things being equal) it is: in the poorest decile; rural; remote; poorly educated. However, many indicators, for example differential mortality, show that requirements are reduced less than consumption.

21 J. von Braun, J. McComb, B. Fred-Mensah and R. Pandya-Lorch. 1993. *Urban food insecurity and malnutrition in developing countries: trends, policies and research implications.* Washington, DC, IFPRI.

22 Among the Chinese poor, however, rural and urban calorie consumption converged in the 1980s, probably because many hungry rural migrants moved to cities, where they seldom obtain either urban or rural social security benefits. See R. Eastwood and M. Lipton. 2000. Changes in rural-urban inequality and urban bias. *In* G. Cornia, ed. *The upturn in inequality within nations since 1980;* and M. Lipton, A. de Haan and S. Yaqub. 2000. Poverty in emerging Asia. *Asian Development Review* (March).

23 WHO. 1991. *Country studies in nutritional anthropometry: Brazil.* Geneva.

24 M. Livi-Bacci and G. de Santis, eds. 1998. *Population and poverty in developing countries.* Oxford, UK, Clarendon Press.

25 A. Bhargava and S. Osmani. 1997. Health and nutrition in emerging Asia. Background paper for *Emerging Asia: changes and challenges.* Manila, AsDB.

26 Bagchi, op. cit., note 10.

27 B. Harriss. 1986. *The intra-family distribution of hunger in South Asia.* Helsinki, World Institute for Development Economics Research; M. Lipton. 1983. *Poverty, undernutrition and hunger.* Staff Working Paper No. 597. Washington, DC, World Bank; P. Svedberg. 1989. *Undernutrition in Africa: is there a sex bias?* Stockholm, Institute for International Economic Studies.

28 Bhargava and Osmani, op. cit., note 25.

29 M. Lipton. 1993. Land reform as commenced business: the evidence against stopping. *World Development,* 21(4): 641-57.

30 Net remittances of urban incomes to the rural poor are important in a small, although growing, number of exceptional areas, but the cost of an urban workplace – capital, infrastructure and congestion – is much higher, even in the informal sector, than in rural areas.

31 Unless such growth is induced by a labour-displacing technology.

32 C. Taylor *et al.* 1978. The Narangwal project on interactions of nutrition and infections: 1. Project design and effects upon growth. *Indian Journal of Medical Research,* 68 (Suppl.) (December).

33 ACC/SCN. 2000. *Fourth Report on the World Nutrition Situation.* Geneva.

34 ACC/SCN, op. cit., note 11.

35 ACC/SCN. 1992. *Second Report on the World Nutrition Situation.* Geneva.

36 ACC/SCN, op. cit., note 33.

37 Ibid.

38 M. Lipton, A. de Haan and E. Darbellay. 1999. Food security, food consumption patterns and human development. In *Human Development Papers 1998: consumption and human development*. New York, UN, Human Development Office.

Agricultural production and productivity in developing countries

INTRODUCTION

In the second half of the twentieth century, farmers were presented with an unprecedented increase in the demand for food. In the first half of the century, the world's population grew by 960 million people. In the second half, the increase was 3 690 million people. The population of the developing countries as a whole increased from 1.8 billion to 4.7 billion during the second half of the century, an increase of 260 percent. In addition, per caput income, another factor that affects food demand, also grew in many developing countries over the period.

Farmers were presented with this demand challenge at a time when much of the land suited for cultivation was already used for crop production. In 1950, farmers in many countries were farming land intensively, with significant levels of irrigation and multiple cropping. In most areas it was not feasible to meet the demand challenge simply by expanding cultivated area. (Some regions, however, did have the potential for cropland expansion, e.g. part of Africa and the Cerrado region in Brazil.)

Figure 21 shows cereal production, imports and food aid per caput for the periods since 1961. While these data do not cover all categories of food or agricultural production, they do reflect the main trends of recent decades in five developing and four developed country regions.

These data are reported in per caput terms, allowing comparison by both region and time period. It may be noted that the apparent per caput consumption of cereal grains is highest in developed countries. This reflects high rates of cereals fed to livestock (and the fact that feed conversion to livestock product rates are low).[1] For developing regions, where cereals are mostly consumed as foodgrains, per caput consumption is lower. Sub-Saharan Africa has the lowest levels because root crops are important in Africa. In South Asia, per caput consumption is also low, reflecting the fact that low levels of cereal grains are fed to livestock

Over the periods depicted, cereal production per caput rose significantly in Latin America, South Asia and the Far East. It

243

Figure 21
CEREAL PRODUCTION, TRADE AND FOOD AID, 1961-1997

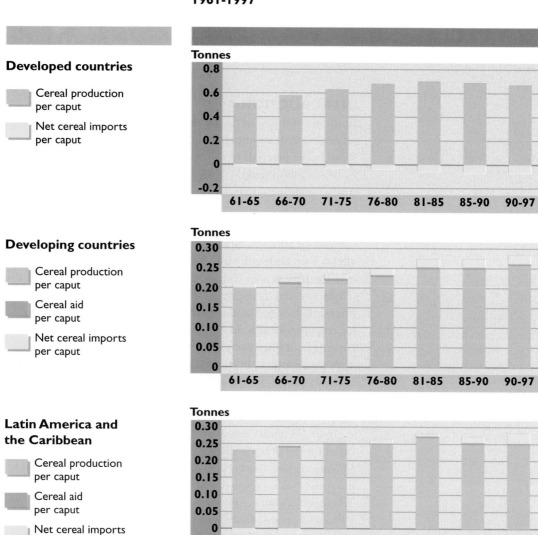

Developed countries

- Cereal production per caput
- Net cereal imports per caput

Developing countries

- Cereal production per caput
- Cereal aid per caput
- Net cereal imports per caput

Latin America and the Caribbean

- Cereal production per caput
- Cereal aid per caput
- Net cereal imports per caput

Sub-Saharan Africa

- Cereal production per caput
- Cereal aid per caput
- Net cereal imports per caput

Figure 21 (continued)

CEREAL PRODUCTION, TRADE AND FOOD AID, 1961-1997

Near East

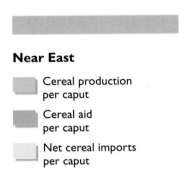

Cereal production
per caput

Cereal aid
per caput

Net cereal imports
per caput

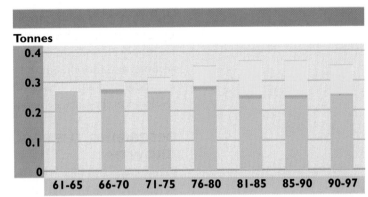

Far East

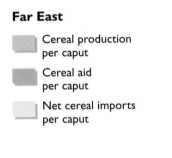

Cereal production
per caput

Cereal aid
per caput

Net cereal imports
per caput

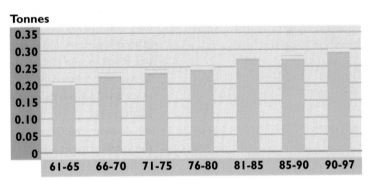

South Asia

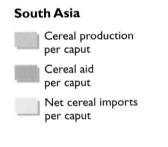

Cereal production
per caput

Cereal aid
per caput

Net cereal imports
per caput

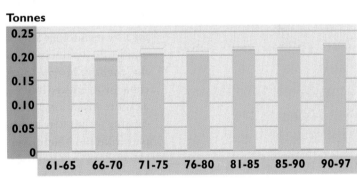

East and Southeast Asia

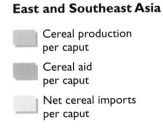

Cereal production
per caput

Cereal aid
per caput

Net cereal imports
per caput

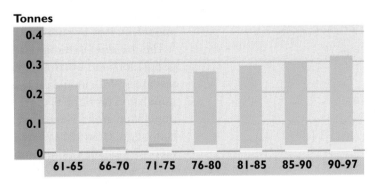

Source: FAO

Agricultural production has increased enormously but unevenly over the past 50 years.

declined in sub-Saharan Africa and the Near East from 1961 to 1981 but has risen in subsequent periods (note that the largest increase in population in these regions occurred after 1981).

Such a per caput production performance can be characterized as both extraordinary and uneven. Extraordinary in view of the massive increase in population; uneven because it has not been uniform over all regions and countries. This section examines the production record and the developments in productivity that lie behind it, both at the aggregate or global level and at the local or national level.

DESCRIBING THE PROCESS OF AGRICULTURAL GROWTH

Economists and historians have offered several different perspectives on the agricultural growth process. These include:

- the *Malthusian-resources* perspective,[2] stressing limited land and water resources and diminishing returns to labour as the labour force per unit of resources increases;
- the *institutional change* perspective, stressing reductions in transaction costs and improved economic efficiency associated with legal systems, property rights and other institutions;
- the *human capital* perspective, stressing improvements in the management and production skills of farmers and of the providers of services to farmers;
- the *best practice* (technology diffusion) perspective, stressing the organizational capacity (agricultural extension) to search for new technology and enable farmers to adopt more rapidly the technology available to them;
- the *adaptive invention* perspective, stressing the building of capacity to engage in technology development through adaptive invention, i.e. through modifying and improving existing technology to adapt it to local conditions.

Apart from the Malthusian-resources perspective, these perspectives are not mutually exclusive. The Malthusian-resources perspective, however, focuses on the economic growth process when institutions and human resources are unchanging and technology invention and diffusion are not taking place.

The *Malthusian-resources* perspective draws attention to both population (and workforce) growth and available land and water resources. With abundant land and water resources, the ratio of population (workforce) to resources need not decline as the population grows, since more land can be brought under cultivation. However, as land (and water) frontiers are closed, the ratio of population to resources will rise and bring about a

The "demographic gift" allows a country to increase investment and savings while its workforce grows.

decline in per caput production. The Malthusian-resources perspective leads to a policy emphasis on population growth reduction. It does not formally recognize the *demographic burden/gift.*

The demographic burden/gift effect is based on differences in the growth rates of population and of the workforce. When growth rates rise, as they did in virtually all developing countries during the 1940s and 1950s, population growth exceeds workforce growth for a number of years simply because of the fact that children and young people do not become workers until they reach a certain age. This creates a consumption burden. Conversely, when population growth rates decline, as they have in most developing countries since the 1950s and 1960s, a demographic consumption gift occurs as growth in the workforce exceeds growth in population. Most developing countries have experienced (at different times) a burden-gift cycle since 1950. The demographic gift is important, even when the Malthusian-resources perspective is valid.

An extension of the Malthusian-resource model recognizes that population growth or population density may actually stimulate investments in institutional and technological change, thus providing its own "antidote" to the diminishing returns feature of the model.

The institutional change, human capital, best practice and adaptive invention perspectives all depart from the Malthusian-resources perspective by introducing dynamics that enable producers to produce more with the same amount of resources (labour, land, etc.). That is, they introduce productivity change (see Box 21 for the arithmetic of agricultural productivity). Each of these perspectives is associated with the development of what here will be referred to as technological capital (TC), which represents a country's capacity to implement, adapt and develop productivity-enhancing technology.

The *institutional change* perspective addresses inefficiencies associated with transaction costs and imperfect markets. Infrastructure investments reduce transport and other costs, and can reduce transaction costs as well. Investments in institutions (credit institutions and legal systems) have been important for agricultural economies. Improved institutions and infrastructure provide a source of growth in per caput food production even in Malthusian-type economies, where few or no changes take place in the technology actually available to farmers.

The *human capital* perspective stresses that farm management skills and farm production skills (farmer human capital) can be improved through investment in training

Box 21

THE ARITHMETIC OF GROWTH IN AGRICULTURE

Crop production (P) can be expressed as area (A) times production per unit area or yield (Y):

$$P = A \times Y$$

The rate of growth in P (G_P) is simply the sum of the rate of growth in area (G_A) and the rate of growth in yield (G_Y):

$$G_P = G_A + G_Y$$

Production of crops (or livestock) (P) can also be expressed as a function of inputs, such as area (A), workers (W), machine services (M) and fertilizers (F):

$$P = F (A, W, M, F)$$

The rate of growth in production (G_P) can then be expressed as the cost-share weighted sum of the rate of growth in the production inputs plus a residual term measuring growth in total factor productivity (TFP) (G_{TFP}):

$$G_P = S_A\, G_A + S_W\, G_W + S_M\, G_M + S_F\, G_F + G_{TFP}$$

This expression effectively defines TFP, which is the ratio of production (P) to an aggregated factor index (I). The growth in I is:

$$G_I = S_A\, G_A + S_W\, G_W + S_M\, G_M + S_F\, G_F$$

$$G_{TFP} = G_P - G_I$$

TFP growth is, therefore, the difference between actual production growth (G_P) and the production growth that would have occurred (G_I) if farmers had not changed the technology of production or their own efficiency behaviour. Growth in production can be achieved through increased factor use or through a more efficient use of production factors. It is the latter that is expressed by the TFP growth.

(schooling) programmes, experience and agricultural extension programmes. Investments in farming human capital can thus produce growth in per caput food production.

The *best practice* perspective focuses on the fact that, at any given time, farmers may not yet have tested and adopted existing technology that would reduce costs and produce growth because of failures in the information and demonstration systems available to them. Investments in agricultural extension systems will then produce growth in food production per caput by bringing farmers closer to best practice technology use.

Finally, the *adaptive invention* perspective emphasizes that agricultural technology is location-specific to a considerable degree. Biological processes are sensitive to soil, climate and even economic conditions. Natural "Darwinian" evolutionary change produced a rich diversity of species, resulting in natural differences in plant and animal life in each ecological niche. Farmers only partially overcame this niche phenomenon when they selected the landraces (farmers' varieties) that today constitute the genetic resource stock utilized by modern plant (and animal) breeders as they search for varietal (and breed) improvements. Modern plant breeders must also respect soil and climate factors and tailor varietal improvements to regions or niches. This means that technology that is valuable in one location may not be valuable in another. It also means that targeted invention (plant breeding) programmes can produce growth in per caput food production.

The Malthusian-resource perspective has, however, been linked to the other perspectives in a number of economic studies that address the relationships between population growth (relative to resources) and the policies and investments inherent in the institutional change, human capital, best practice and adaptive invention perspectives. One linkage is through population-induced changes and investments.[3] Studies of this linkage usually focus on the demographic burden. The second linkage is through the complementary relationship between the demographic gift and institutional changes and investment.[4]

THE ROLE OF INVESTMENTS IN INCREASING AGRICULTURAL PRODUCTIVITY

It must be emphasized that even the institutional change perspective is linked to investments, particularly investments in the production of public goods.[5] The proper role of government in a market economy is to devise and administer institutions

Agricultural sector growth requires investments from the public sector.

(legal systems, regulations, competition policy) that provide incentives for efficient private (farm) production while, at the same time, investing in the provision of public goods where appropriate. In practice, governments in many developing countries have often intervened in markets in inappropriate ways and have invested in state-owned production enterprises that have been inefficient. In recent decades, reform movements have been undertaken in many countries to privatize inefficient state-owned enterprises and to eliminate marketing boards and other cumbersome regulatory agencies. Some of these reform movements, however, have not fully appreciated the historical role of public goods in agriculture in all economies. Public sector investment in rural schools, agricultural extension and applied agricultural research has been vital to agricultural development in every economy in the world. Institutional reform without investment in these public goods does not produce economic growth in the agricultural sector. Growth is not produced by passive "let the markets work" policies that do not include critical public investment programmes.

The interrelationships between these public good investments are illustrated in Figure 22, which depicts schematically the process of improving agricultural productivity through technological progress, represented by five subsequent levels of technological capital (TC). For each TC level, four crop yield levels are shown for a given location. These are: (A) actual farm yield in this location; (BP) best practice yields, i.e. the profit-maximizing yields that are achieved when farmers use the best practices and technology suitable for this location; (RP) research potential yields, i.e. the yields that could be best practice yields if an applied adaptive research programme targeted to this location were in place; (SP) science potential yield, i.e. the yield level that could be the best practice yield if the applied adaptive research programme were supported by international and national "pre-invention science" programmes.

Associated with these yields, three "gaps" can be defined:
- The *extension gap* (BP − A) is the difference between best practice (BP) and average (A) yields. Extension programmes and infrastructure investments are designed to close this gap.
- The *research gap* (RP − BP) is the difference between research potential (RP) yields and best practice (BP) yields. Applied research programmes, if successful, will close this gap.
- The *science gap* (SP − RP) is the difference between science potential (SP) and research potential (RP) yields. To close

this gap, applied adaptive research programmes must be supported by international and national pre-invention science programmes.

The process of improving agricultural productivity is associated with the progressive reduction of each of these gaps — starting with the extension gap, moving on to the research gap and then to the science gap — as the country's capacity improves for adopting and developing improved technologies, represented by the gradual movement from TC I to TC V.

In Figure 22, TC I is a level where little extension, research or science is being undertaken and where the research that is producing technology for other regions is not producing technology for the TC I region. Farmers' schooling levels are low, markets are poor and infrastructure is lacking. The extension gap is large in this stage, and thus investment in extension and infrastructure has a potentially high pay-off, even though there are few effective research programmes to raise best practice yields. Through extension programmes, the extension gap can be reduced to a fraction of its original size, represented by the transition to TC II. In order to move on from TC II to TC III, the economy must rely on the closing of the next gap, the research gap. This depends on the forging of a direct link between research and extension, where extension

Figure 22
SCHEMATIC CROP YIELDS (AND GAPS) BY TECHNOLOGICAL CAPITAL (TC) LEVEL

Science gap

Research gap

Extension gap

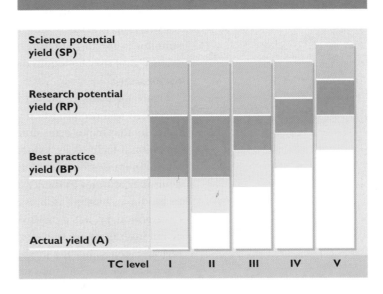

Science potential yield (SP)

Research potential yield (RP)

Best practice yield (BP)

Actual yield (A)

TC level   I   II   III   IV   V

Source: FAO, based on author's elaboration

programmes are responsible for extending the results of applied adaptive research programmes to farmers. The further move from TC III to TC IV is associated with raising the research potential yield (RP), as the applied adaptive research programme is supported by international and national pre-invention science programmes. Further progress, i.e. to TC V, where the science potential yield can also be increased, depends on increasingly effective pre-invention science, research and extension programming.

Although most of Africa is at the level of TC II, some African countries have not yet made the transition from TC I and a few have achieved the transition to TC III, where research systems are producing significant flows of new technology suited to farmers in many regions. This is in contrast to the situation in both South and Southeast Asia where, by the mid-1960s, many economies were already at TC II. Since then, green revolution technology in rice, wheat, maize and other crops has enabled these economies to make the transition to TC III, and today, in many Asian and Latin American countries, there is the potential to reach TC IV.

It is possible that research systems in other regions can raise best practice yields in TC I economies before they have made the transition to TC II. In practice, most research gains have been realized in economies that have already achieved TC II or III market, infrastructure and skill levels. In some cases this has been induced by the development (often in international centres) of genetic resources and methods that increase the research potential (RP) yield levels. In some African countries, RP yield levels may be quite low because of limited genetic resources and difficult disease and insect problems, so the research gap is actually quite small. When this is the case, stimulus in the form of improvements in science (closing of the science gap) may be required to achieve better research performance.

Figure 23 provides further insights into the location specificity and pre-invention science issues. The figure comes from the first major economic study of the economics of agricultural technology, written by Zvi Griliches.[6] It illustrates the adoption (in percentages of area) of hybrid maize by farmers in a number of states in the United States. Griliches noted that the technique of hybridization is actually the invention of a method of invention, i.e. it is a pre-invention science discovery. The actual inventions are the hybrid maize varieties targeted to regional niches, but the method itself is a product of pre-invention science (the modern counterpart of this is the development of biotechnology methods). Although the method has some location specificity, it is far less location-specific than the actual inventions. Thus, the inventions (hybrid maize varieties) suited to Iowa were not valuable (hence not adopted) in Alabama. It was only when breeding programme capacity in Alabama was improved and hybrid maize varieties had been developed for local conditions that the technology was made available to Alabama. Similarly, hybrid maize technology was not available to the Philippines or India until research stations were built in those countries. As will be seen below, this "Alabama effect" has been operative in all developing countries. Countries that do not have the capacity to adapt inventions have gained little from technology produced outside their own boundaries.

Productivity gains from technology occur in developing countries that have the capacity to adapt inventions from outside their own boundaries.

MEASURING PRODUCTIVITY GROWTH IN AGRICULTURE

Productivity growth entails achieving increased production per unit of resource used to produce goods and services. Two types of indicator have been used to measure increases in productivity: partial factor productivity (PFP) indexes and total factor productivity (TFP) indexes. These indexes enable comparisons among regions (and countries) and time periods.

Figure 23
PERCENTAGE OF TOTAL MAIZE AREA PLANTED WITH HYBRID MAIZE SEED IN SELECTED AREAS OF THE UNITED STATES

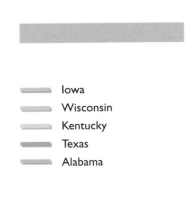

Iowa
Wisconsin
Kentucky
Texas
Alabama

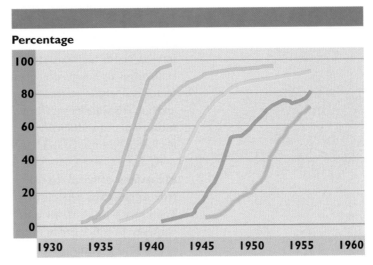

Source: Griliches, 1957, op. cit. note 6.

253

Measures of partial factor productivity

PFP measures are ratios of output to a single production factor. The most widely used PFP for the general economy is the labour productivity index, production (P) per worker (W) or P/W. Production can be measured in terms of a single product, in which case it can be measured in quantity units, or as an aggregate of products, meaning prices must be used to aggregate products into a constant price value. For the purposes of comparison over time, the prices used must be real or constant prices.

The most widely used PFP index for agriculture is production per unit of land, or crop yield. This index has been in standard usage for centuries and allows comparisons among locations and among time periods. Comparisons between locations must take soil and climate differences into account. Yield changes in a given location over time are widely used as indicators of improved economic efficiency.

Figure 24 portrays the yields of major crop groups in developed and developing countries for each decade from the 1950s until the 1990s. This Figure shows that, while crop yields are typically higher in developed countries, the rate of change in yields has been higher in developing countries.

A concern that is often expressed regarding yield increases is that the variability of yields seems to have increased as yields have increased. Increased yields are thus generally associated with increased farm income variability. To clarify this issue, the coefficient of variation[7] is included in Figure 24. Coefficients of variation show no trends, and it appears that higher yields are not associated with higher variability in yields or production.

The chief limitation of PFP measures is that they can be affected by changes in factors other than the factor in the index. For example, increases in fertilizer applications per unit of land will increase yields, so it could not be inferred that an increase in crop yields is the result of genetic improvement or of reductions in transaction costs unless some control for other factor use (either statistically or experimentally) is utilized in the analysis. In spite of this limitation, yield indexes are very useful indicators of productivity change, as they are generally available for specific crops, enabling comparisons by crop.

Measures of total factor productivity (for aggregate agriculture)

Total factor productivity (TFP) measures are sometimes used to compare productivity in different locations, but they are chiefly suited to comparing productivity gains over time. They differ

Yields have grown faster in developing countries than in developed countries but have not become more variable.

from PFP measures in that they are expressed as the ratio of production to a cost-share weighted index of different factors of production.

That is, TFP is the ratio of an index of production to an index of aggregate inputs. The rate of growth in TFP is the rate of growth in production minus the rate of growth in the aggregate input index. This corresponds to the difference between actual production growth and the production growth that would have occurred under conditions in which no productivity change occurred. (See Box 21, p. 248, for an arithmetic presentation of the concept.) Changes in TFP can also be interpreted as changes

Figure 24

TOTAL CEREALS: DECADE AVERAGES OF AREA HARVESTED AND YIELD

Developed countries

Area harvested

Yield

9.34% Coefficient of variation

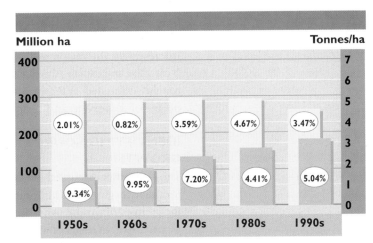

Developing countries

Area harvested

Yield

5.71% Coefficient of variation

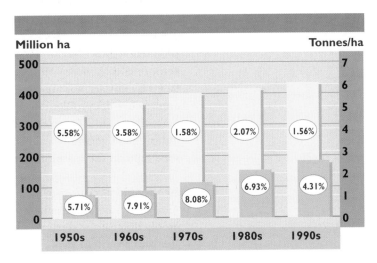

Source: FAO

in the cost of producing a unit of the product, holding input prices constant.

A number of studies have measured TFP changes in different countries, but these are generally difficult to compare because studies and countries follow different practices regarding adjustments for changes in the quality of production factors and have different available data. However, data available from FAO sources allow the calculation of TFP growth rates for the 1961-1996 period for 89 developing countries, based on seven factors of production (see Box 22 for details of the calculations).

The results from these calculations are displayed in Figure 25 by region. Of the 89 countries, 14 had negative TFP growth rates over the 1961-1996 period. Of these, 11 were in sub-Saharan Africa and three in the Caribbean region. Given the crudity of the measurement, these negative TFP growth rates may be owing to error (only six were more than minus 0.5 percent). However, it is possible that some "real" TFP decreases have occurred where land degradation has taken place (discussed with the other unfavourable factors on p. 282). Interestingly, the region with the highest mean TFP growth is the Near East and North Africa. Perhaps the chief feature of these roughly estimated TFP growth rates is that they display a high degree of dispersion and variability from region to region.

IDENTIFYING SOURCES OF PRODUCTIVITY GROWTH

The indicators discussed above are designed only to measure productivity growth. Additional methods are required to identify the sources of productivity changes. Four bodies of evidence can be used to gain insights into the sources, i.e. the investments, policy actions and institutions that produce productivity growth in agriculture. The simplest approach to identify sources is area-yield accounting. Area-yield accounting studies enable production growth to be separated into area and yield components. A more complex form of accounting are product-factor quality accounting studies. A third body of studies approaches the problem from a return to investment perspective. Finally, correlations between TFP growth and indicators of technological capital levels by country can also shed light on the question of sources of productivity growth.

Area-yield accounting

Area-yield accounting is based on the simple fact that growth in production can be separated into two components: growth in area and growth in yield.

Box 22

MEASUREMENT OF TFP GROWTH RATES

FAO AGROSTAT data allow the calculation of the TFP growth rate for 1961-1996 based on seven factors of production. First, rates of growth for production and for each factor are statistically estimated. Second, factor shares are estimated for three periods (1961-1976, 1971-1986 and 1981-1996) using factor-output ratios and estimates of factor shares from independent studies for India and Brazil. The arithmetic of the calculations is explained in the following.

Growth in TFP (G_{TFP}) is defined as growth in production (G_P) minus growth in production inputs (G_I) (see also Box 21, p. 248):

$$G_{TFP} = G_P - G_I$$

Growth in production can be estimated for three periods (1961-1976, 1971-1986 and 1981-1996) from FAO AGROSTAT data as the coefficient b in a regression for each country.

$$\log (P) = a + b \text{ year}$$

Growth in inputs is defined as:

$$G_I = S_A G_A + S_I G_I + S_W G_W + S_{AN} G_{AN} + S_T G_T + S_H G_H + S_F G_F$$

where:
G_A is growth in cropped area, S_A is the cost share;
G_I is growth in irrigated area, S_I is the cost share;
G_W is growth in agricultural workers, S_W is the cost share;
G_{AN} is growth in work animals, S_{AN} is the cost share;
G_T is growth in number of tractors, S_T is the cost share;
G_H is growth in number of harvesters, S_H is the cost share;
G_F is growth in fertilizer and S_F is the cost share.

Growth rates for each factor were estimated for the three periods using the same procedure as for production. Factor shares were estimated by calibration to TFP studies in India for several periods and in Brazil for several periods.

Sources: Factor shares for India: R.E. Evenson and Y. Kislev. 1975. *Agricultural research and productivity.* New Haven, Connecticut, USA, Yale University; R.E. Evenson and M.W. Rosegrant. 1995. *Total factor productivity and sources of long-term growth in Indian agriculture.* EPTD Discussion Paper No. 7, Washington, DC, IFPRI. Factor shares for Brazil: A.F.D. Avila and R.E. Evenson. 1998. Total return productivity growth in Brazilian agriculture and the role of Brazilian agricultural research. *Economia Applicada.*

Figure 25
DISTRIBUTION OF COUNTRIES BY INCREASE IN TOTAL FACTOR PRODUCTIVITY (NUMBER OF COUNTRIES)

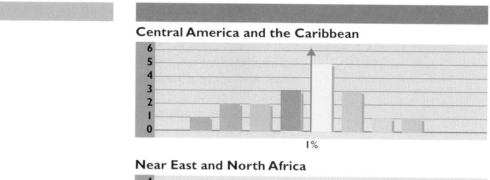

Central America and the Caribbean

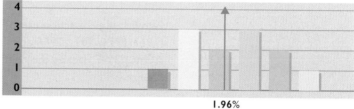

Near East and North Africa

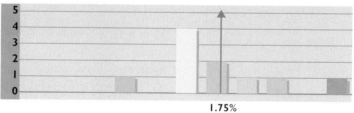

Latin America

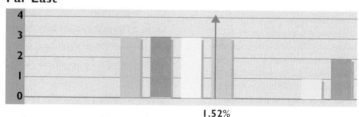

Far East

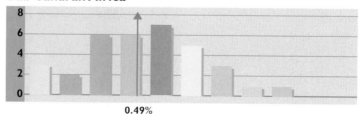

Sub-Saharan Africa

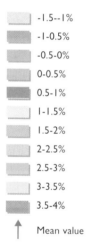

- -1.5--1%
- -1-0.5%
- -0.5-0%
- 0-0.5%
- 0.5-1%
- 1-1.5%
- 1.5-2%
- 2-2.5%
- 2.5-3%
- 3-3.5%
- 3.5-4%

↑ Mean value

Source: FAO, based on author's elaboration

258

Improvement in genetically determined plant performance, in particular, results in yield growth. Yield growth measures have been used as indicators of the contribution of the green revolution associated with improved (semi-dwarf high-yielding) varieties of wheat and rice in the late 1960s in South and Southeast Asia. These improved varieties are credited with increased yield and production and with saving millions of poor families from the dismal prospect of the Malthusian-resources development perspective.

Figure 26 displays area-yield production accounting by decade for major crops in developed and developing countries. Briefly the comparisons show:

- Wheat production increased very rapidly in developed countries in the 1960s and 1970s, but slowly thereafter with yield increases accounting for all growth after the 1950s. For developing countries, the most rapid growth occurred in the 1970s and 1980s. The growth rates were very high. Most of the growth in production was the result of yield growth. Green revolution studies usually regard the late 1960s and the 1970s as the green revolution period, although rates of yield growth continued to be high in the 1980s and 1990s. Studies of varietal production also show that new varieties were being developed at a high rate in the 1990s.

- Rice production shows a similar pattern; rapid growth in production in developed countries during the 1950s and 1960s and slow growth thereafter. For developing countries, high growth continued throughout all the decades considered. Green revolution gains in rice are evident for the 1960s and 1970s, but were not confined to these periods. It should be noted, however, that yield gains were highest in irrigated rice production. Few new varieties of upland rice were produced, but the rate of new variety development for paddy rice remained high over all periods.

- Maize production also increased most rapidly in developed countries in the 1960s and 1970s, with small increases in the 1980s and 1990s. All production growth was caused by yield growth. For developing countries rapid yield growth continued throughout all decades. Yield increases are responsible for between two thirds and three quarters of production growth after the 1950s. (It is generally thought that the green revolutions in developing countries occurred only in wheat and rice. These data show that it also occurred in maize.) Since the mid-1980s, production gains have been more rapid in maize than in rice and wheat.

Improvements in developing countries' agricultural yields did not stop with the green revolution but continue to grow.

Figure 26

ANNUAL AVERAGE GROWTH RATES OF OUTPUT FOR SELECTED CROPS

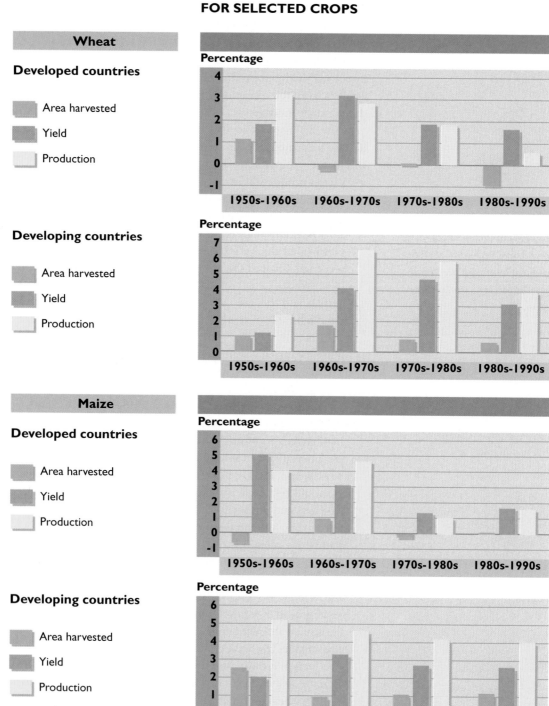

Figure 26 (continued)
ANNUAL AVERAGE GROWTH RATES OF OUTPUT FOR SELECTED CROPS

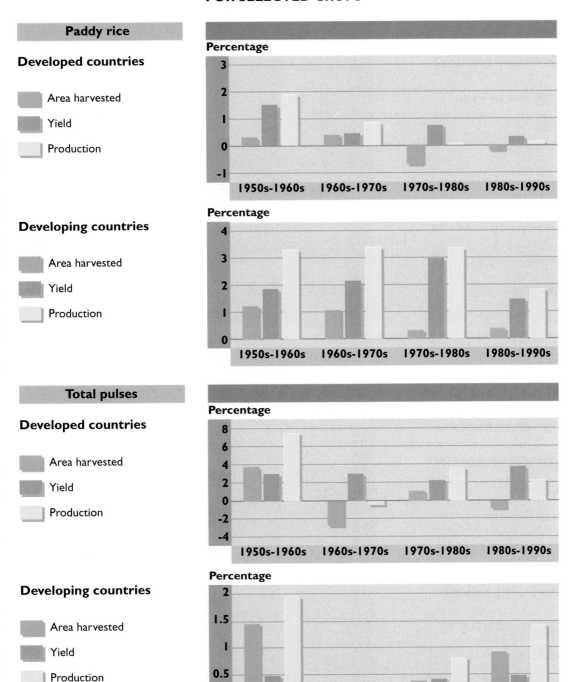

Paddy rice

Developed countries

- Area harvested
- Yield
- Production

Developing countries

- Area harvested
- Yield
- Production

Total pulses

Developed countries

- Area harvested
- Yield
- Production

Developing countries

- Area harvested
- Yield
- Production

Figure 26 (continued)
ANNUAL AVERAGE GROWTH RATES OF OUTPUT FOR SELECTED CROPS

Soybeans

Developed countries

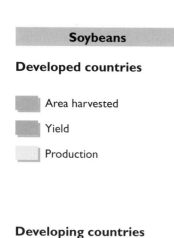

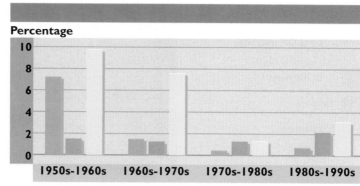

Developing countries

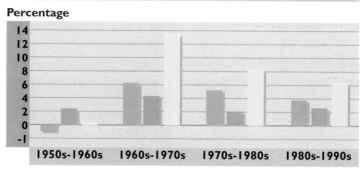

Roots and tubers

Developed countries

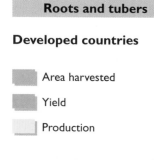

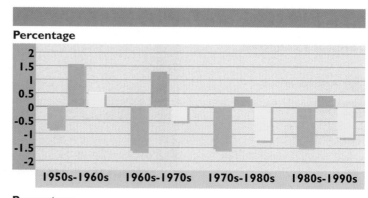

Developing countries

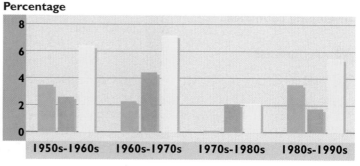

Source: FAO

- For pulses in developed countries, production growth was high in the 1950s and 1960s, but has been slow since then as area changes have been negative. For pulses in developing countries, area expansion fuelled high growth in the 1950s and 1960s. In the 1970s, pulses were effectively crowded out by increased cereal production. Growth in production has picked up in recent years, but yield improvements in pulses have been slow.
- Soybean production grew very rapidly in developed countries in the first three decades of the half century, mostly owing to area expansion. In developing countries, growth has also been rapid since the mid-1960s. Yield growth was especially rapid in the 1960s and 1970s.
- Roots and tubers in developed countries have experienced negative production growth since the 1950s. In developing countries, production and yield growth rates were high throughout the 1970s then declined.

Studies of returns to investment in agricultural productivity

An alternative approach to TFP source identification is to measure the growth contribution of investments in production growth. Two different types of method have been applied: project evaluation methods and statistical methods.

Project evaluation methods. This approach attempts to measure benefits in the form of growth components that can be attributed to investments in agricultural research programmes, agricultural extension programmes, farmer training programmes and infrastructure. A number of studies attempting to measure the benefits attributable to agricultural research and extension programmes have been completed utilizing project evaluation methods. These allow the internal rate of return (IRR) of the project to be identified, among other indicators. The IRR is the rate of discount for which the present value[8] of the benefits is equal to the present value of the costs. It can be interpreted as the rate of return or interest rate realized on investments in the programme, evaluated over a long period of time.

Statistical studies of returns to investments. A second body of return to investment in agriculture and agricultural extension is based on statistical estimates of coefficients in PFP and TFP decomposition studies (see Box 23 for technical details). The basic idea of these studies is to identify, statistically, the contributions to growth in PFP or TFP with variables that are based on investments. Research programmes typically affect productivity with a time lag, which results from time lags between expenditure and discovery and between discovery and diffusion. Studies have estimated this time lag to be between five and ten years from spending to full productivity impact. Decomposition studies can then compute an estimated benefits stream associated with a one-unit investment in a given period (or over several periods). This enables the analyst to calculate a marginal internal rate of return to investment which can be interpreted as the returns to public investment in the programme, where benefits are measured as the total benefits to producers and consumers.

Studies on returns to investments (project methods and statistical methods). IRRs from studies of returns to extension and research based on both project evaluation and statistical methods are summarized in Table 16.[9] While most studies on extension used statistical methods, studies on applied research used both methods. Distributions of IRRs for a number of study categories are presented. Two features characterize virtually every category. The first is that the IRRs are high – 74 percent of the extension IRRs and 82 percent of the research IRRs exceed 20 percent. The second feature is that the IRRs have a broad range of estimates.

Table 16
IRR ESTIMATES SUMMARY

	Number of IRRs reported	Percent distribution						Approx. median IRR
		0-20	21-40	41-60	61-80	81-100	100+	
Extension	81	0.26	0.23	0.16	0.03	0.19	0.13	41
By region:								
OECD	19	0.11	0.31	0.16	0	0.11	0.16	50
Asia	21	0.24	0.19	0.19	0.14	0.09	0.14	47
Latin America	23	0.13	0.26	0.34	0.08	0.08	0.09	46
Africa	10	0.40	0.30	0.20	0.10	0	0	27
Applied research	375	0.18	0.23	0.20	0.14	0.08	0.16	49
By region:								
OECD	146	0.15	0.35	0.21	0.10	0.07	0.11	40
Asia	120	0.08	0.18	0.21	0.15	0.11	0.26	67
Latin America	80	0.15	0.29	0.29	0.15	0.07	0.06	47
Africa	44	0.27	0.27	0.18	0.11	0.11	0.05	37
Pre-invention science	12	0	0.17	0.33	0.17	0.17	0.17	60
Private sector R&D	11	0.18	0.09	0.45	0.09	0.18	0	50
Ex ante research	87	0.32	0.34	0.21	0.06	0.01	0.06	42

Box 23

RETURNS TO INVESTMENT:
TFP (AND PFP) STATISTICAL DECOMPOSITION METHODS

Statistical decomposition methods require that variables for a region and time period of the following general types be defined:

$$G_{TFP} = a + b_1 Res + b_2 Ext + b_3 Sch + b_4 Inf$$

Where:
G_{TFP} is a measure of TFP (when PFP measures are used, input prices should be used as independent variables);
Res, Ext, Sch, Inf are variables corresponding to research, extension, schooling and infrastructure services respectively.

The method enables the analyst to identify TFP growth contributions statistically with variables that are based on investments. Each of the explanatory variables is designed to reflect TFP services for the unit of observation. These services have both time and spatial dimensions which should be estimated and included in the statistical design.

For example, the research programmes servicing a region in the period t to t+1 will be based on investments made before period t. Research programmes typically affect productivity with a time lag, not only from expenditure to discovery, but also from discovery to diffusion. Studies have estimated this lag to be five to ten years for full TFP impact. Research service variables are constructed accordingly as time-weighted cumulations of prior investment.

Spatial dimensions must also be addressed because a region may benefit, not only from the research station associated with the region, but also from research findings from other stations and from private firms. This requires estimation of spill-in weights (although few studies have actually estimated these).

With time and spatial weights and estimates of b_1, b_2, etc., decomposition studies that compute an estimated benefits stream associated with a unit of investment in a given period can cover several periods. This enables the analyst to calculate a marginal internal rate of return to investment.

The estimates of b_1, b_2, etc., combined with changes in the Res, Ext, etc. variables, can also be used to attribute portions of TFP growth to each investment (see Table 17, p. 267).

It should be noted that TFP growth needs to be measured consistently as regards factor quality treatment. It is inappropriate to mix "raw" TFP estimates with quality adjustment estimates.

Returns to public investments in agricultural research and extension are very high.

Given the breadth of the range of IRRs in each category, it is difficult to draw strong conclusions regarding differences in means between categories. It can be noted, however, that the categories with the greatest proportions exceeding 40 percent are pre-invention science, private sector research and development, rice research, and fruits and vegetables research. A slightly higher proportion of research studies exceed 40 percent (59 percent) than is the case for extension studies (51 percent).

Regional distributions vary, with studies of both research and extension in Africa having lower proportions exceeding 40 percent than in other regions. Asian research IRRs are especially high.

There does not appear to be a time trend in the IRRs reported. Studies for later periods show IRRs similar to those in studies of earlier periods.[10] This body of evidence indicates that both research and extension programmes are high pay-off investments for taxpayers.

Many studies have made comparisons between improved and modern varieties and traditional varieties (see Box 24). Plant and animal breeders have contributed to productivity growth by developing plant cultivars and animal breeds (and individual animals) that are more productive and less susceptible to damage by pests and pathogens (see Box 25).

Accounting for contributions to productivity growth. The statistical studies summarized in Table 16 can also be used to account for PFP or TFP growth. Each variable (research, extension, etc.) in the statistical model has an estimated coefficient (or coefficients). These coefficients indicate how much PFP or TFP growth is associated with a given change in the same variable. Thus, it is possible to compute the contribution to growth produced by each source over a particular period.

Table 17 reports such growth accounting calculations based on studies for the United States, India and Brazil. For India, the contribution of high-yielding varieties is measured; these varieties were a major source of growth in the 1970s. The accounting structure used identifies several sources of TFP growth, including research programmes, extension, schooling and market developments. Such accounting, it should be noted, does not indicate that each source of growth is independent of other sources. In fact, the sources complement one another.

Empirical evidence on the role of technological capital
In Figure 22, p. 251 productivity gaps were conceptually

Table 17
TFP GROWTH ACCOUNTING

	US agriculture (1950-1982)		Brazilian agriculture (1970-1985)			1956-1965	Indian agriculture 1966-1976	1977-1989
	Crops	Livestock	Crops	Livestock	Aggregate	Crops	Crops	Crops
Annual TFP growth	**0.63**	**0.51**	**1.11**	**0.9**	**1.00**	**1.27**	**1.49**	**1.14**
Proportion resulting from:								
-Public sector research	0.36	0.09	0.23	0.55	0.30	0.22	0.38	0.45
(High-yielding varieties)	...	...	...	...	...	0	0.20	0.04
-Industrial R&D	0.24	0.54	0.17	0	0.31	0.07	0.18	0.07
-Agricultural extension	0.25	0.17	0.07	0.05	0.02	0.66	0.16	0.43
-Farmers' schooling	-	0.08	...	...	...	0.01	0.01	0.01
-Government programmes	0.02	0.06	...	...	...			
-Markets	...	...	...	...	...	0.04	0.04	0.05
-Other	0.30	0.13	0.45	0.40	0.37	0	0.19	0

Sources: United States data: W.E. Huffman and R.E. Evenson. 1993. *Science for agriculture,* p. 212, Table 7.10. Ames, Iowa, USA, Iowa University; Brazil data: A.F.D. Avila and R.E. Evenson. 1998. Total return productivity growth in Brazilian agriculture and the role of Brazilian agricultural research. *Economia Applicada,* Table 13; India data: R.E. Evenson, C.E. Proy and M.W. Rosegrant. 1999. *Agricultural productivity growth in India.* IFPRI Report No. 109. Washington, DC, IFPRI.

defined in terms of technological capital (TC) classes. Box 26, p. 273 provides an empirical methodology for classifying countries into different TC classes based on eight TC indicators. Using this classification method, it was possible to place 89 developing countries into one of four TC classes in each of three different periods (1961-1976, 1971-1986, 1981-1996). Most countries achieved an improvement in TC class over the three periods, as indicated in Box 27, p. 274 where countries are identified in terms of their technological capital in each period.

Figure 27 displays distributions of TFP growth rates by TC change classes. First consider the 21 countries that have not advanced beyond TC II (i.e. 112 and 222). These countries effectively inherited little (TC I) or poor (TC II) technological capital and have achieved little improvement over the 1961-1996 period. Seventeen of the 21 countries are in sub-Saharan Africa. The sample of countries does not include several

Box 24

PRODUCTIVITY AND VARIETAL IMPROVEMENT

The green revolution, popularized in the media in the late 1960s and early 1970s, associated productivity gains with high-yielding or modern crop varieties of wheat and maize. There is little question that improved varieties were important and that they were a catalysing force in productivity improvement. The images created by the popular press, however, were misleading in many respects. They left the impression that the green revolution was created by the exceptional insights of a small group of scientists in IARCs, and that the modern varieties produced as a consequence were confined to rice and wheat varieties developed in the late 1960s and diffused during the 1970s.

In reality, there were many breeding programmes in developing countries for a number of crops before the IARCs were established. These programmes developed many rice and wheat varieties for tropical and subtropical climate regions in developing countries. In rice breeding, for example, programmes to bring Japonica (temperate) genetic resources into Indica (tropical) rice cultivars had already achieved success in the 1960s. Progress in bringing temperate zone wheat genetic material into subtropical wheat cultivars had also been made in Mexico (led by a Rockefeller Foundation programme that was a predecessor of CIMMYT).

The IARCs brought more concentrated and directed attention to the plant breeding challenges presented by tropical and subtropical production conditions. They facilitated the exchange of genetic resources and of advanced breeding lines used as parents in national agricultural research systems (NARS) breeding programmes. Access to genetic materials was improved by the establishment of IARC gene banks and international nursery systems. IARC programmes complemented NARS breeding programmes and stimulated their expansion.

Recent studies of varietal production and release show that the rate at which new varieties were being developed increased during the 1960s and 1970s in several crops and that this rate of varietal production has been maintained since then. In rice, for example, more than 2 000 modern varieties have been released in more than 100 breeding programmes. New traits (disease resistance, drought tolerance, etc.) have enabled the expansion of high-yielding varieties into more production environments over time.

Many of the studies of returns to research are based on the contribution model by improved crop varieties. The development of improved crop varieties appears to be the key to moving from TC II to TC III in the technological capital formulation. A recent study of rice research concluded that roughly one half to two thirds of the productivity gains produced by rice research programmes was attributable to genetic improvements.

The International Agricultural Evaluation Group (associated with the Consultative Group on International Agricultural Research [CGIAR]) has undertaken a recent study of crop genetic improvement in developing countries. The study reports the following findings:

- Crop breeding programmes in IARCs complement the crop breeding programmes in NARS by providing advanced breeding lines and varieties that have been extensively used as parent materials by NARS.
- The rate of development of new crop varieties rose for wheat, rice and potatoes from the 1960s until the 1980s and remained constant in the 1990s. For other IARC crops, the rate of new varietal development continued to increase throughout the 1990s.
- The complementarity between IARC breeding programmes and NARS breeding programmes has stimulated higher levels of investment in NARS breeding programmes.
- New crop varieties have continued to make significant impacts on crop productivity as recently released improved varieties replace earlier improved varieties. Different rates of diffusion of improved crop varieties have been observed in different crops and regions, however. Some regions are disadvantaged because their soil and climate conditions are such that new crop varieties have little or no impact. This is a factor in the unevenness of productivity change.
- Returns to investment in plant breeding programmes have been very high.

countries that have probably remained at TC I over the period, notably Somalia, the Congo and Ethiopia. Dispersion in TFP growth for this group is high with seven negative TFP growth rates, possibly reflecting soil depletion, but probably also problems of social stability, including civil strife. Many of these countries have limited capacity to provide basic services for their populations, none are industrialized. Five countries in the group had TFP growth rates of over 1 percent, but the group mean was only 0.2 percent. It would be reasonable to infer that these countries are still governed by Malthusian conditions.

Box 25

PRODUCTIVITY AND GENETIC RESOURCES

Prior to the advent of modern biotechnology methods, which enable genetic material from one species to be transformed into another species, breeders were constrained to searching for better genetic combinations within the existing cultivated crop and livestock species. For most of these species, rich within-species diversity is available to breeders in the form of landraces in crops and breeds in livestock. The diversity was created by farmers over previous centuries as they selected new types to suit new conditions in new locations and for expanding populations.

This legacy of farmer-selected biodiversity plus mutants and wild or weedy related species is of great value to breeders today. Many of the productivity

gains in agriculture can be attributed to genetic improvements. *Ex situ* gene bank collections of genetic resources have been developed for all major crop species. These collections hold a high proportion of potentially collectable material, for which a policy of exchange has been maintained.

To date, several studies of genetic resource value have been made. Most work has been done on rice.[1] These studies conclude that genetic resources have high economic value and that further collection, evaluation and prebreeding (to identify parental values) are economically justified. The studies also conclude that, as breeding moves into the biotechnology era, traditional genetic resources will be enhanced in value.

[1] R.E. Evenson and D. Gollin. 1997. Genetic resources, international organizations and improvement in rice varieties. *Economic Development and Cultural Change*, 45: 471-500.

The second panel in Figure 27 displays TFP growth rates for 24 countries that moved from TC II in the first period to TC III in the second or third period (14 of these countries are in sub-Saharan Africa). This group of countries has an average TFP growth of 0.6 percent. Eighteen of them showed positive TFP growth, with three countries in the 1 to 2 percent range. This means that the average country in this group is realizing approximately enough TFP growth to prevent production per caput from declining, and a few countries are realizing good economic growth rates.

The third cluster of 29 countries were at TC III in the first and second periods. Twelve of them moved to TC IV in the third period. The mean TFP growth for this group was 1.53 percent, a very respectable rate. Only one country had negative TFP growth and nine had more than 2 percent TFP growth per year.

The fourth group of 14 countries includes countries that either inherited TC IV levels or had moved into them by the second period. This group includes China, India and Brazil. It has performed extremely well, with a mean TFP growth of 2.3 percent and four countries achieving more than 3 percent. This set of countries has R&D capacity in industry.

While these TFP measures are crude and the TC classes somewhat arbitrary, the TFP-TC correlations tell a powerful story.[11] The story, simply put, is that countries in TC I realize little or no TFP growth. Moving to TC II, where basic government institutions are in place and some agricultural research capacity exists, modest growth is achieved. Countries with TC III capabilities can realize high rates of TFP growth and have significant agricultural research and extension systems. Countries with TC IV capabilities can realize super growth in agriculture. Since TC IV encompasses R&D capabilities in the agricultural supply sector, part of this super TFP growth is a spillover from industrial TFP growth.

OTHER ISSUES IN AGRICULTURAL PRODUCTIVITY CHANGE
Productivity changes and resource degradation
The sustainable development movement of the past two decades draws attention to the possibility that productivity gains in many countries may have been realized at the expense of degrading resources. It is often not recognized, however, that resource upgrading, either through investment in drainage and irrigation or through farming practices (crop rotation, fertilizing, liming), also occurs.

It is important to note that the TFP measures reported in the previous section, in principle, do take account of net degradation or net upgrading of the resource base. It is quite plausible that countries with low TFP growth rates are experiencing net degradation, and that countries with high TFP growth rates are experiencing net upgrading. To the extent that this is the case, resource degradation is inversely related to technological capacity and per caput income.

The literature on resource degradation rates identifies several problem areas, including salinization, soil erosion and intensification.

Salinization problems have been severe in some locations (e.g. Pakistan). In some cases, better management would have prevented these problems. In other cases, management may not have prevented the problem and, with hindsight, it can be concluded that irrigation should have been controlled.

Soil erosion occurs continuously; some areas benefit from erosion, others lose. Erosion on some soils translates into reduced natural productivity. In others this is not the case. Soil erosion can be, and in many countries has been, controlled and managed, in particular where households have secure property rights. (Crosson[12] provides a useful survey of soil erosion and productivity effects.)

Intensification, i.e. the use of fertilizer and other chemicals and improved varieties to achieve high yields, is seen by some as damaging to land productivity. There is concern that such agriculture in the tropics may have negative environmental effects that have not been realized in high-yielding agriculture in the temperate zones. The experience with high-yielding agriculture in temperate zones is that, with proper management, even poor natural soils can be improved. This requires investments, and most soils in tropical regions, especially in Africa, have not benefited from these investments. The majority of soils in Africa have large unexploited potential for improvement through investment.

Productivity changes and income distribution
The benefit from productivity gains can be distributed in different ways among producers and consumers and across locations, according to circumstances. Productivity gains lower costs, which leads to increased supply. In a small economy open to international trade, domestic prices are determined by international market prices, so prices do not fall when production costs fall. In this case, consumers do not gain from productivity change and producers capture all the benefits. For an economy that is closed to international trade (or for non-traded goods), on the other hand, prices will fall when

Box 26

**TECHNOLOGY
CAPITAL INDEXES**

Developing countries were classified according to technology capital (TC) classes in three different periods (1961-1976, 1971-1986, 1981-1996). Four TC classes were defined, based on eight indicators as shown below. The criteria ensure that countries are included in only one TC class in each period. Most countries achieved TC improvements in recent decades (see Box 27).

Indicators[1]	TC I	TC II	TC III	TC IV
Adult male illiteracy	=50%	<50%	<50%	<35%
Proportion of labour force in industry	<10%	<15%	>15%	>15%
Foreign direct investment/GDP	Little or none	<0.5%	=0.5%	0.25% or more
R&D in manufacturing firms/manufacturing value added	None	None	<0.25%	=0.25%
Royalties and licence fees paid	None	None	Minor	Substantial
Royalties and licence fees received	None	None	None	Minor
Agricultural research investment intensity	Low <0.25% of agricultural production	Moderate 0.25-0.5% of agricultural production	High =0.25% of agricultural production	High =0.5% of agricultural production
Intellectual property rights	None	None	Weak protection	Moderate protection

[1] Indicator data are drawn from the World Bank Development Indicators database.

Box 27

DYNAMICS OF TECHNOLOGICAL CAPITAL ACCUMULATION

Over recent decades most countries have changed their TC levels through investments and institutional development. Below countries are listed according to their classification by TC levels in each of the three periods 1961-1976, 1976-1986 and 1986-1996 (e.g. 112 indicates TC I in the first two periods and TC II in the third period).

Most of the countries in the 111, 112 and 222 categories inherited TC I levels in the 1950s; the countries in the 222 classification had upgraded their TC rating to TC II by about 1970, but have remained there since. Only a few countries have achieved more than one TC upgrade over the 40 years covered. More than half have achieved one upgrade.

COUNTRY CLASSIFICATIONS (1961-1976, 1976-1986, 1986-1996)

111	112	222	223	233	333	334	344	444
Zaire	Angola	Burkina Faso	Bangladesh	Dominican Rep.	Barbados	Algeria	Bahamas	Argentina
Congo	Benin	Côte d'Ivoire	Botswana	Gabon	Cyprus	Bolivia	Belize	Brazil
Ethiopia	Burundi	Guatemala	Cameroon	Ghana	Guadaloupe	Ecuador	Chile	Costa Rica
Somalia	Cambodia	Lao People's Dem. Rep.	Guyana	Kenya	Indonesia	Egypt	China	Korea, Rep.
	Chad	Malawi	Madagascar	Nigeria	Iran, Islamic Rep.	El Salvador	Colombia	Singapore
	Gambia	Sudan	Mali	Paraguay	Iraq	Honduras	India	
	Guinea	Togo	Mongolia	Peru	Jordan	Jamaica	Malaysia	
	Guinea-Bissau	Uganda	Namibia	Senegal	Libyan Arab Jam.	Saudi Arabia	Mexico	
	Haiti		Nicaragua	Sierra Leone	Martinique	Tunisia	Morocco	
	Mauritania		Swaziland	Sri Lanka	Mauritania	Turkey	Thailand	
	Mozambique		Tanzania, United Rep.	Suriname	Pakistan	Uruguay		
	Nepal			Viet Nam	Panama	Zimbabwe		
	Niger			Zambia	Philippines			
	Rwanda				Réunion			
	Yemen				Syrian Arab Rep.			
					Trinidad and Tobago			
					Venezuela			

Figure 27
DISTRIBUTION OF TOTAL FACTOR PRODUCTIVITY GROWTH BY TC CLASSIFICATION (NUMBER OF COUNTRIES)

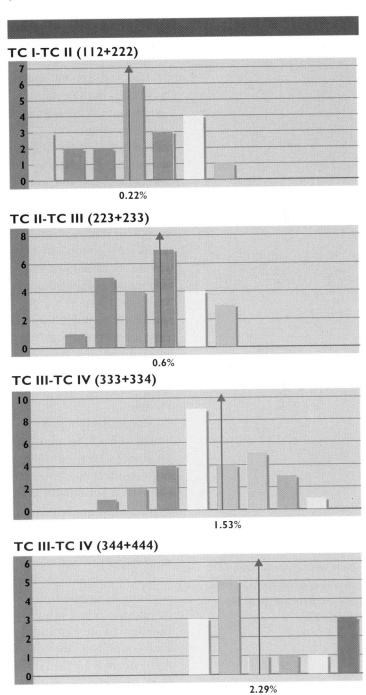

Source: FAO, based on author's elaboration

productivity gains lower costs. This produces gains to consumers, while individual producers will gain or lose according to whether their average costs declined by more or less than prices declined.

Cost declines may vary among producers, and farmers may differ in adoption patterns. Early adopters will then have cost declines before they accrue to late adopters. Credit-constrained farmers may have slower cost declines than farmers with good access to credit. These factors appear to have been of importance in developing countries, but extension and infrastructure programmes have had a levelling effect on them.

The most important factor affecting cost declines in an economy, however, is the nature of biotechnology and its interaction with soil and climate conditions. The first modern green revolution rice varieties were adopted on only about 30 percent of India's irrigated and rainfed rice land. Even though they were very productive under certain conditions (e.g. with good water control) their advantage was reduced or lost under other soil, climate and pest/pathogen conditions. Several generations of breeding for host plant resistance to insect pests and diseases and for host plant tolerance to abiotic stresses (e.g. drought stress) produced rice varieties that are now planted on roughly 90 percent of India's irrigated/rainfed rice area. But this high-yielding varietal technology still remains unavailable to many farmers in upland, deepwater and other unfavourable production conditions for rice.

Technology-induced declines in production costs may benefit only some farmers and may harm farmers who do not have access to the technology.

This favourable-unfavourable production environment situation has been an important element in most developing economies. It creates serious inequities and conditions where improved technology benefits all consumers and some producers, but actually harms producers who do not have access to cost-reducing technology for reasons of location. There are some remedies for this situation, although they will not necessarily create equal access to productivity gains. The most important one is to develop research and experiment station systems designed to serve all regions. This can then be supported by extension, schooling and infrastructure investments. Plant breeding programmes, as noted in the Indian example, can and do tailor genetic improvements to local conditions. Another remedy is the movement of people. A recent study by IRRI[13] concluded that labour mobility enabled workers to avoid the unfavourable environment effects on wages.

SOURCES OF PRODUCTIVITY GAINS

Economic studies of productivity gains in agriculture show considerable variation in productivity performance across countries and periods; but patterns do exist. Studies of productivity change (and the TFP-TC correlations reported above) are consistent in showing that technological capital is critical in determining productivity performance. Technological capital is cumulated over long periods of time. Developing countries differ greatly as regards the capacity inherited from colonial regimes in the early part of the second half of the twentieth century, and also in their investment in upgraded capacity over the half-century.

From the agricultural development models discussed earlier in this chapter, the following generalizations appear to be supported by the experience of the past several decades.

The Malthusian-resource model could be considered valid for a subset of developing countries. Those economies that did not invest in a minimal level of TC realized few or no productivity gains and experienced declining per caput incomes unless they had abundant land resources. Of the 21 developing countries failing to move beyond TC II over the past half-century, none appear to have attempted to solve their problems with the classic Malthusian remedy – population control. Had they done so without investing in technological capacity, it appears that little income growth would have been achieved. Some studies nevertheless conclude that high population densities stimulate investments in technological capital.

Some of the TC II countries attempted to achieve productivity growth by stressing the best practice model. This model calls for investment in agricultural extension as the lead TC strategy and has had rather limited success. When countries have moderate levels of literacy, extension "mining" (see Figure 22, p. 251) to improve farmer productivity by using existing technology more effectively produces only limited growth for a limited period of time.

It is the adaptive invention model that enables countries to achieve high productivity growth. This means building a research capacity. It also means building a capacity to train researchers. With the development of IARCs and their support of TC III national agricultural research programmes, high rates of productivity growth have been realized. As the programmes are complemented by institutional investments in markets and infrastructure, their effectiveness increases.

However, super productivity growth in agriculture takes place only when productivity growth is being realized in the industrial sector. This occurs in TC IV countries and, when it occurs, there can be massive poverty reduction. There is little or no evidence for leaping from TC I to IV – countries do not achieve TC IV without having first achieved III. This indicates that the agricultural sector is an important catalyst for TC IV development.

LESSONS FOR POLICY-MAKING

The production and productivity performance of the agricultural sector in developing countries over recent decades was both extraordinary and uneven; extraordinary because of the magnitude of the production and productivity gains achieved, and uneven because production and productivity gains were realized at different rates in different regions and countries. The extraordinary quality of the production performance in today's relatively open and globalized economy has been a factor in the realization of low food prices. In fact, the real prices of most cereal grains in 1999 were roughly half their 1950 levels.

Real prices of most cereal grains have dropped by about 50 percent over the past 50 years.

As for investments, the experience of the past half-century has been very different for investments in true public goods production for agriculture (research, schooling and extension) and for investments in most state-owned enterprises. Investments in public good production have yielded high returns to taxpayers, while investments in most state-owned enterprises have not. Governments in developing countries and development agencies have not always been able to distinguish between productive and essential public investments, and unproductive and non-essential public investments where the private sector is the efficient form of economic organization.

There are many lessons from the events of the past half-century. Experiences differ by country, period and commodity, but certain patterns stand out and are of relevance in the context of future planning. The following are some of the general lessons that can be drawn.

Productivity gains require investments. It simply is not the case that countries can achieve productivity gains via technological spillovers ("spill ins") without investing in technological capital.

Investment can be achieved via two means. The first is to provide an institutional and policy environment that provides incentives for private sector investment, including foreign direct investment. The second is to engage in public investment and, in many cases, public sector control of activities that the private sector does not invest in (and cannot be encouraged to do so). This balancing of public and private investment is not easy. It requires careful evaluation and planning.

Population control programmes based on the Malthusian-resource model will not, in and of themselves, produce real welfare improvement. They must be complemented with investments in technological capital.[14]

Most inventions in developing countries are adaptive inventions, i.e. adaptations of inventions made in developed countries. In public sector agricultural research programmes, IARCs facilitate adaptive inventions, as do private multinational firms. Developing countries can exploit international productivity sources if these are accessible to them and if they have invested in domestic capacity.

There is a sort of technological sequencing within productivity improvement. Genetic improvement appears to be central in that it provides a complementary relationship with extension and agronomy, pathology, entomology, economics and other research fields. Once an economy reaches an advanced level of technology capacity, the effectiveness of extension and management advice depends on investment in research.

The full effects of productivity improvement are realized through broader economic changes. Agricultural productivity gains may not accrue exclusively, or even primarily, to farm producers. Markets distribute the gains to both producers and consumers and enable the general population to benefit.

As developing countries seek to move to TC IV, they must first progress through I, II and III. For most countries in TC I and II, the agricultural sector is the dominant sector of the economy and obviously critical to development. The technological capital investments required in agriculture to move to TC III are investments in public sector agricultural research and extension.

PROSPECTS FOR AGRICULTURAL PERFORMANCE

As the twenty-first century begins, there are both favourable and unfavourable factors which will play a role in agricultural performance. Several recent studies by the World Bank, FAO and the International Food Policy Research Institute (IFPRI) have projected global production trade and prices for agricultural products. All agree that for the next 25 years or so the favourable factors will outweigh the unfavourable factors and that per caput food production will increase sufficiently to prevent food prices from rising. In fact, all three models project declining real food prices. Thus the extraordinary nature of the food and agriculture sector performance is likely to continue for some time. (These models take into account the fact that very new technology will become effective in the near future.) The unevenness of food and agricultural performance is, unfortunately, also likely to continue.

Projections suggest that productivity growth in agriculture will continue for the next 25 years.

Favourable factors

Virtually all developing countries experienced high rates of population growth in the 1950s and 1960s. Declines in death rates, especially of infants, had occurred in the 1940s and 1950s producing a population boom. This also gave rise to a population burden, because populations grew faster than the workforce (it takes 15 years for the newly born to become workers) i.e. the dependency ratio rose.

Partly for policy reasons (family planning programmes, rural health progress, etc.) and partly for economic reasons, families began to reduce fertility rates and thus enter the second phase of demographic transitions. The fertility rate began to decline in different countries at different times, with Taiwan Province of China, Singapore, Hong Kong and the Republic of Korea – the "Asian Tigers" – leading the way. By the 1970s, most Latin American countries and other countries in Asia were also experiencing fertility declines and, by the 1990s, they had spread to virtually all developing countries. For developed countries the fertility decline was truly astounding; by 1995 almost all developed countries were below replacement fertility levels.

There is still considerable population momentum associated with the fact that more children in the last generation means more mothers in this generation, but the largest global population increments occurred a few years ago and further increments will become smaller each year. As fertility declines and population growth slows, a demographic gift in the form of a falling dependency ratio takes place because the workforce grows more rapidly than the population. This gift is very favourable for agriculture, since workers are vital to agricultural production.

At the beginning of this half-century, the technological capital of developing countries was very limited. Only a few had achieved productive research capacity (TC III) in 1950. By 1990, most developing countries had technology capital levels of TC III or IV.

In 1950, the CGIAR system of IARCs had not yet been developed. By the 1990s, several IARCs had produced important research and technological findings, many modern high-yielding variety programmes were being developed by IARCs, and the exchange of genetic resources, including advanced breeding lines, was facilitated by the IARC gene bank and international nursery systems. This made NARS more productive.

The development of IARC-NARS programmes is still not complete, however. Progress in increasing the technological

FAO/19480/G. BIZZARRI

The green revolution

High-yielding varieties of rice are now planted in 90 percent of India's irrigated and rainfed rice area

capacity of countries with limited capacity has not been particularly good in the past decade or so, as international support for the programmes has diminished. Nonetheless, the existing capacity and the development of improved varieties, agronomic practices (integrated pest management), etc. provide technological momentum that will ensure further productivity growth probably at something like the growth record of the 1990s.

The biological sciences that provide the scientific foundation for the agricultural sciences have also made extraordinary progress in recent decades. Fundamental scientific discoveries in the basic fields of science are occurring at unprecedented rates and it is no exaggeration to suggest that a scientific revolution has been under way in recent years. This scientific revolution has stimulated a technological revolution in the form of biotechnology, which is still in its formative stages and has accumulated a broad array of critics. The most aggressive investors and developers of biotechnology products for agriculture have been private companies. Transgenic products are now widely used in a number of developed countries, and stronger intellectual property right (IPRs) are critical to private investors in these countries.

The public sector research system in developed countries is also responding to pressures created by advances in science, by strengthened IPRs and by the rapidly growing private sector research and development activities. The response is seen in graduate study programmes, research project selection and design and a research system culture in which free exchange of scientific information is possibly being curtailed. Public research systems see both threats and potential in the biological science revolution.

To date, the response of agricultural research systems in developing countries has been very slow, and developing country access to biotechnology products from the private sector will be more difficult than in developed countries. At present, the TC IV developing countries are realizing some of the benefits of biotechnology, but the TC III countries (and certainly the TC I and II countries) have yet to build capacity to benefit from this scientific advance.

Productivity experience over recent decades clearly shows that the agricultural sector benefits from robust growth and development in the industrial sector in both developed and developing countries. The agricultural sectors in developed countries are undergoing structural change (farm size, specialization, contracting, etc.) as a result of industrialization, but structural change has been less important in developing countries. Industrial growth provides improved factors of production to agriculture. It also improves the functioning of labour markets and provides income growth which stimulates improved market efficiency. Industrialization in developing countries, notably in East and Southeast Asia, has proceeded rapidly. The crisis of the late 1990s in Southeast Asia appears to be subsiding and the next decades are likely to be decades of rapid industrialization.

Unfavourable factors

Land degradation has probably occurred at a substantial rate in some countries over recent decades. Land improvement has as well. In almost all countries, good management of lands leads to net improvements. It will be the case, however, that not all countries will have good management in future decades. This is especially important for countries where the long process of developing practices to raise soil productivity is in its early stages. Land degradation and land improvement take place in all countries, but in countries with high TC levels and supporting institutions, land tends to be managed more efficiently.

In developed countries, cropland expansion has virtually

ceased (and actually reversed in most cases). With investments in drainage and soil conservation measures, land is more productive than it was half a century ago. In developing countries with low levels of technological capital, poor institutional conditions and high rates of population growth, cropland expansion and fallow period reduction are occurring. Land improving investments are, however, also occurring – especially irrigation investments. It is possible that some of the negative TFP performances realized in some countries reflect significant land degradation.

Water is scarce in some regions, abundant in others. Irrigation systems have expanded over the past half-century in most developing countries, but it is probably the case that irrigation investment opportunities have been exhausted in many regions. Furthermore, irrigation system management has not been ideal in many regions. But water scarcity is similar to land scarcity; productivity gains, especially genetic improvement gains, that enable more production per unit of land also enable more production per unit of water.

A lack of capital and favourable institutions in poor countries impedes solutions to resource degradation problems.

When referring to resource constraints, however, it is important to emphasize that technological capital and supporting institutions can alleviate such constraints. Resource scarcity and degradation are, therefore, most important in the poorest countries.

Most TC I and II developing countries have been losing ground to developed countries for the past half-century. These countries face difficult political and policy environments, both domestically and internationally. The biotechnology revolution will almost certainly mean that they will lose further ground, given today's political and policy climate and the failure of these countries to make the investments required to achieve productivity growth.

Those developing countries that have achieved TC III status have generally gained ground on developed countries over most of the past half-century. They have reduced their technological lag through adaptive invention programmes and have been aided by IARCs. For the past decade, however, they have been losing ground as biotechnology inventions at the frontier have been made and put into practice. The political hostility to biotechnology has contributed to this by inhibiting the IPR reforms and other policies important to gaining access to this technology. It has also contributed by inhibiting investment in training required to modernize the agricultural sciences in both NARS and IARCs.

Many developing countries that have achieved TC IV status,

however, do have the institutional backing to enable them to benefit from advances in biological sciences and the associated biotechnology inventions and are less likely to lose ground to the developed countries because of delayed implementation of these advances.

NOTES

1 For the developed countries overall, total feed use in 1997 corresponded to 60 percent of domestic supply of cereals, as against only 21 percent for the developing countries.

2 Thomas Robert Malthus (1766-1834), in his *Essay on the principle of population as it affects the future improvement of society,* discussed the interaction between an exponentially growing population and a linearly growing natural resource base which, without restraints on population growth, would lead to continued pressure on living standards.

3 J. Simon. 1977. *The economics of population growth.* Princeton, New Jersey, USA, Princeton University; E. Boserup. 1981. *Population and technological change: a study of long-term trends.* Chicago, Illinois, USA, University of Chicago Press.

4 D.E. Bloom and J.G. Williamson. 1998. *World Bank Economic Review,* 12: 419-456.

5 Public goods are goods that cannot be withheld from single individuals without being withheld from everybody (classic examples are national defence, police protection, street lighting). For this reason they cannot be provided by private entrepreneurs (who would not be able to impose a payment for the public good on its beneficiaries, and would thus have no incentive to provide it) and must, therefore, generally be provided by the public sector.

6 Z. Griliches. 1957. Hybrid corn: an exploration in the economics of technological change. *Econometrica,* 25: 501-522.

7 The standard deviation divided by the mean for each decade, the coefficient of variation is a statistical indicator of the degree to which the various observations in a sample are dispersed around its mean. The smaller the coefficient of variation, the closer the observations on the whole are to the mean; the larger the coefficient of variation, the more they are dispersed around the mean value of the sample.

8 The present value is the value today of a future sum or flow of money. It is calculated by discounting, from the future sum or flows, an interest rate equivalent to the interest at which the sum could have been invested.

9 R.E. Evenson. 1999. Economic impact studies of agricultural research and extension. New Haven, Connecticut, USA, Yale University (mimeo).

10 Ibid.

11 Note 27, however, that the TC classes are actually quite firm, regardless of the indicators on which they are based. Fewer or alternative indicators and indicator criteria would not change the membership in the clusters in Figure 27 very much.

12 P. Crosson. 1995. *Soil erosion and its on-farm productivity consequences: what do we know?* Resources for the Future Discussion Paper No. 95/29; and P. Crosson. 1997. Will erosion threaten agricultural productivity? *Environment,* 39: 4-9, 29-31.

13 C.C. David and K. Otsuka, eds. 1994. *Modern rice technology and income distribution in Asia.* Los Baños, the Philippines, IRRI.

14 Boserup, op. cit., note 3.

Political economy in the alleviation of poverty and food insecurity

INTRODUCTION

The previous sections review various technological and socio-economic aspects of agriculture, rural development and food security from a historical perspective. The picture that emerges is one of major achievements in terms of increased agricultural production and productivity and greater food security for large parts of humanity. However, poverty and food insecurity continue to affect a large share of the world's population. This section completes the historical analysis of the preceding sections by focusing on political economy and governance factors that, rather than reducing such situations of poverty and food insecurity, help to perpetuate them.

The principal politico-economic question is why the escape routes from poverty are often blocked. It is important to identify the political and institutional mechanisms that prolong poverty and draw lessons from the few cases among less developed countries where the blocks have been successfully removed so as to consider the context-specific prospects of replicating such cases. The focus in this section will be more on conceptual issues than on descriptive or prescriptive details.

There is now a large literature on the processes that generate poverty traps, although attention has shifted from the traditional discussion of Malthusian demographic traps and the physiological traps that cause undernutrition to reproduce itself as a result of low work capacity, towards imperfections in credit and insurance markets. Here, wealth constraints (and the usually costly private adjustments to those imperfections) severely restrict the ability of the poor to enlarge their scale of production, buy or lease land and equipment, take up high-return high-risk projects or occupational choices, avoid shortsighted strategies and invest in productivity-raising human and physical capital formation.

COORDINATION FAILURES

Low-level equilibrium traps suggest some kind of coordination failure. This implies failures in a society's various coordination mechanisms at the level of the *market, the government, or the*

FAO/16961/KNIGHT

Poverty trap
A lack of coordination among markets, governments and local institutions blocks the escape routes from poverty

Wealthy and powerful interests in developing countries often obtain subsidies intended for the poor.

local community institutions. Failures at these three levels are often interconnected. Credit market failures, for example, are crucial to our understanding of the origin and perpetuation of poverty, but attempts to correct them through various credit subsidy programmes in poor countries have been beset by political and governance failures. This is illustrated by the mixed results of the Integrated Rural Development Programme in India, which is one of the world's largest credit programmes for asset-building by the rural poor.

There is a similarly disappointing history of subsidized rural credit programmes in Latin America.[1]

Wealthier borrowers (and entrepreneurs) often appropriate the credit subsidies intended for the poor. Credit administered through government or parastatal agencies weakens incentives to invest wisely or repay promptly, and the formation of political connections to obtain debt relief and rent-seeking sometimes becomes more important than responsible investment behaviour. It is also a case of local institutional failure, as community organizations that have the local knowledge to overcome the inherent enforcement and information problems related to official credit agencies are not deployed in many cases. The relatively successful cases such as the Grameen Bank

Microcredit uses participatory processes that ensure only targeted groups benefit.

in Bangladesh and the Self-Employed Women's Association (SEWA) in Gujarat, India, are still few and far between. SEWA is a self-help organization for poor women, now encompassing more than 200 000 members. The Grameen Bank aims to reach the poorest and most vulnerable women. For the period 1985-1996, it had an adjusted repayment rate of 92 percent, a real interest rate of 10 percent and a subsidy of 11 percent per loan.[2] From a panel data set in two villages surveyed in northwestern Bangladesh, Amin, Rai and Topa[3] show quite convincingly that subsidized credit is largely successful in reaching the poor and the vulnerable under the Grameen and other microcredit programmes. Selection devices such as offering only small loans, requiring weekly attendance, and providing only moderate subsidies may have discouraged the rich from participating and diverting the credit in these programmes. However, as Morduch[4] points out, the microcredit movement worldwide has yet to make significant inroads in areas where agriculture is the primary activity of the borrowers.

Failures of the insurance market, in addition to those of the credit market (originating in similar information problems), make the life of the poor extremely vulnerable to temporary shocks (weather or market price fluctuations, illness, pests, etc.). Movement in and out of poverty is sometimes as common as chronic poverty. Data from the International Crops Research Institute for the Semi-Arid Tropics (ICRISAT) covering six Indian villages over the period 1975 to 1983 showed that, while half of the population was poor in a typical year, only 19 percent was poor every year. In a panel data set in rural China covering the period 1985 to 1990, Jalan and Ravallion[5] found that transient poverty, defined as poverty that can be attributed to intertemporal variability in consumption, accounted for 37 percent of total poverty for those households that were below the poverty line on average.

Poor people use low-return income strategies to reduce vulnerability.

Faced with pervasive risks, the poor try to follow *ex ante* risk management strategies (including crop diversification, use of low-yield drought-resistant varieties, protective irrigation, sharecropping, migration of family members, etc.) or *ex post* risk-coping strategies to smooth consumption intertemporally (dissaving, sales of assets, borrowing from relatives and other informal sources, remittances, withdrawing children from school, etc.). Yet these attempts are often costly and insufficient. For example, Morduch (1995)[6] has shown from ICRISAT data in India that households that are more vulnerable to income shocks devote a much smaller share of their land to risky high-yielding varieties compared with less vulnerable households.

Thus, a low-return low-risk approach tends to prolong poverty.[7] Attempts at local, informal risk pooling have proved insufficient, particularly when there are systemic and covariate risks at the village and region levels. In general, the difficulties in enforcement and information dissemination associated with both insurance and credit transactions frustrate poor households in their efforts to insulate their consumption from income shocks.

Some microcredit programmes, such as that of Burkinabé Caisse Villageoise d'Épargne et de Crédit den Bangh in Burkina Faso, SEWA in India, the Grameen Bank and Bangladesh Rural Advancement Committee (BARC) in Bangladesh, explicitly provide simultaneous access to credit and insurance. Loan defaults by poor women members in SEWA declined significantly after there was a provision of insurance against health and other risks. In order to diversify its own risks, the SEWA Bank has now arranged for group insurance contracts with a large state-run insurance company. Joint arrangements between state and community organizations mitigate different kinds of information problems and risks faced by both types of organization, for example the local community organization can provide group screening and monitoring services while the state organization can cover for covariate risks. Such arrangements are crucial in building viable credit and insurance programmes for the poor but, as yet, there are too few of them in developing countries.

GOVERNMENT INTERVENTION TO ALLEVIATE FOOD INSECURITY

One of the main ways in which governments in some countries have tried to alleviate food insecurity is to make available subsidized food at authorized points of public distribution. India, for example, has a large programme of public food distribution through "fair price" shops, accounting for a significant part of the government's budgetary subsidies. It is a very costly programme, as an estimated 72 percent of the food subsidy is taken up by overheads, storage, freight and interest costs, etc.) and its benefits reach only a tiny fraction of the rural poor in the whole country.[8]

A much more cost-effective way of reaching the poor (specifically the able-bodied adults) is through public works programmes where work is made available for low wages whenever the worker wants. This is an arrangement offered by the Employment Guarantee Scheme (EGS) in the state of Maharashtra in India, for instance. Since the poor, particularly in lean agricultural seasons, can self-target themselves in such works programmes, the leakage of the benefits to the non-poor is relatively small (bogus master rolls may, of course, divert some funds to the non-poor entrepreneurs). A detailed comparative study, carried out by Guhan,[9] of the cost-effectiveness of EGS *vis-à-vis* the public food distribution programme in India suggests that the former is twice that of the latter (even after taking into account the foregone earnings of those participating in EGS). In addition, there are secondary benefits of EGS, including asset creation (roads, irrigation, etc.) and increased bargaining power of peasant farmers in the agricultural labour market. Other studies to determine the cost-effectiveness of alternative anti-poverty programmes in India – by Radhakrishna *et al.*[10] and Dev[11] – show that the cost per rupee of transfer to the poor was Rs 5.37 for the public food distribution scheme, Rs 2.28 for an India-wide public works programme (called JRY) and Rs 1.87 for EGS in Maharashtra.

Of course, programmes such as EGS are more effective in relieving transient poverty and providing a floor to agricultural wages than in improving skills, sustainability of income or autonomy. Self-employment on farms and in artisan shops is a better avenue for the latter purposes. Regarding self-employment, while those who emphasize market failures point to the constraints posed by credit, marketing and physical infrastructure (e.g. roads or electricity supply), those who emphasize government failure point to cumbersome regulations and state interventions in pricing. The latter also show that serious underpricing of scarce inputs – such as capital, energy, water and environmental resources – often leads to the adoption of capital-intensive and environment-damaging projects, which ultimately hurt the poor. In addition, the requisite government subsidies drain the public treasury of funds that could have been much better invested in infrastructure and public investment in agriculture. Those who emphasize local institutional failures point to the fact that inappropriate technology and disenfranchisement of the poor from their traditional access to environmental resources are often the outcome of distant centralized decision-makers not being sensitive to local information on methods of production, traditional arrangements and particularistic needs.

Government interventions to address transient poverty are different from those aimed at long-term income sustainability.

ECONOMIC AND SOCIAL FUNCTIONS OF THE GOVERNMENT

It is now generally agreed that, while the government often plays an obtrusive role in areas where it usually performs poorly (e.g.

Lagging support for needed public goods and infrastructure has slowed technological progress in agriculture.

in certain lines of manufacturing or trade, including regulations in foodgrain marketing and pricing),[12] it frequently does not play an important role where it should (e.g. providing basic education, research and extension services, public health and sanitation and roads). In particular, falling public investment in agricultural research and development in many countries is slowing the rate of technological progress in agriculture, while the decline of investments in the maintenance and repair of irrigation and drainage systems and rural roads as well as in the prevention of soil erosion have curtailed the effectiveness of earlier investments in agriculture. In Africa, public agronomic research aimed at locally specific technological improvements has been seriously deficient. In China, recent projections by IFPRI suggest that every yuan renminbi invested in research and irrigation over the coming decades could yield returns of between Y 3.6 and Y 4.8.

Those who emphasize the role of local institutions underline the importance (from the point of view of both targeting and cost-effectiveness) of local governments, accountable to the local people, in the provision of public goods and services. Standard examples of this are the serious problems of absenteeism of salaried teachers in village public schools and doctors in rural public health clinics – a situation that may be mitigated by making the teachers and doctors answerable to local village councils and dependent on them for at least part of their salary. The same applies to the accountability to local farmers of government officers such as extension agents, irrigation engineers, water guards and veterinarians for farm animals.

Accountability usually brings responsibility in decision-making and in implementation, which helps in improving quality and cost-efficiency. There is some scattered evidence of such quality improvement and cost savings. The *World Development Report 1994*[13] on infrastructure reports several cases. In Mexico, under the municipal fund project introduced in 1990, community committees (Comites de Solidaridad) manage rural investment in simple infrastructure such as small water supply systems, rural roads and bridges and school buildings. Studies have found that these projects often cost one half to two thirds as much as similar projects managed by state or federal agencies. A review of World Bank data for 42 developing countries found that, where road maintenance was decentralized, backlogs were lower and the conditions of roads better. Data for a group of developing countries reveal that per caput costs of water in World Bank-funded water projects are

FAO/17418/H. WAGNER

Members of a village committee discuss anti-erosion measures in a maize field

Local social capital results from a shift in emphasis from massive state interventions to better local resource management

Local participation in projects vastly increases their chance of success.

four times higher in centralized than in fully decentralized systems. An econometric study by Isham, Narayan, and Pritchett[14] of 121 completed rural water supply projects in 49 countries showed that seven out of every ten projects succeeded when the intended beneficiaries took an active part in project selection and design, but that only one in ten succeeded when they did not.

With the aim of improving the effectiveness of investments, the emphasis of public investments in agriculture is shifting from massive state investment in large dams (which often cause large displacements of people, environmental damage, waterlogging and salinity and arbitrary water control operations run by a corrupt and distant bureaucracy) to better local management of existing irrigation systems and minor irrigation projects under some form of community control. In a comparison of the mode of operation of canal irrigation bureaucracy in the Republic of Korea and India, Wade[15] finds the former to be more sensitive to the needs of the local farmers, and thus more effective. The Indian canal systems are large, centralized hierarchies in charge of all functions (operations and maintenance as well as design and construction). Their ways of operating (including promotion and transfer rules for officials, rules designed to minimize identification between the irrigation patrollers and the local farmers, and the frequent use of low-trust management and supervision methods) and their sources of finance (most of the irrigation department's budget is in the form of a grant from the state treasury) are totally insensitive to the need for developing and drawing on local social capital. In contrast, in the Republic of Korea there are functionally separate organizations in the canal systems: the implementation and routine maintenance tasks (as opposed to policy-making and technical design work) are delegated to the Farmland Improvement Associations (one per catchment area), which are staffed by local part-time farmers (selected by the village chiefs). These farmers have knowledge of changing local conditions, are largely dependent for their salary and operational budget on the user fees paid by the farmers and continually draw on local trust relationships.

In government transfer programmes to the poor or the provision of safety nets, again, issues of local accountability are considered important for reducing leakages (in the form of both misappropriation by non-target groups and failure to reach all members of a target group). While the literature on targeting emphasizes the administrative and incentive aspects of targeted interventions, some politico-economic discussion suggests that a transition from a universal to a more narrowly targeted anti-poverty programme designed to minimize leakages may seriously erode its political support base and worsen the condition of the poor. Examples may be cited from the food subsidy programmes in Sri Lanka and Colombia, where episodes of increased targeting have been followed by reductions in overall benefits.

Alliances among different groups in a country are required to mobilize political support for poverty reduction programmes.

Concerning political support for anti-poverty programmes, it is generally agreed that the poor are not usually sufficiently organized to mobilize political pressure and need explicit or tacit alliances with other groups in society to push for these programmes. It often requires astute political leadership to organize short-term sacrifices on the part of wealthier taxpayers to fund anti-poverty programmes that will generate positive externalities also for the élite groups in the long term (less crime and public squalor, a better-educated and healthier populace and labour force, a larger demand base for industries, etc.). Policies that combine growth with redistribution (i.e. sharing in the increments rather than in the existing pie) soften the opposition to public anti-poverty programmes. In general, democracies provide a more hospitable environment for support to such programmes (there seems to be some cross-country evidence[16] of a positive correlation between democratic regimes and the human development indicators, controlling other factors). More generally, regimes that are characterized by transparency and accountability in their institutions may have a better chance of reaching out to the intended beneficiaries of such programmes.

Going beyond the impact of local accountability on the quality of service in publicly supplied facilities, it is important to note that, if a local community organization has a stable membership and well-developed structures for transmitting private information and norms among the members, it may have the potential for better management of common property resources (e.g. forests, grazing lands, fisheries and minor surface irrigation works). These are resources on which the rural poor are vitally dependent for their daily livelihood and also for insurance in the form of a fallback source of food and fodder in bad crop years. There are several documented examples in different parts of the world of successful and autonomous local community-level management of commons – see Ostrom,[17] Tang,[18] Baland and Platteau,[19] and Lam.[20]

Nevertheless, there are also many cases of failure of cooperation in the management of common resources in poor countries, leading to an anarchical regime in the scramble for these resources. With the erosion of the local commons – the decimation of forests and grazing lands, silting and increasing toxicity of rivers and ponds, the depletion of aquifers, soil erosion and desertification – the life of the rural poor in many parts of the world has become more insecure and impoverished in ways that are not captured in the usual poverty estimates based on private consumer expenditure data. Many countries actually have a long history of balanced resource management under highly informal local community arrangements.

The erosion of the commons set in only with the major demographic and institutional changes that occurred in recent decades, often accelerated by commercial or bureaucratic appropriation of the common resources, supplanting the traditional historical rights of local communities over these resources. A devolution of power back to these communities can succeed in regulating, conserving and maintaining these resources. In some cases, for example in forest protection and regeneration and wasteland development in India, there have been successful instances of joint management by the state and the local community, with the latter taking major responsibilities.

DEFINING THE ROLE OF THE STATE

The state has an important role in catalysing public involvement and decision-making.

The implication of the foregoing is that a more nuanced theory of the state is required than is usually available from the age-old state-versus-market debate. On the one hand, factors limiting the state's capacity as an economic governance structure should be recognized, for example its lack of access to local information, its lack of local accountability and its vulnerability to wasteful rent-seeking processes. On the other hand, the state is not to withdraw into its minimalist role of classical liberalism but, instead, should play an activist role (if only as a "catalyst") in enabling the mobilization of people in local participatory development; in providing supralocal support by pump-priming local finance and underwriting risks (but at the same time avoiding the associated moral hazard of encouraging dependency); supplying technical and professional services to build local capacity (including in accounting and bookkeeping); acting as a watchdog for service quality standards, evaluation and auditing; investing in larger infrastructure; and providing some coordination in the face of externalities[21] across localities. This is a complex but necessary task for any state, but it is often unappreciated by proponents of decentralization.

Advocates of decentralization sometimes also ignore the fact that problems relating to distributive conflicts are a major hindrance to most schemes of decentralized governance. In areas of high social and economic inequality, the "capture" of local governing agencies by the local élite group can be severe, and the poor and the weaker sections of the population may be left grievously exposed to their mercies and malfeasance. The central government can also be "captured", but there are many reasons why the problem may be more serious at the local level. For example, there are certain fixed costs of organizing resistance groups or lobbies: as a result, the poor may sometimes be less organized at the local level than at the national level, where they can pool their organizing capacities. Similarly, for a number of reasons, collusion among the élite groups may be easier at the local level than at the national level. Policy-making at the national level may indeed represent a greater compromise among the policy platforms of different parties and such "capture" may be subject to greater media attention at the national level. When a local government is captured by the powerful and the wealthy, instances of subordinate groups appealing to supralocal authorities for protection and relief are not uncommon. In such cases, interventions by the long arm of the state in remote corners of poor countries have been by invitation, and not always by arbitrary imposition. Ultimately, tendencies of the élite to capture local bodies and use them for their own purpose can be kept in check only as accountability mechanisms and local institutions of transparency and democracy take root (and as experience in self-management acquired by the poor − e.g. in cooperatives, unions and other rural social and political organizations − starts spilling over from one activity to another).

The same problem clearly afflicts local (non-governmental) community organizations in management of the commons. Extreme social fragmentation in a country, for example, makes cooperation in community institution building much more difficult than in more socially homogeneous countries. One beneficial by-product of land reform, frequently underemphasized in economic analyses of the issue, is that, by changing the local political structure in the village, such reform gives more "voice" to the poor and induces them to become involved in local self-governing institutions and the management of local commons.

ISSUES OF GOVERNANCE

The relationship between the state and local governance is also important in thinking about the question of why progress in the alleviation of poverty and food insecurity in recent decades seems to have been slower in some regions than in others. This is a complex question, and it is difficult to give a satisfactory answer. Only one broad aspect is touched on here: while geography and climate, droughts and disease and declining and volatile terms of trade for commodity export-based economies have been emphasized in the recent literature, the issue of governance may also be important. It is possible to argue that regions with slower growth in general may have seen no more government interventionism than other regions. More important than the quantity of intervention, however, is the quality of intervention. The quality of governance in some countries has been directly affected by rampant ethnic conflicts and civil wars. With weak and fragmented governments (even under authoritarian rulers), the state often may not enforce the laws or property rights that provide the minimum underpinnings of a market economy. The problem in slower-growing regions may to a large extent be linked with state capacity and social integration within the boundaries of the state, with the disjunction between state and community or civil society being much more egregious.

Under these circumstances, in centralized regimes where power is in the hands of dominant ethnic groups or regions, *decentralization* in the sense of the devolution of power to local units and communities and the local accountability of officials delivering public services is crucial in defusing ethnic tensions that often arise from minority groups and regions fearing discrimination and permanent exclusion. A system of checks and balances against the arbitrary abuse of power to the detriment of minorities and regional autonomy in major political and economic decisions can go a long way to creating institutions of trust and commitment. Under the pressure of reducing fiscal deficits in a structural adjustment programme (SAP), the central government often tries to shift the fiscal responsibility of some redistribution programmes to the underfunded local units, with serious implications for poor ethnic groups and backward regions. As Azam, Berthelemy and Calipel[22] show in their econometric tests on the basis of a large sample of African countries, political unrest is often triggered by wrong government decisions regarding redistributive versus repressive expenditures.

The context of sharply demarcated ethnic groups or regions also raises the issue of the possible need for group-specific public interventions. In situations of historically disadvantaged groups (differentiated by ethnicity or gender, for example) and backward and remote geographical areas locked into poverty, anti-poverty programmes in poor countries may have to go beyond the usual policies addressed to individuals and households *per se*, and policies aimed at poor areas and groups as a whole may be fruitful in terms of equity, efficiency and intergroup harmony. Of course, preferential policies towards some groups or areas designed to cope with historical handicaps can carry the risk of being difficult to reverse, once adopted, and of having perverse incentive effects. A particularly important aspect of the problems relating to disadvantaged groups or areas refers to opportunities for intergenerational social mobility. The data on poverty and inequality in poor countries are generally remarkably deficient in indicators of such intergenerational social mobility for different social and economic groups. Yet some of the intense democratic struggles and ethnic movements in poor countries are less about income distribution and poverty lines, and more about opportunities for such intergenerational mobility.

Obstacles to collective action for change

Finally, in trying to understand why dysfunctional institutions that perpetuate poverty persist, one cannot avoid the general issue of power constellations in a society and the difficulties of

Extension services

Trainers convey integrated pest management techniques to improve local management skills

changing them, even when such changes may be shown to be beneficial for the majority of the people. The crux of the problem is in organizing collective action that orchestrates the movement from a "bad" equilibrium to a "good" equilibrium. Sometimes the gains from such a movement are diffuse or uncertain in the perception of the gainers. But even if everyone were to know that the social gain from an institutional change clearly outweighed the loss, and that gainers could compensate the losers, potential gainers cannot credibly commit themselves to compensating the losers *ex post.* Ideally, the state would issue long-term bonds to buy off the losers and tax the gainers to repay. But in most poor countries there are serious limitations to the government's ability to tax as well as to keep inflation under control, and so the bond market is thin.

The classic example of inefficient institutions persisting as the lopsided outcome of distributive struggles relates to the historical evolution of land rights in developing countries. In most of these countries the empirical evidence suggests that economies of scale in farm production are insignificant (except in some plantation crops), and the small family farm is often the most efficient unit of production. Yet, the violent and tortuous history of land reform in many countries suggests that there are numerous roadblocks on the way to a more efficient reallocation of land rights put up by vested interests for generations. Why do the large landowners not voluntarily lease out or sell their land to small family farmers and take much of the surplus arising from this efficient reallocation? Clearly there has been some leasing out of land, but monitoring problems, insecurity of tenure and the landowner's fear that the tenant will acquire occupancy rights on the land have limited the efficiency gains from and the extent of tenancy. The land sales market has been particularly thin (and in many poor countries the sales go the opposite way, from distressed small farmers to landowners and moneylenders). With low household savings and severely imperfect credit markets, even the potentially more efficient small farmer is often unable to afford the market price of land.

The creation of productive small farms is impeded by rigidities in landownership.

Landowners also resist land reforms because the levelling effects reduce their social and political power and their ability to control and dominate even non-land transactions. Large landholdings may confer on their owners a disproportionate degree of social status or political power (so that the status or political effect of owning 100 ha is larger than the combined status or political effect accruing to 50 new buyers owning 2 ha each). Thus, the social or political rent of landownership for the large landowner will not be compensated by the offering price of the numerous small buyers. Under these circumstances, the former will not sell, and land concentration – which may be inefficient from a purely productivity perspective – will persist.

Even in the context of increasing returns to landownership in terms of political rent, land concentration is not always the unique or stable political equilibrium. Much depends on the nature of political competition and the context-specific and path-dependent formations of political coalitions. An interesting example, in terms of comparative institutional-historical analysis, is provided by Nugent and Robinson.[23] Holding constant both colonial background and crop technology, they compare the divergent institutional (particularly in terms of smallholder property rights) and growth trajectories of two pairs of former Spanish colonies in the same region (Costa Rica and Colombia, on the one hand, and El Salvador and Guatemala, on the other) producing the same principal crop (coffee).

In general, an important aspect of political rent is that both sides are really interested in *relative*, rather than absolute, gain or loss. In a power game, as in a winner-take-all contest or tournament, it is not enough for an institutional change to increase the surplus for all parties concerned. One side may gain absolutely, and yet it may lose relative to the other side and thus may resist change.

Given the strength of opposition of vested interests, many regard the political prospects for land reform in most poor countries as bleak, and therefore drop it altogether from the agenda of poverty alleviation. This is not always wise. Some aspects of land reform (e.g. extension of tenurial security) may be less difficult to implement than others (e.g. land ceilings). Furthermore, in the dynamics of political processes and shifting coalitions, the range of feasibility often changes, and options that are left open contribute to the political debate and may influence the political process. Some policy advisers (in international lending agencies) who rule out land reform as politically infeasible are at the same time enthusiastic supporters of other policies that may be no less politically difficult; an example is the strict targeting of food subsidies (that we have already alluded to) and thus cutting the substantial subsidies to the vocal urban middle classes. In the context of political coalitions, a radical policy sometimes becomes feasible if it helps cement strategic alliances between, for example, sections of the urban upper classes (including white-collar workers) and the rural poor.

Some methods of land reform can be counterproductive, particularly in situations of land scarcity and weak organization of land-poor groups. Well-intentioned measures such as the abolition of tenancy often end up driving tenancy underground or leading to large-scale eviction of tenants, and they take away the part of the agricultural ladder by which the landless could formerly climb out of poverty. Redistributing land without adequate provision of credit and marketing facilities and extension services may make land recipients worse off as they are obliged to burn their bridges with the erstwhile landlord-creditor patron. In recent years, there has been increasing support for "market-assisted land reforms" (as opposed to confiscatory land reforms), whereby the government assists voluntary transactions in the land market through credit and subsidies to the small buyers.

CONCLUSIONS
Reducing poverty and food insecurity is not simply a question of enhancing agricultural productivity and production or of generating more income. Institutions are the structuring features that command access of people to assets, to voice and to power over their lives and that regulate competing claims to limited

resources. It is fundamental to address those institutional, governance and politico-economic factors that tend to exclude individuals and population groups from progress. This section has assessed the experience in this regard and suggested avenues for reorganizing governance and institutions (particularly in agriculture and the rural economy in general) with this purpose in mind.

NOTES

1 See, for example, J. Yaron, B. McDonald and S. Charitonenko. 1998. Promoting efficient rural financial intermediation. In *World Bank Research Observer*, and R. Vogel. 1984. The effect of subsidised agricultural credit on income distribution in Costa Rica. *In* D.W. Adams, D. Graham and J.D. von Pischke. *Undermining rural development with cheap credit.* Boulder, Colorado, USA, Westview Press.

2 See J. Morduch. 1998. The microfinance promise. Princeton University (unpublished paper).

3 S. Amin, A.S. Rai and G. Topa. 1999. *Does microcredit reach the poor and vulnerable? Evidence from northern Bangladesh.* CID Working Paper, Harvard University (October 1999).

4 Morduch, op. cit., note 2.

5 J. Jalan and M. Ravallion. 1998. Transient poverty in post-reform rural China. *Journal of Comparative Economics*, 26(2): 338-357.

6 J. Morduch. 1995. Income smoothing and consumption smoothing. *Journal of Economic Perspectives.*

7 For a similar effect on the adoption or the spread of new technologies for grain production in semi-arid Africa, see J. Sanders, B. Shapiro and S. Ramaswamy. 1996. *The economics of agricultural technology in semi-arid sub-Saharan Africa.* Baltimore, Maryland, USA, Johns Hopkins University Press.

8 In many states (including some of the poorest) it has been found that more than 95 percent of the population does not receive any of their foodgrain supplies from the public distribution system.

9 S. Guhan. 1994. Social security options for developing countries. In *International Labour Review.*

10 R. Radhakrishna and K. Subbarao with C. Indrakant and C. Ravi. 1997. *India's Public Distribution System: a national and international perspective.* World Bank Discussion Paper No. 380. Washington, DC, World Bank.

11 S.M. Dev. 1998. Rising food prices and rural poverty: going beyond correlations. *Economic and Political Weekly*, 39.

12 For examples from the United Republic of Tanzania and Kenya of how heavy government regulations in grain marketing made food prices more volatile, and how the adoption of cash crops by smallholders – a main source of agricultural growth – was slowed by government pricing policies, see D.L. Bevan, P. Collier and J.W. Gunning. 1993. *Agriculture and the policy environment.* Paris, OECD.

13 World Bank. 1994. *World Development Report 1994.* Washington, DC.

14 J. Isham, D. Narayan and L. Pritchett. 1995. Does participation improve performance? Establishing causality with subjective data. In *World Bank Economic Review*, May 1995.

15 R. Wade. 1997. How infrastructure agencies motivate staff: canal irrigation in India and the Republic of Korea. *In* A. Mody, ed. *Infrastructure strategies in East Asia.* Washington, DC, Economic Development Institute, World Bank.

16 See, for example, A. Przeworski and F. Limongi. 1997. Development and democracy. *In* A. Hadenius, ed. *Democracy's victory and crisis.* New York, Cambridge University Press.

17 E. Ostrom. 1990. *Governing the commons: the evolution of institutions for collective action.* New York, Cambridge University Press.

18 S.Y. Tang. 1991. Institutional arrangements and the management of common pool resources. *Public Administration Review,* January/February 1991.

19 J.M. Baland and J.-P. Platteau. 1996. *Halting degradation of natural resources: is there a role for rural communities?* Rome, FAO.

20 W.F. Lam. 1998. *Governing irrigation systems in Nepal: institutions, infrastructure, and collective action.* Oakland, USA, ICS Press.

21 An externality, or an external effect, refers to a situation in which the production or consumption of a good or service by one individual consumer or producer directly affects the welfare of some other consumers or the costs of production of other producers. Such externalities can be either positive (when they reduce costs or improve the welfare of other economic agents) or negative (when they raise costs or reduce the welfare of others).

22 J.-P. Azam, J.-C. Berthelemy and S. Calipel. 1996. Risque politique et croissance en Afrique. *Revue Économique,* 47 (3): 819-829.

23 J.B. Nugent and J. Robinson. 1998. *Are endowments fate? On the political economy of comparative institutional development.* Department of Economics Working Paper. Los Angeles, USA, University of Southern California.

What have we learned?

Humanity is forgetful. Today, many are unaware of the fact that, until recently, the risk of extensive famines was a stark reality. This was the case half a century ago, when the founders of FAO raised the Organization's flag – committing themselves to ensuring humanity's freedom from hunger.

> *"The nations accepting this Constitution ... promote the common welfare ... for the purpose of: raising levels of nutrition and standards of living...; securing improvements in the efficiency of the production and distribution of all food and agricultural products; bettering the condition of rural populations; and thus contributing towards an expanding world economy and ensuring humanity's freedom from hunger;"*
>
> **Constitution of FAO, Preamble – as amended in 1965**
> **In *Basic Texts of the***
> ***Food and Agriculture Organization of the United Nations***

In the late 1940s, parts of the world were recovering from devastating war damages and others struggling against colonialism. The majority of the world's population was poor and powerless and agricultural productivity was low. Famines threatened, particularly in the densely populated continent of Asia, and in some tragic cases became a reality.

Looking back 50 years later, however, we can see that humanity as a whole has achieved considerable progress in the battle against hunger. The average food intake and standard of living have improved substantially, despite the fact that there are 2.5 times more mouths to feed, and the undernourished population has declined in both absolute and percentage terms.

Yet this overall performance is gravely inadequate, as more than 800 million people are still chronically undernourished. It also masks enormous regional disparities. Since 1970, the number of undernourished has doubled in Africa, while it has been halved in East and Southeast Asia. Country performances also vary greatly within regions and hunger also persists among the poorer and vulnerable groups in rich countries.

As noted at the beginning of this review, the past 50 years have been extraordinarily eventful and have brought about wide-ranging and rapid changes to humanity. Progress has been spectacular in such areas as agricultural technology and productivity, but disappointing with regard to poverty alleviation, especially in rural areas. New issues such as sustainability and environmental impacts have gained prominence as agricultural production has expanded, with a greater use of inputs and resources.

This special chapter has investigated some of the major factors that explain these positive and negative changes. To conclude, the main findings have been summarized with a view to deriving some general conclusions.

KEY FINDINGS

Food and agriculture over the past 50 years. The past half-century has seen evolving perceptions regarding development, including its promises and constraints, ways to achieve it and the role that the public and private sectors should play in accelerating it. For a long time, the key contribution made by agriculture to economic and social development has not always been recognized. Moreover, world hunger has failed to attract the sustained attention it warrants. Against a rapidly accelerating process of international integration and interdependence, a flurry of national and international initiatives in the past decade have borne witness to greater public interest in problems and issues relating to poverty reduction, sustainable development and food security. Furthermore, it has been recognized that, because of the interdependence of such issues, concerted action is required to address them.

Figure 28

UNDERNOURISHMENT IN THE DEVELOPING REGIONS

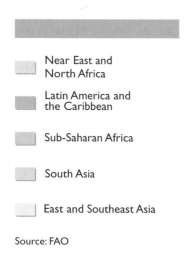

Near East and North Africa

Latin America and the Caribbean

Sub-Saharan Africa

South Asia

East and Southeast Asia

Source: FAO

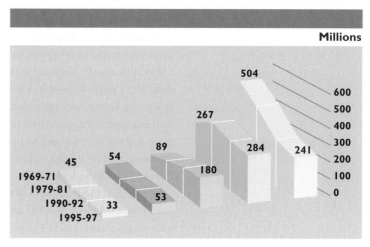

Millions

1969-71
1979-81
1990-92
1995-97

45
54
89
267
504
284
241
180
33
53

600
500
400
300
200
100
0

Social and economic impact of agricultural modernization.
The process of agricultural modernization has enabled major
gains in agricultural output overall but has had very asymmetrical
effects on rural societies and on the income and productivity
levels of small-scale traditional farmers *vis-à-vis* those involved in
industrial agriculture. A continuation of this process could have
detrimental economic and social effects on poor farmers and
rural societies. It would also accelerate rural migration, thus
accentuating the negative effects of rapid urbanization.

Food and nutrition security: why food production matters.
Development strategies that emphasize staple food production
have proved to be cost-effective in providing the poor with
entitlement to food. For most of the undernourished who live in
rural areas, extra employment and income derived from staple
food production has been – and will continue to be – the key
to enhanced food entitlements. While food availability must be
secured, it is equally important for consumers to have access to
a safe, varied and nutritionally balanced diet that ensures them
an active and healthy life.

Agricultural production and productivity. Extraordinary but
uneven gains in agricultural production and productivity have
been achieved, largely as a result of different approaches to
augmenting countries' "technological capital". Technological
advancements, rendered possible by research and investment
efforts and by support from national and international
agricultural research centres, have played an irreplaceable role.
Changes in the relationship between population and resources
have also been important factors; the worker-population ratio,
which had been declining in many countries, is now growing in
most, thus allowing these countries to benefit from the
"demographic gift" that has already helped some of the most
populous countries to address the challenge of development
and increasing food supplies. Prospects for a continuation of
the productivity growth seen in the past are hindered in many
countries by land degradation, strained water resources and
reduced irrigation investment opportunities. However, there is
now evidence that biotechnology can contribute substantially to
overcoming these problems, provided adequate precautions are
taken against properly assessed negative outcomes.

Political economy issues, poverty and food security. "Poverty
traps" continue to plague large segments of populations in all
societies, and they are perpetuated or even accentuated by

failures in various political, institutional and coordinating mechanisms – at the level of the market, the government or the local community. Imperfections in the credit and insurance markets severely restrict the ability of the poor to invest in and expand production. Where success has been achieved in poverty alleviation, governments have played a fundamental role in helping the poor to escape the poverty trap, by enabling them to have access to basic education, health, research and extension services, roads and marketing infrastructures. On the other hand, the removal of costly and distortive government regulations and market interventions has boosted economic and agricultural development.

CONCLUSIONS

Common to the findings listed here is the fact that progress achieved in the reduction of hunger over the past 50 years has been insufficient, and much is still to be accomplished before hunger, a scourge as ancient as humanity, is finally eradicated.

> It is humankind that is responsible for having imposed hunger on itself for so long, but humankind is also capable of eliminating this burden. There can be no greater challenge than this.

Improving access to food

It has become progressively clear that hunger results not so much from insufficient food supplies, as from people's lack of access to those supplies. In fact, the world already had a problem of food "surpluses" owing to insufficient purchasing power 50 years ago.

Nobel Prize laureate Amartya Sen[1] has analysed the causes of famines and observed cases in which people starved to death in spite of food availability – because they had no "entitlement".

> "What we can eat depends on what food we are able to acquire. The mere presence of food in the economy, or in the market, does not entitle a person to consume it. In each social structure, given the prevailing legal, political and economic arrangements, a person can establish command over some alternative commodity bundles ... [i.e.] this person's entitlements. *A person's entitlements depend on what she owns initially and what she can acquire through exchange. For example, a wage labourer owns her labour power, and by exchanging that for a wage... she acquires some money, which she can exchange for some commodity bundle or other....*"
>
> **Hunger and public action**

Promoting growth with equity

In improving access to food by the poor, two factors are of prime importance: economic growth and equity. For a poor household whose major endowment is its labour force, economic growth with equity can offer a favourable market for its products, more employment opportunities, a greater capacity on the part of society to support the needy and, thus, increased *entitlements*.

While economic growth obviously matters in reducing hunger, optimism regarding how widely and rapidly its benefits are spread is often challenged. Indeed, poverty and hunger do not always retreat as a national economy grows. Growth often bypasses, and can even harm, some groups, and recent economic growth at the international and national levels has frequently been accompanied by growing inequalities.

There is a strong case for resource-poor farmers who are unable to keep up with the competition of modern agriculture, especially in the face of declining output prices. All reviews of rural poverty, particularly women's poverty, point to a common factor – unequal access to land, compounded by unequal access to water, credit, knowledge and markets. This underlines the importance of agrarian reform. Although politically difficult, successful agrarian reforms have not only rectified income distribution but also resulted in sharp increases in productivity.

Improving the distribution of wealth, resources and opportunities is a key factor in the fight against hunger. Extreme inequity and poverty result in desperate people and destabilizing tensions in rural and urban societies. This also points to the need for targeted measures that not only address the immediate food and health care requirements of disadvantaged groups, but also provide them with developmental means, i.e. access to inputs, infrastructure, services and, most important, education.

The importance of food and agricultural production

In pursuance of economic growth, many countries, particularly during the first part of the past 50 years, endeavoured to accelerate industrialization in the hope that earnings from industrial exports would enable them to import food to complement domestic production. This hope was fuelled both by the fact that food supplies in world markets were adequate to meet import needs and by an observed declining trend in real food and agricultural prices in world markets. However, such a strategy, based on industry-led growth and often accomplished through an urban bias in fiscal and social policies, largely failed, leaving behind vast rural poverty and food insecurity while accentuating problems linked to rapid urbanization.

Policies based on this strategy failed mainly because they overlooked the importance of agricultural production, particularly of staple foods, as a critical source of entitlements for the many food producers, who were also consumers. In predominantly agrarian economies, there is no mechanism for distributing entitlements to peasant farming populations other than that of enabling them to develop their food and agricultural production.

Building technological capital

The unprecedented increase in crop yields over the past 50 years has been the main source of growth in the world's food supplies, as the global expansion of arable land has been limited. Nevertheless, there have been dramatic shifts in land use. Deforestation has fed a good part of the increase in arable land − with well-documented negative consequences on the environment − while, on the other hand, previously productive farmland has been taken up by urban and infrastructure development as well as by desertification and other forms of land degradation and conversion.

Behind the yield increases are major technological forces, including increased inputs of fertilizers and pesticides, genetically improved seeds, irrigation and drainage. Improved infrastructure, such as rural roads, has also contributed to the increase in agricultural productivity. Such advances were made possible by public and private investments. However, the drawback with increased inputs, i.e. physical investments, is that they bring diminishing returns. In this context, research leading to technological development and its dissemination has been crucial. National research capacities to adopt and disseminate technological developments have proved a crucial factor in the performance of yield increases.

The most remarkable agricultural achievement of the past 50 years has been the green revolution, combining coordinated agricultural research and policy effort. It was particularly successful in large parts of Asia, although initial enthusiasm later waned with the growing awareness of some of its negative social and environmental impacts. Given the absence of a comparable technological development suitable for the conditions and crop composition prevailing in most of Africa, the green revolution bypassed most of that region's farmers.

Investment in research, rural infrastructure and extension services, as well as human capital development, has proved indispensable to technological progress and the development of social and physical infrastructure.

Developing human capital

Human capital in the form of knowledge and skills has been vital for reducing poverty and improving food security. Many studies have demonstrated the effect of education, especially for women, on farm and off-farm output and productivity, as well as on health and nutrition. The provision of basic education constitutes the best long-term investment, favouring the most disadvantaged groups in particular. Training and the development of skills are also fundamental, as farmers with good knowledge and skills are better able to respond to new technology, market opportunities and risks. Training activities can be very costly, however, and so the suitability and rapid application of new skills taught must be a prime consideration in their design.

The importance of sound and stable institutions

The institutional framework that governs a people's collective behaviour and social relations is crucial in enabling the expression of individuals' capacities for their own betterment as well as for the collective welfare, encompassing food security and sustainable agriculture. Institutions can either help shape or prevent solidarity relations, sustainable management of common resources, risk pooling and responsible behaviour. Institutions are also crucial in giving a voice to the weak and in checking the damaging effects of excessive power differences within a society. Moreover, sound institutional frameworks and capacity are naturally conducive to good governance.

Sound institutions are also required to secure minimum conditions of political stability and social cohesion. In addition to their direct and dramatic impacts on the populations concerned, civil strife and conflicts have long-term negative effects on development and food security – clearly indicated by the high proportion of conflict-affected countries among those with the highest incidence of undernourishment. Even when conflicts have been resolved, they leave behind a terrible inheritance that can last many years, including land mines, loss of human capital and demolished infrastructure.

Making incentives work

Perceptions of the responsiveness of agriculture to economic incentives have evolved dramatically over the past 50 years. In contrast to the old view that farmers are traditional and, therefore, not economically minded or responsive to incentives, there is now a general understanding that agriculture is responsive to economic incentives and is best run under private operations. China's experience in shifting from a collective farm system to one of household responsibility is, among other things, a shining example of incentives having resulted in a historical upsurge in agricultural production.

Yet incentives fail where the risks cannot be afforded. This is one element of the poverty trap, referred to under Key findings, p. 306. Many poor farmers cannot adopt higher-return crops or new technology because the change entails risks, and failure would be fatal for their livelihood. They therefore continue low-risk, low-return farming activities.

Unless effective incentives and a minimum level of protection against risk are available to farmers, agricultural capacity cannot be fully exploited − adequate credit and insurance markets are crucial in this regard.

Keeping pace with globalization

Over time, impressive structural changes occur that affect all people. Positively, population growth is slowing down, bringing with it a "window of opportunity" as the active-dependent population ratio starts to increase after a long decline. Negatively, the depletion of resources, deforestation, the emission of wastes, climate change, etc. may become serioius threats to the livelihood of humankind.

Currently, the dominant phenomenon is accelerating globalization. Without a historical precedent, goods and services, money and information are crossing borders in increasing amounts and with greater speed. This extraordinary process is not without costs, however. Globalization, or borderlessness, does not automatically benefit the poor. The fact that labour, the chief resource in early stages of development, is among the least mobile (in terms of crossing borders) of all production factors means that globalization can lead to greater inequalities as well as to greater progress. The capability of humankind to accompany globalization with the required understanding of its impact, as well as the collective capacity to harness its strength for the common good, will be crucial in the years to come.

NOTE

1   A. Sen. 1989. *In* J. Dreze and A. Sen, eds. *Hunger and public action.* Oxford, UK, Clarendon Press.

ANNEX

TABLE

COUNTRIES AND TERRITORIES USED FOR STATISTICAL PURPOSES IN THIS PUBLICATION

Developed countries	Countries in transition	Developing countries			
		Sub-Saharan Africa	Asia and the Pacific/ Far East and Oceania	Latin America and the Caribbean	Near East and North Africa
Albania	Albania	Angola	American Samoa	Anguilla	Afghanistan
Andorra		Benin	Bangladesh	Antigua and Barbuda	Algeria
Armenia	Armenia	Botswana	Bhutan	Argentina	Bahrain
Australia		Burkina Faso	British Virgin Islands	Aruba	Cyprus
Austria		Burundi	Brunei Darussalam	Bahamas	Egypt
Azerbaijan	Azerbaijan	Cameroon	Cambodia	Barbados	Gaza Strip
Belarus	Belarus	Cape Verde	China	Belize	Iran, Islamic Rep.
Belgium/ Luxembourg		Central African Rep.	Cocos Islands	Bermuda	Iraq
Bosnia and Herzegovina	Bosnia and Herzegovina	Chad	Cook Islands	Bolivia	Jordan
Bulgaria	Bulgaria	Comoros	East Timor	Brazil	Kuwait
Canada		Congo, Rep.	Fiji	Cayman Islands	Lebanon
Croatia	Croatia	Côte d'Ivoire	French Polynesia	Chile	Libyan Arab Jamahiriya
Czech Republic	Czech Republic	Democratic Republic of the Congo	Guam	Colombia	Morocco
Denmark		Djibouti	India	Costa Rica	Oman
Estonia	Estonia	Equatorial Guinea	Indonesia	Cuba	Qatar
Faeroe Islands		Eritrea	Kiribati	Dominica	Saudi Arabia
Finland		Ethiopia	Korea, Dem. People's Rep.	Dominican Republic	Syrian Arab Republic
France		Gabon	Korea, Rep.	Ecuador	Tunisia
Georgia	Georgia	Gambia	Lao People's Dem. Rep.	El Salvador	Turkey
Germany		Ghana	Macau	Falkland Islands (Malvinas)	United Arab Emirates
Gibraltar		Guinea	Malaysia	French Guiana	West Bank
Greece		Guinea-Bissau	Maldives	Grenada	Yemen
Greenland		Kenya	Marshall Islands	Guadeloupe	
Hungary	Hungary	Lesotho	Micronesia, Fed. States	Guatemala	
Iceland		Liberia	Mongolia	Guyana	
Ireland		Madagascar	Myanmar	Haiti	
Israel		Malawi	Nauru	Honduras	
Italy		Mali	Nepal	Jamaica	
Japan		Mauritania	New Caledonia	Martinique	
Kazakhstan	Kazakhstan	Mauritius	Niue	Mexico	

Developed countries	Countries in transition	Developing countries			
		Sub-Saharan Africa	Asia and the Pacific/ Far East and Oceania	Latin America and the Caribbean	Near East and North Africa
Kyrgyzstan	Kyrgyzstan	Mozambique	Norfolk Islands	Montserrat	
Latvia	Latvia	Namibia	Northern Mariana Islands	Netherlands Antilles	
Liechtenstein		Niger	Pakistan	Nicaragua	
Lithuania	Lithuania	Nigeria	Palau	Panama	
Malta		Réunion	Papua New Guinea	Paraguay	
Monaco		Rwanda	Philippines	Peru	
Netherlands		Saint Helena	Samoa	Puerto Rico	
New Zealand		Sao Tome and Principe	Singapore	Saint Kitts and Nevis	
Norway		Senegal	Solomon Islands	Saint Lucia	
Poland	Poland	Seychelles	Sri Lanka	Saint Vincent and the Grenadines	
Portugal		Sierra Leone	Taiwan Province of China	Suriname	
Republic of Moldova	Republic of Moldova	Somalia	Thailand	Trinidad and Tobago	
Romania	Romania	Sudan	Tokelau	Turks and Caicos Islands	
Russian Federation	Russian Federation	Swaziland	Tonga	United States Virgin Islands	
San Marino		Togo	Vanuatu	Venezuela	
Slovakia	Slovakia	Uganda	Viet Nam		
Slovenia	Slovenia	United Republic of Tanzania	Wallis and Futuna Islands		
Saint Pierre and Miquelon		Zambia	Tuvalu	Uruguay	
South Africa		Zimbabwe			
Spain					
Sweden					
Switzerland					
Tajikistan	Tajikistan				
The Former Yugoslav Republic of Macedonia	The Former Yugoslav Republic of Macedonia				
Turkmenistan	Turkmenistan				
Ukraine	Ukraine				
United Kingdom					
United States					
Uzbekistan	Uzbekistan				
Yugoslavia	Yugoslavia				

Special chapters of
The State of Food and Agriculture

In addition to the usual review of the recent world food and agricultural situation, each issue of this report since 1957 has included one or more special studies on problems of longer-term interest. Special chapters in earlier issues have covered the following subjects:

1957   Factors influencing the trend of food consumption
       Postwar changes in some institutional factors affecting agriculture
1958   Food and agricultural developments in Africa south of the Sahara
       The growth of forest industries and their impact on the world's forests
1959   Agricultural incomes and levels of living in countries at different stages of
       economic development
       Some general problems of agricultural development in less-developed countries
       in the light of postwar experience
1960   Programming for agricultural development
1961   Land reform and institutional change
       Agricultural extension, education and research in Africa, Asia and Latin America
1962   The role of forest industries in the attack on economic underdevelopment
       The livestock industry in less-developed countries
1963   Basic factors affecting the growth of productivity in agriculture
       Fertilizer use: spearhead of agricultural development
1964   Protein nutrition: needs and prospects
       Synthetics and their effects on agricultural trade
1966   Agriculture and industrialization
       Rice in the world food economy
1967   Incentives and disincentives for farmers in developing countries
       The management of fishery resources
1968   Raising agricultural productivity in developing countries through technological
       improvement
       Improved storage and its contribution to world food supplies
1969   Agricultural marketing improvement programmes: some lessons from recent
       experience
       Modernizing institutions to promote forestry development
1970   Agriculture at the threshold of the Second Development Decade
1971   Water pollution and its effects on living aquatic resources and fisheries
1972   Education and training for development
       Accelerating agricultural research in the developing countries
1973   Agricultural employment in developing countries
1974   Population, food supply and agricultural development
1975   The Second United Nations Development Decade: mid-term review and appraisal
1976   Energy and agriculture
1977   The state of natural resources and the human environment for food
       and agriculture

1978   Problems and strategies in developing regions
1979   Forestry and rural development
1980   Marine fisheries in the new era of national jurisdiction
1981   Rural poverty in developing countries and means of poverty alleviation
1982   Livestock production: a world perspective
1983   Women in developing agriculture
1984   Urbanization, agriculture and food systems
1985   Energy use in agricultural production
        Environmental trends in food and agriculture
        Agricultural marketing and development
1986   Financing agricultural development
        1987-88 Changing priorities for agricultural science and technology in
        developing countries
1989   Sustainable development and natural resource management
1990   Structural adjustment and agriculture
1991   Agricultural policies and issues: lessons from the 1980s and prospects
        for the 1990s
1992   Marine fisheries and the law of the sea: a decade of change
1993   Water policies and agriculture
1994   Forest development and policy dilemmas
1995   Agricultural trade: entering a new era?
1996   Food security: some macroeconomic dimensions
1997   The agroprocessing industry and economic development
1998   Rural non-farm income in developing countries

FAO Agricultural Policy and Economic Development Series

AGRICULTURAL AND ECONOMIC DEVELOPMENT ANALYSIS DIVISION AND POLICY ASSISTANCE DIVISION

1 Searching for common ground – European Union enlargement and agricultural policy (K. Hathaway and D. Hathaway, eds, 1997)
2 Agricultural and rural development policy in Latin America – New directions and new challenges (A. de Janvry, N. Key and E. Sadoulet, 1997)
3 Food security strategies – The Asian experience (P. Timmer, 1997)
4 Guidelines for the integration of sustainable agriculture and rural development into agricultural policies (J.B. Hardaker, 1997)

In preparation

- Farm-nonfarm linkages and income diversification in the developing countries: case studies in Africa and Latin America (T. Reardon and K. Stamoulis, eds)
- Perspectives on agriculture in transition: analytical issues, modelling approaches and case study results (W.-R. Poganietz, A. Zezza, K. Frohberg and K.G. Stamoulis, eds)

FAO Economic and Social Development Papers

AGRICULTURAL AND ECONOMIC DEVELOPMENT ANALYSIS DIVISION*

65 Agricultural stabilization and structural adjustment policies in developing countries (A.H. Sarris, 1987)
66 Agricultural issues in structural adjustment programs (R.D. Norton, 1987)
84 Measures of protection: methodology, economic interpretation and policy relevance (P.L. Scandizzo, 1989)
90 The impact of stabilization and structural adjustment policies on the rural sector – case-studies of Côte d'Ivoire, Senegal, Liberia, Zambia and Morocco (P. Salin and E.-M. Claassen, 1991)
95 Guidelines for monitoring the impact of structural adjustment programmes on the agricultural sector (A.H. Sarris, 1990)
96 The effects of trade and exchange rate policies on production incentives in agriculture (C. Kirkpatrick and D. Diakosavvas, 1990)
98 Institutional changes in agricultural products and input markets and their impact on agricultural performance (A. Thomson, 1991)
99 Agricultural labour markets and structural adjustment in sub-Saharan Africa (L.D. Smith, 1991)
100 Structural adjustment and household welfare in rural areas – a micro-economic perspective (R. Gaiha, 1991)
103 The impact of structural adjustment on smallholders (J.-M. Boussard, 1992)
104 Structural adjustment policy sequencing in sub-Saharan Africa (L.D. Smith and N. Spooner, 1991)

105 The role of public and private agents in the food and agricultural sectors of developing countries (L.D. Smith and A. Thomson, 1991)

107 Land reform and structural adjustment in sub-Saharan Africa: controversies and guidelines (J.-Ph. Platteau, 1992). French version: Réforme agraire et ajustement structurel en Afrique subsaharienne: controverses et orientations

110 Agricultural sustainability: definition and implications for agricultural and trade policy (T. Young, 1992)

115 Design of poverty alleviation strategy in rural areas (R. Gaiha, 1993)

124 Structural adjustment and agriculture: African and Asian experiences (A. de Janvry and E. Sadoulet, 1994)

121 Policies for sustainable development: four essays (A. Markandya, 1994)

125 Transition and price stabilization policies in East European agriculture (E.-M. Claassen, 1994)

128 Agricultural taxation under structural adjustment (A.H. Sarris, 1994)

131 Trade patterns, cooperation and growth (P.L. Scandizzo, 1995)

132 The economics of international agreements for the protection of environmental and agricultural services (S. Barrett, 1996)

133 Implications of regional trade arrangements for agricultural trade (T. Josling, 1997)

134 Rural informal credit markets and the effectiveness of policy reform (A.H. Sarris, 1996)

135 International dynamics of national sugar policies (T.C. Earley and D.W. Westfall, 1996)

136 Growth theories, old and new, and the role of agriculture in economic development (N.S. Stern, 1996)

138 Economic development and environmental policy (S. Barrett, 1997)

139 Population pressure and management of natural resources. An economic analysis of traditional management of small-scale fishing (J.M. Baland and J.P. Platteau, 1996)

141 Economies in transition – Humgary and Poland (D.G. Johnson, 1997)

142 The political economy of the Common Market in milk and dairy products in the European Union (R.E. Williams, 1997)

143 Growth, trade and agriculture: an investigative survey (P.L. Scandizzo and M. Spinedi, 1998)

144 Rural poverty, risk and development (M. Fafchamps, 2000)

Note: Up to 1996, these papers were published by the former Policy Analysis Division.

To obtain the publications listed, please contact:
Sales and Marketing Group, Information Division
Food and Agriculture Organization of the United Nations
Viale delle Terme di Caracalla, 00100 Rome, Italy

E-mail: publications-sales@fao.org
Tel.: (39 06) 57051; Fax: (39 06) 5705 3360

TIME SERIES FOR SOFA 2000 – ON DISKETTE
Instructions for use

As in the past years, *The State of Food and Agriculture 2000* includes a computer diskette containing time series data for about 150 countries and the necessary software, FAOSTAT TS, to access and display these time series.

FAOSTAT TS

FAOSTAT TS software provides quick and easy access to structured annual time series databases. Even inexperienced computer users can use FAOSTAT TS, which does not require spreadsheet, graphics or database programs. FAOSTAT TS is fully menu-driven, so there are no commands to learn. Users can browse through and print graphs and tables, plot multiple-line graphs, fit trend lines and export data for use in other programs. FAOSTAT TS is trilingual (English, French, Spanish) and uses a standard menu format.

FAOSTAT TS software is in the public domain and may be freely distributed. The data files accompanying the software, however, are under FAO copyright, and users must attribute FAO as the source. FAO may provide only very limited support to users of this software and the accompanying data and cannot assist users who modify the software or data files. FAO disclaims all warrants of fitness for the software or data for a particular use.

Technical requirements

FAOSTAT TS software requires an IBM or compatible PC with a hard disk, DOS 3.0 or later version, 300 KB of available RAM and graphics capability. Graphics support is provided for all common graphics adapters (VGA, EGA, MCGA, CGA and Hercules monochrome).

FAOSTAT TS will print graphs on Epson dot matrix, Hewlett-Packard and compatible laser printers. To use FAOSTAT TS with other printers, users can enable their own graphics printing utility before starting the program. One such utility is GRAPHICS.COM in DOS 2.0 or later version.

Because of its use of DOS graphics modes, if FAOSTAT TS is run under MS-Windows or OS/2, it should be set to run in a full screen DOS session.

Installation

Before running FAOSTAT TS you must install the software and data files on your hard disk. Installation is automated through the INSTALL.BAT utility on the diskette.
- To install from drive A: to drive C:
- Insert the diskette in drive A:
- Type A: and press ENTER.
- Type INSTALL C: and press ENTER.
- Press any key.

A C:\SOFA00 directory is created and, after installation, you will already be in this directory.

Entering **FAOSTAT TS**

- To start the FAOSTAT TS software, if you are not already in the C:\SOFA00 directory (as after installation):
  - Change to this directory by typing CD\SOFA00 and pressing ENTER.
  - From the command prompt in the SOFA00 directory, type SOFA00 and press ENTER.

A graphics title screen will be displayed, followed by the main menu screen.

If FAOSTAT TS does not start, graphs do not display correctly or the menus are difficult to read, your computer may not be compatible with the default functions of FAOSTAT TS. The use of a command-line option may help. You may try to start FAOSTAT TS with the -E parameter (by typing SOFA00-E) to disable its use of expanded memory. You may also force the use of a particular graphics or text mode by typing its name as a parameter (e.g. -EGA would force the use of EGA mode graphics).

Language choices

- The initial default language for FAOSTAT TS is English. To change the default language to French or Spanish:
  - Go to the FILE menu
  - Select LANGUAGE using the Arrow key ($\downarrow$) and pressing ENTER.
  - Select your choice of language and press ENTER.

The language selected will remain the default language until another is selected.

Navigating the menus

The main menu bar consists of FILE, DATA, GRAPH, TABLE and HELP menus. Most menu options are disabled until you open a data file. Navigate the menus by using the ARROW keys ($\uparrow\downarrow\leftrightarrow$) and make a selection by highlighting an item and pressing ENTER. To back out of a selection, press the ESC key.

- If you have a mouse, menu items can be selected with the mouse cursor. The left mouse button selects an item and the right mouse button acts as the ESC key.

After you have made a menu selection, the menu will redraw and highlight a possible next choice.

- Several short-cut keys are available throughout the program:

Key	Action
F1	HELP: Displays context-sensitive help text
ESC	ESCAPE: Backs out of the current menu choice or exits the current graph or table
ALT+N	NOTES: Displays text notes associated with the current data file, if the text file is available. This text may be edited. Notes will not appear while a graph is displayed.
ALT+X, ALT+Q	EXIT: Exits FAOSTAT TS immediately, without prompting.

Help

- You will see context-sensitive help displayed at the bottom of each screen. Press F1 for more extensive help on a highlighted option.
- Select HELP from the main menu to access the help information. Introductory information on the software, help topics and an "About" summary screen are available from the HELP menu.
- The HELP menu options call up the same windows obtained by pressing the F1 key at any of the menu screens:
  - FAOSTAT TS displays the top-level help page.
  - TOPICS lists the help contents.
  - ABOUT shows summary program information.

Opening a data file

- To display a list of FAOSTAT TS data files:
  - Go to the FILE menu.
  - Select OPEN.

All of the FAOSTAT TS data files in the current directory are displayed. Initially, only SOFA00 will be present. Other FAOSTAT PC data files, version 3.0, can be used with FAOSTAT TS.

- Use the ARROW keys to highlight the file you wish to view and press ENTER to select it. Files are shown with the date of their last revision. You can also highlight your choice by typing the first letters of the file name. The current search string will appear in the lower left corner of the list.
- You can change the default data drive and directory from the file list by selecting the directory or drive of your choice.

If a current data file is open, loading in a new file will return FAOSTAT TS to its defaults (time trend, no trend line, no user-specified units or scalar). Only one file can be loaded at a time.

Once you have made a file selection, all the menu selections are activated.

Selecting a data series

- Use the DATA menu to select or modify a data series or to fit a statistical trend.
- Select a data series by choosing the name of a country and a data element from scrolling menus. The first entry displays a list of country names, the second entry displays a list of data item names and the third displays a list of data element names.

If you type the first letters of a name in a list, the menu selection bar will jump to the matching name. For example:
  - Type NEW to skip to New Zealand.
  - Press ENTER to select the highlighted name

Displaying graphs and graph options

The GRAPH menu allows you to view the data in chart form. You can display time trends and table or column profiles. Options under the GRAPH menu change the data series shown as well as its display.

For example, to show a plot of the data selected:

- Go to the GRAPH menu.
- Select DISPLAY.

Many options to modify, save or print a graph are available only while the graph is on-screen. Remember to use the F1 help key for a reminder of your options.

Graph action keys. You have several options when a graph is displayed:

- Press ESC to exit the graph and return to the main menu.
- Press F1 for help on the graph action keys. The help box lists the choices available while a graph is on-screen. You must exit the help box before making a selection.
- Press the ARROW and (↑↓) PAGEUP, PAGEDOWN keys to change the series displayed.
- The plus key (+) allows you to add from one to three additional series to the one displayed. Press the MINUS key (-) to remove a series. To create a multiline chart:
  - Display an initial series.
  - Press the + key to add subsequent series to the chart.
- Press A to display a table of the axis data with statistics. Press T to show a table of the fitted trend data, the residuals and fit statistics (if a trend line is selected, see below).
- The INS key permits you to insert text directly on the graph. While inserting text, press F1 for help on your text options. You can type small or large, horizontal or vertical text.
- To print a graph, press P and select your choice of printer from the menu. The print output is only a screen dump of the display, so the quality is limited.
- To save a graph for later printing or viewing, press S. The graph image will be saved in the common PCX bitmap format. You can use the PRINTPCX program or other software to view or print multiple images later. PRINTPCX also permits you to convert colour PCX images into black and white images suitable for inclusion in a word processing document.

Fitting trend lines

- To fit a statistical function to a data series, select FIT from the DATA menu. The options under FIT allow you to select the type of function, data year limits to include in the fit and a final projection year for a statistical forecast.
- By fitting a trend line (selecting the option under FIT) with a projection (selecting PROJECTION under FIT), a statistical forecast can be plotted. Use the + key to add a new data series to the graph, which can be made with only a few key strokes.

Charting profiles

The options under the GRAPH menu allow you to change the year span or style of the graph display (options LIMITS and STYLE, respectively), or to switch from a time trend to a table or column data profile (VIEWPOINT). The VIEWPOINT option is an easy means to compare data for a particular year.

Viewpoint

- If you want to change from a time series display to a country or item profile display for a given year, select VIEWPOINT from the GRAPH menu. Select DISPLAY from the GRAPH menu, and the profile will be drawn. The initial profile display is for the last year of historical data. To change the year, use the ARROW (↑↓) keys. Press F1 for help.
- For a tables profile (profile of data across countries), you can either choose the tables to be displayed or let FAOSTAT TS select the top members and array them in order.

A limit of 50 items can appear in one profile. By selecting TOP MEMBERS instead of SELECTED MEMBERS, FAOSTAT TS will sort the values in the file and display a ranking of table or column values.

Viewing tables

- The TABLE menu allows you to look at data in a tabular format and to define subset tables that may be saved and imported into other software packages.
  - Go to the TABLE menu.
  - Select BROWSE DATA to view individual data tables from the current file.
- When viewing tables, a help bar appears at the bottom of the screen. Press PAGEUP or PAGEDOWN to change the table displayed or press ALT+1 or ALT+2 to choose from a list of tables. Use the ARROW keys (↑↓↔) to scroll the columns and rows.

Series data

- The SERIES DATA option under the TABLE menu displays the last data series selected, including summary statistics. This is the series used to plot a graph. To change the series, you must make a new choice from the DATA menu.
- The SERIES DATA screen can also be displayed while you are in a graph by pressing the letter A. If more than one series has been plotted, only the last series is shown. The range of years used for the series and statistics can be adjusted through the LIMITS option under the GRAPH menu.
- To view country or item profile lists and statistics, select VIEWPOINT from the GRAPH. You can quickly see a list of the tables with the greatest values (for example, countries with the highest commodity consumption) by choosing a table profile from VIEWPOINT and selecting the TOP MEMBERS option. Then select SERIES DATA from the TABLE menu to view the list, or select DISPLAY from the GRAPH menu to plot a chart.

Trend data

- If the FIT option has been selected (from the DATA menu) for a time trend, then the values composing the trend can be displayed with the TREND DATA option. Summary statistics for the original series and for the trend as well as residual values are included. The list scrolls with the ARROW keys, and you can toggle between the axis and trend data with the A and T keys.

Exporting data

- The EXPORT option under the FILE menu allows you to export FAOSTAT TS data into other file formats or to create custom tables for viewing or printing. By selecting EXPORT, you will jump into another set of menus.
- To select the tables and columns you want to view or save, go to the DATA menu. You must mark your choice of options with the + key. To undo all your selections quickly, select RESET MARKS.
- To arrange, view, save or print data, go to the options under EXPORT (in the FILE menu):
  - FAO TABLE creates a table with data from the last four available years.
  - VIEW displays a temporary text file of the data selected. It is a convenient way to view a subset of the tables and columns in a FAOSTAT TS file and can also be used to see the effects of the ORIENTATION or LAYOUT selections before using the SAVE or PRINT option.
  - SAVE displays a list of file formats to let you save your data choices in a file. You will be prompted for a file name. If you need to export FAOSTAT TS data for use with other software, use this menu item. The WK1 and DBF file format selections are not affected by the LAYOUT options (see below).
  - PRINT prints your current table and column selections. Many printers cannot print more than five columns of FAOSTAT TS data. Select VIEW to check the table width before printing.
  - LAYOUT allows you to display years across rows or down columns. The default direction is down columns.
- To get back to the main FAOSTAT TS menu or to clear your selections and create more tables, go the RETURN option.

Making notes

- To read or edit textual information on the current data file, select NOTES from the FILE menu. You can also call up the Notes box by pressing ALT+N at any of the menus. The option NOTES allows you to read or edit text associated with the data file.

DOS shell and exit

The DOS SHELL option under the FILE menu returns you to the DOS prompt temporarily but keeps FAOSTAT TS in memory. This is not the normal way to exit the program. It is useful if you need to execute a DOS command and would like to return to the same data file. The data file itself is dropped from memory and reloaded on return, so default values will be in effect.

Exiting **FAOSTAT TS**

- To exit FAOSTAT TS:
  - Go to the FILE menu.
  - Select EXIT.

The Alt+X or Alt+Q key combinations are short cuts to exit the program from almost any screen.

Sales and Marketing Group, Information Division, FAO
Viale delle Terme di Caracalla, 00100 Rome, Italy
Tel.: +39 06 57051 – Fax: +39 06 5705 3360
E-mail: publications-sales@fao.org

WHERE TO PURCHASE FAO PUBLICATIONS LOCALL
POINTS DE VENTE DES PUBLICATIONS DE LA FA
PUNTOS DE VENTA DE PUBLICACIONES DE LA FA

• **ANGOLA**
Empresa Nacional do Disco e de
Publicações, ENDIPU-U.E.E.
Rua Cirilo da Conceição Silva, Nº 7
C.P. Nº 1314-C, Luanda

• **ARGENTINA**
Librería Agropecuaria
Pasteur 743, 1028 Buenos Aires
World Publications S.A.
Av. Córdoba 1877, 1120 Buenos Aires
Tel./Fax:+54 11 48158156
Correo eléctronico:
wpbooks@infovia.com.ar

• **AUSTRALIA**
Hunter Publications
PO Box 404, Abbotsford, Vic. 3067
Tel.: 61 3 9417 5361
Fax: 61 3 9419 7154
E-mail: jpdavies@ozemail.com.au

• **AUSTRIA**
Gerold Buch & Co.
Weihburggasse 26, 1010 Vienna

• **BANGLADESH**
Association of Development
Agencies in Bangladesh
House No. 1/3, Block F
Lalmatia, Dhaka 1207

• **BELGIQUE**
M.J. De Lannoy
202, avenue du Roi, B-1060 Bruxelles
CCP: 000-0808993-13
Mél.: jean.de.lannoy@infoboard.be

• **BOLIVIA**
Los Amigos del Libro
Av. Heroínas 311, Casilla 450
Cochabamba;
Mercado 1315, La Paz

• **BOTSWANA**
Botsalo Books (Pty) Ltd
PO Box 1532, Gaborone

• **BRAZIL**
Fundação Getúlio Vargas
Praia do Botafogo 190, C.P. 9052
Rio de Janeiro
Núcleo Editora da Universidade
Federal Fluminense
Rua Miguel de Frias 9
Icaraí-Niterói 24
220-000 Rio de Janeiro
Fundação da Universidade
Federal do Paraná - FUNPAR
Rua Alfredo Bufrem 140, 30º andar
80020-240 Curitiba

• **CAMEROUN**
CADDES
Centre Africain de Diffusion et
Développement Social
B.P. 7317, Douala Bassa
Tél.:+237 43 37 83
Télécopie: +237 42 77 03

• **CANADA**
Renouf Publishing
5369 chemin Canotek Road, Unit 1
Ottawa, Ontario K1J 9J3
Tel.: +1 613 745 2665
Fax:+1 613 745 7660
E-mail: renouf@fox.nstn.ca
Website: www.renoufbooks.com

• **CHILE**
Librería - Oficina Regional, FAO
c/o FAO, Oficina Regional para América
Latina y el Caribe (RLC)
Avda. Dag Hammarskjold, 3241
Vitacura, Santiago
Tel.: +56 2 33 72 314
Correo eléctronico:
german.rojas@field.fao.org
Universitaria Textolibros Ltda.
Avda. L. Bernardo O'Higgins 1050
Santiago

• **CHINA**
China National Publications
Import & Export Corporation
16 Gongti East Road, Beijing 100020
Tel.: +86 10 6506 3070
Fax: +86 10 6506 3101
E-mail: serials@cnpiec.com.cn

• **COLOMBIA**
INFOENLACE LTDA
Calle 72 Nº 13-23 Piso 3
Edificio Nueva Granada
Santafé de Bogotá
Tel.: +57 1 2558783-2557969
Fax: +57 1 2480808-2176435
Correo electrónico:
infoenlace@gaitana.interred.net.co

• **CONGO**
Office national des librairies
populaires
B.P. 577, Brazzaville

• **COSTA RICA**
Librería Lehmann S.A.
Av. Central, Apartado 10011
1000 San José
CINDE
Coalición Costarricense de Iniciativas
de Desarrollo
Apartado 7170, 1000 San José
Correo electrónico:
rtacinde@sol.rassa.co.cr

• **CÔTE D'IVOIRE**
CEDA
04 B.P. 541, Abidjan 04
Tél.: +225 22 20 55
Télécopie: +225 21 72 62

• **CUBA**
Ediciones Cubanas
Empresa de Comercio Exterior
de Publicaciones
Obispo 461, Apartado 605, La Habana

• **CZECH REPUBLIC**
Artia Pegas Press Ltd
Import of Periodicals
Palác Metro, PO Box 825
Národní 25, 111 21 Praha 1

• **DENMARK**
Munksgaard, Direct
Ostergate 26 A - Postbox 173
DK - 1005 Copenhagen K.
Tel.: +45 77 33 33 33
Fax:+45 77 33 33 77
E-mail: direct@munksgaarddirect.dk
URL: www.munksgaardirect.dk

• **ECUADOR**
Libri Mundi, Librería Internacional
Juan León Mera 851
Apartado Postal 3029, Quito
Correo electrónico:
librimul@librimundi.com.ec
Universidad Agraria del Ecuador
Centro de Información Agraria
Av. 23 de julio, Apartado 09-01-1248
Guayaquil
Librería Española
Murgeón 364 y Ulloa, Quito

• **EGYPT**
MERIC
The Middle East Readers' Information
Centre
2 Baghat Aly Street, Appt. 24
El Masry Tower D
Cairo/Zamalek
Tel.: +202 3413824/34038818
Fax: +202 3419355
E-mail: mafouda@meric-co.com

• **ESPAÑA**
Librería Agrícola
Fernando VI 2, 28004 Madrid
Librería de la Generalitat
de Catalunya
Rambla dels Estudis 118 (Palau Moja)
08002 Barcelona
Tel.: +34 93 302 6462
Fax: +34 93 302 1299

Mundi Prensa Libros S.A.
Castelló 37, 28001 Madrid
Tel.: +34 91 436 37 00
Fax:+34 91 575 39 98
Sitio Web: www.mundiprensa.com
Correo electrónico:
libreria@mundiprensa.es
Mundi Prensa - Barcelona
Consejo de Ciento 391
08009 Barcelona
Tel.: +34 93 488 34 92
Fax: +34 93 487 76 59

• **FINLAND**
Akateeminen Kirjakauppa Subscription
Services
PO Box 23, FIN-00371 Helsinki
Tel.: +358 9 121 4416
Fax: +358 9 121 4450

• **FRANCE**
Editions A. Pedone
13, rue Soufflot, 75005 Paris
Lavoisier Tec & Doc
14, rue de Provigny
94236 Cachan Cedex
Mél.: livres@lavoisier.fr
Site Web: www.lavoisier.fr
Librairie du commerce international
10, avenue d'Iéna
75783 Paris Cedex 16
Mél.: pl@net-export.fr
Site Web: www.cfce.fr
WORLD DATA
10, rue Nicolas Flamand
75004 Paris
Tél.: +33 1 4278 0578
Télécopie: +33 1 4278 1472

• **GERMANY**
Alexander Horn Internationale
Buchhandlung
Friedrichstrasse 34
D-65185 Wiesbaden
Tel.: +49 611 9923540/9923541
Fax: +49 611 9923543
E-mail: alexhorn1@aol.com
S.Toeche-Mittler GmbH
Versandbuchhandlung
Hindenburgstrasse 33
D-64295 Darmstadt
Tel.: +49 6151 336 65
Fax: +49 6151 314 043
E-mail: triops@booksell.com
Website: www.booksell.com/triops
Uno Verlag
Poppelsdorfer Allee 55
D-53115 Bonn 1
Tel.: +49 228 94 90 20
Fax:+49 228 21 74 92
E-mail: unoverlag@aol.com
Website: www.uno-verlag.de

• **GHANA**
SEDCO Publishing Ltd
Sedco House, Tabon Street
Off Ring Road Central, North Ridge
PO Box 2051, Accra
Readwide Bookshop Ltd
PO Box 0600 Osu, Accra
Tel.: +233 21 22 1387
Fax: +233 21 66 3347
E-mail: readwide@africaonline.cpm.gh

• **GREECE**
Papasotiriou S.A.
35 Stournara Str., 10682 Athens
Tel.: +30 1 3302 980
Fax: +30 1 3648254

• **GUYANA**
Guyana National Trading
Corporation Ltd
45-47 Water Street, PO Box 308
Georgetown

• **HONDURAS**
Escuela Agrícola Panamericana
Librería RTAC
El Zamorano, Apartado 93, Tegucigalpa
Oficina de la Escuela Agrícola
Panamericana en Tegucigalpa
Blvd. Morazán, Apts. Glapson
Apartado 93, Tegucigalpa

• **HUNGARY**
Librotrade Kft.
PO Box 126, H-1656 Budapest
Tel.: +36 1 256 1672
Fax: +36 1 256 8727

• **INDIA**
Allied Publisher Ltd
751 Mount Road
Chennai 600 002
Tel.: +91 44 8523938/8523984
Fax: +91 44 8520649
E-mail:
allied.mds@smb.sprintrpg.ems.vsnl.net
EWP Affiliated East-West
Press PVT, Ltd
G-I/16, Ansari Road, Darya Gany
New Delhi 110 002
Tel.: +91 11 3264 180
Fax: +91 11 3260 358
E-mail: affiliat@nda.vsnl.net.in
Oxford Book and Stationery Co.
Scindia House
New Delhi 110001
Tel.: +91 11 3315310
Fax: +91 11 3713275
E-mail: oxford@vsnl.com
Periodical Expert Book Agency
G-56, 2nd Floor, Laxmi Nagar
Vikas Marg, Delhi 110092
Tel: +91 11 2215045/2150534
Fax: +91 11 2418599
E-mail: oriental@nde.vsnl.net.in
Bookwell
Head Office:
2/72, Nirankari Colony, New Delhi - 11000
Tel.: +91 11 725 1283
Fax: +91 11 328 13 15
Sales Office:
24/4800, Ansari Road
Darya Ganj, New Delhi - 110002
Tel.: +91 11 326 8786
E-mail: bkwell@nde.vsnl.net.in

• **IRAN**
The FAO Bureau, International
and Regional Specialized
Organizations Affairs
Ministry of Agriculture of the Islamic
Republic of Iran
Keshavarz Bld, M.O.A., 17th floor
Teheran

• **ISRAEL**
R.O.Y. International
PO Box 13056, Tel Aviv 61130
E-mail: royil@netvision.net.il

• **ITALY**
FAO Bookshop
Viale delle Terme di Caracalla
00100 Roma
Tel.: +39 06 5705 2313
Fax: +39 06 5705 3360
E-mail: publications-sales@fao.org
Libreria Commissionaria Sansoni
S.p.A. - Licosa
Via Duca di Calabria 1/1
50125 Firenze
Tel.: +39 55 64 8 31
Fax: +39 55 64 12 57
E-mail: licosa@ftbcc.it
Libreria Scientifica Dott. Lucio de Biasio
"Aeiou"
Via Coronelli 6, 20146 Milano

• **JAPAN**
Far Eastern Booksellers
(Kyokuto Shoten Ltd)
12 Kanda-Jimbocho 2 chome
Chiyoda-ku - PO Box 72
Tokyo 101-91
Tel.: +81 3 3265 7531
Fax: +81 3 3265 4656
Maruzen Company Ltd
PO Box 5050
Tokyo International 100-31
Tel.: +81 3 3275 8585
Fax: +81 3 3275 0656
E-mail: h_sugiyama@maruzen.co.jp

• KENYA
Text Book Centre Ltd
Kijabe Street
PO Box 47540, Nairobi
Tel.: +254 2 330 342
Fax: +254 2 22 57 79
Inter Africa Book Distribution
Kencom House, Moi Avenue
PO Box 73580, Nairobi
Tel.: +254 2 211 184
Fax: +254 2 22 3 5 70
Legacy Books
Mezzanine 1, Loita House, Loita Street
Nairobi, PO Box 68077
Tel.: +254 2 303853
Fax: +254 2 330854

• LUXEMBOURG
M.J. De Lannoy
202, avenue du Roi
B-1060, Bruxelles (Belgique)
Mél.: jean.de.lannoy@infoboard.be

• MADAGASCAR
Centre d'Information et de
Documentation Scientifique et
Technique
Ministère de la recherche appliquée
au développement
B.P. 6224, Tsimbazaza, Antananarivo

• MALAYSIA
Southbound
Suite 20F Northam House
55 Jalan Sultan Ahmad Shah
10050 Penang
Tel.: +60 4 2282169
Fax: +60 4 2281758
E-mail: chin@south.pc.my
Website: www.southbound.com.my

• MALI
Librairie Traore
Rue Soundiata Keita X 115
B.P. 3243, Bamako

• MAROC
La Librairie Internationale
70, rue T'ssoule
B.P. 302 (RP), Rabat
Tél./Télécopie: +212 7 75 01 83

• MÉXICO
Librería, Universidad Autónoma de
Chapingo
56230 Chapingo
Libros y Editoriales S.A.
Av. Progreso N° 202-1° Piso A
Apartado Postal 18922
Col. Escandón, 11800 México D.F.
Mundi Prensa Mexico, S.A.
Río Pánuco, 141 Col. Cuauhtémoc
C.P. 06500, México, DF
Tel.: +52 5 533 56 58
Fax: +52 5 514 67 99
Correo electrónico:
1015452361@compuserve.com

• NETHERLANDS
Roodveldt Import b.v.
Brouwersgracht 288
1013 HG Amsterdam
Tel.: +31 20 622 80 35
Fax: +31 20 625 54 93
E-mail: roodboek@euronet.nl
Swets & Zeitlinger b.v.
PO Box 830, 2160 Lisse
Heereweg 347 B, 2161 CA Lisse
E-mail: infono@swets.nl
Website: www.swets.nl

• NEW ZEALAND
Legislation Services
PO Box 12418
Thorndon, Wellington
E-mail: gppmjxf@gp.co.nz
Oasis Official
PO Box 3627, Wellington
Tel.: +64 4 499 1551
Fax: +64 4 499 1972
E-mail: oasis@clear.net.nz
Website: www.oasisbooks.co.nzl

• NICARAGUA
Librería HISPAMER
Costado Este Univ. Centroamericana
Apartado Postal A-221, Managua

• NIGERIA
University Bookshop (Nigeria) Ltd
University of Ibadan, Ibadan

• PAKISTAN
Mirza Book Agency
65 Shahrah-e-Quaid-e-Azam
PO Box 729, Lahore 3

• PARAGUAY
Librería Intercontinental
Editora e Impresora S.R.L.
Caballero 270 c/Mcal Estigarribia
Asunción

• PERÚ
INDEAR
Jirón Apurímac 375, Casilla 4937
Lima 1
Universidad Nacional «Pedro Ruiz Gallo»
Facultad de Agronomía, A.P. 795
Lambayeque (Chiclayo)

• PHILIPPINES
International Booksource Center, Inc.
1127-A Antipolo St, Barangay Valenzuela
Makati City
Tel.: +63 2 8966501/8966505/8966507
Fax: +63 2 8966497
E-mail: ibcdina@webquest.com

• POLAND
Ars Polona
Krakowskie Przedmiescie 7
00-950 Warsaw

• PORTUGAL
Livraria Portugal, Dias e Andrade
Ltda.
Rua do Carmo, 70-74
Apartado 2681, 1200 Lisboa Codex

• REPÚBLICA DOMINICANA
CUESTA - Centro del libro
Av. 27 de Febrero, esq. A. Lincoln
Centro Comercial Nacional
Apartado 1241, Santo Domingo
CEDAF - Centro para el Desarrollo
Agropecuario y Forestal, Inc.
Calle José Amado Soler, 50 - Urban.
Paraíso
Apartado Postal, 567-2, Santo Domingo
Tel.: +001 809 544-0616/544-0634/
565-5603
Fax: +001 809 544-4727/567-6989
Correo electrónico: fda@Codetel.net.do

• SINGAPORE
Select Books Pte Ltd
03-15 Tanglin Shopping Centre
19 Tanglin Road, Singapore 1024
Tel.: +65 732 1515
Fax: +65 736 0855

• SLOVAK REPUBLIC
Institute of Scientific and Technical
Information for Agriculture
Samova 9, 950 10 Nitra
Tel.: +421 87 522 185
Fax: +421 87 525 275
E-mail: uvtip@nr.sanet.sk

• SOMALIA
Samater
PO Box 936, Mogadishu

• SOUTH AFRICA
David Philip Publishers (Pty) Ltd
PO Box 23408, Claremont 7735
Tel.: Cape Town +27 21 64 4136
Fax: Cape Town +27 21 64 3358
E-mail: dpp@iafrica.com
Website: www.twisted.co.za

• SRI LANKA
M.D. Gunasena & Co. Ltd
217 Olcott Mawatha, PO Box 246
Colombo 11

• SUISSE
UN Bookshop
Palais des Nations
CH-1211 Genève 1
Site Web: www.un.org
Van Diermen Editions Techniques
ADECO
41 Lacuez, CH-1807 Blonzy

• SURINAME
Vaco n.v. in Suriname
Domineestraat 26, PO Box 1841
Paramaribo

• SWEDEN
Wennergren Williams AB
PO Box 1305, S-171 25 Solna
Tel.: +46 8 705 9750
Fax: +46 8 27 00 71
E-mail: mail@wwi.se
Bokdistributören
c/o Longus Books Import
PO Box 610, S-151 27 Södertälje
Tel.: +46 8 55 09 49 70
Fax: +46 8 55 01 76 10; E-mail:
lis.ledin@hk.akademibokhandeln.se

• THAILAND
Suksapan Panit
Mansion 9, Rajdamnern Avenue,
Bangkok

• TOGO
Librairie du Bon Pasteur
B.P. 1164, Lomé

• TURKEY
DUNYA INFOTEL
100. Yil Mahallesi
34440 Bagcilar, Istanbul
Tel.: +90 212 629 0808
Fax: +90 212 629 4689
E-mail: dunya@dunya-gazete.com.tr
Website: www.dunya.com

• UGANDA
Fountain Publishers Ltd
PO Box 488, Kampala
Tel.: +256 41 259 163
Fax: +256 41 251 160

• UNITED ARAB EMIRATES
Al Rawdha Bookshop
PO Box 5027, Sharjah
Tel.: +971 6 734687
Fax: +971 6 384473
E-mail: alrawdha@hotmail.com

• UNITED KINGDOM
The Stationery Office
51 Nine Elms Lane
London SW8 5DR
Tel.: +44 20 7873 9090 (orders)
     +44 20 7873 0011 (inquiries)
Fax: +44 20 7873 8463
and through The Stationery Office
Bookshops
E-mail: postmaster@theso.co.uk
Website: www.the-stationery-
office.co.uk
Electronic products only:
Microinfo Ltd
PO Box 3, Omega Road
Alton, Hampshire GU34 2PG
Tel.: +44 1420 86 848
Fax: +44 1420 89 889
E-mail: emedia@microinfo.co.uk
Website: www.microinfo.co.uk
Intermediate Technology Bookshop
103-105 Southampton Row
London WC1B 4HH
Tel.: +44 20 7436 9761
Fax: +44 20 7436 2013
E-mail: orders@itpubs.org.uk
Website: www.oneworld.org/itdg/
publications.html

• UNITED STATES
Publications:
BERNAN Associates (ex UNIPUB)
4611/F Assembly Drive
Lanham, MD 20706-4391
Toll-free: +1 800 274 4447
Fax: +1 800 865 3450
E-mail: query@bernan.com
Website: www.bernan.com
United Nations Publications
Two UN Plaza, Room DC2-853
New York, NY 10017
Tel.: +1 212 963 8302/800 253 9646
Fax: +1 212 963 3489
E-mail: publications@un.org
Website: www.unog.CH
UN Bookshop (direct sales)
The United Nations Bookshop
General Assembly Building Room 32
New York, NY 10017
Tel.: +1 212 963 7680
Fax: +1 212 963 4910
E-mail: bookshop@un.org
Website: www.un.org
Periodicals:
Ebsco Subscription Services
PO Box 1943
Birmingham, AL 35201-1943
Tel.: +1 205 991 6600
Fax: +1 205 991 6602
The Faxon Company Inc.
15 Southwest Park
Westwood, MA 02090
Tel.: +1 617 329 3350
Telex: 95 1980
Cable: FW Faxon Wood

• URUGUAY
Librería Agropecuaria S.R.L.
Buenos Aires 335, Casilla 1755
Montevideo C.P. 11000

• VENEZUELA
Fundación La Era Agrícola
Calle 31 Junín Qta Coromoto 5-49
Apartado 456, Mérida
Fudeco, Librería
Avenida Libertador-Este
Ed. Fudeco, Apartado 254
Barquisimeto C.P. 3002, Ed. Lara
Tel.: +58 51 538 022
Fax: +58 51 544 394
Librería FAGRO
Universidad Central de Venezuela (UCV)
Maracay
Librería Universitaria, C.A.
Av. 3, entre Calles 29 y 30
N° 29-25 Edif. EVA, Mérida
Fax: +58 74 52 0956
Tamanaco Libros Técnicos S.R.L.
Centro Comercial Ciudad Tamanaco
Nivel C-2, Caracas
Tel.: +58 2 261 3344/261 3335
Tecni-Ciencia Libros S.A.
Torre Phelps-Mezzanina
Plaza Venezuela
Apartado Postal: 20.315, 1020
Caracas
Tel.: +58 2 782 8698/781 9945
Correo electrónico: tchlibros@ibm.net

• ZIMBABWE
Grassroots Books
The Book Café
Fife Avenue, Harare;
61a Fort Street, Bulawayo
Tel.: +263 4 79 31 82
Fax: +263 4 72 62 43